NEW ZEALAND IN WORLD AFFAIRS

New Zealand in World Affairs III
1972–1990

EDITED BY

BRUCE BROWN

VICTORIA UNIVERSITY PRESS
in association with
THE NEW ZEALAND INSTITUTE OF INTERNATIONAL AFFAIRS

VICTORIA UNIVERSITY PRESS
Victoria University of Wellington
PO Box 600 Wellington
http://www.vup.vuw.ac.nz

Copyright © The New Zealand Institute of International Affairs 1999

ISBN 0 86473 372 0

First published 1999

This book is copyright. Apart from
any fair dealing for the purpose of private study,
research, criticism or review, as permitted under the
Copyright Act, no part may be reproduced by any
process without the permission of
the publishers.

The cartoons by Bromhead on pp.8 and 20,
originally published in the *Auckland Star*,
are reproduced with permission.

The New Zealand Institute of International Affairs
is an independent body which seeks to promote an
understanding of international issues, particularly
as they concern New Zealand. The Institute does not
advocate any particular policy nor does it express
opinions. The views expressed in this publication
are, therefore, those of the authors.

Printed by Publishing Press Ltd, Auckland

CONTENTS

Sir Frank Holmes
Preface — 7

Merwyn Norrish
Introduction — 9

Bruce Brown
New Zealand in the World Economy:
Trade Negotiations and Diversification — 21

Malcolm Templeton
New Zealand and the Development of International Law — 62

W. David McIntyre
From Singapore to Harare:
New Zealand and the Commonwealth — 85

Ian McGibbon
New Zealand Defence Policy from Vietnam to the Gulf — 111

Malcolm McKinnon
Realignment: New Zealand and its ANZUS Allies — 143

Stephen Hoadley
Trans-Tasman Relations: CER and CDR — 177

Ann Trotter
An Evolving Relationship: New Zealand and Japan — 205

John McKinnon
Breaking the Mould: New Zealand's Relations with China   226

John Henderson
New Zealand and Oceania   267

Roderic Alley
The Public Dimension   295

Editorial note   319

List of Acronyms   320

Notes on the authors   323

Index   327

SIR FRANK HOLMES

Preface

THIS IS THE THIRD VOLUME IN THE INSTITUTE'S SERIES *New Zealand in World Affairs*. Volume I, covering the period 1945–1957, was first published in 1977 and reprinted in 1991 along with Volume II, covering the years 1957–1972. Both, incidentally, are still in print and available from the Institute.

This third volume is timely. The years from 1972 to 1990 saw dramatic changes in New Zealand's political, economic and strategic circumstances – from the Kirk Government which took office in 1972 through the Muldoon years until the Lange–Palmer–Moore administrations of the later 1980s. It is history recent enough to remain topical and distant enough to allow us some better perspective.

The gratitude of the Institute is due to the Ministry of Foreign Affairs and Trade, both for their generous grant to assist the publication of the book and for their ready help in much of the necessary research work of the authors. We are grateful also for the continued interest and support of the Victoria University of Wellington, which houses the Institute, and for the enthusiastic co-operation and the professionalism of the Victoria University Press which succeeded in getting the book out within the University's busy centennial year.

Our thanks go also to the editor and the authors, all experts in their fields, for their skilled and voluntary labour. I believe the book will meet the Institute's objective of reaching a wide audience, from those who lived through the events it describes to today's students.

Sir Frank Holmes
President
New Zealand Institute of Interational Affairs

MERWYN NORRISH

Introduction

THIS PUBLICATION COMPLEMENTS TWO EARLIER VOLUMES covering the period from World War II to 1972. Collectively, they enable readers to see in the round the changes that have taken place in New Zealand's foreign interests and its relations with other countries over almost half a century. Each of the chapters in the present volume speaks of change in the 1970s and 1980s. Approached separately, they portray aspects of the overall picture. Taken together, they demonstrate that the 18 years from 1972 to 1990 encompassed a near revolution in New Zealand's foreign relations.

Although its first application was made as early as 1961, Britain did not join the European Community until 1 January 1973. Until that point, New Zealand's trading position had seemed secure. Britain did not announce its withdrawal from east of Suez until 1968. The Cold War still raged. New Zealand was comfortably ensconced as a member of the ANZUS alliance and found it natural to align its foreign policies for the most part with those of the major Western and Old Commonwealth powers. Its military forces exercised and operated freely with their British, American and Australian counterparts. Although there were persistent calls for progress in disarmament and the cessation of nuclear testing, neither the New Zealand Government nor the vast majority of the public would contemplate putting relations with United States and the West in jeopardy by pressing too hard.

In 1972, New Zealand had only a partial free trade arrangement with Australia, distinguished as much by the bickering it produced as by its limited trading advantages. New Zealand governments up to that time had made little effort to get the best out of relations with their near neighbour. While there were many and various links, we took most of them for granted. Stephen Hoadley, in the chapter 'Trans-Tasman Relations', goes so far as to describe the relationship as having been one of 'mutual disregard'.

In 1972, New Zealand's approaches to Asia were piecemeal. There was little talk then of Asia as the great new area of opportunity. The war in Vietnam was not quite over; New Zealand had still not recognised the Government of China; relations with Japan, though smooth enough, were not far developed. Although New Zealand had begun to cultivate the new Southeast Asian grouping, ASEAN, that relationship also was in its infancy.

In 1971, the Commonwealth had only 32 members and, as David McIntyre points out in his chapter on New Zealand and the Commonwealth, decolonisation in the Pacific had just begun.

In the early part of the period covered by this book, apartheid remained firmly entrenched in South Africa. The horrors of the Springbok rugby tour of New Zealand in 1981 symbolised a relationship fraught with difficulty and devoid of profit.

By 1990, all of these things had changed, all of them dramatically.

Norman Kirk, coming to power as Prime Minister late in 1972, had articulated an enhanced sense of nationhood. His government, too, had moved towards foreign policy positions that were sometimes at odds with those of New Zealand's traditional friends and this was spectacularly advanced by the fourth Labour Government in the mid-1980s.

With Britain throwing in its lot with the European Community, New Zealand's gradual move away from its historical dependence rapidly accelerated. By the end of the period, the proportion of New Zealand's trade with Britain had declined dramatically. More than that, many New Zealanders, far from continuing to turn instinctively to Britain for advice and support or just for feelings of 'family' comfort, had moved to the point of questioning whether it was any longer appropriate that their Head of State and their court of last resort should be domiciled on the other side of the world.

By 1990 also, New Zealand had carried anti-nuclear policies to the point where its membership of ANZUS was suspended and its military forces could no longer exercise with American forces. Fortuitously, the end of the Cold War rendered the anti-nuclear issues less acute between New Zealand and its friends. But New Zealanders came to recognise, more quickly than they might otherwise have done, that foreign policy now meant drawing their own conclusions about where New Zealand's interests lay and how best to advance them, without the advantages conferred by full membership of a somewhat monolithic Western club.

New Zealand's passive attitude towards Australia disappeared in the 1970s and 1980s. Politically, New Zealand recognised publicly that its relationship with Australia was more important to it than with any other country in the world. New Zealand ministers joined their Australian Federal and State counterparts in the regular discussion of common problems. Economically, the free trade area was made much more comprehensive and extended to cover a much wider area of economic activity than just trade in goods. And to this Closer Economic Relations cluster of agreements was added a series of cooperative military arrangements under the heading of Closer Defence Relations.

As for Asia, not even the recent economic crisis can obscure the magnitude of the changes that have taken place in New Zealand's approaches to that continent, both politically and economically. Ann Trotter's and John McKinnon's chapters illuminate developments in relation to Japan and China. Bruce Brown's paper on trade negotiations and diversification charts the growth that has come about through New Zealanders' willingness (both the government and the private sector) to seize opportunities that have appeared throughout the region. Who would have thought, in the early 1970s, that by 1999 New Zealand would be playing host to a massive gathering of heads of state and government from the Asia-Pacific region (not a European amongst them) in an Asia-Pacific Economic Co-operation (APEC) conference?

Who would have thought, also, that by the end of the period covered by this book Nelson Mandela would have been released from prison in South Africa and President de Klerk would have opened negotiations for new constitutional arrangements leading, inevitably, to an end to apartheid? Before long sporting contacts between New Zealand and South Africa would resume and New Zealand would appoint an Ambassador in Pretoria. The foundations of a friendly and profitable relationship were laid where none could previously exist.

In the South Pacific, almost all the former British, Australian and New Zealand colonial territories had become self-governing or independent. Some had become full members of the Commonwealth and all were benefiting from assistance through the Commonwealth, the United Nations and other international bodies.

This was a period, too, when far-reaching changes took place in areas of foreign affairs that are less tangible perhaps than those above but no less significant. Malcolm Templeton, in his chapter on the development of international law, makes the point that 'more international law has been developed or codified since the Second World War than in all of previous recorded history'. He goes on to show just how important this has been for New Zealand – in the field of human rights, for example, the law of the sea and, indeed, in contributing to the cessation of nuclear testing in the atmosphere.

At the end of the 1990s, New Zealand was readying itself to claim resource control, in accordance with the Law of the Sea Convention, over a massive area of the seabed beyond the 200-mile limit which currently applies. That is a graphic example of the practical advantages that can flow from developing international law. More than that, the progressive codification of international rules is of clear benefit to small countries insofar as it limits the freedom of action of bigger players who do not always take adequate account of small country interests.

Immense changes such as these – and there were still more – called for considerable adaptability in both policy and practice if they were to be swiftly accepted, digested and turned to advantage. Most of the changes were not of New Zealand's making, though the ANZUS and Australian developments very largely were. How has New Zealand fared in this respect?

Public opinion was no barrier to New Zealand's making many of the major adjustments which circumstances demanded. In the economic field, if the government sometimes took the lead, the business community did not lag behind. The diversification of trade in agricultural products away from the British market is a classic case where the government, producer boards and traders worked in co-operation with one another to find and exploit other markets. There was full bipartisan support in Parliament. Ministers of Foreign Affairs and Overseas Trade, the diplomatic and trade promotion arms of the government service and the private sector shared a common goal. In the 1960s fears had often been expressed that alternative markets would simply not be available, at least not on remunerative terms, for the large quantities of butter, cheese and lamb likely to be displaced from Britain. A combination of hard work and the time cushion given by the gradual application of the British cuts proved those fears to have been excessive.

The issue of nuclear ships visiting New Zealand fell into a different category. There was little division of opinion on the desirability of ceasing nuclear testing and reducing, if not eliminating, nuclear weapons in the world. In principle, that was fine by almost everyone. Opinion divided sharply, however, over how hard New Zealand should push for these objectives to be attained, at a time when world peace was often said to depend on the maintenance of a strong nuclear deterrent. The divisions deepened when, in the mid-1980s, a Labour Government moved towards a ban on visits by nuclear-armed and nuclear-powered ships to New Zealand ports.

This was not a case where Parliament, the Government and the general public pulled together. For a time, the Opposition in parliament sharply criticized the Government's moves on the grounds that they endangered the ANZUS relationship with the United States and Australia. It was not always clear, moreover, just what the Government did intend or how far it was prepared to go. There was confusion, or at any rate lack of certainty, within the Government service as well as among the public. Rod Alley's paper 'The Public Dimension' documents the activities of the popular movement against nuclear ship visits, which gained strength as time moved on. In the end, public support for the Government's anti-nuclear legislation proved to be massive and from that point neither the Opposition nor any other major interest felt able to continue in disagreement. The idealistic stream in New Zealand's foreign policy thinking had perhaps its greatest time of triumph.

With the end of the Cold War, New Zealand governments did not have to face up to potentially far reaching consequences of the anti-nuclear stand. Strong fears had earlier been expressed about the consequences of a break with ANZUS but, with the collapse of the Soviet Union, alliances assumed less critical importance. New Zealand was out of ANZUS for all practical purposes, limitations were placed on intelligence co-operation, joint military exercising and the like, but otherwise New Zealand's foreign relations were little affected. New Zealand remained a Western country strongly supportive of Western values and Western interests. And at home, once the ANZUS break had actually taken place, public acquiescence quickly followed.

Chapters contributed to the book by Malcolm McKinnon and Ian McGibbon cover from different perspectives the moves and countermoves which led to these results. McGibbon, in addition, traces the chequered course of attempts to adapt the New Zealand armed forces to a role more in keeping with their limited size and strength and with New Zealand's place in the post-Cold War world. He notes as significant the National Government's willingness, from 1990, to endorse more active participation by New Zealand and its armed forces in United Nations peacekeeping missions.

It was sometimes claimed, during the 1980s in particular, that a large body of opinion wished New Zealand to turn away not just from nuclear weapons but also from a wide range of contacts with Western countries. This 'isolationist' stream of opinion was thought to prefer New Zealand to turn inwards and to play little part in the affairs of the wider world. No doubt some people did so wish. For most, however, the rhetoric was little more than the exaggeration common to a public campaign such as that against visits by nuclear ships. Many of the people involved were active at the same time in pushing for more intervention, not less, in the affairs of other countries – South Africa and East Timor are examples – and more broadly over human rights and environmental issues everywhere.

Any move that there may have been towards isolation on the foreign policy front, moreover, was being decisively countered by dramatic changes taking place in the economy. The massive restructuring of the late 1980s, matched by moves towards 'globalisation' elsewhere in the world, meant inevitably that New Zealand would be more affected by external events than previously and would be obliged in its own interest to engage more, not less, with the outside world.

On many other aspects of foreign policy, the Government and the public found little reason to differ. Although bipartisanship in foreign affairs disappeared at the time of the Vietnam war and was of course absent during the nuclear ships controversy, on numerous issues (relations with Australia, the South Pacific, approaches to Asia, anticommunism . . .) the political parties differed, if at all, only in matters of degree.

The Government's handling of issues arising from the military coups in Fiji, to take a specific example, was not seriously contested or criticised by Opposition parties. Nor was it among the general public, apart from hotheads who felt that New Zealand should sail its military forces into Fiji and 'sort Rabuka out'. Curiously, some of these hotheads, who should have known that what they called for would constitute aggression in terms of the United Nations Charter, were at the same time strongly opposed to the proposition that the Navy should have a frigate force adequate to do what they asked. John Henderson's chapter 'New Zealand and Oceania' includes a fascinating discussion of the Government's moves at the time of the Fiji coups. Coming as it does from one who was at the heart of Government policy making, Henderson's account should lay to rest some of the far-fetched notions that were given currency at the time and indeed since.

Two specific examples where the Government of the day did come under strong criticism from the Opposition in Parliament and from large sections of the public were the 1981 South African rugby tour of New Zealand and the settlement of the Rainbow Warrior affair.

It is now widely accepted that the issue of the 1981 rugby tour was used by the then Prime Minister as a political tool with an imminent general election in mind. Given that he won that election, Prime Minister Muldoon may have been right in assessing that rather more New Zealanders wanted the tour to take place than wanted it cancelled. The latter group, however, was not a run-of-the-mill protest group that could be ignored with impunity. It was large, organised and included many people of senior standing and real influence in the community. The tour damaged New Zealand's reputation abroad for non-racialism and high standards of human rights observance. The strength and nature of the opposition to it, however, were also widely noted abroad – to such an extent that when, three years later, the government changed and Prime Minister Lange set out to repair New Zealand's reputation, he found a ready willingness to accept that nothing of the sort would happen again.

The sinking of the Rainbow Warrior in Auckland harbour outraged all New Zealanders. There was initially no division of opinion here, whether in Parliament, in the media or among the public. There was unanimous satisfaction that two of the perpetrators had been caught and sentenced to 10 years imprisonment. As time passed, Prime Minister Lange often asserted in public that the full terms of imprisonment would be served in New Zealand jails. It was these assertions that came to cause political problems for the Government as it gradually became clear that, in the wider interests of New Zealand's foreign policy and its economic and trading relations, some realistic settlement would have to be reached with the Government of France. That settlement eventually included an agreement by New Zealand to the transfer of the two prisoners to serve out the remainder of their sentences, not in New Zealand but on the French Pacific island of Hao. Not surprisingly, when this part of the settlement became public, honourable though it was, much criticism resulted. It is seldom wise for a government to be saying one thing in public while authorising something different in private, in this case the negotiation of a settlement package.

The beginning of this Introduction drew comparisons between New Zealand's place in world affairs in 1972 (the close of the period covered by Volume II) and 1990. Dramatic changes had taken place. It is also instructive to compare the position reached in 1990 with that covered by Volume I, namely, the period from about 1945 to 1957.

Volume I records the origins of the New Zealand Foreign Ministry and 'the formulation of an independent foreign policy', to quote from the title of a chapter contributed by the first Secretary of External Affairs, Sir Alister McIntosh. Other chapters record the means by which New Zealand began to assert itself as a nation and to adjust to the need to seek security under an American rather than a British umbrella. For a time, predominantly during the term of Peter Fraser as Prime Minister and Minister of External Affairs, the steps taken in these directions were vigorous. So much so, that Professor F. L. W. Wood later described New Zealand's stance in those days as that of a 'small power rampant'. There was, however, a long way to travel and the speed of change slackened as New Zealand entered a phase characterised more by comfortable membership of a system of alliances than by radical policies or actions. Thus, New Zealand's membership of a new alliance, the South-East Asia Treaty Organisation (SEATO), was occasioned not by a desire to enter into co-operative relations with Asian countries – that came much later – but as a part of the Western system to curb the expansion of communism. And few moves were made to adapt New Zealand's defence policies and defence forces to emerging new needs. Compared with all this, the chapters in the present volume show how far New Zealand has moved since those formative years.

No country can be fully independent in foreign policy terms. Like virtually everyone else, New Zealand's interest continues to lie largely in co-operation with other countries. Like everyone else, New Zealand's foreign policy must strike a balance between the ideal and the realistic. These things are not new. What is new is that New Zealand now reaches its foreign policy decisions after careful consideration of its own direct national interests, less influenced than before by a willingness to follow the lead of others.

A topic not covered in the chapters which follow is the development of New Zealand's Foreign Ministry during the period to 1990. Sir Alister McIntosh's paper in Volume I recorded the early years of a tiny Department of External Affairs, first established in 1943. McIntosh covered the period to 1957, by which time, he wrote, the Department had not yet come of age. For its size, nevertheless, it had been astonishingly active and influential in the immediate post-war years. Malcolm Templeton, in his introduction to Volume II, traced the gradual development of the Department from 1957 to 1972 and the up-and-down nature of its relations with the Ministers for whom it worked. Neither Walter Nash nor Keith Holyoake, the Prime Ministers during most of those years, felt much need for a well-founded and vigorous Foreign Ministry. Indeed, wrote Templeton, it sometimes seemed that the Holyoake Government regarded the New Zealand diplomatic service 'as an unaffordable luxury'. Reality did prevail, however, to a sufficient degree for the Department gradually to consolidate its position and, indeed, to demonstrate (in cases such as the campaign over Britain's application to join the European Community) both the need for it and its capacity for effective operation abroad. The Department was ready, therefore, Templeton concluded, 'to cope with the changed and more active foreign policy that a new government brought into office at the end of 1972'.

Three Prime Ministers during the 1972–1990 period took a very active interest in New Zealand's relations abroad. Two of the three, Norman Kirk and David Lange, were also the Foreign Ministers. One, Robert Muldoon, although never holding the portfolio of Foreign Affairs, was nevertheless the chief decision maker and often the executant of the Government's policies. Kirk and Lange believed that New Zealand should be active in promoting 'moral' foreign policies, so far as that was realistic, and in cultivating the best possible relations with many other countries. Kirk's extensive visit to South and Southeast Asia in 1973–74 and Lange's to Africa in 1985 were examples of activist policies designed in the one case to open up new possibilities for New Zealand and in the other to repair relationships that had been badly damaged by the Springbok rugby tour affair. Muldoon was conservative in matters such as these and indeed he exacerbated foreign policy difficulties for New Zealand over the rugby issue and on occasion through less than cordial relationships with governments in, for example, Australia and Japan. He was nevertheless active and in some degree forward-looking in international economic and financial matters and, notably, in preserving excellent relations with Britain and throughout the South Pacific.

These were busy times for the Foreign Ministry. Its continued development was hampered or set back at times by periods of financial stringency. In one notable case, budget cuts required the closing of several missions abroad, including the High Commission in New Delhi, which brought down much heavier criticism than he apparently expected on the head of the Minister then responsible. Nevertheless, the network of posts did gradually expand to meet new needs, notably in China, the Soviet Union, the Middle East and Southern Africa.

At the same time, the Ministry at home moved towards a structure that better fitted it to carry out a role in which New Zealand's foreign political and economic interests were intertwined and in defence of which overseas operations had perforce to be conducted on a shoestring. Three major changes of structure took place during the period. The first involved the separation of the Foreign Ministry from the Prime Minister's Department. This change was not at the Ministry's instigation but it was no doubt inevitable at some stage. Then, in the 1980s, the Secretary of Foreign Affairs became also the Head of the Overseas Service, which meant that the management and administration of posts abroad could be carried out by one team rather than in the disparate way that had applied before, when several departments claimed the right to manage and direct their own officers serving as temporary diplomatic personnel. Finally, the biggest development of all took place when the political and the trade aspects of foreign policy were brought together under a unified administration. The trade policy functions of the then Department of Trade and Industry were merged with Foreign Affairs to create the new Ministry of External Relations and Trade, later renamed Foreign Affairs and Trade, while trade promotion became the responsibility of a newly established Trade Development Board. These changes may perhaps be seen in retrospect as marking the coming of age of the Ministry, just a few years before the 50th anniversary, in 1993, of its founding.

The establishment of the Ministry of Foreign Affairs and Trade brought the civil service apparatus responsible for the political and trade aspects of foreign policy into line with the realities of New Zealand's place in the world. Prime Minister Muldoon once famously asserted that 'New Zealand's foreign policy is trade'. Others have claimed that the reverse is true. The argument is specious. Several of the chapters in this book demonstrate – surely beyond argument – that the political and the economic in foreign policy are for New Zealand inextricably intertwined. They are not separate; neither takes precedence over the other; they are simply the major components of a seamless whole. New Zealand depends on foreign trade for its economic well-being to a greater extent than most countries in the world. Any New Zealand government that attempted to push the country's trading interests without at the same time nurturing its political relationships would be ill-advised indeed, as would any government pursuing political relations at the expense of trading interests.

The next volume in this series, whenever it is produced, may be expected to trace a different course of events from the three volumes to date. These three record processes of development away from dependence and major adaptations to new realities. Predictions are hazardous, perhaps foolish, but it may be that by the 1990s New Zealand had reached a position in its relations with the rest of the world that would serve it well enough for some time to come.

BRUCE BROWN

New Zealand in the World Economy: Trade Negotiations and Diversification

THE YEARS 1972–90 SAW DRAMATIC CHANGES IN BOTH NEW Zealand's trading environment and economic management. First, New Zealand was hurt by the oil price shocks of 1973 and 1979. As a consequence of events in the Middle East, the price of oil, long stable and cheap, was quadrupled within a short timeframe. This had both internal and external repercussions for New Zealand. The high oil prices lifted our import bill, increased our domestic cost structure, and fattened our export freight costs.

The year 1973 also saw a steep fall in the levels of other commodity prices, including New Zealand's principal primary exports, and signalled the end of a period of relatively good export prices which, with some ups and downs, had lasted from the end of World War II in 1945. An earlier precursor, a collapse of wool prices in 1967, had already shaken New Zealand's economic confidence. After a short commodity price boom in 1972–73 the drop in New Zealand's terms of trade – the ratio of export prices to import prices – from 1973 to 1975 (41.5 per cent) was steeper than that in the worst years of the Great Depression of the 1930s (39.1 per cent from 1929–33).[1]

Then, from January 1973, Britain entered the European Economic Community (EEC – now termed the European Union, EU) and New Zealand entered a five year transitional period for the access to Britain of our exports of butter, cheese and lamb. Thereafter, in fact from 1977 –93, quantities for butter exports had to be negotiated with the EEC in three or five year cycles.

The impact of Britain's decision at a time when it still took some

90 per cent of our butter exports, 88 per cent of lamb, and 78 per cent of cheese – and these exports alone represented 25 per cent of our total exports[2] – stimulated greater efforts towards diversification of both products and markets, notably in Australia, Asia (especially Japan) the Middle East and Latin America.

In terms of global access for our principal exports, New Zealand entered two negotiating rounds of the General Agreement on Tariffs and Trade (GATT) in this period, the Tokyo Round (1973–79) and the Uruguay Round (1986–94), the latter being of greater importance.

Within this period the Labour Government, elected in July 1984 and holding office until 1990, carried out what amounted to a revolution in economic policy and government management, opening up the economy to imports and capital, floating the currency, removing domestic primary producers' subsidies, reorganising government administration and privatising parts of it. By the mid-1980s New Zealand had sustained budget deficits, accumulated massive overseas debt, and suffered serious balance of payments problems. The new Government's policies wrought the most fundamental alterations to the structure of New Zealand's economy since the first Labour Government imposed foreign exchange control and the import licensing system in 1938.

Finally, a word on the role of governments in international trade relations. Government to government negotiations are involved wherever market access is controlled in one way or another by governmental regulations or decisions, whether by tariffs, quantitative restrictions (such as import licensing) or plant and animal health regulations and quarantine requirements. In New Zealand's case, our principal exports have long been primary products – agricultural, pastoral, horticultural – and trade in such products has been much more subject to government regulation and restrictions than manufactured goods which are traded more freely. (The industrial nations have seen to that while protecting their agriculture.) It has also been subject to the trade-distorting impact of government mandated subsidies. For New Zealand therefore, government to government negotiation has always been important in our export trade. It has not only been a case of selling but of getting rights of access to a market in the first place – and also of reducing or eliminating trade distortions that affect the free flow of that access.[3] The account which follows of New Zealand's trading relations reflects this fact of our economic life.

New Zealand, Britain and Europe

Britain's entry into the European Economic Community (EEC) in 1973 was the culmination of stop and start negotiations over some 10 years. The Conservative Government of Harold Macmillan first applied to join in 1961 only to have that application in effect vetoed by President de Gaulle of France in 1963; the second application, by Harold Wilson's Labour Government in 1967, was also opposed by France and soon lapsed; the third application, by Ted Heath's Conservative Government in 1970, was finally successful in negotiations concluded in Luxembourg in June 1971. New Zealand thus had, in effect, a decade's breathing space.[4]

Already New Zealand had had cause for concern about the future capacity of the British market. As early as 1932, Gordon Coates, then Minister of Finance, had said that with the development of refrigerated shipping 'in 1882 we discovered in Britain a bottomless market; in 1932 we discovered that the market was not a bottomless one'.[5] In the later 1950s, after the easy years of bulk purchase contracts with Britain from 1940–54, New Zealand again made the same discovery.

Britain's decision to seek entry into the Community therefore shocked a New Zealand still heavily dependent on the British market. The New Zealand National Government of Keith Holyoake, in office from 1960–72, decided that it should not seek to obstruct British entry but rather to seek special arrangements which would safeguard our important export trade. In this respect we took a more constructive and cooperative line than Australia or Canada, neither of which gained much from their more assertive approach.[6]

In the three negotiations with the Community spread over 10 years, New Zealand's original list of exports to be safeguarded was gradually eroded, from butter, cheese, casein, beef, sheepmeat (principally lamb), apples and pears in 1961; to butter, cheese and sheepmeat in 1967; to butter and cheese in 1972; and finally by 1977, to butter alone. New Zealand's case, led by Deputy Prime Minister and Minister of Overseas Trade John Marshall, sought continued access to the British market after Britain joined the Community, despite the EEC contention that there was a principle of 'Community preference' in trade. Negotiations were conducted with and through the British Government and the (then) six existing members of the EEC were also lobbied directly. New Zealand

also conducted political and public relations campaigns in Britain.
The final agreement of June 1971 was set out in Protocol 18 to the Treaty of Rome (the founding document of the EEC), sometimes termed the 'Luxembourg Protocol'. Under the protocol, New Zealand was granted continuing access rights for butter and cheese to a milk equivalent of 71 per cent of its then current level of sales of butter and cheese. This arrangement would last for a transitional period of five years, from 1973–77. France resisted any prior agreement for an extension of this arrangement beyond the transitional period, but eventually accepted the formula 'a continuing arrangement subject to review'.

Under the protocol, annual quantities for the importation of New Zealand butter and cheese were set for the five year transitional period, diminishing each year under the Community principle of 'degressivity' (a Euro-euphemism if ever there was one, meaning continued progressive reductions). Those for butter were reduced from some 166,000 tonnes in 1973 to 138,000 in 1977 and for cheese from 68,500 to a little over 15,000 tonnes in the same period.[7]

Protocol 18 also provided (in Article 5) for a review arrangement in 1975 which should consider progress towards 'an effective world agreement on milk products' (a doubtful goal which the EEC held out as one solution for New Zealand's dairy export problems) and New Zealand's progress in diversifying its economy and exports. It further provided that 'appropriate measures' to ensure the maintenance after 1977 of special arrangements for New Zealand would be decided by the EEC in light of this review.

In this respect, the Dublin Summit of March 1975, a meeting of all EEC heads of government, was of great importance to New Zealand. In the Dublin Declaration of 10 March 1975 the enlarged Community[8] confirmed the provisions in Article 5 of Protocol 18 in terms which clearly envisaged a continuation beyond 1977 of the special arrangements for New Zealand and they invited the European Commission to prepare the review '. . . and to submit as soon as practicable a proposal for the maintenance after 31st December 1977 of special import arrangements as referred to in that article'.

Continued access, in principle, was one thing. The quantities to be permitted was quite another. In this respect, the Declaration was also helpful: 'As regards the annual quantities to be established by the Community institutions in the framework of the special arrangements after 1977, these should not deprive New Zealand of outlets which are essential to it. Thus for the period up to 1980, these annual quantities depending upon future market developments, could remain close to effective deliveries in 1974 and the quantities envisaged for New Zealand in 1975'. Finally, the Declaration gave a nod towards the prospect of co-operation between the EEC and New Zealand 'in the orderly operation of world markets' and the prospect of an effective world (dairy) agreement.

The Declaration was an important political platform for the first review in 1977 and for the subsequent reviews for butter access thereafter until Protocol 18 was overtaken by the agreements under the GATT Uruguay Round in 1994. From 1977–93, New Zealand's butter access to Britain was negotiated in a serious of three- or five-year cycles: 1978–80, 1981–83, 1984–88, 1989–92, and a one-year term in 1993. All of these reviews were subject to EEC 'degressivity' and the total butter tonnage permitted was reduced from 125,000 in 1978 to 51,380 by 1993. The Declaration also provided the framework within which higher prices were later negotiated as a trade-off for lower quantities.[9]

The reduced quantities were not altogether a disadvantage in that they encouraged New Zealand to diversify both its dairy markets and dairy products. Butter, for example, is now a much smaller percentage of dairy exports than once it was. In any case, the British butter market for imports itself steadily declined, both because of increased British production and declining British consumption. For example, in 1975, total British butter consumption – or 'disappearance' in the official phrase – was 470,000 tonnes. British butter production was 47,000 tonnes. By 1985, annual consumption had dropped to some 311,000 tonnes and was falling. British production, however, had reached over 240,000 tonnes and was rising. The imposition of EEC milk quotas in 1984 checked the rise in production, but consumption continued to fall. Nonetheless the European Union market remains a very important butterfat market for New Zealand. In the case of cheese, no special arrangement was continued for New Zealand exports to Britain after 1977, but subsequently, in the GATT Tokyo Round (1973–79) a quantity of 9,500 tonnes per year was negotiated.

In the case of lamb, New Zealand's bargaining position was much stronger than for either butter or cheese. This was because in the GATT Dillon Round (1961) New Zealand had acquired a tariff binding of 20 per cent for unrestricted access to the EEC which could not be altered to our disadvantage without New Zealand being offered some equivalent compensation. The EEC then had no sheepmeat regime under its Common Agricultural Policy (CAP) and there was therefore no basis for a special arrangement. Moreover, the Community was only 70 per cent self-sufficient in sheepmeat, which probably accounts for the access rights New Zealand secured in 1961. However, in 1980, the enlarged Community decided to introduce a sheepmeat regime. New Zealand argued that there was no need for one, but if there was to be one, it should be a light one, with no provision for intervention stocks under the CAP. On both counts, we were unsuccessful and the regime, intervention and all, was established.[10] New Zealand then mounted a combined government and meat industry campaign in Britain reaching politicians, shipping interests, meat importers and consumers and was successful in negotiating a Voluntary Restraint Agreement (VRA) with the Community for lamb exports. A maximum of 245,500 tonnes per year was accepted (and even as late as 1970, New Zealand had exported over 300,000 tonnes to Britain) in return for a reduction in the Community's standard rate of tariff from 20 per cent to 10 per cent – which as Prime Minister Muldoon remarked in a speech in London to the Butchers Company on 18 June 1981 still meant that 'we lost one lamb in ten'. Subsequently in 1991, New Zealand agreed to a further reduction of tonnage, to 205,000, in return for a reduction in the tariff to zero.

While the VRA was in theory Community-wide, in practice 'sensitive market' agreements were negotiated with France and Ireland, to which volumes were to be limited to an agreed and low level – which meant, in the case of Ireland, none. Later, there were restrictions on the volume of chilled lamb New Zealand could send, since it was the chilled product which competed most directly with European fresh lamb and was therefore feared by European producers. The Community also agreed that it would not use intervention stocks to upset the market and that it would limit the use of export subsidies to the Community's traditional market share.[11]

One other effect of the Community's regime, as New Zealand had predicted, was a spectacular rise in the sheep population in Britain and the Community as a whole. Numbers almost doubled within a period of ten years, from 56 million in 1984 to 100 million in 1993, a graphic illustration of the power of CAP production subsidies as opposed to the deficiency payments to farmers Britain had previously used from 1934. There was a similar expansion in Community milk production and the EEC soon became the world's largest dairy exporter, pushing New Zealand well down to second place.[12]

The negotiations with the Community for our continued access to the British butter market – five in all from 1977 to 1993 – absorbed much political and diplomatic effort.[13] Protocol 18 had provided (in Article 5(2)) that approval of post-1977 arrangements for New Zealand required unanimity in the EEC Council of Ministers – in other words, any Community member could veto a proposal from the European Commission. This provision, incidentally, was inserted in the text of the Protocol by the Community without consultation with New Zealand, to the considerable annoyance of the New Zealand Government when it learned of it.[14] In practice, this meant that France and Ireland could and did on occasion hold up decisions for months, in which case New Zealand was placed on month to month rollovers of the preceding year's quantities, with a subsequent adjustment when a new proposal was approved – a precarious situation.

In the negotiations, New Zealand discussed with the British Government what quantity it wanted in the next cycle and the British Government would then informally give the European Commission in Brussels a steer as to what quantity would be acceptable to them. New Zealand also lobbied the Commission and all EEC members to ensure our position was understood. The Commission would then draft a proposal for future access for the approval of the EEC Council of Ministers, which was never known to increase the quantities recommended and sometimes reduced them. Sometimes, also, the Council approved only part of a proposal, as was the case with the recommendation for the five year period 1984-88. The Council approved the 1984-86 figures in July 1984 (after Ireland had been the lone holdout for some six months) but did not approve the 1987-88 figures until July 1986.

Because of our GATT-bound rights governing access to the Community for lamb, New Zealand's bargaining power in that respect was much greater than for butter. It was for a long time New Zealand policy to avoid any trade-offs between access for butter and for lamb, no doubt because of New Zealand governmental sensitivity to the two differing farming constituencies at home. We expressly avoided 'linkage' and were instructed there should be none. In 1980, New Zealand declined a Commission offer of more generous terms on lamb in return for a lower quantity of butter.

In May 1984, however, when the proposals for 1984–88 butter quantities were still being blocked by France and Ireland, Prime Minister Robert Muldoon soon realised (as his officials had) how nervous the French were that New Zealand would not agree to renew the 'sensitive market' agreement on lamb which restricted our lamb sales to France, and was soon to expire. He quickly linked the two questions, stating that New Zealand would initial but not sign that agreement until the New Zealand butter quantities were approved, and so brought the French on board. The Irish held out a little longer.

Muldoon also tried to stop 'degressivity', calling the quantities proposed for 1984 the 'irreducible minimum'. In January 1983, to mark the tenth anniversary of Britain's entry to the Community, he wrote an article for *The Times* of London attacking the CAP, which *The Times* headlined 'Can Ties of Blood Survive These Selfish Policies?'. He had also appealed to British public sentiment during the Falklands war between Britain and Argentina, in May 1982, agreeing to lend a New Zealand frigate to Britain to free an equivalent Royal Navy ship for service in the Falklands. That was more than just sentiment – it was sentiment plus self-interest, since we were then at a critical stage in post-1983 butter access negotiations.

British support, in fact, was vital to the success of the New Zealand case and over the years it was given, both by the Labour Government of the late 1970s and the Conservative Government of Mrs Thatcher, which won office in 1979. She was, we were told by British officials, the strongest supporter of New Zealand in her cabinet.

On one occasion, however, British support was less than robust. Britain's relations with New Zealand were affected to some degree by the anti-nuclear policy of the Lange Government, following that Government's refusal to accept a visit by the USS *Buchanan* in February 1985. Although it received much less publicity, and was a lesser target for the protest movement – if only because visits by British warships had become increasingly rare – the New Zealand policy on nuclear-powered and nuclear capable ships meant that the Royal Navy as well as US Navy ships could no longer visit, since neither Government was prepared to submit themselves to a determination of their nuclear status, or lack thereof, by the New Zealand Prime Minister. (It was, and is, a common misapprehension that New Zealand required a visiting warship to declare its nuclear status. Under the legislation that determination remains the responsibility of the New Zealand Prime Minister).

In the course of his visit to New Zealand in May 1987, Sir Geoffrey Howe, Britain's Secretary of State for Foreign Affairs, made some linkage between visits by warships and the question of butter access, and reiterated this to the New Zealand Foreign Minister, Russell Marshall, in London in March 1988. He said that attitudes in Britain were bound to shift anyway, what with the imposition of Community milk quotas, the growth of dairy surpluses, and the growing antagonism of British farmers, but New Zealand's nuclear policies could be seen as a large straw on the other (for us, the wrong) side of the wagon.[15]

Mike Moore, Minister of Overseas Trade and Marketing (MOTM) had written to John MacGregor, British Minister of Agriculture, asking him to present New Zealand's view on what post-1988 butter quantities should be, but in his reply MacGregor made no commitment. MacGregor did not support the quantities New Zealand wanted in prior consultation with the European Commission before its recommendations were publicly formulated. As Bryce Harland, then New Zealand's High Commissioner to Britain, has recalled:

> As a result, our Trade Minister had to negotiate with the Commission entirely on his own and the Commission did not neglect the opportunity the British had given it. Once Moore had struck a deal, involving sheepmeats as well as butter, MacGregor supported it strongly, against British farmers and their political spokesmen. Mrs Thatcher stood behind him . . . But she did not make MacGregor support Moore in his approach to the Commission. Moore got the best deal going in the circumstance but it involved further heavy reduction in imports of butter, as well as lamb, from New Zealand.[16]

In his book *Nuclear Free – The New Zealand Way* David Lange contended that it was 'the British consumers who put pressure on the British Government to keep taking our agricultural products' not 'our wartime sacrifices or our support for Western interests'. As for the Europeans, he argued that they accepted that New Zealand was still aligned with the West and were more concerned about 'the strength of their farm lobby and the size of the wine lake and butter mountain' of their own surplus stocks.[17]

Certainly, there was a warmth of sentiment among the British public towards New Zealand, a substantial brand loyalty to New Zealand butter and lamb built up over 100 years of trade, and some strong consumer groups. But political and producer opinion also carries great weight, especially in continental Europe where farmers have wielded great political power. When it comes to staying power, producers are an army, consumers are a mob.

It was for these reasons that over the years following British entry – indeed before – New Zealand consciously began to develop its wider links with Europe, opening embassies in Community capitals – Brussels (1961) Athens (1964) Rome(1965) Bonn (1966) – to add to existing posts in London, Paris and The Hague. Europeans, understandably, became tired of hearing about New Zealand's special relationship with Britain. What now became increasingly important was New Zealand's relationship with the Community. A New Zealand officials' delegation, led by Secretary of Foreign Affairs Frank Corner, began talks in Brussels to develop that relationship in November 1975. Annual talks have followed ever since. In the consideration of post-1980 access, the political and strategic arguments were further developed and became an important element in the New Zealand case thereafter. In essence the theme was that New Zealand, as a member of the Western alliance through the ANZUS Treaty (in effect a Pacific partner of NATO) was a contributor to stability in the Pacific region. Our economic viability was therefore relevant to the Community in this broader sense.

That argument was certainly damaged at the time by the anti-nuclear policy which annoyed some of the Europeans (and worried some of the Asians). It has since been overtaken by other events notably, in political terms, the ending of the Cold War in 1989–90, and in economic terms by New Zealand's success during the GATT Uruguay Round in 1993– 94 in putting increased access for butter and lamb to the enlarged Community on a stronger political and legal basis.

There was a school of thought in New Zealand, and amongst anti-Community politicians of both the Conservative and Labour parties and others in Britain, that had New Zealand directly opposed British entry in the long-drawn-out negotiations from 1961–71 it might have influenced British parliamentary and public opinion to defeat approval of the British application. The vote in the House of Commons in 1972 in favour of entry had been a narrow one. Perhaps such a New Zealand campaign directed to both political and public opinion in Britain over the heads of the British Government might have helped defeat the entry application in 1972. But for how long and at what cost? The British political, and much of the financial and commercial, establishment would have been antagonized to a dangerous degree by such a course. And as the British economy faltered in the 1970s (remember, the IMF had to be called in to rescue British finances in 1976) New Zealand might well have become a scapegoat and British public opinion towards us rapidly soured. It is salutary to remember too that Harold Wilson's Government held a referendum in June 1975 as to whether Britain should remain in the Community. The result was a two-thirds majority, 67 per cent to 33 per cent, for staying in.

In retrospect, New Zealand's long rearguard action over 30 years and more to maintain the right of access to Britain was, in my view, one of the two most significant New Zealand political and diplomatic achievements since the Second World War (the other being the negotiation of Closer Economic Relations, CER, with Australia). Protocol 18 was a lifesaver for the New Zealand dairy industry which would have collapsed without it. It was only because we were still there in that market, although at greatly reduced quantities, throughout the long negotiation of the GATT Uruguay Round from 1986 to 1994, that we were able to put our access on a firmer, permanent political and legal basis – and with increased quantities.

To some degree, the relationship has changed in consequence. It is now a New Zealand–European Union legal relationship, not simply a New Zealand–Britain family relationship, and our exports, including butter and lamb, have access to the whole Union. But Britain and the European Union market as a whole remain a major market for New Zealand butter and lamb and are an important and growing market for wool, apples, wine, manufactures and tourism. Britain is also important for investment in New Zealand and in banking, insurance, funds management, and shipping. Britain itself remains our fourth largest market and the European Union is one of the big four in that respect along with Australia, Japan, and the United States. At time of writing (1999) the EU as a whole is second to Australia.

Trade Diversification – Australia

Australia, as well as New Zealand, was shaken by Britain's decision to join the European Community. Because it had a stronger, more varied economy – and perhaps also because it over-estimated its bargaining power and took a tougher line with Britain than New Zealand did – Australia did not secure any special access arrangements with the Community. Like New Zealand, Australia too was shaken by the first oil shock of 1973 and later that of 1979, following the fall of the Shah of Iran.

The first British application to join the Community contributed to the decision of Australia and New Zealand to begin negotiating a trade agreement in the early 1960s. In the 19th century, Australia had been for a time New Zealand's principal trading partner, until the era of refrigerated shipping which began in 1882 led to the rapid growth of dairy and meat industries, turning the trade of both countries towards Britain. In a sense, they came to sit back to back in the Pacific, Australia trading to Britain through the Suez Canal and later, New Zealand doing likewise through Panama. Thereafter, for many years – with the notable exception of World War II, and its aftermath – both official and trading relations between the two were surprisingly slight. The British decision in 1961 did much to alter that.

In 1961, New Zealand suggested a limited trade arrangement, covering forest products only. Australia rejected this and counter-proposed a wider arrangement based on a positive list. Nothing was to be included unless agreed. Negotiations were completed in 1965 and the New Zealand–Australia Free Trade Agreement (NAFTA) came into force in January 1966. It was accepted by GATT on Australian and New Zealand assurances that it was a transitional arrangement towards a wider agreement, a generous interpretation at that time.

In practice NAFTA, which lasted from 1966 to 1983, when it was replaced by the Australian–New Zealand Closer Economic Relations Trade Agreement (ANZCERTA) proved to be more an instrument for managed trade than free trade. Industry groups on each side had to be consulted about what items could be included in Schedule A, which provided for the gradual reduction and elimination of duties, and both were extremely cautious about doing so. The result was annual haggles between governmental and industry representatives on each side. Few agricultural products were included. Another provision, Article 3(7), provided for reciprocal trading deals, company to company. Schedule A did not come to cover much more than 60 per cent of trans-Tasman trade, encouraging the quip 'All the way with Schedule A' to change to 'Half the way with Schedule A'. In retrospect, however, NAFTA served a useful purpose. While it may not have made a great contribution directly to the substantial increase in trans-Tasman trade which followed – it may be that the 1967 devaluation of the New Zealand dollar was more important – it got both the two governments and the two business communities talking to each other much more than before. New Zealand awoke to the potentialities of the Australian market, and Australia to the fact that New Zealand had become its biggest market for manufactures.[18]

By the late 1970s it became clear that NAFTA had bogged down and the Australians, irritated by the minutiae involved in the annual negotiations and frustrated by the New Zealand import licensing system, became increasingly impatient with it. Matters came to a head in 1979 when Australian Deputy Prime Minister and Trade Minister Doug Anthony declared he was no longer prepared to deal with such trivia.

At this time, both New Zealand and Australia were concerned by the fall of the Shah of Iran and the Iranian revolution, which threatened what had developed into a highly promising primary products market for both, and also by the second oil price hike imposed by the Middle East-dominated Organisation of Petroleum Exporting Countries (OPEC). New Zealand's recognition of Australia's growing significance had also been cogently expressed by Brian Talboys, Deputy Prime Minister and Minister of Overseas Trade, in a speech on 14 September 1977: 'The time has come for New Zealand to recognize that our relationship with Australia is more important to us than our links with any other country in the world. I believe we do recognise this fact instinctively, at the back of our minds. We have to bring it to the forefront, make it explicit in our thinking and in our actions. It has to be the cornerstone of New Zealand's external policies'.[19]

Talboys followed up this thinking by an extensive official visit to Australia in March 1978, in which, for the first time by a New Zealand foreign minister, he visited every state capital as well as Canberra. This visit concluded with a meeting with Prime Minister Malcolm Fraser, and a joint statement, the 'Nareen Declaration', was issued. It affirmed that the futures of the two countries were 'inextricably linked' and in a cautious way pointed towards a closer trading relationship.[20]

In June 1979, the political initiative was taken by the Minister of Customs, Hugh Templeton, in a speech in Wellington urging a closer economic relationship. His message was well received. The Australians responded by sending Minister of Trade Vic Garland to New Zealand in September. So ensued what amounted to a three-way negotiation: firstly, within the New Zealand Government, where Prime Minister Muldoon, a 'doubting Robert', blew hot and cold on the issue over the three years or more that the negotiations ground on; between the Government and New Zealand interest groups, essentially the manufacturers and especially those in Auckland; and between the New Zealand and Australian Governments. The personal animosity between Muldoon and Malcolm Fraser, exacerbated by the controversial Springbok rugby tour of New Zealand in 1981 and its potential threat to the success of the Brisbane Commonwealth Games of 1982, in the judgement of Templeton delayed the conclusion of the negotiation by at least a year.[21] Finally, agreement was reached and the Closer Economic Relations Agreement (CER for short) came into force. The negotiations, the provisions of the agreement, and progress in the subsequent reviews are described in detail in a later chapter.[22]

In brief, CER reversed the NAFTA 'positive list' principle under which nothing was to be included unless agreed, by a 'negative list' approach under which everything was to be included unless it was agreed that it should be excluded – and the 'too hard' list was to be short. The agreement came into force on 1 January 1983. The first review, in 1988, widened its scope and accelerated its timetable. The target date for dutyfree goods across the Tasman was advanced to 1 January 1990 and effected. 'Second generation' issues – for example, services, shipping, civil aviation, telecommunications, investment, and the harmonisation of commercial law – were all addressed with varying degrees of progress. The 1992 review was disappointing and the later Australian decision to renege on an agreement under which each country's airlines were to be allowed to compete in the other's domestic market, particularly so.

Nonetheless, under CER trans-Tasman trade has boomed. Australia is now New Zealand's biggest export market and New Zealand is Australia's fourth largest – and its second largest market for manufactures. The imbalance in the value of trade between the two countries, which at one time in the 1970s was 4:1 in Australia's favour, closed to 1:1 for a time and later turned again in Australia's favour – but much less so than in earlier years. By the 1980s, Australia had also become the principal source of overseas investment in New Zealand and the principal destination of New Zealand investment abroad. CER also had the effect, much in the mind of New Zealand officials, of leading the way in opening up New Zealand's protected economy.

In political terms, the web of consultation – ministerial and official – between the two governments is now far greater than it has ever been.

The election in December 1972 of Norman Kirk's Labour Government in New Zealand and Gough Whitlam's Labor Government in Australia – was a catalyst which created considerable interest on each side. Both parties had been out of office for a long time, New Zealand Labour since 1960 and Australian Labor even longer, since 1949. Early Prime Ministerial visits were exchanged and there were some 14 New Zealand ministerial visits to Australia and 9 Australian to New Zealand in the two governments' first year.[23] That set a pace which has since rarely slackened. An important development has been the acceptance of New Zealand in the Council of Australian Governments, the structure for Federal–State ministerial meetings.

Japan

Japan has a long trading record with New Zealand. In the 1920s the New Zealand dairy industry developed an interest in the potential of the Japanese market and it was pressure from that quarter which was largely responsible for the decision of the New Zealand Government, in 1928, to negotiate a trade agreement with Japan – New Zealand's first commercial treaty with a state not a member of the (British) Commonwealth.

By 1937, Japan was New Zealand's third largest export market although well behind the United States in second place and a long way behind Britain in first. Wool became the principal New Zealand export to Japan, and textiles Japan's principal export to New Zealand. The outbreak of the Pacific war in 1941 stopped the trade until 1952, after the signing of the Japanese Peace Treaty in 1951. Japanese shipping, which had first started a direct service to New Zealand in 1935, resumed sailings in 1952.

In 1954, New Zealand negotiated another trade agreement with Japan but the Government – facing a general election and some opposition (for differing reasons) from Britain and the United States – did not sign it until 1958. It was not until Britain had decided to seek entry into the EEC that British officials began to take the view that Japan was a logical market for New Zealand. Until then it was seen as a rival. New Zealand saw the potential of the Japanese market but became well aware of its difficulties. The wider relationship is described in detail in a later chapter.[24] What follows is a summary of principal developments in the trading relationship.

Under the 1958 agreement New Zealand obtained rights to compete for the foreign exchange available for Japan's imports of meat and wool. However, full GATT rights were not granted to Japan until 1962, when the agreement was revised and renewed. New Zealand agreed to grant Japan full GATT Most Favoured Nation (MFN) status, although with some safeguards against damage to New Zealand industry. For its part, Japan also obtained safeguards, to protect its (high cost) agriculture. The fact that New Zealand granted Japan MFN status before Australia, and relatively early in international terms, helped to produce a cordial atmosphere for New Zealand in Tokyo.[25]

Trade steadily increased thereafter and a number of agreements followed. By 1966, Japan was once again New Zealand's third largest export market and by 1976 our third largest trading partner, for both exports and imports. A double taxation agreement was concluded in 1963; fisheries agreements in 1967 and (not without difficulty) 1978; and an air services agreement, providing for direct flights, in 1980. The New Zealand Dairy Board was the first to establish an office in Japan, in Tokyo in 1952, and the New Zealand Meat Producers Board did likewise in 1954. Both Boards later entered into joint ventures in Japan, a convenient way of doing business there.

All of New Zealand's major primary industries sought to export to the Japanese market – dairy products (cheese, for which Japan is now our largest market, skim milk powder [SMP] and casein); meat (initially mutton, for which Japan was our largest market in the 1960s, and also beef and lamb); forest products; horticultural products; and wool (once our major export, now less important in direct exports). But a major export to Japan became and remains aluminium produced at the Comalco Plant at Tiwai Point, a joint venture launched by Comalco, Sumitomo Chemicals KK and Showa Denka KK. (Aluminium is, in fact, New Zealand's largest single manufactured export and most of it has been bought by Japan and Korea). From 1980, when the direct air services began, tourism from Japan also became a major foreign exchange earner and the number of Japanese tourists visiting New Zealand increased from 5441 in 1972 to 108,000 in 1990.[26]

Japan's exports to New Zealand also grew substantially. Japanese motor vehicles, cars especially, came to dominate New Zealand roads and Toyota, Mitsubishi, Honda, Nissan and Mazda established assembly plants here. These have been phased out (in 1998) as New Zealand's tariffs have been lowered to the level at which small scale local production became uneconomic (although it may be expected that continued imports from Japan of both new and used vehicles will remain dominant). Japanese investment, while modest in relative terms, has made important contributions in computers and communications equipment, forest and timber processing, fishing and tourism facilities, as well as transport and aluminium previously mentioned – although not to any extent in the food processing industries. In the 1970s and early 1980s, Japan also became a source of borrowing for the New Zealand Government, but after 1984 the Government ceased to borrow abroad and concentrated on repaying foreign debt.

Despite the growth of two-way trade over the years there have been serious and frustrating problems for New Zealand in gaining access to the huge Japanese market. An underlying problem was the immense disparity in size between the two economies so that while the Japanese market became of vital importance to New Zealand the New Zealand market remained of only peripheral interest to Japan. To this disparity must be added the fact that, especially following the liberalisation of the New Zealand economy since 1984, with a unilateral lowering of tariffs, access to the New Zealand market has become easier for exporters from all regions.

A particular problem was the irregularity of Japanese imports of key New Zealand exports – meat, wool, dairy, and forest products. Prime Minister Muldoon raised this question in Tokyo on his first visit to Japan in April 1976, shortly after he had been elected. He stressed New Zealand's long term expectations on the basis of reciprocity '. . . unless New Zealand is granted opportunities to place trade with Japan on a stable and expanding footing real doubt will arise in the longer term about our ability to go on importing increasing quantities of manufactures from Japan, which would otherwise seem a logical source of them'.²⁷ He said that New Zealand would like to see quotas available for exports of butter and SMP and was ready to establish joint ventures in fishing, fish processing, and research.

In 1977, dissatisfied with the Japanese response, Muldoon sought to link the renewal of Japanese fishing rights in New Zealand's Exclusive Economic Zone (EEZ) with better access for New Zealand beef to Japan. In a speech on 10 May 1977, he said he had made it clear to Japanese authorities that the New Zealand meat trade could not operate on the basis of 'reluctant issues of arbitrary quotas from time to time with no guarantee of regular access'. The message had been understood but there had been no response. He therefore determined that no agreement on fishing would be signed with Japan until New Zealand could get an assurance of regular access for its farm products to Japan.

The 'Fish for Beef' dispute, as it became known, (or 'Squid-Pro-Quo') was not settled until July 1978, when despite Prime Ministerial conditions, New Zealand eventually reached a fishing agreement without any commitment on access.²⁸ This affair illustrated New Zealand's lack of bargaining power *vis-à-vis* Japan, although it might also have served some purpose in reminding Japanese officialdom that the interests of even small trading partners need to be taken into account. In later years, New Zealand has sought to gain leverage by joining a quadripartite grouping within the GATT disputes procedure – the United States, Canada, Australia and New Zealand – in seeking better beef access to both Japan and Korea and some progress has been made, although there is a risk in these tactics that the most powerful player, the United States, might be tempted to do bilateral deals. For a variety of reasons therefore, New Zealand has sought to improve its access to major markets of interest to it through both multilateral and bilateral negotiations within GATT, as is described in a later section.

To sum up, despite continuing access problems and frustration to New Zealand exporters, Japan remains a market of the highest importance to us, one of the 'Big Four', and will continue to be so.

The United States

The United States has been a major trading partner of New Zealand since World War I. Substantial American investment began in New Zealand in the 1920s and 30s in the motor and tyre industries, and the oil industry. Again, New Zealand faces a huge disparity in economic strength and bargaining power, and access for primary exports to America has been at the centre of New Zealand's economic diplomacy. One problem has been the fact that in 1955 the United States obtained a GATT waiver on the use of quantitative restrictions on agricultural imports, which lasted throughout the period under review.[29] Some other countries, notably Canada, also applied similar restrictions to keep out agricultural imports. The European Union did it by variable levies at the border, which could price imports out of the market.

The New Zealand dairy trade was frustrated by American embargoes but from about 1952, New Zealand rapidly developed an export beef trade to the United States so that the United States soon became by far our largest beef market. This situation prevailed through the 1970s and 80s, when the American market took over 70 per cent of our export beef and Canada, our second largest market, some 10 per cent. In later years conscious efforts were made by the New Zealand industry to diversify exports to Asia, especially Japan and Korea. New Zealand's grass-fed beef exports to North America are principally devoted to manufacturing beef and the hamburger trade. Grain-fed beef is still preferred in that market as in Asia for the restaurant trade.

The beef trade too has been subject to American restrictions from time to time. The Meat Import Law (MIL) adopted in 1964 and revised in 1979 permitted the United States Government to control the volume and could be triggered once set quota levels were exceeded. In consequence, New Zealand and Australia negotiated 'Voluntary' Restraint Agreements (VRAs) from time to time under which voluntary quotas were accepted by exporters to avoid formal quotas which would have been more disadvantageous. Canada had a similar Meat Import Act (MIA) but differed in that its application was not mandatory but at ministerial discretion.

The United States, like Japan, the European Union, Canada and all too many others also has a highly protected and subsidised agricultural industry only now coming within the disciplines of the GATT Uruguay Round. Not only has the United States protected its agricultural industries from imports but under the Export Enhancement Programme (EEP) it exports subsidised products abroad. For example, in 1986 the United States Congress passed the Food Security Act, as a result of which the Commodity Credit Corporation (CCC) was required to export from its stocks 150,000 tonnes of butter per year, tonnage which competed with New Zealand commercial exports on the world market. It must be said, however, that in dairy exports the United States has often been more careful to consult with New Zealand than has the European Union, which exported much larger volumes of subsidised product.[30]

The New Zealand meat industry has also worked to develop lamb exports in a North American market unreceptive to the product – consumption in both the United States and Canada is only of the order of 1.5kg per head per year. The New Zealand Lamb Company set up by the Meat Board to develop this trade has had its ups and downs – a down period being in the late 1980s when sales in the United States were only some 4,000 tonnes, about half those in Canada. Sales have since revived significantly. Over the years, New Zealand exports have run into the opposition of American lamb producers from time to time, despite efforts to cooperate with them in increasing lamb consumption. In 1983, countervailing duties were imposed on New Zealand lamb, on the representation of the American lamb lobby. At that time, lamb was the recipient of Supplementary Minimum Prices (also known as SMPs) – in other words subsidies – from the Muldoon Government (of which more later). That policy was dropped by the Lange Government after 1984. In 1988 the United States Omnibus Trade and Competition Law removed previous legislative provisions to impose quotas on lamb and casein. The law required the United States International Trade Commission (ITC) to monitor New Zealand lamb imports and allowed the domestic producers to petition if a case of 'injury' to their industry could be claimed.[31]

As was the case with Britain and the European Union, New Zealand has sought to use political arguments from time to time with the United States to reinforce the economic ones, contending that as an American ally under the ANZUS Treaty, New Zealand's economic viability was of political and strategic as well as economic relevance to the United States. Prime Minister Holyoake tried this line of argument on the Nixon Administration in 1969–70, seeking to avert the imposition of quotas on New Zealand lamb exports by a piece of Congressional legislation. In the event they were not imposed.[32]

An interesting case was that of another Muldoon Government subsidy, the Export Market Development Tax Incentive (EMDTI) adopted in 1980, which the Lange Government continued until 1990. In 1985, the United States suspended New Zealand's right to an 'injury test' in all countervailing duty cases – which would have made our defence more difficult – because of the export incentive schemes. A New Zealand request for reinstatement of the 'injury test' because the other six of the seven practices the United States considered breached the GATT Subsidies Code had been phased out, including SMPs, was rejected. This was of concern to lamb and steel exporters although it is doubtful if it cost much in practice. But the American position was that New Zealand had signed the code and all such practices should be ended, whereas the EMDTI was twice extended and not ended until March 1990. The American decision was then rescinded. Despite the frequent disparities between American political and trade policies, this tough American line suggests that it also had a political–foreign policy ingredient, in view of the differences then existing between New Zealand and the United States over nuclear policies. The Muldoon Government might have expected to be able to keep the measure and get away with it. In the event, the Lange Government could not.[33]

To sum up, despite these difficulties from time to time the United States remains one of New Zealand's four biggest markets for both exports and imports. Whereas in earlier years, especially the 1960s and 70s, New Zealand had substantial balance of payments surpluses with the United States, in more recent years the reverse has been the case. Beyond bilateral trade New Zealand has worked closely with the United States in international economic forums, notably the GATT Uruguay Round in which the strong American position was a key factor in a successful outcome.

The Middle East and Other Markets

The 1970s were a decade of political, financial and economic turmoil. In 1971, President Nixon devalued the American dollar (the most important world trading currency) and ended the United States commitment to buy gold at a fixed price, which brought an end to much of the basis of the Bretton Woods financial system set up after World War II. Further, he slapped a 10% special duty on all imports to the United States and banned the export of soy beans to Japan. No wonder the Japanese termed these measures the 'Nixon Shokku'.

Then in 1973, in part as a consequence of the Arab-Israeli war of that year, the Organisation of Petroleum Exporting Countries (OPEC) – dominated by the large Middle East producers such as Saudi Arabia,

Iran and Iraq – succeeded in lifting the international price of oil some fourfold after it had remained stable and relatively cheap for decades. The result was oil shortages and raised costs, producing outbreaks of inflation in many countries around the world. The heavy additional costs the oil importing countries (including New Zealand) incurred was, of course, substantial extra income for the oil exporting countries, whose purchasing power rose astonishingly – a dramatic transfer of wealth. The result was what might be termed an 'oil rush', equivalent to a gold rush, as many countries sought to develop their relations and expand their exports to the new El Dorado in the Middle East.

Iran and *Iraq* were prime New Zealand targets, both because of their new riches and their relatively large populations. New Zealand's high level political contacts with Iran began at the UN General Assembly in late 1973, when Prime Minister Norman Kirk met Iranian Foreign Minister Abbas Ali Khalatbari. This led to an exchange of ministerial and official visits in 1974 and then to a state visit to New Zealand (as to Australia) in September that year by the Shah and Shabanou of Iran. The visit led the New Zealand Government, then under Prime Minister Bill Rowling, to establish embassies in Tehran and also Baghdad in early 1975.

The Shah's interest in Australia and New Zealand was both political and economic. Politically, he saw the two countries as potential partners across the Indian Ocean, an aspect about which New Zealand had little enthusiasm. More to our taste was his concern to find reliable sources of food supplies for his still undeveloped country. (Iranian Prime Minister Hoveyda later remarked to Brian Talboys, when the New Zealand Deputy Prime Minister visited Iran, that Tehran was a city with all the problems of the 20th century while 50 kilometres away people were still riding around on the backs of donkeys, as they did in the Middle Ages.) For New Zealand it seemed almost a form of divine compensation after Britain's entry to the EEC that so much oil should be found under the soil of all those people who ate lamb and cheese and made beautiful carpets out of wool. With, then, some 34 million people (at time of writing now 60 million) and a Gross Domestic Product (GDP) increasing by phenomenal percentages, (the Iranians claimed something around 38 per cent in the 1974–75 year), the Iranian market was an exciting prospect.[34]

A frozen lamb export trade to Iran began on a small scale in 1972 and burgeoned rapidly thereafter, as fast as cold storage facilities could handle it. In the 1977–78 year, some 26,000 tonnes of lamb were delivered and some 40,000 tonnes were on order. By the September year 1984, the total of New Zealand lamb exports reached about 149,000 tonnes, more than we exported to Britain (123,000 tonnes).[35] The New Zealand freezing industry adapted its plants to facilitate 'halal' slaughter, to meet Islamic requirements. There was also a substantial trade in live sheep shipments to Iran and other Middle East countries, although much greater from Australia than New Zealand. The New Zealand Dairy Board was also active in selling skim milk powder and cheese in Iran and secured the first contract of SMP for the Shah's school milk programme, for which 16 milk reconstitution plants were under construction. A potential milk powder market of some 30,000 tonnes per year was an exciting prospect. New Zealand wool too was in demand, for both handmade traditional Persian carpets and machine-made carpets to Persian patterns, which the Iranians concluded they could make as well as the Belgians, then the world's largest manufacturer of them. By 1980, Iran had become New Zealand's sixth biggest export market. Also important, it was a market for lamb, dairy products and wool, traditional New Zealand exports for which new markets had become urgent. The trade was lopsided, and we came under Iranian pressure from time to time to source more of our oil imports from them.

This flourishing export trade was then damaged by the Iranian revolution of 1978–79 (the Shah left Iran in January 1979 and the spiritual leader of the revolution, Imam Khomeini, returned from exile that February) and worse, by Iraq's invasion of Iran in 1980 which led to a cruel, wasteful eight years war. Saddam Hussein, Iraq's leader, thought he could seize the adjoining rich Iranian oil producing province of Khuzistan while Iran was embroiled in the revolution. He made a great mistake and was fought to a stalemate.

The result, for New Zealand's trade, was greatly reduced purchases from an Iran impoverished by the war. If one reflects on the vicissitudes of New Zealand's sheep industry over recent decades one must accord a significant place to the contraction of the Iranian market which occurred during that war and after. Yet the overall trade was still maintained, although at lower levels – itself a considerable political and commercial achievement – and in my view Iran remains a market of potential importance for our primary products. Much the same may be said of

Iraq, which in 1979-80 had ordered a substantial quantity of New Zealand lamb (my recollection is 35,000 tonnes) but the war stopped this development too.[36] In later years trade with other Middle East countries, including Saudi Arabia and the Gulf States has also grown, although at relatively modest levels.

Another important market which also has been subject to political vicissitudes was the former *Soviet Union*, which in the 1970s succeeded Japan as New Zealand's biggest buyer of mutton, a product difficult to dispose of profitably in the modern world. The Soviet Union also became New Zealand's second largest butter market after Britain. The Dairy Board established an agency to import Lada cars (Russian-built Fiats) to help develop reciprocal trade. The last major sale the Dairy Board made to the Soviet Union, 100,000 tonnes in 1990, encountered payment problems consequent upon the dramatic political changes which led to the break-up of the Soviet Union. Subsequently, exports have been sold virtually on a cash basis. Again, the potentialities of the Russian market and those of the other states of the former Soviet Union are substantial but await better political and financial circumstances.

In the early 1970s, *Latin America* offered encouraging prospects as a dairy market, especially for SMP and, in consequence, New Zealand opened embassies in Chile and Peru in 1972. Later in 1983, as the Mexican market also looked promising, Mexico City was added. Cross-accreditations from these posts also covered many other countries of the continent. The 1980s, however, proved a very difficult decade for most Latin American states, with severe debt and inflation problems and while trade continued, volumes languished. The 1990s has seen some revival.

It was *Asia*, which, especially in the 1980s, began to show the most exciting prospects. The booming economies of Northeast Asia – China, Korea, Taiwan and Hong Kong – and the ASEAN countries of Southeast Asia (then Malaysia, Singapore, Indonesia, Thailand, the Philippines and Brunei) grew at remarkable rates and New Zealand exports to them surged accordingly. The trade included a wide spectrum of foodstuffs, timber (to Korea and also Japan) and consultancy services. That boom was sustained throughout the 1980s. The *South Pacific* also became a useful market, Fiji especially, particularly for manufactures. In more recent years exports to the South Pacific have exceeded those to the Middle East.

Looking back, New Zealand has had both considerable achievements and some bad luck with alternative markets. In the 1970s, the Middle East and Latin America looked especially promising until political turmoil and war in one case, and inflation and debt in the other, contracted these opportunities. The Soviet market for primary products looked bigger and bigger as Soviet agriculture failed, until the Soviet state failed too. The Asian boom was sustained throughout the period under review, in fact until the late 1990s when financial collapses produced severe problems and contraction in many Asian economies. In all these cases, a greater trading potentiality is there when recovery comes, as it will.

In hindsight, Britain's decision to join the European Community was probably to New Zealand's long term advantage. Had Britain not done so, New Zealand would have had much less incentive to seek new markets and to diversify products, and might well have remained more dependent on a declining British butter and lamb market than is now the case. In fact, despite the disappointments, New Zealand has succeeded in diversifying its markets and to some extent its products to a remarkable degree. We now export to over 140 countries. Exports to Britain, still almost 36 per cent of our total exports in 1970, were a little over 14 per cent in 1980 and some 6 per cent in the 1990s (although still a high proportion of lamb and butter). Primary products have been processed to a greater degree to meet consumer demand – some 80 per cent of lamb exports are now cuts rather than carcasses. Further, chilled meat rather than frozen – a more competitive product thanks to refrigerated container technology – is becoming gradually a higher proportion of meat exports. Manufactures have also developed significantly and as a group are now one of the biggest foreign exchange earners, as are horticultural and forest products, and tourism.

The question of access to markets, however, remains of critical importance. New Zealand has sought to achieve this through bilateral and regional agreements, and through multilateral trade negotiations in GATT.

GATT and All That

New Zealand became a founding, if initially unenthusiastic, member of the General Agreement on Tariffs and Trade (GATT) in 1948. The agreement reached in Havana in 1947 emerged as a substitute for the proposed International Trade Organisation (ITO). Opposition in the United States Congress to the ITO and its proposed coverage of agricultural commodities had proved too strong and that proposal lapsed.[37] GATT was destined to remain, in theory at least, an interim contractual arrangement between member states (technically 'contracting parties') until the completion of the Uruguay Round in 1994 and the formation of World Trade Organisation (WTO) as its successor. So, about 50 years later, many of the intentions of the 1947 Havana Conference were realised.

Walter Nash, New Zealand Minister of Finance (1935–49) was present at Havana and succeeded in inserting in the GATT text the right to use quantitative restrictions (rather than tariffs) for balance of payments reasons – thus protecting the import licensing system the Labour Government had introduced in 1938.[38] Although the Labour Party was initially wary of GATT – despite Nash's participation in its founding – New Zealand under successive governments gradually realised the advantages for a small country with little international bargaining power but highly dependent on external trade of an international system of rules which might protect their trading rights against stronger states. For example, as earlier commented, it was in an early GATT negotiating round, the Dillon Round in 1961, that New Zealand won the GATT binding governing access for lamb to Europe, which later put us in a much stronger position for lamb than for butter in our access negotiations with the European Community.[39]

But a serious weakness in the GATT structure from its foundation was that while the major industrial states which dominated world trade were ready to see rules laid down to liberalise access for industrial exports, they were not prepared to do likewise for agricultural exports since most followed protected and subsidised agricultural policies. The most visible example was the United States which in 1955 secured a waiver from GATT rules for agriculture which lasted as long as GATT did. Over the years, various devices – particularly 'Voluntary' Restraint Agreements – were used to restrict agricultural imports and there were suggestions from time to time that GATT rules might be changed or stretched to accord more closely with current practices. The New Zealand delegation summed up this trend nicely on one occasion: 'It's rather like saying that as the Ten Commandments are not being fully observed, we should write them so they accord with human behaviour and that, in this way, we would have abolished sin'.[40]

The Tokyo Round negotiations lasted from 1973–79 with the participation of 102 countries, although serious negotiations did not begin until 1975. The round succeeded in further reducing, by one third, custom duties in the world's nine major industrial markets, but on other issues it was, on the whole, disappointing. Agricultural trade was on the agenda and tackled seriously for the first time, but the results were meagre. New Zealand did gain cheese quotas in the United States and the EEC. There was also some improvement in the rules governing subsidies (for the existing rules were regarded as virtually no rules). While the use of agricultural subsidies was still permitted under new rules, they could not (if observed) be used to displace the exports of another country from its export market. There were improvements also in Sanitary and Phytosanitary Standards (SPS) involving plant and animal health in that an orderly procedure was required for changes and it was prohibited to set higher such standards for imports than for domestic products. The round also set up two consultative arrangements, involving exporters and importers, for beef and dairy exports respectively. An International Dairy Arrangement (IDA) was agreed in which New Zealand became an active member. It set agreed minimum prices among the world's leading dairy exporters for butter, cheese and SMP.[41] But the Tokyo Round failed to achieve greater liberalisation of access in agricultural trade when the United States, the most powerful bargainer in the Round, accepted a compromise deal with the European Community which fell well short of that.

The Uruguay Round was launched at Punta del Este, Uruguay in September 1986 and proved to be the largest (126 countries) and longest (1986–94) GATT negotiation, and also the most complex and the most successful. For New Zealand it was of great importance because, at last, agricultural trade became central to the outcome.

Much credit for the eventual outcome of the Round goes to the United States for tougher bargaining with the European Union over agricultural exports than before, and a group of agricultural exporters, including New Zealand, which became known as the Cairns Group. The formation of this group, at first calling itself the 'Fair Traders in Agriculture' (that is, unsubsidised) was an Australian initiative which New Zealand strongly supported – indeed, helped to promote. It first met at officials level in Pattaya, Thailand in July 1986 preparatory to a ministerial level meeting in Cairns, Australia that August, which in turn preceded the Punta del Este meeting in September. It consisted of 14 countries drawn from Asia, the Pacific, North America, Latin America and Eastern Europe.[42] There were some conflicts of interest within the group, with Australia, Canada and New Zealand being principally interested in temperate products and Indonesia, Malaysia and Thailand in tropical products. Canada was sometimes an odd man out in the group, because of its heavy subsidisation of its domestic agriculture (especially its dairy industry) and it would not accept the group position on the ending of all quantitative import restrictions. But by and large the group held together well.

The negotiating agenda adopted in the Ministerial Declaration at Punta del Este, to which New Zealand had made a significant contribution, was the widest ever attempted by GATT. It covered virtually every outstanding trade policy issue and extended the GATT system into new areas such as intellectual property and services, and also to reforms in the sensitive trade sectors of textiles and agriculture. It provided that there should be 'Standstill' (under which participants would agree not to take any trade measures inconsistent with GATT during the negotiations) and 'Rollback' (under which trade restricting or distorting measures should be brought within the provisions of GATT inside an agreed timeframe). It stated, in Section D, 'that there was an urgent need to bring more discipline and predictability to world agricultural trade by preventing and correcting restrictions and distortions including those relating to structural surpluses ...' Further, 'negotiations shall aim to achieve greater liberalisation in agriculture and bring all measures affecting import access and export competition under strengthened and operationally more effective GATT rules and disciplines'. Good stuff for New Zealand and other efficient primary product exporters. Fifteen negotiating groups were then set up, of which the most important for New Zealand was the group negotiating agriculture.[43]

In New Zealand's view the strong position taken by the Cairns Group at this Punta del Este meeting (and, one should add, by the United States) was largely responsible for the strong mandate on agriculture being accepted in the Ministerial Declaration.[44] At meetings of ministers and officials the group fleshed out its tactics. It was agreed it should develop long term GATT rules for agricultural trade; that they should build on the acceptance of Producer Subsidy Equivalents (PSEs) as the best measure of the true level of subsidies; that they should ensure there was not too much 'flexibility' in national implementation plans (they particularly disliked the European Union's idea of 'rebalancing' subsidies which would permit it to increase some by reducing others, within a permitted overall level); and that they should ensure that the Group's proposals did not undercut the position of the United States.[45]

The American position on agriculture was of critical importance to the whole negotiation. It was, on the surface, a tough one, the 'Zero Option', which provided for the phasing out of all trade distorting subsidies and import barriers within a period of 10 years. The United States held to this position until a late stage of the negotiations although some key players, including the European Union and Japan, could not believe they really meant it since the position did seem politically extreme in terms of America's own domestic policies. Nonetheless, the United States took a much firmer line on agriculture in the negotiations than in previous rounds. The Cairns Group also made its own proposals for cuts in domestic and export subsidies which were demanding but, on the face of it, more realistic than the American. The net result was probably to push the European Union and others further towards agricultural trade liberalisation than they would otherwise have gone.

Progress in negotiations was slow. The scheduled mid-term Ministerial meeting in Montreal in December 1988 broke up without full agreement after five Latin American countries threatened to walk out in protest at lack of progress on agriculture. They made it clear they would not accept agreement on any aspect of the negotiations unless and until measures for agriculture were agreed – a position supported more or less explicitly by other agricultural exporters. A 'final' ministerial meeting in Brussels in December 1990 also ended in deadlock – neither the European Union nor Japan would move far enough on agriculture – and the negotiations were at a low ebb. Various strategies were tried to achieve a breakthrough. For agriculture, the Dutch official Art de Zeeuw, chairman of the agriculture negotiating group, produced a compromise paper, which however was not accepted by the European Union. Finally, matters were left to the GATT Secretary-General, Arthur Dunkel, and later his successor, Peter Sutherland, to produce a full compromise proposal, which was accepted in December 1993 (after the

United States and the European Union had settled most of their differences on agriculture in November 1992, in the 'Blair House Accord') and formally concluded at Marrakesh, Morocco, in April 1994.

In brief, the final Uruguay Round Agreement on agriculture provides that in the five years 1995–2000 firstly, internal (financial) support for agriculture will be reduced by 20 per cent from 1986–88 base levels; secondly, that all non-tariff barriers (that is, particularly quantitative restrictions or import controls) will be replaced by tariffs, or 'tariffied' and reduced by at least 15 per cent from 1986–88 base levels; and thirdly that the volume of subsidised agricultural exports will be cut by 21 per cent and budgetary expenditure on export subsidies by 36 per cent from 1986–90 base levels.

If fully observed, there provisions should benefit non-subsidised commercial primary product exporters such as New Zealand. But the end result may not be as good as it may look. The process of conversion of a quantitative restriction to a tariff, on a commodity which had never been subject of a tariff before, led to the setting of some very high tariffs – 'dirty tariffication' as it has been termed[46] – as a one-off exercise. But this does expose the importing country to a degree of ridicule when some tariffs are set at hundreds of percentage points, revealing the true extent of protection, and should therefore help to increase pressure for their eventual reduction.

The Round also provided for country-to-country deals – 'coordinated horse-trading' as it has been called – and New Zealand conducted bilateral negotiations with more than 50 countries which led, in many cases, to the granting of Country Specific Tariff Quotas (CFTQs) to protect existing trade rights or allow increased or new rights of access.

New Zealand's negotiations with the European Union in this context were of the utmost importance and very successful. They increased rights of access for butter, lamb and to a more limited extent, cheese, to the whole of the European Union. The butter quantity permitted was 76,667 tonnes per year (compared to 51,830 tonnes under the last year of Protocol 18 access); for lamb 225,000 tonnes per year (compared to 205,500 tonnes previously); and for cheese, 11,000 tonnes per year (compared to 9,500 tonnes previously) and the right to tender for additional imports, in which New Zealand has been successful. These rights are not subject to 'degressivity'. They are bound under the rules of the new World Trade

Organisation (WTO), the successor to GATT, and cannot be removed or reduced without New Zealand being granted equivalent compensation. They replace Protocol 18.[47]

APEC

The regional grouping Asia-Pacific Economic Co-operation (APEC) was another Australian initiative, by Prime Minister Bob Hawke, in 1989. In many ways it revived the idea of a Pacific economic community which Prime Minister Ohira of Japan had first floated in 1980. The group which Hawke first proposed included selected Asian countries and Australia and New Zealand, but not the United States and Canada. The reaction of both was such as to lead to their inclusion in the founding ministerial conference in Canberra in November 1989.

A second problem was the cautious attitude of some of the six ASEAN countries,[48] especially Malaysia under Prime Minister Mahathir Mohamad, who tended to see the new organisation as a rival which might subsume ASEAN. Mahathir counter-proposed a purely Asian grouping, first termed the East Asia Economic Group (EAEG) which excluded not only the United States and Canada but also Australia and New Zealand. After some hard and confidential lobbying of potential members of this group, by the Americans especially, it was renamed the East Asian Economic Caucus (EAEC) a change which presumably was intended to convey a less institutionalised aspect.[49] The EAEC survives with a purely Asian membership, although New Zealand and Australia have indicated their interest in joining and there is some sympathy for this among the members. But the opposition of Mahathir so far has been decisive. Mahathir's suspicion of APEC survived for some years and he did not attend the first meeting of leaders of APEC convened by President Clinton in Seattle in 1993, but came to that hosted by President Suharto of Indonesia in 1994.[50] APEC's membership soon increased from those countries which founded it in 1989 to a total of 21 members in 1998. A 10 year period of consolidation before any new members are admitted is now proposed.[51]

Because of their economic strength it was thought that China, Taiwan (termed Chinese Taipei) and Hong Kong – then sometimes called the 'three Chinas' – should all be members. To negotiate this successfully it was necessary to assert that members were 'economies' rather than states (because China's claim to sovereignty over both Hong

Kong and Taiwan was internationally recognised) and the meetings are of 'leaders' rather than of heads of government – a convenient political device. Malaysia and the other ASEAN countries were also safely brought on board.

APEC is a regional grouping focused on the liberalisation of trade amongst its members (an early and important decision),[52] the facilitation of intra-regional trade, and economic and technical co-operation. Its leaders meet every year and it was agreed, as a compromise with the ASEAN states, that every second meeting (rather than every meeting as initially they wished) should be held in an ASEAN country – a sequence which will now be altered because of the larger membership. There is a small secretariat, based in Singapore, and a whole raft of committees to consider all aspects of trade, including one of business leaders, the APEC Business Advisory Council (ABAC).

Early meetings included discussion on the best tactics to secure a successful outcome of the GATT Uruguay Round. APEC's own programme, however, was stimulated by the first leaders meeting, convened by President Clinton in Seattle in November 1993, and especially at the next such meeting, in Bogor, Indonesia in November 1994. The Bogor Declaration of Common Resolve set targets for the progressive liberalisation of trade within the grouping – developed members to achieve the goal of free and open trade and investment within the region no later than 2010 and developing economies by 2020.[53] These goals are not mandatory – they are targets and each member is responsible for formulating and implementing its own Individual Action Plan (IAP). The process has been termed 'voluntary co-ordinated liberalisation' or 'concerted unilateralism', a new concept.[54] It is New Zealand policy to encourage the formal binding within the WTO of the voluntary measures for liberalisation agreed within APEC, so that they cannot then be reversed or withdrawn without compensation. New Zealand's current policy is to reach the developed country target by 2006.

For New Zealand, APEC has been important in that it opens up the prospect of better access to markets in the Asia-Pacific region which by the late 1980s accounted for almost 70 per cent of New Zealand's exports and imports. Since many of the Asian, as well as the North American, markets for key primary products of interest to New Zealand were well protected, their future liberalisation within APEC was an enticing prospect. At the same time, New Zealand officials were aware of a certain frailty in some of the fastest growing Asian economies (the NIEs, newly industrialised economies) because of their very high dependence on exports (over 50 per cent of GDP in some cases), especially to the American market.[55] That underlying concern has become a reality in the late 1990s. It remains to be seen to what extent the Asian financial crisis, which began in 1997, affects export prospects in the shorter term – it may well induce greater caution. The longer term prospects still look attractive. APEC therefore remains of great interest to New Zealand which will host the 1999 Leaders Meeting.

The New Zealand Scene

In 1973, New Zealand was hit by a 'triple whammy' – Britain's entry to the European Community; the first oil price hike; and the collapse of our terms of trade. This had been preceded by a collapse of wool prices in 1967, which shook confidence in the economy, followed by a brief commodity boom in 1972–73. These pressures led to heavy foreign borrowing by the Rowling Labour Government in 1974–75, and by the Muldoon National Government after 1975.

Inflation was also a severe problem for New Zealand in those years. The early 70s saw wage-price or price-wage spirals and there was another burst of high inflation in the mid-1980s. The result was that New Zealand's rate of inflation was substantially higher than that of our principal trading partners, an added burden on exporters.[56]

In order to stimulate the economy and also render it less dependent on imported oil, the Muldoon Government launched a series of major projects, the 'Think Big' policy (later headlined by *The Economist* of London 'Sink Big?') particularly in the energy field. The projects included the Marsden Point oil refinery; the Motanui methanol plant (which unlike the refinery was completed on time and within budget); the electrification of more of the North Island main trunk railway; and the Clyde Dam. These projects involved heavy borrowing. The Muldoon Government also implemented a wage-price freeze in an attempt to control inflation in the year preceding its electoral defeat in July 1984. The Lange Labour Government which then took office, after an initial run on the New Zealand dollar which caused a balance of payments crisis, startled many of its own supporters and New Zealand's trading partners by the pace and extent of its economic policy and governmental management reforms.[57] Politicians and officials had begun to realise that the managed economic structure New Zealand had built up since 1938 would not meet New Zealanders' economic aspirations. Consequently, liberalisation of the economy and the dispersal of decision-making to many other, especially private, actors was seen as a better course. The result was an economic revolution.

The new government devalued the New Zealand dollar to US43c and then, in March 1985, floated it (a clean, not a managed float) whereupon it soared up to US70c, as a result of higher interest rates and an inflow of short-term overseas capital. The government removed foreign exchange controls; removed controls over prices and wages; deregulated the financial sector and opened it to greater international competition; liberalised rules for foreign direct investment in New Zealand; steadily removed remaining import controls and unilaterally lowered many tariffs as well; revised the tax structure and with the introduction of the Goods and Services Tax (GST) in 1986, shifted the incidence from direct towards indirect taxation; restructured the public sector and privatised some of its commercial operations; and quickly removed almost all agricultural subsidies.

This last was an important matter in terms of our export trade. The Muldoon Government had introduced Supplementary Minimum Prices for lamb exports, a direct subsidy which was noted adversely by those trading partners abroad, notably in the European Union, whom we were accusing in all appropriate international trade forums of unfair subsidisation of agriculture. Their prompt abolition by Labour was accepted by leaders of the New Zealand farming community, although they disputed the sequence of the Government's reforms and argued that they were being singled out while the labour market, much in need of reform in their view, was relatively untouched. But the abolition of SMPs and other farming subsidies restored the virtue and strength of New Zealand's arguments against agricultural subsidies.[58]

The stock market crash of 1987, precipitated by Wall Street, hit New Zealand hard and checked the benefits of the reform process. There was something of a boom psychology from 1984–87 followed by a distinct bust, from which New Zealand had not fully recovered by the early 1990s. The consequence has been a growing public disenchantment with the free market policies which were continued by the National Government in the years following its election in 1990, years in which

Labour, instigators of the reforms, began to move away from them. Such are the fortunes of political life. Whatever their social impact, however, it must be said that the reforms have made New Zealand exporters more innovative and more competitive. They have also, by opening our economy to almost complete freedom of importing and reducing tariffs unilaterally, encouraged the longstanding New Zealand habit of importing more than we can afford. This has produced once more, at time of writing, a serious balance of payments problem. How future governments will handle this perennial problem remains to be seen.

Notes

1 See Annex I.
2 *New Zealand Foreign Affairs Review* (hereafter *NZFAR*), September 1970, p.16.
3 For a discussion of this point, see also Merwyn Norrish, 'Changes in the Focus of the Foreign Ministry' in Ann Trotter (ed.), *Fifty Years of New Zealand Foreign Policy Making* (Dunedin, 1993), pp.152ff.
4 For an account of the negotiations see Bruce Brown, ' "Foreign Policy is Trade": Trade is Foreign Policy: Some Principal New Zealand Trade Policy Problems since the Second World War', in Trotter, *Fifty Years of New Zealand Foreign Policy Making*, pp.62–83, and Bruce Brown, 'From Bulk Purchase to Butter Disputes: New Zealand's Trading Relations with Britain' in Robert Patman (ed.), *New Zealand and Britain: A Special Relationship in Transition* (Palmerston North, 1997), pp.44–50.
5 *NZFAR*, October–December 1980, p.21.
6 See, for example, Miriam Camp's *Britain and the European Community 1955–64*, (London, 1964) pp.347, p.350.
7 The quantities were as follows:

	Butter (tonnes)	**Cheese** (tonnes)
1973	165,811	65,580
1974	158,902	60,960
1975	151,994	45,720
1976	145,085	30,480
1977	138,176	15,240

Source: *Protocol 18, Article I(2)*.
8 The six founder members of the EEC which signed the Treaty of Rome in 1957 were France, Germany, Italy and the three 'Benelux' countries (Belgium, the Netherlands and Luxembourg). Britain, Denmark and Ireland joined in 1973 and Greece in 1979. Spain and Portugal were admitted in 1986.
9 For details of the annual butter quantities, see Annex II.
10 Under the CAP intervention schemes, the EEC set very high domestic price levels for the various agricultural products subject to such regimes, to an extent

which encouraged greatly increased domestic production and probably also discouraged consumption. The price levels necessitated high levels of subsidies. Unsold product was then bought by the EEC at highly subsidised prices and much of it disposed of abroad at much lower levels, to the detriment of more efficient commercial exporters, such as New Zealand. The Community's subsidised exports have been of such volumes as effectively to set world market prices.

11 'The Sheepmeat Regime', New Zealand High Commission Memorandum to the House of Lords European Communities Sub-Committee, May 1984. House of Lords 21st Report, London, June 1984.

12 For sheep numbers, see Brian Chamberlin, former President of Federated Farmers of New Zealand and New Zealand Agricultural Counsellor in London, in *North and South*, February 1993, p.28. In the case of butter, the Community's share of the world market increased from 22 per cent in 1972 to 65 per cent in 1980. See MFAT 607/5/1 Pt.5, p.114.

13 As Deputy High Commissioner in London from 1981–85, I had the carriage of these access issues.

14 *NZFAR*, September 1972, p.19.

15 Brief on New Zealand–United Kingdom Trade Relations, for Minister of Overseas Trade and Marketing, March 1988, MFAT 607/8/3. Pt.9, p.72.

16 Bryce Harland, *On Our Own* (Wellington, 1992), pp.25–6. Harland was New Zealand High Commissioner to Britain from 1985–91.

17 David Lange, *Nuclear Free – the New Zealand Way* (Auckland, 1990), pp.111-12.

18 Peter Lloyd, 'Australia–New Zealand Trade Relations: NAFTA to CER', in Keith Sinclair (ed.), *Tasman Relations* (Auckland, 1987), pp.143–5, 151–4.

19 *NZFAR*, July–September 1977, pp.27–8.

20 For report of the visit and text of the Declaration, see *NZFAR* January–March 1978, pp.16–29.

21 See Hugh Templeton, *All Honourable Men – Inside the Muldoon Cabinet 1975–84* (Auckland, 1995), especially ch.13. As a personal recollection from my time as Deputy High Commissioner in London, New Zealand came very close to being expelled from the Commonwealth Games Association at a special meeting in London because of the anger of the many African members, supported by Asian and Caribbean associations, at New Zealand's acceptance of the Springbok tour. That would have caused a serious split in the Commonwealth and probably wrecked the Brisbane Games.

22 See Stephen Hoadley, 'Trans-Tasman Relations', pp.177–204 below.

23 Personal recollection, as Deputy High Commissioner, Canberra, 1972–75.

24 See Ann Trotter, 'An Evolving Relationship', pp.205–25 below.

25 Personal recollection of Rob McLuskie, then a New Zealand Meat Producers Board official.

26 Ian Kennedy, *Japan and New Zealand: Adding Value* (Wellington, 1992), p.122.

27 *NZFAR*, April–June 1976, pp.29–33

28 See *NZFAR*, April–June 1977, pp.10-11. A further discussion follows in Trotter, 'An Evolving Relationship', pp.205–25 below.

29 The waiver applied from 1955 until 1994, when it was removed, along with all quantitative restrictions in agriculture in the GATT Uruguay Round and replaced by tariffs.

30 In 1981, the New Zealand Dairy Board bought 100,000 tonnes of US CCC butter, in order to process it and market it abroad in a way which would do least damage to the world market and prices. The move raised some eyebrows in the European Union (which did however, gain some of the processing work) but on the whole seemed a successful manoeuvre. Personal recollections as DHC London, 1981–85.
31 At the time of writing, in 1999, American producers had taken such action and won a decision from the United States International Trade Commission that a 20 per cent tariff should be placed on New Zealand lamb for four years. The New Zealand Meat Industries Association and the New Zealand Government lobbied the United States Administration urging that this judgment should not be enforced but the Administration decided to impose tariffs declining over three years from 9 per cent to 6 per cent and 3 per cent on quantities up to the 1998 level of exports and of 40 per cent, 32 per cent and 24 per cent on quantities above that level, all to be reviewed within 18 months. New Zealand has initated consultations under the WTO disputes procedures. *Source:* New Zealand Meat Industries Association.
32 See, for example, Ray F. Goldstein, 'New Zealand Lobbies America', in *Political Science*, December 1969, pp.18–35 and Bruce Brown, 'New Zealand Lobbies America: A Comment' and Ray Goldstein, 'A Rejoinder', in *Political Science,* July 1970, pp.26–39.
33 Frank Holmes and Clive Pearson, *Meeting the European Challenge – Trends, Prospects and Politics* (Wellington, 1991), pp.183–5 and Paul L. Laase, 'United States Bilateral Economic Relations with Australia and New Zealand' in Richard Baker and Gary Hawke (eds.), *ANZUS Economics: Economic Trends and Relations among Australia, New Zealand and the United States* (Westport, 1992), pp.202; plus personal recollections.
34 *NZFAR*, June 1974, pp.28–30 and October 1974, pp.11–19. Also, personal recollections as the first New Zealand Ambassador to Iran, 1975–78.
35 New Zealand Meat Producers Board.
36 It was in an attempt to recoup his losses in the war with Iran, reputed to have cost Iraq some US$30 billion, that Saddam Hussein invaded the rich oil producing state of Kuwait in 1990, only to be pushed out by international action in the 1991 Gulf War.
37 The ambitious draft charter of the ITO covered not only world trade disciplines but also rules on employment, commodity agreements, restrictive business practices, international investment, and services. *MFAT Brochure: Basics*, p.1.8
38 It was inserted as a footnote to Article XXI. Keith Sinclair, *Walter Nash* (Auckland, 1976), p.254.
39 See p.26 above. GATT negotiating rounds took place in 1947 (23 countries), 1949 (13), 1951 (38), 1956 (26), 1960–61 Dillon Round (26), 1964–67 Kennedy Round (62), 1973–79 Tokyo Round (102) and 1986–94 Uruguay Round (125). *MFAT Brochure: Basics* p.1.8.
40 New Zealand statement in GATT meeting, 28–30 April 1971, which noted that the Kennedy Round's virtual neglect of agriculture meant that concessions agreed in the Round covered only 3.6 per cent of New Zealand's export trade. MFAT PM 104/48/1 Vol.2, 1 January 1971–30 June 1973.

41 *MFAT Brochure: Basics*, pp.1.9–1.10 and MFAT 104/48/5 Pt.11, 1 October–31 December 1975.
42 Membership of the Cairns Group was as follows:
Argentina	Columbia	New Zealand
Australia	Fiji	The Philippines
Brazil	Hungary	Thailand
Canada	Indonesia	Uruguay
Chile	Malaysia	
43 MFAT 607/5/1 Pt.5, 1 December 1986–31 March 1987 and *MFAT Brochure: Basics* pp.1.12–13. The fifteen groups were:
Tariffs	Anti-Dumping
Non-Tariff Barriers	Subsidies
Natural Resource Products	Intellectual Property
Textiles and clothing	Investment Measure
Agriculture	Dispute Settlement
Tropical Products	The GATT System
GATT Articles	Services
Tokyo Round Codes	
44 New Zealand Statement at the 2nd Cairns Group SOM, Bangkok 9–11 February 1987. MFAT 607/5/1 Pt.5.
45 Cairns Group SOM 22–23 September 1987, MFAT 607/5/1 Pt.6. Producer Subsidy Equivalents measured the percentage of farm income derived from subsidies. New Zealand has consistently had the lowest level for many years, Japan and many European countries amongst the highest.
46 During my time as New Zealand High Commissioner to Canada, 1988–92, it was reported that Canadian officials had calculated they would need a tariff of 240 per cent to keep out New Zealand butter and 178 per cent for New Zealand cheese. Later estimates, I understand, were higher.
47 MFAT, *Trading Ahead – The GATT Uruguay Round Results for New Zealand*, pp.22–33 especially. The report covers a wide range of the negotiations. There were many other gains for New Zealand, including increased beef access rights to the United States and Canada.
48 The Association of Southeast Asian Nations, (ASEAN) then consisted of Brunei, Indonesia, Malaysia, the Philippines, Singapore and Thailand. Vietnam, Myanmar (formerly Burma) and Cambodia have since been added.
49 See MFAT 604/1/7/16, APEC Regional Trade Liberalisation, 1 January 1991–31 July 1992.
50 MFAT brief for New Zealand – Australia talks, 10 December 1993, MFAT 604/1/7/3. Later Mahathir's attitude changed to the point where he hosted the 1998 APEC meeting in Kuala Lumpur.
51 Australia, Brunei Darrusalam, Canada, Chile, China (Peoples Republic), Chinese Taipei, Hong Kong, Indonesia, Japan, Korea (Republic of), Malaysia, Mexico, New Zealand, Papua New Guinea, Peru, the Philippines, Russia, Singapore, Thailand, United States, and Vietnam.
52 See MFAT 301/1/2, October 1989–January 1990.
53 *Asian-Pacific Co-operation*, 1997, Ministry of Foreign Affairs and Trade p.2ff.

54 The APEC Committee on Trade and Investment considers a wide range of issues covering all aspects of regional trade and there are also a number of working groups of officials dealing with specific issues. The Committee considers Tariffs and Non-Tariff Measures; Services; Investment; Standards and Conformity; Customs Procedures; Intellectual Property Rights; Competition Policy; Governmental Procurement; Deregulation; Rules of Origin; Dispute Mediation; Mobility of Business People (i.e. visa requirements etc); Implementation of Uruguay Round Outcomes; and Early Voluntary Sectoral Liberalisation (EVSL). Working groups cover Energy; Fisheries; Human Resources Development; Industrial Science and Technology; Marine Resource Conservation; Telecommunications; Tourism; Trade and Investment Data Review; Trade Promotion; and Transportation – a formidable list. *MFAT Update of Activities within APEC, Special Edition*, November 1998.

55 See MFAT Brief, October 1989, for the first APEC Ministerial Meeting, Canberra, November 1989, MFAT 301/1/2. The shift in New Zealand's trade pattern towards the APEC region was shown by the changes from 1970–87: New Zealand exports increased from 23 per cent in 1970 to 63 per cent in 1987; and imports from 52 per cent in 1970 to 67 per cent in 1987.

56 From 1974–87, comparative figures for inflation were: New Zealand 430 per cent; Britain 240 per cent; Australia 180 per cent; United States 140 per cent; Japan 78 per cent. Brian Chamberlin, President of New Zealand Federated Farmers, to the World Food Conference, Brussels, April 1988. MFAT 607/8/3 Pt.9.

57 For a full account of these and earlier developments in the New Zealand economy, see Gary Hawke, 'Economic Trends and Economic Policy, 1938–92', in Geoffrey W. Rice (ed.), *The Oxford History of New Zealand* (second Edition, Auckland, 1992), pp.412–50.

58 As DHC, London, I encountered arguments from British and European Union officials that 'everybody subsidises their agriculture – including New Zealand. It's just a matter of degree'. The SMPs received unfortunate publicity in *Agra-Europe*, the leading European journal of agriculture, published in Brussels and circulated widely in the European Union, as a result of the holding of the world conference of the International Federation of Agricultural Journalists (IFAJ) in New Zealand in November 1982. No doubt that had seemed a good idea when it was first decided upon some years earlier. For the conference, see *NZFAR*, October–December 1982, pp.12–15.

I am indebted to Professor Gary Hawke, Professor Sir Frank Holmes, Peter Kennedy, Professor Ralph Lattimore, Stuart McMillan, Merwyn Norrish and Ted Woodfield who read and commented on my draft. Responsibility for the content, however, remains with me.

Annex I:
New Zealand's Comparative Terms of Trade 1929–33 and 1973–75

1. **1929–33**
(Base: 1977 = 100)

1929	138
1930	109
1931	90
1932	86
1933	84

Percentage fall = 39.1%

Source: Peter Nicholl and Alan Boaden, 'New Zealand' in Baker and Hawke (eds) *ANZUS Economics*, p.93.

2. **1973–75**
(Base: 1957 = 100)

1973 (June quarter):	124
1975 (March quarter):	70

Percentage fall = 43.5%

Source: John Gould, *The Rake's Progress* (Auckland 1982), pp.127–30.

3. **Comment**
The figures are obviously not an exact comparison, because of the differing composition of the indices and the differing base years. Nonetheless they do serve to illustrate that the depth of the fall in 1973–75, over a period of only 21 months, was even steeper than between 1929 and 1933, the depth of the Great Depression.

Annex II:
New Zealand's Butter Access Entitlement to the European Community 1973–93

	European Commission Recommendation (tonnes)	European Council Decision (tonnes)
a) Transitional Period – Five-year Proposal, 1973–77		
1973		165,811
1974		158,902
1975		151,994
1976		145,085
1977		138,176

(Protocol 18 to the Treaty of Rome, adopted 1971)

NEW ZEALAND IN THE WORLD ECONOMY

	European Commission Recommendation (tonnes)	European Council Decision (tonnes)

b) Post–1977 Access – Three-year Proposal, 1978–80

	Original	Revised*	
1978	129,000	125,000	125,000*
1979	121,000	120,000	120,000
1980	113,000	115,000**	95,000**

* Revised proposal approved June 1976
** An agreed later volume reduction set-off against a levy reduction which lifted the price.

c) Post–1980 Access – Three-year Proposal, 1981–83

1981	94,000	94,000*
1982	92,000	92,000*
1983	90,000**	87,000**

* Approved April 1981
** The Council decision on the 1983 total was delayed until 16 March 1983

d) Post–1983 Access – Five-year Proposal, 1984–88

1984	83,000	83,000*
1985	81,000	81,000*
1986	79,000	79,000*
1987	77,000	76,500**
1988	75,000	74,500**

* Approved 12 July 1984
** Approved July 1986

e) Post–1988 Access – Four-year Proposal, 1989–92

1989	64,500	64,500
1990	61,340	61,340
1991	58,170	58,170
1992	55,000	55,000

Approved 26 September 1989

f) Post–1992 Access – One-year Proposal, 1993

1993	55,000	51,830

Approved 17 December 1992

Sources: New Zealand Foreign Affairs Review; New Zealand Dairy Board; Juliet Lodge, *The European Community and New Zealand* (London, 1982).

MALCOLM TEMPLETON

New Zealand and the Development of International Law

AS THIS TOPIC WAS NOT DEALT WITH IN THE FIRST TWO volumes of *New Zealand in World Affairs*, I may stray a little outside the temporal limits of Volume III. Instead of attempting comprehensive coverage, I shall concentrate on three major issues and developments in international law with which New Zealand has been involved between 1970 and 1990; human rights, nuclear weapons tests, and the law of the sea.

It is safe to say that more international law has been developed or codified since the Second World War than in all previous recorded history. Since virtually every treaty imposes obligations as well as establishing rights, the body of new law taken as a whole has created an extensive regulatory system within which states exercise their sovereignty. It is also safe to say that this development has failed to penetrate the consciousness of the New Zealand public, whose attitude to international law might be described as pragmatic. When a piece of international legislation confers a benefit on New Zealand, it welcomes it. When that benefit disappears, or a treaty provision collides with a domestic policy, the instinctive reaction is to ignore, reject or even abuse the provision in question. The Law of the Sea Treaty, for example, confers great benefits on New Zealand as a coastal state with a vast exclusive economic zone and continental shelf. At the same time, the Treaty codifies traditional freedoms of the sea, including the right of innocent passage,[1] but there were many, especially in the anti-nuclear movement and the left wing of the Labour Party, who were prepared to argue that New Zealand should ignore the Treaty and legislate to exclude nuclear armed ships from its territorial seas.[2] I have recorded elsewhere how, when it appeared that the International Labour Organisation might issue a critical report about the New Zealand Government's labour legislation, there was an outraged response from New Zealand ministers: if New Zealand was in breach of its obligations under ILO Conventions, the Conventions must be outdated and the ILO a dinosaur.[3] More recently, there have been claims from interest groups in New Zealand that the proposed OECD Multilateral Agreement on Investment would restrict the exercise of New Zealand sovereignty. Of course it would. But the real question, which the opponents of the MAI tended to avoid, was whether the benefits to be conferred did or did not outweigh the obligations the parties would be required to assume.

International law may be, and has been, viewed in two ways: it can be regarded as providing the *foundation* of state rights, or simply as imposing a restriction on the unfettered exercise of state sovereignty, so that anything which cannot be shown to be forbidden by some rule of international law is *ipso facto* allowable. In the opinion of a distinguished British jurist, Sir Gerald Fitzmaurice, the latter view is a retrograde and unscientific one, not in accordance with the real spirit or best interests of the development of international law. Yet there is an obvious temptation for a government to embrace that view when, in a particular set of circumstances, it appears to offer that government a short term advantage. The interests of a small country such as New Zealand are better served, I suggest, by support for the former approach and by active participation in the ongoing treaty-making process, so as to progressively reduce the areas in which the latter view can plausibly be invoked.

Human Rights

> Let us not pretend. We do not have any profound national commitment to anything in the civil liberties field. Pragmatism is dearer to us than principle.
>
> Geoffrey Palmer[4]

The United Nations Charter of 1945 called for the promotion of human rights without discrimination, and pledged its members to work for their universal observance. Not only that, but it established machinery to make specific recommendations in the field of human rights and, if necessary, to prepare draft conventions giving effect to them. While the International Labour Organisation had shown the way in respect of labour law, the broad sweep of the Charter provisions was a giant step forward into a field of law-making that governments had tended to treat as within their domestic jurisdiction. At the founding UN Conference in San Francisco, New Zealand supported the strengthening of the human rights provisions of the Charter,[5] without perhaps appreciating all the implications of their implementation. New Zealand governments of the time would not, for example, have considered their discriminatory immigration policies an appropriate topic for international review, and for some years New Zealand ministers did not consider the racially discriminatory policies of other UN members to be within the United Nations' legal competence to examine.[6]

As a first step towards the codification of human rights, the United Nations General Assembly adopted the Universal Declaration of Human Rights in 1948. This was not a binding treaty: that was to follow. New Zealand supported the broadening of the Declaration to include economic and social as well as civil and political rights.[7] It would have preferred the treaty commitment and implementation measures to be adopted simultaneously with the Declaration, but in fact the two Covenants, on Civil and Political and on Economic and Social Rights, were not completed until 1966. New Zealand signed the Covenants in 1968, but did not ratify them until 10 years later.

Surprisingly, perhaps, the third Labour Government showed no particular interest in ratification. The Prime Minister, Norman Kirk, was content, in response to correspondents urging that New Zealand take this step, to sign letters indicating that early action was unlikely. 'It is our preliminary conclusion', Kirk wrote in July 1973, '. . . that ratification . . . would raise juridical difficulties for us'.[8] Two years later, his successor, Bill Rowling, took a somewhat less negative stand: 'we are committed to ratification . . . but the actual legal processes involved for a country with a legal system such as ours are both involved and prolonged'.[9] There is no indication that the task of scrutinising New Zealand's legislation to ensure its conformity with the Covenants was being pursued with any sense of priority.

The National Party, however, had included in its manifesto for the 1975 elections an undertaking to introduce into Parliament a Human Rights Bill which would establish a New Zealand Human Rights

Commission, and in the course of a visit to Britain in April 1976, the newly elected Prime Minister, Robert Muldoon, announced a firm intention to proceed with such a measure.[10] The Foreign Ministry took the opportunity to propose that the Bill should provide a basis for ratifying the Covenants. By this time the Covenants had entered into force,[11] and Britain, Australia and Canada were actively considering ratification. There were still, in the view of Ministry lawyers, a number of potential difficulties for New Zealand. Article 13 of the Civil and Political Covenant would give aliens the right to challenge decisions expelling them from New Zealand: at the time, deportation of aliens was at the discretion of the appropriate Minister. Article 14(6) would establish a right to compensation for a person whose criminal conviction was subsequently overturned. (The compensation was to be provided 'according to law": this would seem *prima facie* to suggest a requirement for appropriate legislation). Legislation might also be needed, the Ministry thought, to guarantee freedom of peaceful assembly (Article 21) and the anti-discriminatory provisions in both Covenants.[12]

In March 1977, reporting to the Foreign Ministry in my capacity as New Zealand representative on the UN Economic and Social Council (ECOSOC), I drew attention to President Carter's announcement that he intended to seek Congressional approval for him to sign the Covenants, the Genocide Convention and the Treaty for the Elimination of Racial Discrimination. I sought approval to inform the Council that the New Zealand Government also had in mind legislation to permit early ratification of the Covenants and the Genocide Convention.[13] The Government was not, however, ready to take this step. It had been decided by the Justice Department that the Covenants could not be dealt with in the Human Rights Commission Bill, although Foreign Ministry lawyers felt that only minor elaboration of the Bill would be required.[14] Addressing the UN General Assembly in October 1977, the Foreign Minister, Brian Talboys, 'expected' that New Zealand would ratify both Covenants and the Genocide Convention no later than 1978.[15]

Nothing happened until September 1978, when the General Debate speech was delivered by the Prime Minister. The two Covenants and the Genocide Convention, he announced, would be ratified by New Zealand *during the current Assembly*.[16] Muldoon being Muldoon, this self-imposed time limit kindled a fire under the ratification process. After rather desperate efforts (the Cook Islands and Niuean Governments had to be consulted) the ratification instruments were delivered to a somewhat elusive UN Secretariat between Christmas and the New Year.[17]

A number of reservations were entered to the Covenants, in regard to trade union rights, paid maternity leave, the segregation of adult and juvenile prison inmates, compensation for wrongful imprisonment, advocacy of religious hatred, and freedom of association.[18] These reservations, which were given no publicity, still stand today. What the reader may find remarkable, 20 years later, is that the ratification process was conducted without any thought of consulting Parliament, still less the general public, either in regard to the very extensive obligations accepted or the quite significant reservations entered. Moreover, while the Economic, Social and Cultural Covenant admittedly envisaged gradual rather than immediate implementation, the whole underlying philosophy was one requiring state intervention and regulation to promote the rights in question. At the time it is doubtful that even the Cabinet looked closely at the fine print of the Covenants. While Muldoon was condemning in the Assembly those countries which denied the right to freedom of opinion and expression, Cabinet was considering a move to restrict the freedom of Southern African students awarded scholarships in New Zealand to express themselves publicly on controversial issues, such as apartheid and sports contacts with South Africa.[19]

An Optional Protocol to the Civil and Political Covenant permitted individuals claiming to be victims of human rights violations to complain to an international body, the Human Rights Committee established by that Covenant. New Zealand did not ratify this Protocol until 1989. (It simultaneously ratified a second protocol outlawing the death penalty.) In 1990, in the last days of the fourth Labour Government, the New Zealand Parliament passed a Bill of Rights Act, designed 'to affirm New Zealand's commitment' to the Civil and Political Covenant.[20] This Act, it should be noted, is an ordinary repealable piece of legislation; New Zealand's Bill of Rights is not, as in some countries, embodied in an entrenched Constitution.

In 1994, the New Zealand Court of Appeal declared that the Human Rights Committee was 'in a sense part of this country's judicial structure in that individuals subject to New Zealand jurisdiction have direct rights of recourse to it'.[21] While to some this might seem a statement of the obvious, others regard it as controversial, since the Committee is not constituted as a judicial organ, and cannot therefore pronounce judgments: and there is no certainty that the Privy Council (to which New Zealand retains an anachronistic right of ultimate appeal) or a more conservative New Zealand Appeal Court, would necessarily uphold the position taken in the 1994 judgment.

Few people, perhaps, would now endorse the argument of Richard Mulgan, 30 years ago, that the Universal Declaration of Human Rights 'is a dangerous and hypocritical document which is likely to exacerbate the situation it was intended to improve'.[22] Nevertheless, I suggest, the collective will of New Zealanders to give effect to the provisions of the Declaration and the Covenants, by imposing effective remedies for their violation, is at best shaky. New Zealand's foremost living jurist, Lord Cooke, has noted the 'weakness' of the New Zealand Bill of Rights. The attempts of the New Zealand courts to give it teeth, he observes, have been seen abroad as the best evidence that it works 'up to a point', but have been the subject of criticism within New Zealand.

'The enactment of a legal right is meaningless and window dressing without a legal remedy . . . it is the duty of the courts to provide legal remedies for the breach of legal rights.' The more influential the opposition to this view, says Lord Cooke, 'the more out of touch we will be with the trend towards internationally recognised human rights'.[23] One can only agree.

What international developments – in addition, one hopes, to greater compliance – may be expected in the future? The Declaration and the Covenants have not been without their critics. The Declaration, it is suggested, is essentially a 'Western' document, which takes insufficient account of other cultures. The Prime Minister of Malaysia has proposed that it be 'reviewed'. The United States Secretary of State has rejected that suggestion.[24] Critics argue that 'Western' countries put excessive emphasis on civil and political rights, paying scant attention to economic and social rights. There is some justice in this criticism. Active implementation of the Economic Social and Cultural Covenant would require a degree of intervention by the state which does not appeal to devotees of the market.

If the rights in that Covenant are to be implemented progressively, as New Zealand understood when it ratified, can they be enforced? Are they, in legal terminology, justiciable?[25] At the time of the adoption of the Declaration, New Zealand went out of its way to emphasise that it regarded all the rights it proclaimed, not least the economic, social and cultural rights, as of equal importance. Nevertheless it would have come as a considerable and unwelcome surprise to the Government that ratified the Covenants some 30 years later, had it been told that the rights in the second Covenant might be legally enforceable. For that proposition to become widely adopted would require a much greater willingness to accept international intervention in domestic policy than is evident at present. After all a number of important and populous states, including China, Indonesia, Pakistan and the United States, have still to ratify the Economic, Social and Cultural Covenant.[26] And although ECOSOC established a Committee on Economic, Social and Cultural Rights in 1985 to make recommendations about the implementation of that Covenant, it is not empowered to receive and consider complaints about its violation.[27]

Prominent as Article I in *both* Covenants is an assertion of the right of all peoples to self-determination. This right differs from other rights in the Covenants in focussing on *peoples* rather than individuals. For some years the Western colonial powers resisted the inclusion of this right in the Covenants (it does not appear in the Declaration), claiming that self-determination was a principle rather than a right: New Zealand joined in the opposition to its inclusion, but the developing countries, most of them former colonies, insisted and had their way. By the time New Zealand decided to ratify the Covenants, the United Nations had been persuaded to accept acts of self-determination by two island territories administered by New Zealand – the Cook Islands and Niue – that enabled them to retain constitutional links with New Zealand. The self-determination article did not, therefore, cause the New Zealand Government to enter a reservation when it ratified the Covenants. The article again became the focus of contention, however, when ECOSOC initiated an examination of the rights of indigenous peoples (or populations) by a Working Group (WGIP) in 1982. Between 1985 and 1993, the Group worked on a draft declaration on the rights of such peoples. The Commission on Human Rights in 1995 established another Working Group (WGDD) to continue work on the draft. Contentious issues, including the applicability or otherwise of the right of self-determination to indigenous peoples, have slowed progress towards its completion.

Between 1970 and 1993, New Zealand ratified several other United Nations Conventions dealing with aspects of human rights, including the International Convention on the Elimination of All Forms of Racial Discrimination (November 1972), the Convention on the Elimination of All Forms of Discrimination Against Women (January 1985), the Convention on the Rights of the Child (May 1993) and the Convention Against Torture and Other Cruel, Inhuman or Degrading Treatment or Punishment (December 1989).[28]

Nuclear Weapons Tests

The testing of nuclear weapons in the Pacific, which the New Zealand Government and most of its citizens tended to accept without too much fuss while the tests were being conducted by Britain and the United States, became the object of acute concern when, after those two countries had ended their test programmes in the atmosphere (and in the Pacific), France embarked on what seemed a never-ending series of tests conducted in its South Pacific island territories.

Diplomatic protests having proved singularly ineffective, New Zealand from about 1970 onwards, sought to bring about an end to nuclear weapons testing by legal means, with special focus on the French tests. It took the offensive on three fronts, collaborating closely with Australia on two of them.[29] In the United Nations General Assembly, it sought to promote and accelerate the negotiation of a comprehensive test ban treaty (CTBT). In 1973, with Australia, it undertook, for the first time, a case in the International Court of Justice (ICJ) to have the French tests declared illegal. With two Pacific Island countries, Fiji and Papua New Guinea, but without Australia, it sought the endorsement of the UN General Assembly in 1975 for a South Pacific Nuclear Weapon Free Zone (SPNFZ). Later, it collaborated *with* Australia and other South Pacific countries in drawing up a SPNFZ Treaty.

In the General Assembly, New Zealand worked closely with Australia, Sweden and sometimes Mexico, in seeking the support of as large a majority as possible for resolutions condemning (or failing that, deploring) the continuance of nuclear weapons testing, including underground tests, and calling for the early conclusion of a CTBT. Lopsided majorities were, in fact, secured: but to no avail. The nuclear weapon states variously opposed, abstained or even on occasion (but not in concert) supported the resolutions. But on the actual negotiations, which were supposed to take place in Geneva in the Conference on Disarmament (CD), no progress was made in the 1970s and 1980s. New Zealand's participation in the disarmament debates was limited by its non-membership of the CD, (it did not become a member until 1996)[30] but its presence would have made no difference. A CTBT was finally concluded in 1996, but its entry into force has been stymied by India.[31]

The ICJ case against France was an Australian initiative. The New Zealand Prime Minister, Norman Kirk, was at first unenthusiastic. His pet project was to send a frigate to the island of Mururoa, where France was conducting its tests, to make them a focus for international attention and, he hoped, condemnation. But the British-built RNZN frigates lacked the necessary range, and the support of an Australian naval tanker was needed to keep one on station near Mururoa. So a deal was done between Kirk and the Australian Prime Minister, Gough Whitlam. The tanker was made available, and New Zealand joined in the Court action. (It could scarcely have stood aside, but Kirk played his cards well). The New Zealand and Australian legal teams presented separate cases, not always in full harmony. The New Zealand team, led by the Attorney-General, Martyn Finlay, was entirely indigenous, but had the benefit of the advice of eminent international lawyers from abroad, hired at great expense by Australia. After more than a year of judicial manoeuvring, in which the Court joined the two cases together for the purposes of a hearing, refused the French demand that they be thrown out, and issued an interim injunction (which France ignored), France announced that the atmospheric tests it intended to conduct in 1974 would be the last. In December of that year the Court, without giving the plaintiffs an opportunity to argue the point, decided that the French decision to cease atmospheric testing meant that the Australian and New Zealand complaint 'no longer had any object'. If France resumed atmospheric testing, it would be open to the plaintiffs to come back to the Court, but for the time being at least the majority of the judges had managed to avoid pronouncing on whether the Court indeed had jurisdiction to hear the case.[32]

Whether the possibility that the Court might accept jurisdiction *caused* France to cease atmospheric testing and to conduct future tests underground, or whether it intended to do so anyway, is a matter on which there can be two opinions. The New Zealand Government, however, had no hesitation in claiming victory. The Prime Minister, Bill Rowling, asserted that 'there was now the highest authority for the proposition that any resumption of atmospheric nuclear testing in the South Pacific would be in breach of an international obligation'.[33]

In the absence of discernible progress towards a global prohibition of nuclear weapons testing, the New Zealand Government decided in 1975 to approach the problem on a regional basis, by promoting a treaty-based nuclear weapon free zone in the South Pacific. For this the Antarctic Treaty offered one paradigm, the Treaty of Tlatelolco another. But a SPNFZ would be more ambitious. Antarctica is virtually uninhabited. In Latin America, the Treaty of Tlatelolco applied predominantly to a continent in which the nuclear powers had relatively minor territorial interests. The South Pacific area, on the other hand, includes vast areas of high seas, and the question whether a treaty would apply to maritime areas was initially obscure. It is not surprising that the reaction of the Nuclear Weapon States (NWS) to the proposal was negative. More surprising to the New Zealand Government was the attitude of the Australian Labor Government which, attaching prime importance to its alliance relationship with the United States, sought to dissuade the New Zealand Government from proceeding with its initiative. Rowling was not deterred, and with support from Fiji and Papua New Guinea, New Zealand introduced a resolution in the UN General Assembly to endorse the concept. Australia agreed reluctantly to vote in favour, but declined to speak or to cosponsor.[34] The resolution was adopted by a large majority,[35] but its adoption coincided with the fall of both Governments. The newly elected Prime Ministers, Muldoon in New Zealand and Malcolm Fraser in Australia, combined to kill the initiative off at the next meeting of the South Pacific Forum, without appearing too blatantly to do so.[36]

There was a certain irony in the fact that when the proposal was officially revived eight years later, it was a newly elected Labor Government in Australia that took the lead.[37] After the accession to office in New Zealand of the fourth Labour Government in 1984, the two Governments collaborated, sometimes harmoniously, to negotiate a treaty which would attract the support of their fellow-members in the South Pacific Forum. It was now made clear that the proposed treaty would apply only to the sovereign territory of the parties, which would be free to decide whether to admit the nuclear-armed ships of foreign governments to their ports. This did not satisfy the NWS, however. France, of course, was conducting a vigorous programme of *underground* tests at Mururoa.

After a lengthy process of negotiation among the members of the Forum, a regional treaty, which became known as the Treaty of Rarotonga, was opened for signature on Hiroshima Day, 6 August 1985.[38] New Zealand ratified the Treaty on 13 November 1986 and it entered into force a month later. In the drafting of the Treaty and of three Protocols intended for signature by the five NWS, Australia and New Zealand had done their best to secure formulations which would be acceptable to those states, and in particular to the United States. France, of course, could not be expected to sign up while it continued to test its nuclear weapons in the South Pacific, but when the Treaty entered into force the United States and the United Kingdom wasted little time in making known their unwillingness to adhere to the Protocols. While the United States simply cited its global security interests as the basis for its decision, it may reasonably be supposed that its concurrent breach with New Zealand over naval ship visits, and a wish not to isolate France, also played a part in reaching that decision. The position of the Western NWS was bolstered, it must be added, by the slowness of some of the South Pacific Island countries to ratify the Treaty. Tonga has still to do so.[39] The three Western NWS waited until France had completed its test programme at Mururoa before jointly signing the Protocols on 25 March 1996.

Some 21 years after New Zealand had first broached the idea, the South Pacific was effectively nuclear free.

Law of the Sea

> It will always be in New Zealand's fundamental interest to work for a legal régime which is universally acknowledged and applied.
> R Q Quentin-Baxter, May 1970[40]

> The international community expressed its collective will to cooperate in this effort on a scale the magnitude of which was unprecedented in treaty history.
> Bernardo Zuleta, Special Representative of the Secretary General to the Law of the Sea, 1983[41]

The Third United Nations Conference on the Law of the Sea met throughout the first decade of the period covered by this book. This had not been the intention. Lengthy preparations had been made, and when the Conference convened in Caracas in mid-1974 for a 10-week session, the participating governments were expecting it to produce a comprehensive treaty bringing together all aspects of maritime law.[42] Some of the old hands among the delegates perhaps knew better. In six years the preparatory body, known as the Sea-bed Committee, had not got very far on questions of substance. The first session of the Conference, which had met in New York in 1973, had argued for months about the rules of procedure. It had been decided that the Conference should proceed by way of consensus, resorting to voting only when all efforts to reach a consensus had been exhausted. This was wise, but did not offer the prospect of speedy decision making. Even the most pessimistic delegation, however, could scarcely have expected that the Caracas session would be unable to agree on even one article, and could only produce a framework for future negotiation. Nor could they have predicted that it would take another eight years of negotiation, session upon session, before a treaty – the United Nations Convention on the Law of the Sea (UNCLOS) – could be completed and opened for signature in December 1982.

Why was this, and what was New Zealand's interest in the matter?

The task of the Conference was not merely to update and codify traditional maritime law, but, in addition, to give legal form to revolutionary new concepts and incorporate them with existing elements into one comprehensive instrument. In 1970 the UN General Assembly declared (the United States dissenting) that the sea-bed and the ocean floor, and the resources of the area beyond the limits of national jurisdiction, were the common heritage of mankind, not subject to appropriation by states or persons.[43] But this of course raised the question, particularly for coastal states such as New Zealand, what should be the limits of national jurisdiction?

Traditionally, the territorial seas of coastal states had been limited to three nautical miles. Beyond that were high seas, on which freedom of navigation was a right jealously guarded by the major maritime nations, and whose living resources could be exploited by anyone – but in practice, by industrialised nations with distant water fishing fleets. There was mounting dissatisfaction among coastal states at the ruthless plundering of fish stocks relatively close to their shores. Some countries, especially in Latin America, unilaterally proclaimed 200 mile territorial seas. But the First and Second LOS Conferences had failed to agree on broader limits for the territorial sea. At the Second Conference, in 1960, a proposal for a six mile territorial sea, plus a six-mile fishing zone, failed by one vote to secure a two-thirds majority.

New Zealand's initial position was to support the maritime powers in their determination to preserve traditional high seas freedoms: as a member of Western alliances and a nation dependent on its overseas trade, it took this stand for both strategic and commercial reasons. But there was increasing pressure to act to protect its coastal fisheries. In 1965, New Zealand – 'stretching' existing international law – legislated to establish a twelve mile fishing zone.[44] By 1974, it had embraced the more ambitious concept of extending coastal state ownership of living resources for 200 nautical miles, in what was to be known as the exclusive economic zone (EEZ). At Caracas, the New Zealand delegation took a leading role in urging that this concept be incorporated in the new treaty, asserting its belief – with perhaps more confidence than it actually felt – that it already had the necessary backing.

From the beginning New Zealand recognised, and acknowledged in this early statement, that agreement could only be reached, and its most important interests preserved, by a readiness to compromise. The New Zealand delegation therefore indicated its readiness to accommodate the interests of landlocked countries and those 'geographically disadvantaged' countries whose maritime zones were limited by the proximity of other states; as a country with an extensive continental shelf it was prepared to consider compromise proposals for the treatment of areas of the shelf (the 'natural prolongation' of the land territory) that extended beyond the boundaries of the proposed EEZ; it was willing to contemplate allowing distant water fishing nations (DWFNs) to enter the 200-mile zone to take the balance of the allowable catch not harvested by the local industry; and it supported the right of non-self-governing territories to enjoy the benefits to be derived from the resources of their EEZs and continental shelves, free from exploitation by colonial or foreign governments.[45]

New Zealand continued to support freedom of navigation, including the right of innocent passage through territorial seas, EEZs and international straits; but these issues were no longer at the forefront of its concerns. By contrast to the geographically disadvantaged states, whose maritime zones were in some cases severely curtailed through contiguity with those of other states, New Zealand is highly 'advantaged' by its geographical isolation. Not only is it situated far from its nearest neighbours, but its territory includes a chain of small islands to the north, east and south of the principal islands. Should these islands generate the same maritime spaces as other land territory, as New Zealand strongly contended, New Zealand would have one of the largest EEZs in the world, approximately 1.4 million square miles. But elsewhere one could find islands belonging to state A situated in the territorial waters of state B (for example, Greek islands off the coast of Turkey) creating serious delimitation problems and disadvantaging still further states which in some cases were disadvantaged already. There was thus strong opposition on the part of a few states to giving small islands any maritime spaces at all; and it was difficult initially to engage the attention to this issue of other states which had more pressing concerns.

New Zealand was pursuing a strong national interest: but it was an interest shared with a number of island states in the South Pacific for whose welfare New Zealand felt a responsibility. The interests of some island states were eventually to be protected by what came to be accepted as the 'archipelagic principle', but others (eg Cook Islands, Kiribati) were too scattered to come within the definition of an archipelago negotiated during the course of the Conference.

Other governments took a more hard-nosed stand in defence of their national interests. Broad shelf states, such as Australia, were determined to establish (or retain, according to the point of view) sovereign rights over the mineral resources in their continental shelves, if not to 'the last grain of sand', nevertheless to the outer edge of the continental margin, however far beyond the EEZ boundary that might extend. Coastal states with important fishing industries, such as Norway, were determined to protect their sovereign rights to exploit the living resources of their EEZs, strictly limiting any participation in that exploitation by distant water fishing states, however geographically disadvantaged or dependent on fishing as a food resource those states might claim to be.

As the Conference dragged on, New Zealand's position tended to harden. New Zealand joined the relatively small group of broad shelf states – the 'margineers' – although it remained more ready than some to contemplate an acceptable compromise. What finally emerged, at a very late stage, was an extremely complicated formula for establishing the legal boundary of the continental shelf, with a limited provision for revenue sharing from minerals extracted from the shelf outside the 200 mile boundary of the EEZ.

New Zealand likewise took part in the efforts of the coastal states to secure control of the living resources of their EEZs. In the end, each coastal state was given the right to determine the allowable catch of such resources within its EEZ and to take the whole of the catch itself if it had the capacity to do so. Other states, whether landlocked or geographically disadvantaged, were to be permitted to take part in the exploitation of the EEZs of coastal states only in the same region or subregion, and only by agreement with the coastal state. New Zealand has taken full advantage of these provisions as its own national fishing industry has developed.

In 1977 the New Zealand Government, no doubt impatient with the slow progress of the negotiations, and concerned to protect nearby fish stocks against the depredations of the fishing fleets of DWFNs, proceeded with legislation to establish an EEZ, taking into account the maritime spaces generated by all its outlying islands.[46] In doing so it anticipated agreement on the islands article, which was included in the 'package' at a very late stage. The article provides that islands should generate the same territorial seas, EEZs and continental shelves as other land territory, except for uninhabitable rocks, which have a territorial sea only.[47] Uninhabitable rocks would be a fair description of the Bounty Islands, which are included in the New Zealand zone.

Another contentious issue that was settled only at a late stage was the method of delimiting boundaries between maritime spaces where these would otherwise overlap. A different method was provided for the delimitation of EEZ and shelf boundaries from that for boundaries between territorial seas. In the latter case, equidistance was to be the guide; in the former, agreement is to be sought, on the basis of international law, 'in order to achieve an equitable solution'. In other words, equitable principles are to be applied, of which equidistance is only one. This raises the possibility of a more complex negotiation when New Zealand comes to settle its maritime boundaries with Australia.

During the years when the Convention was being negotiated, there was a widespread belief that the potential mineral wealth that lay, in the form of metallic nodules, on the deep sea-bed, was or soon would be physically and economically exploitable. Since then the cost of such exploitation, in comparison with that of land-based minerals, would seem to have deferred large-scale sea-bed mining to some indefinite future date. At the time, however, the developing countries (known as the group of 77, but actually more numerous) were determined to secure a fair share of that wealth – the 'common heritage of mankind' – and to prevent its monopolisation by multinational mining companies owned by a few industrialised countries. The developing countries were all the more determined to pursue that objective since through the accident of geography, many of them were unable to secure the benefits the treaty would confer on the coastal states.

New Zealand did not take a prominent part in the tortuous negotiations that eventually resulted in apparent agreement on the relevant provisions of the Convention (Part XI). Its main concern was to secure agreement on the Convention as a whole, thus protecting its extensive interests as a coastal state. It supported the concept of the common heritage of mankind. It did not expect to benefit significantly from deep sea-bed mining either as a participant in mining ventures or through the receipt of revenue. It was nevertheless prepared to contribute to the cost of running the International Sea-bed Authority which was to control the exploitation of deep sea-bed resources.

Part XI of the Convention is immensely complex, and possibly unworkable. The aim was to establish a parallel system designed to give the commercial arm of the Sea-bed Authority – 'the Enterprise' – an equal opportunity with state-sponsored companies or consortia to mine the deep sea-beds. Special provisions to counterbalance the advantages enjoyed by such companies included a start-up fund for the Enterprise, to which all parties to the Convention – including, of course, New Zealand – would be required to contribute, and a requirement for the transfer of technology from the private companies to the Enterprise on fair commercial terms. Revenues would be distributed for the most part to developing countries.

By the end of the ninth session of the LOS Conference in 1980, most of the difficult issues relating to sea-bed mining had been resolved. The leading industrialised countries, such as the United States, had participated actively in the negotiations. The chief United States delegate, Elliott Richardson, said it was all but certain that a convention would be ready for signature in 1981. He spoke too soon. The Republican administration elected at the end of 1980, under the leadership of President Reagan, found the provisions of Part XI of the draft Convention politically and ideologically repugnant; it was under great pressure from the mining companies to reject these provisions, but in any case it could not stomach the 'collectivist' philosophy underlying the aim of Part XI to place the resources of the deep sea-bed under international control. Abortive efforts to find a compromise, in which New Zealand took part, ended in April 1982 when the United States and three other countries voted against the adoption of the Convention, while a number of industrialised countries abstained. On 10 December 1982, however, 119 countries signed the Convention, including a number of those that had abstained in April: but the United States maintained its opposition.

There followed eight years of stalemate. Not only the United States, but most developed countries, refrained from ratifying the Convention. New Zealand, which was already enjoying the benefits conferred on coastal states by the Convention on a *de facto* basis, was reluctant to risk having to pay a disproportionate share of the costs of setting up the Enterprise. In 1990 the United Nations Secretary-General, Perez de Cuellar, took the initiative in seeking to broker a compromise aimed at breaking the deadlock. With encouragement from him and his successor, Boutros Boutros-Ghali, a compromise was eventually agreed, if compromise it could be called. The Agreement Relating to the Implementation of Part XI of the LOS Convention, opened for signature on 29 July 1994, was indissolubly linked to the principal Convention, Part XI of which it drastically amended. It could, perhaps, be said to have effectively gutted those provisions in Part XI which were designed to ensure an equitable share of the benefits of the exploitation of seabed resources for the developing countries. De Cuellar had commented on the transformation in the general economic climate that had taken place 'as a result of the changing perception with respect to the roles of the public and private sectors'. As he put it, 'there was a discernible shift towards a more market-oriented economy'.[48] Indeed there was. While some of those involved in the original negotiations may have been surprised that the developing countries were prepared to give away much of what had been gained in years of hard fought negotiation, it would seem that they came to see ratification of the Convention by the industrialised countries as essential if there were to be any form of international oversight of the exploitation of seabed resources. The prospective entry into force of the Convention, which took place on 16 November 1994 with 60 ratifications mainly from developing countries, underlined the need for a 'realistic' compromise. The alternative would be open slather for the multinational mining companies. New Zealand for its part welcomed the conclusion of the Agreement and promptly signed it.[49]

On 19 July 1996, it ratified the Convention itself, thereby consenting to be bound by the Agreement as well. Among the obligations assumed by New Zealand was an undertaking to submit to a Commission on the Limits of the Continental Shelf the particulars of the limits of New Zealand's shelf where it extends beyond the EEZ, with supporting data, within a 10-year period. Work on the formidable task of delineating this boundary is now in progress. New Zealand also undertook to make contributions to the International Seabed Authority from any revenue it may derive from exploitation of the non-living resources of its shelf beyond 200 miles (eg petroleum). More immediately, New Zealand makes an assessed contribution to the expenses of the Authority.

Much of New Zealand's attention since UNCLOS was signed in 1982 has been devoted to the conservation and management of fish stocks, especially in the South Pacific region. The Forum Fisheries Agency established by the South Pacific Forum, which assists the member countries in the delineation of their EEZs, the development of their fisheries policies and the protection of their zones from poaching, has had from the beginning New Zealand's active support.

Although under the Convention coastal states manage the exploitation of fish stocks within their EEZs, problems remain. Some fish stocks 'straddle' the boundaries between EEZs and the high seas. Others, such as tuna, migrate at will in and out of coastal state jurisdiction. Overfishing these species on the high seas in the vicinity of EEZs means that the catch within EEZs is in danger of unacceptable damage. One problem of special concern to South Pacific countries was driftnet fishing by DWFNs in nets up to 50 kilometres in length. The practice was prohibited in the South Pacific by the Wellington Convention on Drift Net Fishing in 1991, and discouraged more generally by resolutions of the UN General Assembly. The problems of straddling stocks and highly migratory species were addressed initially in the context of the UN Conference on Environment and Development (UNCED) which met in 1992. After lengthy negotiations an Agreement for the Implementation of the Provisions of UNCLOS Relating to the Conservation and Management of Straddling Fish Stocks and Highly Migratory Fish Stocks was concluded in August 1995 and is to enter into force when 30 states have ratified it. The Food and Agriculture Organisation produced a Code of Conduct for Responsible Fisheries and an Agreement to Promote Compliance with International Conservation and Management Measures by Fishing Vessels on the High Seas.

The mere existence of UNCLOS and these important subsidiary agreements does not, of course, guarantee the sustainability of marine fish stocks for the benefit of future generations. Many fish stocks of the world's oceans are now wholly or partly to be found in EEZs, subject to the exercise by coastal states of their sovereign rights over living resources within such zones. Responsibility for the preservation of these stocks is thus a matter for national governments: if coastal states fail to protect them from over exploitation, even extinction, they have only themselves to blame, and it is their own nationals in succeeding generations who will be the ones to suffer. Fish stocks in the high seas beyond national jurisdiction are another matter. There are concerns that DWFNs are cleaning out important ocean fisheries. The LOS Convention contains Articles imposing a duty on all states to regulate fishing by their own nationals to the extent necessary to conserve high seas stocks, to negotiate with other states exploiting the same stocks, and to establish regional fisheries organisations for that purpose. It is an open question whether these provisions, and the supplementary agreements I have described, will suffice to deter predatory fishing by vessels from Northern Hemisphere developed countries in the South Pacific and Southern Oceans. Since the discovery of the Patagonian toothfish in Antarctic waters, for example, fishermen from as far away as Spain and Norway have declared open season on this lucrative resource. New Zealand and Australia may invoke the provisions of the Convention for the Conservation of Antarctic Marine Living Resources (CCAMLR) against such uncontrolled fishing; but its effectiveness has still to be tested. As for the Agreement on Straddling Stocks and Highly Migratory Species, this Agreement is not yet in force, and its effectiveness will obviously depend on whether DWFNs decide to ratify it and conscientiously police fishing by vessels flying their flags. Even New Zealand, an architect of the Agreement, has still (at the time of writing) to put in place the legislation required to enable this country to become a party. In the next millennium, more determined action to enforce the law will be needed if the sustainability of one of the world's more important sources of food is to be assured.

Also in the next millennium, exploitation of the 'common heritage of mankind' may be expected to begin. It remains to be seen whether the 1994 Supplementary Agreement will permit the resources of the deep sea-bed to be shared equitably with developing countries, or whether in the 'more market-oriented economy' noted by the UN Secretary-General, multinational companies owned by advanced industrialised countries will grab the lion's share. To the extent that New Zealand has influence as a member of the International Sea-bed Authority, it will – one may hope – oppose any such trend and uphold the original concept of the common heritage.[50]

Notes

1. See Pt.2, Section 3 of the LOS Convention.
2. Helen Clark persuaded the Labour Party Conference to reject a remit to this effect, *Dominion*, 1 September 1986.
3. Ramesh Thakur (ed.), *The United Nations at Fifty: Retrospect and Prospect* (Dunedin, 1996), p.56.
4. *Evening Post*, 27 July 1976, reporting a seminar on human rights at Victoria University of Wellington.
5. See Malcolm Templeton (ed.), *New Zealand as an International Citizen* (Wellington, 1995), p.17.
6. For example, New Zealand voted against the inscription of the apartheid item in the UN General Assembly in 1952 and 1953, citing the domestic jurisdiction clause in the UN Charter (Article 2(7)).
7. Speech by NZ representative, Colin Aikman, in the UNGA on 10 December 1948. (Official records 181st meeting, pp.887–9.)
8. MFAT PM 108/11/13/1 Pt.14, letters of 26 July 1973 from Kirk to Hon David Thomson.
9. MFAT PM 108/11/13/1 Pt.14, letter of 15 May 1975 from Rowling to Rev J S Thomson.
10. MFAT PM 108/11/13/1 Pt.14, memorandum of 26 April 1976 from NZ High Commission, London, to Secretary of Foreign Affairs (SFA).
11. On 23 March 1976.
12. MFAT 108/11/13/1 Pt.14, memorandum of 18 May 1976 from SFA to Secretary of Justice.

13　MFAT 108/11/13/1 Pt.15, telegram 171 of 23 March 1977 from Permanent Representative, New York, to Wellington.
14　MFAT 108/11/13/1 Pt.15, telegram 232 of 7 April 1977 from Wellington to Permanent Representative, New York.
15　*New Zealand Foreign Affairs Review* (hereafter *NZFAR*), October–December 1977, pp.67, speech to UNGA on 10 October 1977.
16　*NZFAR*, July–September and October–December 1978, pp.26–7, speech to UNGA on 25 September 1978.
17　MFAT 106/26/2/1 Pt.1, telegram 1297 of 28 December 1977 from Permanent Mission, New York, to Wellington, reported that instruments of ratification had been deposited that day.
18　MFAT 106/26/2/1 Pt.1, letter CN329. 1978. Treaties – 15 from UN Legal Counsel to member states set out these reservations, and noted that the Covenants would enter into force for New Zealand on 28 March 1979. The reservations applied to Articles 8 and 10(2) of the Economic Social and Cultural Covenant, and to Articles 10(2)(b), 10(3), 14(6), 20 and 22 of the Civil and Political Covenant respectively.
19　108/11/13/1, Pt.16, memorandum of 15 September 1978 from SFA to Minister.
20　Helen Fawthorpe, in Templeton, *International Citizen*, ch.6, p.101.
21　Tavita v Minister of Immigration [1994] *NZLR* 257.
22　In K. J. Keith (ed.), *Essays on Human Rights* (Wellington, 1968), p.13.
23　Paper by Lord Cooke, NZIIA seminar of 15 April 1998, reproduced in *New Zealand Independent*, 20 May 1998.
24　*Business Times* (Malaysia) 31 July 1997. Albright was reported by the paper as having told the Indonesians during an ASEAN Post-Ministerial Meeting that the US would be 'relentless in its opposition to any attempt to water down the Declaration'.
25　Among others Paul Hunt, Senior Lecturer in Law at Waikato University, has written extensively on this subject. See his article 'Reclaiming Economic Social and Cultural Rights' (*Waikato Law Review*, Vol. 1, 1993, p.141), his book *Reclaiming Social Rights* (Dartmouth, 1996), pp.24–31 and his lecture to the Otago University Foreign Policy School on 'Social Rights: Building a Legal Tradition', in Robert G. Patman (ed.), *Universal Human Rights?* (Macmillan Press, forthcoming).
26　UN Document ST/HR/4/Rev 16, Chart of ratifications as at 31 December 1997.
27　See *United Nations Handbook 1997* (MFAT) p.136, for the constitution of the Committee.
28　See *New Zealand Handbook on International Human Rights* (MFAT, 1998) for details and texts.
29　For a more comprehensive account of New Zealand's disarmament policy, including its policy on nuclear tests, see Roger Ball's account in Templeton, *New Zealand as an International Citizen*, ch.5, pp.81–96.
30　The membership of the Conference on Disarmament was increased in June 1996 from 38 to 61, after which NZ became a member (*United Nations Handbook 1997*, pp.32–4).
31　The CTBT was adopted by the UNGA on 11 September 1996; opened for signature on 24 September; and signed by New Zealand on 27 September. India was one of three countries voting against adoption.

32 For a published account of and commentary on the Court case, see K. J. (now Sir Kenneth) Keith, 'The Nuclear Test Case after Ten Years', in *Victoria University of Wellington Law Review* 1984 (14), and 'The ICJ and Nuclear Weapons', in *New Zealand International Review*, January–February 1996.
33 Press statement by PM, 21 December 1974.
34 Australian objections culminated in a letter from Whitlam to Rowling on 7 October 1975 (MFAT PM 121/12/36/2 Pt.6) in which he repeated Australian criticisms of the initiative and reiterated Australia's refusal to give it verbal support.
35 UNGA resolution 3477 (XXX) of 11 December 1975, adopted by 110 votes to none, with 20 abstentions.
36 The Forum communiqué in March 1976 implied that there would be further consultations on the basis of the Assembly resolution, but emphasised that in seeking the cessation of nuclear weapons testing in the Pacific, the principle of freedom of navigation in the high seas would be respected and in developing the zone concept there would be no incompatibility with existing security arrangements. In the privacy of the meeting, however, Muldoon and Fraser made clear their concern that the initiative should go no further. Fiji was unhappy, but no member of the Forum raised the issue at the next meeting in July 1976.
37 Labor was returned to office in Australia in March 1983. In New Zealand, the Government had taken no action in 1979 on a Parliamentary Petition, sponsored by CND and supported by some 20,000 signatures, which called for a SPNFZ. In 1982 Richard Prebble introduced a bill to make New Zealand a NFZ, from which nuclear armed ships and aircraft would be excluded: but this pioneering effort did not get past first base. In New Zealand, of course, a Labour Government was not returned until July 1984. In August 1983, however, Muldoon had been obliged to accept a consensus which effectively revived consideration of the SPNFZ concept in the South Pacific Forum.
38 For a comprehensive description of the Treaty, see article in *Victoria University of Wellington Law Review* 1987 (17) pp.33–51, by Christopher Beeby and Nigel Fyfe, both of whom were closely involved in the negotiations. Other MFA officials who took part were Kennedy Graham and Allan Bracegirdle.
39 Tonga signed the treaty on 2 August 1996 but has still to ratify (as at August 1999).
40 Paper given to the NZ Institute of Public Administration by Professor Quentin-Baxter, May 1970, 'Legal Aspects of Exploiting Maritime Resources'.
41 *Official Text of the UN Convention on the Law of the Sea* (United Nations, 1983), Introduction, p.XIX.
42 Like other countries with important maritime interests, and in the expectation of rapid progress towards the conclusion of a treaty, New Zealand sent a (relatively) large delegation to the Caracas meeting. (The numbers diminished at later sessions). The delegation comprised:
Malcolm Templeton, Permanent Representative to the United Nations, Chairman
F. A. Small, Head, UN Division, MFA
C. D. Beeby, Head, Legal Division, MFA
W. R. Mansfield, First Secretary, NZ Mission to the UN
T. B. Caughley, Legal Division, MFA

B. T. Cunningham, Director of Fisheries, MAF
Capt D. H. Donaghue, Director of Defence Plans, MoD
and a supporting staff of three.
43 UNGA Resolution 2749 (XXV), 17 December 1970.
44 See Quentin-Baxter, 'Legal Aspects'. *The Territorial Sea and Fishing Zone Act 1965* established a nine-mile fishing zone beyond the three-mile territorial sea. Other countries, including Britain, had already in place twelve-mile fishing zones. Japan, whose fishing vessels were those principally affected, nevertheless threatened to take New Zealand to the International Court. It was placated by giving Japanese fishermen fishing rights within the New Zealand zone for a five-year period. By 1970 a majority of coastal states had adopted some form of twelve mile limit. But the demand for a 200-mile zone was still largely confined to Latin America.
45 UN document A/CONF.62/C.2/SR of 31 July 1974 contains a summary of the NZ statement.
46 *The Territorial Sea and Exclusive Economic Zone Act 1977* (New Zealand Statutes 1977 Vol.1 No.28).
47 UNCLOS, Article 121.
48 UN Document containing official text of the Agreement Relating to the Implementation of Part XI of UNCLOS, Introduction, p.208.
49 On 29 July 1994.
50 The Convention thus became effective for New Zealand on 18 August 1996, and the latest date for submission of shelf boundary data 18 August 2006.

W. DAVID MCINTYRE

From Singapore to Harare: New Zealand and the Commonwealth

BETWEEN 1971 AND 1991 THE COMMONWEALTH EVOLVED from being an ambiguous legacy of empire into a principles-based multilateral international association. For New Zealand this organisation, which had provided our original window on the world and our first forum for exercising a voice in international affairs, became only one (and not the most important) of the myriad of organisations through which we sought to foster our interests. In 1971 the Commonwealth had 32 members and decolonisation in the Pacific had only just begun. By 1991 the total membership of 50 was only one short of the UN at the time of its birth, and decolonisation was virtually complete. In 1971 Cold War tensions were rampant in Africa and even in the Pacific. By 1991 the Soviet Union had collapsed and the rehabilitation of Eastern Europe appeared set to consign the development needs of the small states of the Commonwealth to the shadows.

In 1971, in her book *The 'Open' Commonwealth*, American political scientist Margaret Ball used the image of an iceberg.[1] Most of the Commonwealth's activities were beneath the water line of public and media attention. The tip of the iceberg consisted of the symbolic Head of the Commonwealth (HoC); the biennial Heads of Government Meetings (Chogms), which began in 1971, and the Commonwealth Games. Below the water line were regular ministerial and officials' meetings. There were also the inter-governmental organisations (IGOs) – the Commonwealth Secretariat and its new operational arm the Commonwealth Fund for Technical Co-operation (CFTC); the Commonwealth Foundation; the Commonwealth Agricultural Bureaux, and several other technical organisations. The Commonwealth of

Learning (COL) joined these in 1989. Then, there were the numerous non-governmental organisations (NGOs). Some had started as imperial organisations in the hey-day of empire before the 1914–18 war. Most of them were in the process of formation with the assistance of the Foundation. The most popular activities were to be found in the sporting arena, especially the Commonwealth Games, but also in the great team sports, notably cricket and rugby football. This whole area of the non-official Commonwealth began to be referred to as the 'Peoples' Commonwealth'. Indeed, by 1991, Ball's iceberg metaphor was ripe for duplication. If the Chogms were the tip of the political Commonwealth, the Games were the peak of the Peoples' Commonwealth, with the symbolic HoC common to both. Elements of these visible and invisible activities and organisations will form the basis of the analysis which follows.

The Head of the Commonwealth

Queen Elizabeth II, as HoC, was forging a new symbol in international affairs. The title was barely two years old when she acceded to the throne in 1952. It had been included in the London Declaration of 1949 to facilitate India's continued membership after it became a republic. At the same time, in unpublished minutes it had been agreed that other aspiring republics would receive the same consideration. While the other members retained the British monarch as head of state, India agreed to accept King George VI as 'the symbol of the free association of its independent members and as such the Head of the Commonwealth'. The formula was a triumph of compromise chiefly attributable to Clement Attlee and Jawaharlal Nehru, with significant contributions from Canada's Lester Pearson and South Africa's Daniel Malan. Peter Fraser had been the most reluctant leader to agree, but he made some significant contributions to the meeting.[2]

This symbolic headship was quite new. George VI had little chance to develop it before his sudden death in 1952. The question of the succession to the HoC, which might have been tricky and given rise to controversy about an election, was neatly solved by Nehru, Prime Minister of the one republic, who, in his telegram of condolence to the young Queen, also congratulated her on becoming the new HoC.[3] The other seven members endorsed this. As a precedent for any future succession, 1952 hardly rated.

In her long reign, Elizabeth II created the pattern of HoC activities, a role quite separate from that of monarch. In 1971 there were 17 republics and only 10 members recognised the Queen as Head of State. Another five had their own monarchs. By 1991, 27 were republics and only 16 outside Britain recognized the Queen as Head of State. All recognised the symbolic HoC. In this role, specifically Commonwealth activities included messages broadcast on Christmas Day and others published on Commonwealth Day (which began in 1977); visits, receptions and banquets at the time of Chogms, and opening or closing the Commonwealth Games. As patron of the Games she provided the baton for the Queen's relay as part of the run-up. The Duke of Edinburgh was President of the Games from 1955 to 1990, but Winston Churchill's fanciful idea that he should be made 'Prince of the Commonwealth' was not followed up.

The first Chogm in 1971 provided the one breach in this HoC procedure. The social hosting which had been normal when Commonwealth leaders went to London, could not occur because Prime Minister Edward Heath advised the Queen that she should not go to Singapore because Britain (as will be seen) was in bad odour over Southern African issues. But before the next Chogm in Ottawa in 1973, the Secretary-General, Arnold Smith, ensured that the Canadian Prime Minister, Pierre Trudeau, arranged a visit to Canada so the Queen could be present at Ottawa and she indicated she was keen to do this. A pattern of region or country visits to coincide with Chogms became established.[4] In 1979 Mrs Thatcher again warned the Queen of possible dangers in visits to Botswana, Malawi, Tanzania and Zambia because of the Zimbabwe guerrilla war. However the Queen was determined to go. Her presence gave an added touch of normality to the Lusaka Chogm and led to a brief truce in the war.[5] In 1986, when Southern Africa issues looked like wrecking the Commonwealth Games, there were rumours of a serious rift between Buckingham Palace and No. 10. By the 1990s, it was well established that the HoC was deeply committed to the Commonwealth role.

The nature of royal visits to Commonwealth countries changed after 1970 following a notable experiment first tried in New Zealand. When the Queen visited Wellington Town Hall on 12 March 1970 it was arranged that, instead of being taken inside by the mayor to meet dignitaries, the Queen would walk around outside to meet ordinary people. Those most doubtful about this idea had been the police, who said they would not have enough constables. They were told politely that the Queen was not coming to meet policemen. They then claimed there would not be enough ceremonial cord to restrain the crowd, so it was decided that a line would be drawn on the pavement and people be asked to stay behind it. On the day, the Queen and Mayor walked around for half-an-hour and the visit was deemed a success. A veteran English journalist headlined the event in the *Daily Mail* with the words 'Queen goes Walkabout'. In spite of ironies recognised by her Australian press secretary, 'walkabouts' caught on.[6] Henceforth, before each Chogm the HoC did a walkabout around the conference venue and talked to people involved in the running of the meetings. Although present at the time of the Chogms only in symbolic and social capacities, on at least one occasion, the Gleneagles Agreement of 1977, the HoC probably exerted a political influence as will emerge later.

Heads of Government Meetings

In an age renowned for its 'summitry', the Chogms were the oldest, largest, and longest meetings of Heads of Government. They were the contemporary successors of the Colonial Conferences 1887–1907, Imperial Conferences 1911–37, and the Commonwealth Prime Ministers' Meetings (PMM) 1944–69. Most of these meetings had been held in London, in the Cabinet Room in No. 10, or in Marlborough House or Lancaster House, except for two special economic meetings, in Ottawa in 1894 and 1932, and a special one-issue PMM held in Lagos in 1966. New Zealand was part of the select 'Group of Three' along with Britain and Canada, which was represented at the entire series.

In 1971 the new pattern began. The style 'Commonwealth Heads of Government Meeting' was adopted;[7] the venues began to rotate around large conference centres in different member states; the host Head of Government took the chair. The meeting always began in these years with a *tour d'horizon* of the world scene; moved on to a survey of global economic trends, and ended by reviewing Commonwealth functional co-operation. Each meeting tended to produce a *cause célèbre* played up by the media.

As Commonwealth membership swelled on the tides of decolonisation and Commonwealth organisations proliferated, these meetings covered an ever-wider range of issues. They were dominated, however, throughout the entire period by the quartet of big Southern African issues – apartheid in South Africa; sporting contacts with South Africa; the guerrilla war in Rhodesia; South Africa's occupation of Southwest Africa. These were all overshadowed by the Cold War, which added the issues of nuclear weapons, the development needs of the Third World, and the quest for a New International Economic Order.

Year	Venue	NZ head of delegation	Total delegations	Issue
1971	Singapore	Holyoake	31	British arms sales to South Africa
1973	Ottawa	Kirk	32	French nuclear testing in Pacific
1975	Kingston	Rowling	33	New International Economic Order
1977	London	Muldoon	34	Apartheid and sport – Gleneagles
1979	Lusaka	Muldoon	39	Zimbabwe settlement
1981	Melbourne	Muldoon	42	Springbok tour of N.Z.
1983	New Delhi	Muldoon	42	Grenada invasion
1985	Nassau	Lange	46	Apartheid and sanctions
1987	Vancouver	Lange	45	Apartheid and sanctions
1989	Kuala Lumpur	Palmer	46	Apartheid and sanctions. Environment
1991	Harare	Bolger	47	Apartheid – Nelson Mandela

Although New Zealand was far removed from Africa or the hot spots of the Cold War and could never expect to make much impact on development issues, it could not stand on the sidelines because of two national passions. These were rugby contests with South Africa and opposition to French nuclear testing in the Pacific. Another perplexing factor which New Zealand leaders had to take into account was Britain's disillusionment with the Commonwealth. This arose partly because of bewilderment at the pace of decolonisation, but mainly because Britain was perpetually in the dock over its valuable trade and investment in South Africa and its failure to deal with the Unilateral Declaration of Independence (UDI) by Rhodesia in 1965. Apartheid and UDI were the twin sticks perpetually used to beat Britain from the 1960s to the 1990s. This produced a mainly negative view of the Commonwealth in

Whitehall. Thus British leadership in the Commonwealth lapsed. Ironically, the organisation thus became a more truly multilateral association. But New Zealand's close association with Britain, although eroding, made it one of the few allies of the British at several significant moments.

Singapore in 1971 was a very tense conference. However, there were several promising developments. There was the new type of venue and the vigorous chairmanship of Lee Kuan Yew. The first Pacific Island states attended, welcomed by Keith Holyoake as the 'third generation of members', namely newly-independent Fiji and Tonga, as well as Western Samoa, independent since 1962.[8] The Commonwealth Fund for Technical Co-operation was inaugurated to provide 'Third Party Technical Assistance' whereby members' contributions to the Fund were used to facilitate the work of experts from other member countries giving advice to third countries.[9]

But the inaugural Chogm was dominated by the issue of British arms sales to South Africa. The Conservative government of Edward Heath, elected in 1970, insisted on completing sales of helicopters and spares for frigates in fulfilment of earlier contracts and the agreement permitting Royal Navy use of the Simonstown Naval Base. Heath maintained that a growing Soviet naval presence in the Indian Ocean posed a threat to shipping round the Cape. This strategic and commercial argument did not impress the Third World majority for whom the overriding concern was opposition to apartheid and the withholding of any support to the apartheid regime. Heath obstinately stuck to his guns and boycotted the customary weekend socialising, preferring to relax on his yacht. To salvage something from the impasse, Kenneth Kaunda of Zambia developed an idea, suggested five years earlier by Sir Abubakar Tafawa Balewa of Nigeria, that all members should subscribe to a declaration of basic principles.

The Declaration of Commonwealth Principles approved on 22 January 1971, became a virtual charter document. First it provided a new definition: 'The Commonwealth of Nations is a voluntary association of independent sovereign states, each responsible for its own policies, consulting and co-operating in the common interests of their peoples and in the promotion of international understanding and world peace'. Members then pledged themselves *in favour* of peace, liberty and co-operation and *against* racial discrimination, colonial domination and gross inequalities of wealth. The declaration was not completely anodyne. The anti-discrimination clause was couched in unusually forceful phrases: 'We recognise racial prejudice as a dangerous sickness threatening the healthy development of the human race and racial discrimination as an unmitigated evil of society'. Yet the text was not devoid of mollifying phrases. While each member agreed to 'combat this evil' within its own nation, it would only withhold assistance to such evil regimes '*which in its own judgement*' contributed to that policy.[10] New Zealand's contributions to the document were directed solely at tidying the text. For example, in the second paragraph of the preamble, 'five oceans' was added to 'six continents' in the description and a reference to major faiths, colour, and racial groups was replaced by 'races, languages and religions'.[11]

Heath was so incensed by the Singapore Chogm that he told Secretary-General Arnold Smith that he hoped for a long interval before another. When Smith arranged with Trudeau to call the next meeting two years later in Ottawa in 1973, Heath went only reluctantly and left early. Ottawa was significant for the revival of the weekend retreat (akin to those once held at Chequers and Dorneywood, country houses in the Chilterns, north of London). From Ottawa, Heads of Government and wives, without officials, went to a resort hotel at Mount Tremblant[12], where the weekend was used to good effect by Norman Kirk, the New Zealand Prime Minister, to cultivate friendships with African leaders. Thus when, on the UDI issue, Heath denounced military aid to the African guerrillas in Rhodesia, Kirk supported African feelings while urging negotiation rather than force and suggested a Commonwealth peacekeeping force. In return for his sympathy, Kirk secured African support for New Zealand's opposition to French nuclear testing in the Pacific.

Because Britain was only eight months into its membership of the EEC, Heath refused to countenance any condemnation of France, so Kirk could only get a general declaration against nuclear testing. Somewhat dejected, he wondered what he could tell the press in view of his failure to get a condemnation of France. Frank Corner's suggestion that he should play it as a win, prompted Kirk to declare: 'Boys, we've won!' He was also successful in having the declaration on nuclear testing made public partway through the conference to mark the tenth anniversary of the partial test ban treaty of 1963.[13]

By the next Chogm, at Kingston Jamaica in 1975, Britain's membership of the EEC and adoption of the Common Agricultural Policy had begun to bite and the loss of Commonwealth preferences adversely affected several Commonwealth economies. A bitter debate over trade access, including denunciations of Britain, annoyed Harold Wilson, the British Prime Minister. Bill Rowling, for New Zealand, offered less rhetoric and a more constructive approach and he supported Secretary-General Ramphal's idea of a committee of 'Ten Wise Men' to report on proposals for a New International Economic Order.[14] This became the first of a series of expert groups or commissions, which examined political, economic, social and environmental issues over the next 15 years. New Zealand's representative on the first of these was the University of Canterbury vice-chancellor, Professor A. D. Brownlie.

If New Zealand had emerged as the constructive mediator in 1975, by the time of the 1977 Jubilee Chogm, held at Lancaster House, London, Robert Muldoon appeared as the Commonwealth bad boy. The question of sports contacts with South Africa had simmered since the 1950s. An All Black tour of South Africa in 1970 had been extended to include matches in Southwest Africa and Rhodesia in defiance of a UN General Assembly resolution against sports contacts. A planned Springbok tour of New Zealand in 1973 was postponed on Kirk's insistence lest it prejudice the 1974 Commonwealth Games in Christchurch. However, Muldoon's policy of 'keeping politics out of sport', although popular at home, brought international odium, especially when the 1976 All Black tour of South Africa coincided with the Soweto riots, where over 170 people died. As a result of the tour there were moves to expel New Zealand from the Montreal Olympic Games. The failure of this move led to an almost complete African boycott of the Olympics. Only two (non-Commonwealth) African countries competed. The possibility of another boycott, this time of the Edmonton Commonwealth Games in 1978, indicated an urgent need to get agreement about sports contacts during the 1977 Chogm. However, the Secretary-General's pre-Chogm approach to Muldoon about getting some formula agreed in London was rebuffed.

Muldoon hoped that a general discussion of apartheid and sport could be avoided at the Chogm. Moreover he did not think the Commonwealth Games were sufficiently important to modify his government's position that it would *discourage* sports contacts with South

Africa, but *not interfere* with the right of New Zealand citizens to play games with whomsoever they chose. Yet it was known that Secretary-General Ramphal was working on a general formula about sports contacts. He planned to use the Retreat at the Gleneagles Golf Course in Scotland to finalise the formula. A small committee consisting of the heads of government of Australia, Canada, Jamaica, New Zealand, Nigeria, and Tanzania was mooted. Muldoon refused to join if Malcolm Fraser of Australia was included. Bernard Galvin, of the Prime Minister's Department, was shown a copy of the draft and indicated points where Muldoon would want amendment. Ramphal let Galvin know that the trump card up his sleeve was the attitude of the Queen as HoC. She was disturbed that the sports issue was casting a shadow over the Silver Jubilee. Although she was, reputedly, sympathetic to New Zealand's position, she thought Muldoon was too intransigent.[15]

In the event, Muldoon proved himself a pragmatist. He defused African antagonism about the All Black tour by endorsing the Maputo Declaration supporting the liberation movements in Rhodesia and Southwest Africa. He took part in the Gleneagles Meeting, which he later claimed lasted only an hour and was not confined to the sporting issue. That, he later claimed, took only 15 minutes.[16] He endorsed the *Commonwealth Statement on Apartheid in Sport* (also dubbed The Gleneagles Agreement) reaffirming the 1971 principle about racial discrimination being a dangerous sickness and unmitigated evil and members' support for the international campaign against apartheid. Member governments also pledged themselves to discourage sporting contacts with South Africa.

The Gleneagles text indicated that Heads of Government expected that 'there were unlikely to be future sporting contacts of any significance between Commonwealth countries or their nationals and South Africa while that country continues to pursue the detestable policy of apartheid'. Probably to satisfy Muldoon, certain qualifying phrases were incorporated in the text. In a paragraph indicating that sports contacts with apartheid countries gave the impression that countries which had allowed them were less than totally committed to the 1971 Commonwealth principle, agreement to seek a remedy was put in a context of poor communications. The revised sentence reads: 'Regretting past misunderstandings and difficulties and recognising that these were partly the result of inadequate inter-governmental consultation they agreed that they would seek to remedy this situation in the context of the increased level of understanding now achieved'. After the pledge to combat apartheid vigorously by withholding sports contacts, the vital qualification was inserted that 'it was for each government to determine in accordance with its laws the methods by which it might best discharge these commitments'.[17]

Muldoon, then, for all his obstinate populism at home, could receive international signals and take advice. His conciliatory attitude at Gleneagles was carried over to the 1979 Lusaka Chogm, which played a major role in getting a settlement of the UDI issue. As usual on this issue the British were in the dock. Rhodesian elections held in April 1979 produced an African-majority parliament and a British Conservative Party observer reported that it had been a free and fair election. On 1 June 1979 Bishop Abel Muzorewa took office as Prime Minister of the newly renamed Zimbabwe-Rhodesia. Meanwhile on 4 May 1979 the Conservatives had come to power in Britain under Margaret Thatcher. Would Britain now recognise the Muzorewa regime and grant legal independence? Commonwealth leaders who gathered in Lusaka in August 1979 were determined to restrain Mrs Thatcher. Fraser of Australia led this move. Muldoon, by contrast, stood forth as Mrs Thatcher's main supporter. This probably enabled him to retain an influence with her, which helped move her towards the compromise, which the FCO also advised. It was agreed at Lusaka that Britain would summon a conference of all the parties from Zimbabwe-Rhodesia, including the rival guerrilla groups.[18] During the Lusaka meetings Muldoon pointed to some common ground in the attitudes of Mrs Thatcher and Julius Nyerere of Tanzania. He also visited a refugee camp run by the Zimbabwe African Peoples Union – the only leader from the white Commonwealth to do so – a gesture that made a positive impact.[19]

After an heroic feat of chairmanship by Lord Carrington, the Lancaster House Conference of all the parties, held between October and December 1979, produced an agreement that there would be a cease-fire in the guerrilla war; that sanctions would be lifted; and that Britain would send a governor, who would rule by ordinance and conduct elections. Commonwealth assistance was forthcoming in the form of a 2400-strong army monitoring force to supervise the cease-fire and a Commonwealth observer group to ensure free and fair elections. New Zealand sent a carefully selected 74-man contingent to join

Australian, British, Fijian, and Kenyan troops in the monitoring force. At one point the Zimbabwe nationalists objected to the proposed New Zealand presence, but remembrance of Muldoon's visit to the ZAPU camp and realisation that New Zealand was not solely a 'white' country and that Maori would form part of the contingent, tipped the balance.[20] New Zealand also sent two MPs and an official as its own observer group. Much to Mrs Thatcher's chagrin, Robert Mugabe's Patriotic Front won an overwhelming majority and Zimbabwe became independent in 1980. Six years later New Zealand would open its first diplomatic post in Africa by appointing a High Commissioner located in Harare, accredited to Zimbabwe, Zambia, Kenya, Botswana and Tanzania.

The kudos earned by Muldoon in 1977 and 1979 was soon dissipated by his renewed insistence that politics be kept out of sport. In spite of Gleneagles, a Springbok rugby team toured New Zealand in 1981 and the ensuing domestic strife displayed to the world a media spectacle of helmeted protesters confronting helmeted baton-wielding police in the streets. After one game was cancelled because protesters invaded the field, the South African team received close police protection provided by using army logistic support. Muldoon's principle that the government would try to persuade the Rugby Union to abide by the Gleneagles Agreement but would not order it to cancel the tour, was successfully maintained at the cost of alienating many voters, dividing families, and tarnishing New Zealand's image abroad. The most immediate result of the 1981 tour was that a Commonwealth Finance Ministers' Meeting scheduled to meet in Auckland was switched to the Bahamas. This was decided by High Commissioners meeting as the Commonwealth Committee on South Africa, on 21 July 1981, the day before the first Springbok match.[21]

Muldoon went to the Melbourne Chogm in 1981 very much in the dock for breaking the Gleneagles Agreement. Muldoon, however, was determined to brazen it out. He threatened to reconsider the Gleneagles Agreement. He indulged in some crude talk, including a remark about Robert Mugabe – 'when you have been in the jungles a few years shooting people' it would be difficult to understand the New Zealand Government's unwillingness to use compulsion over sport. He said of Secretary-General Ramphal that he should stick to taking minutes and not act as president.[22] Muldoon was disappointed that the African Heads of Government were prepared to be conciliatory and did not rise to the bait.

The lack of fireworks in Melbourne was, however, deceptive. In 1982 the Organization of African Unity Council of Ministers demanded New Zealand's exclusion from the Brisbane Commonwealth Games. This was not an idle threat. In May 1982 the New Zealand delegates to a Commonwealth Games Federation meeting in Marlborough House found themselves 'virtually ostracised'. A motion from Tanzania and Nigeria called for New Zealand to be expelled from the Federation. In the event, a more moderate motion proposed by Jamaica was substituted only after Roy Dutton, for the New Zealand Olympic and Commonwealth Games Association, read out a grovelling statement, produced in the Secretariat, probably by New Zealanders Chris Laidlaw and Jeremy Pope.[23]

Muldoon's last Chogm was in New Delhi in 1983, by which time he had managed to come round once more to the side of the angels. In his capacity as Minister of Finance he had for some time called for a 'new Bretton Woods' to ensure stabilisation of currencies. His move was partly tactical to mollify African colleagues, but it also stemmed from genuine conviction about the needs of small states. At the Commonwealth Finance Ministers' Meeting in August 1982 it was agreed that another expert group should look at this matter. The Delhi conference, however, was diverted by the recent American invasion of Grenada, which, as well as raising interesting constitutional issues and testing regional alignments, highlighted the plight of many small states which now made up half of the Commonwealth members. Another group of experts was given the task of investigating the vulnerability of small states, a number of which were in the Pacific.[24] The fruit of Muldoon's efforts to get currency stability was the report of a group convened by Gerald Helleiner of Canada, *Towards a New Bretton Woods*, which was received at Delhi. When, in the next year, Muldoon lost office after the snap election, Sir Peter Marshall, Deputy Secretary-General (Economic) said, 'We've lost our locomotive'.[25]

For the rest of the 1980s, the apartheid issue dominated Chogms. With the sudden election of the fourth Labour Government under David Lange in 1984, New Zealand's stand on Southern African issues came into line with the Commonwealth consensus. Lange himself was no devotee of the Commonwealth. The elaboration, expense, pretension, and rhetoric of the Chogms irritated him. He would later dismiss them as nothing more than a series of 'photo opportunities'. But at Nassau in

1985 and Vancouver in 1987 he joined such leaders as Bob Hawke (Australia), Brian Mulroney (Canada) and Rajiv Gandhi (India) in supporting sanctions against South Africa and giving aid for African education and training in the Republic and Southwest Africa.[26]

Commonwealth pressure on South Africa in the second half of the 1980s was directed at opening a new political dialogue; the release of political prisoners such as Nelson Mandela jailed since 1964; the unbanning of the African National Congress and other African parties; dismantling social and economic apartheid; the calling of democratic elections, and granting independence to Namibia. In this Britain, which had for long denounced apartheid, stood apart from the Commonwealth majority on the grounds that it believed sanctions would not work or would adversely affect the ordinary Africans they were supposed to benefit. There were also fears that Germans, Japanese, and others might snaffle British markets. Thus at a mini-summit of seven Commonwealth leaders called in London in 1986 to review the package of economic measures agreed at Nassau in 1985, Mrs Thatcher broke consensus and refused to go along with any new measures not adopted by her EC partners. At Vancouver in 1987 and Kuala Lumpur in 1989 this breach was institutionalised by several insertions of the phrase 'with the exception of Britain' in the communiqués.[27] At Kuala Lumpur in 1989 Mrs Thatcher seemed so to relish her isolation that she declared: 'If it's forty-eight against one, then I'm sorry for the forty-eight.'[28]

By this time, however, the thaw had begun in South Africa. Prisoners from Robben Island had begun to be released. The new State President F. W. de Klerk indicated he was prepared for dialogue about reform. When Mrs Thatcher maintained her 'with the exception of Britain' stance, Geoffrey Palmer was one of the few leaders who did not denounce her and said he felt it was 'not a good idea for the Commonwealth to turn into an organisation to orchestrate hymns of hate against the UK'.[29] He was also part of a new move to highlight environmental threats. The only Minister of Environment present, he led a move to condemn driftnet fishing in the Pacific. At Kuala Lumpur the Heads of Government also took heed, on Canadian insistence, of the problems facing Commonwealth sports. They set up a committee of experts to look into the future of the Commonwealth Games. They also appointed a High Level Appraisal Group (H-Lag), consisting of all previous Chogm hosts, to consider the Commonwealth in the 1990s.[30]

The full H-Lag met only once, on the eve of the 1991 Harare Chogm. Earlier meetings had been postponed, first because of the Gulf War and then by Rajiv Gandhi's assassination. As usual, it was left to senior officials to produce the draft mission statement for the 1990s, which grew into a longish document incorporating all the buzz words of the 1980s about democracy, human rights, gender equality, free trade, the market economy, educational opportunities, sustainable development and environmental protection. The British delegate was Lord Armstrong, the music-loving former Sir William Armstrong, Cabinet Secretary under Mrs Thatcher. When her successor, John Major, asked him if Britain could adhere to the declaration, Armstrong was positive, but felt that the document was unfocused and somewhat prolix. Major asked him to produce a succinct summary. When the H-Lag finally met in Harare on the eve of the 1991 Chogm, they devoted most of their time to considering help for a post-apartheid South Africa in the light of de Klerk's reforms. As they were about to break for lunch, Major reminded them about the document for the 1990s and mentioned that Britain had a shorter version, which contained the main principles. This went through, with minor amendments, more or less on the nod.[31]

Launched publicly after the Retreat at Victoria Falls, *The Harare Commonwealth Declaration* was introduced by the Secretary-General as 'our guide book and beacon for the new century'. Major told his press conference that it was 'not a string of words to forget, but the road map for future progress'. Although the ideas were not new and did not have the memorable ring of the famous 1926, 1949 and 1971 declarations, it did become a significant ideological and institutional landmark. It signified the emergence of a rules-based organisation and the rules came from those who (in the words of Stephen Chan) had won the Cold War.[32] As well as reaffirming the 1971 principles, the Harare Declaration went on to affirm certain fundamental political values: democracy, democratic processes, the rule of law, independence of the judiciary, good governance, human rights, gender equality, and educational opportunity. It called for sustainable development and the abolition of poverty by means of sound economic management, the free market economy, population control, the freest possible flow of trade, environmental protection, and special assistance for small states.[33]

Thus the doctrines of 'the West' were affirmed for the Commonwealth in 1991, with the implication that development assistance would become conditional on adherence to the Harare principles. But the greatest media interest in 1991 focused on Nelson Mandela, only 20 months out of jail after 27 years, who went with an efficient ANC team to Harare as guests of Robert Mugabe. Although not attending the Chogm, Mandela attended the opening ceremony, met with important leaders, and held a large press conference. When he was introduced to Jim Bolger at the Secretary-General's reception, he said he hoped soon to welcome the All Blacks back to South Africa.

For the rest of the 1990s the contours of a rules-based Commonwealth would be fleshed out, using the Harare Declaration as the reference point.

Regional Organisations

If the HoC and the Chogms – the tip of the iceberg – made the headlines, most Commonwealth activities – those below the waterline in the metaphor – went largely unnoticed. From 1973, when officials met before the Ottawa Chogm, such meetings were instituted regularly mid-way between Chogms and became known as the SOM (Senior Officials Meeting). There were also regular ministerial meetings usually associated with meetings of UN and other agencies. Finance Ministers met before the IMF and World Bank, Health Ministers before the World Health Assembly, Labour Ministers before the ILO, Agricultural Ministers before the FAO. There were occasional meetings of Education Ministers and in 1985 Ministers responsible for Women's Affairs began to meet, followed in 1989 by Ministers for the Environment, and in 1992 Ministers of Youth Affairs. Unlike the Chogms, which were usually attended by most of the member states, attendance at the ministerial meetings was more selective.[34]

Of more immediate concern to most countries were the regional organisations in which member states tended to be more intimately engaged. These had begun for New Zealand with the Canberra Pact in 1944 and the South Pacific Forum in 1971. Others of interest to New Zealand included ASEAN, formed in 1967, because of defence commitments to Malaysia and Singapore, and the EEC, because Britain joined in 1973. In the Caribbean, Caricom began in 1973 followed by the Organization of East Caribbean States in 1991. The four Commonwealth West African members joined Ecowas (the Economic Community of West African States) in 1975. SADC (the Southern African Development

Community, 1980) and Saarc (the South Asian Association for Regional Co-operation, 1986) were created in Southern Africa and South Asia respectively.[35]

The South Pacific Forum was a by-product of decolonisation in the Pacific in the 1970s. The initiative came from the Pacific Island Producers' Association, of which the leaders of Fiji, Tonga, and Western Samoa, supported by the New Zealand Ministry of Foreign Affairs, persuaded Holyoake to host a meeting in New Zealand of independent Commonwealth members in the South Pacific. At the inaugural Forum in Wellington in 1971, the delegates were the President of Nauru, the Prime Ministers of Fiji, New Zealand, Tonga, and Western Samoa, the Premier of the Cook Islands, and Australia's Minister of External Affairs. As further Pacific Ocean colonies gained self-government or independence in the 1970s and 1980s, the Forum doubled in membership. The addition of the non-Commonwealth Marshall Islands and Federated States of Micronesia in 1987 brought the total to 15 making it the largest Commonwealth regional organisation. It was exceeded in size only by Ecowas, which had just four Commonwealth members.

While the Forum became one of the more active regional organisations, another regional effort proved short-lived. In 1978 Malcolm Fraser, the Australian Prime Minister, took the initiative in calling Commonwealth Heads of Government Regional Meetings (Chogrms) for Asia and the Pacific in an effort to get away from preoccupation with African issues. He hosted the first Chogrm in Sydney in 1978, but Muldoon was unenthusiastic, partly because of the Australian lead, but mainly because of a possible overlap with the Forum.[36] Chogrms were held in Delhi (1980), Suva (1982) and Port Moresby (1984), but it was decided that regular meetings were not necessary and the experiment was eventually laid to rest. By 1989 a new regional initiative emerged under Australian leadership in the shape of the Asia-Pacific Economic Cooperation conference in Canberra (APEC). However, Malcolm Fraser favoured reviving the Chogrms during an Australian Parliamentary Seminar in 1997.[37]

Inter-Governmental Organisations

New Zealand's contributions to the inter-governmental organisations consisted of modest financial subscriptions, commensurate with our size, and a handful of personnel. The basic support for the Commonwealth Secretariat, the Fund for Technical Co-operation, and the Foundation always came from the 'ABC members' – Australia, Britain, Canada – who contributed over half the funds. Most of the smaller members had basic subscriptions to the Secretariat of either 1.5 per cent or 0.75 per cent of the total budget. In 1971 the total budget was £650,095. Following Britain (30 per cent), Canada (18.20), India (10.48), Australia (9.17) and Pakistan (2.23), New Zealand was sixth with 2.17 per cent, just a little over the basic rate.[38] By 1991 New Zealand was fifth with 2.16 per cent. The sums were not large. The Secretariat's budget by 1990–91 totalled £7,944,520, of which New Zealand's contribution was about $414,000. In addition a sum was assigned to the Commonwealth Science Council of £651,802. New Zealand's contribution was $63,000. There were pledges to the Commonwealth Youth Programme amounting to £1,425,866 (with New Zealand's contribution at $97,000). The CFTC's total budget was £22,383,319 with New Zealand's contribution about $950,000.[39]

From time to time New Zealanders served in the Secretariat. The most senior was Hunter Wade, who became Deputy Secretary-General (Economic) in 1972. Following Gerald Hensley's success as one of the original personal assistants to the Secretary-General, David McDowell followed between 1969 and 1972 and Chris Laidlaw was Assistant Director of the Secretary-General's office from 1978 to 1984. Peter Brooks headed the Youth Division from 1979 to 1981 and Stephen Chan also served in the Division. Jeremy Pope, as Director of the Legal Division, from 1981 to 1993, was the longest-serving New Zealander in the Secretariat, and he had a major hand in drafting numerous Commonwealth Declarations. In 1991 Dr Helen Bichan became Assistant Director of the Health Programme. In financial administration, K. R. Bain was Director of Finance and Research Services in 1979, P. A. Stevens a special assistant on taxation and W. R. Tuck a special adviser on Finance in CFTC in 1981.[40]

The oldest and largest of the IGOs was the Commonwealth Agricultural Bureaux, a group of four research institutes and 10 bureaux, which were clearing houses for disseminating research information covering the whole field of agricultural, veterinary, forestry and food production sciences. As the Imperial Agricultural Bureaux it had come into being as a group in 1929, bringing under its wing earlier organisations. New Zealand was an original member and contributor and therefore had a seat on the governing council. The name was changed to the Commonwealth Agricultural Bureaux (CAB) in 1948. As usual, the 'ABC members' were the largest contributors. But from 1972 the basis of funding changed. Instead of relying for the bulk of its funds on member government subscriptions, an ever-growing proportion came from the sale of publications and services. Two thirds of these sales were to non-Commonwealth countries.

Therefore, in the 1980s it was agreed that the CAB should be converted into an international organisation. It might have reverted to being known as IAB with 'international' in place of 'imperial', but in 1961 it became CAB-International, a not-for-profit international organisation open to all countries on the basis of treaty-level agreements with governments, and self-financing through charges for publications and services. Thus Fiji could remain a member when its membership of the Commonwealth lapsed in 1987. Ireland and Pakistan (former Commonwealth members) could join. In 1988 Hungary became the first non-English-speaking member to join. By 1990 the old Commonwealth relationship was felt to hamper the recruitment of members and a conscious effort was made to project a corporate image which downplayed historic links. The name was subsequently simplified to CABI (referred to as Cabi) and sub-titled 'International Centre for Agriculture and Biosciences'.[41] For a time in the early 1990s New Zealand's membership seemed tenuous because government restructuring had led to the demise of the DSIR, which had been the Cabi link. The problem was resolved when the new Ministry of Research, Science and Technology took over this role.

New Zealanders also had a role in creating the newest and least known of the IGOs – the Commonwealth of Learning (COL) founded in 1989. The proposal arose out of concern about the sudden drop in student mobility in the Commonwealth caused by the adoption of full cost-recovery fee regimes in the developed Commonwealth members in the 1980s. At the Nassau Chogm in 1985 the Secretary-General was instructed to look into filling the gap by distance learning. An expert group under Lord Briggs (provost of Worcester College, Oxford and Chancellor of Britain's Open University) reported to the 1987 Vancouver Chogm in favour of a University of the Commonwealth for Co-operating in Distance Education. This was not to be an institution to enrol students, but an agency that would develop distance learning materials, assemble packages of existing materials, and act as broker on behalf of member countries in their dissemination. A small professional staff of about 20 was envisaged with an annual cost of about £2.4 million. The long term aim was 'that any learner, anywhere in the Commonwealth, shall be able to study any distance-teaching programme available from any bona fide college or university in the Commonwealth'.[42] Sufficient pledges of support were forthcoming at Vancouver for the COL to start work on 1 January 1989. Bill Renwick, former Director of Education in Wellington, was one of the first governors of the COL. Peter McMechan, former Director of the University of Otago and then the University of the South Pacific Extension Programmes, was one of the founder staff members, and served until 1998. By 1991 New Zealand was pledging NZ$50,000 per year towards the COL Budget.

Professional Associations

The Commonwealth Foundation, although an IGO, was largely involved with voluntary non-official organizations. An autonomous body housed within the Secretariat, the Foundation was financed by voluntary contributions of Governments and was governed by a Board of Trustees. The initial fund was only £250,000 (then roughly NZ$500,000) and intended for 'increasing interchanges between Commonwealth organisations in professional fields'.[43] After ten years the fund had risen to £450,000. It did not pass the £1 million mark until the 1980s and peaked at £1.9 million in 1993. New Zealand's contribution at this point was the fifth largest (2.51 per cent of the total) at about £50,000. The original mandate – known as the 'seven commandments' – provided for support for (1) fuller representation at professional conferences, (2) professional bodies holding more conferences, (3) professional exchanges and study visits, (4) exchanges of professional information, (5) setting up new associations, (6) the growth of Commonwealth-wide or regional organisations, and (7) exceptional requests by individuals and associations in other than the professional fields. In the first 10 years the Foundation helped found numerous new professional associations and national professional centres, where groups of professional bodies could share common premises.

By the mid-1970s it was realised that there were many areas where the Secretariat and the Foundation might cooperate, but that governments were often suspicious of non-governmental organisations

(NGOs). At the 1977 Chogm an advisory committee was set up to consider cooperation between the official and non-official Commonwealth. The report, *From Governments to Grassroots*, completed in 1978, indicated that relations between the two were uncoordinated and it suggested that the Foundation's mandate should be expanded to take in cultural, social welfare, and development areas. It also suggested that an NGO Desk should be created in the Secretariat and that governments should create national liaison units to foster and consult with NGOs.[44] The 1979 Lusaka Chogm increased the Foundation's funding to £1 million annually (not actually reached until 1982–83). The Trustees accepted an expanded list of areas of interest in food production, health, education, social welfare, science/technology, culture, the media, and public administration. The Foundation (which had begun as a charity in British law) changed its status and it, like Cabi, became an international organisation with appropriate diplomatic immunities.

In the 1970s and 1980s there was a veritable explosion of voluntary activity. With Foundation support the following new associations were founded in the period under review:

Date	Profession	Acronym
1970	Magistrates	CMagA
1970	Education Administrators	CCEA
1971	Legal Education	CLEA
1971	Planners	CAP
1971	Postal Administrators	CCPA
1972	Librarians	COMLA
1973	Nurses	CNF
1974	Museums	CAM
1974	Science, Technology and Maths Educators	CASTME
1974	Linking Trust for Teachers	CLT
1978	Journalists	CJA
1978	Scientific Agricultural Societies	CASAS
1978	Tax Administrators	CATA
1979	Trade Unions	CTUC
1980	Chess	CCA
1983	Legislative Counsel	CALC
1983	Mental Handicap and Development Disabilities	CAMHDD

1983	Lawyers	CLA
1984	Hansard Editors	CAHE
1984	Archivists and Records Managers	ACARM
1985	Education in Journalism and Communication	CAEJC
1985	Education of Adults	CAEA
1987	Parliamentary Librarians	CAPL
1987	Human Rights Initiative	CHRI
1988	Development	CAD
1989	Local Action and Economic Development	COMMACT.
1989	Historians	CHS

An informal grouping of these bodies known at first as Commonwealth Professional Associations (CPAs) was renamed in 1989 the Organization of Commonwealth Associations (OCA). In one case, the Commonwealth Human Ecology Council (Chec) founded in 1969, the initiative and leadership came from a New Zealander. Zena Daysh, a physiotherapist by training, had worked for the British Ministry of Production during the Second World War on connections between health and productivity, and then for the Committee on Nutrition in the Commonwealth in the 1950s. Chec held its first conference on the problems of development, health and the environment in 1970. In the 1990s, past the age of 80, Mrs Daysh remained an active executive vice-chair of Chec.[45]

As new associations proliferated, the Director of the Foundation, Inoke Faletau (Tonga) moved to create Commonwealth Liaison Units (Clus) in member countries beginning with the Pacific Islands. By 1993, when 40 governments were contributing to the Fund, the Foundation had contributed to the creation of 35 new associations and 40 Clus had come into being.[46] In New Zealand the Foreign Minister, Russell Marshall, said in 1989 that a Clu was unnecessary, but in 1993 the Council for International Development became the base for the Association of NGOs in Aotearoa (Angoa). In 1991 the Foundation moved on from regional consultations to holding the first Commonwealth NGO Forum at Harare a few months before the Chogm. From this came a call for an NGO Charter. In the 1990s considerable discussion would take place about the nature, role and accountability of the NGOs. A draft charter was considered at the second forum in Wellington in 1995. From these discussions a distinction was drawn between 'care and welfare' organisations (voluntary, independent, not-for-profit, not self-seeking) and professional organisations, which had been the Foundation's original raison d'être.[47]

It became very evident that the designation NGO (defining organisations by what they were *not*) was unsatisfactory. Americans preferred Voluntary Agencies (Vol Ags). D.A.Low suggested, 'personal, professional and philanthropic' organisations.[48] But this neglected the whole sporting arena. A much better designation would be 'voluntary, independent, professional, philanthropic and sporting organisations' (Vippsos). This indicates their nature (voluntary and independent) and their main functions (professional, philanthropic and sporting). Moreover, the last represents the most popular part – often the *only* part – of the Commonwealth for many people.

Sport

Although New Zealand was part of the select 'Group of Three' from the original political Commonwealth, it was usually a minor player in the Chogms, the Secretariat, the CFTC, and the Foundation. In the Vippso world, individual New Zealanders had played important roles in several professional organisations and many more benefited from professional conferences. In the sports arena, however, New Zealand had long been a major player.

The 16 Games held since the British Empire Games began in 1930 were hosted by only four countries – Australia, Britain, Canada and New Zealand – except in 1966 and 1998. In the period under review, New Zealand was host twice, at Christchurch (1974) and Auckland (1990). Both were important landmarks. In 1974, 38 countries sent 1,276 competitors. The decision was taken to drop 'British' in the Games title. The 'arrival' of African sporting power was evident in 52 medals won by African athletes – not least the gold won by Filbert Bayi who beat John Walker in the 1500 metres.[49] The New Zealand Olympic and Commonwealth Games Association managed to more than break even on the 1974 Games, to the long-term benefit of the association's funds. In 1990, 55 countries sent over 2,000 athletes. Commercial sponsorships had to be accepted for the first time and even then a government subsidy was needed.

This growing costs crisis cast a shadow over the future of the Games and had already been brought to the attention of member governments.

Indeed, the possibility of boycotts because of sporting contacts with South Africa; the sheer cost of mounting the Games, which seemed to preclude hosting by Third World members; and unevenness in the spread of sporting talent, all raised questions about the future of the Games in the 1980s. Nigeria boycotted the Edmonton Games in 1978. Boycotts of the 1986 Edinburgh Games meant that more countries stayed away than competed. Thus the Canadian Government ensured that sport was placed on the agenda at the 1989 Kuala Lumpur Chogm, where it was agreed to set up an expert group to consider the problem.[50] Mr Justice Roy McMurtry, a former Canadian High Commissioner in London and then Associate Chief Justice of Ontario, headed the group. Bill Garlick, chairman of the Olympic and Commonwealth Games Association, represented New Zealand, and Jeremy Pope represented the Secretariat. The group reported to the SOM in 1990 and the Harare Chogm in 1991. There it was reconstituted as the Chogm Committee on Co-operation Through Sport (CCCS). Over the next few years the CCCS expounded a philosophy as visionary as that of the COL.

It highlighted the fact that of the 1.7 billion people in the Commonwealth, 1 billion were under the age of sixteen. The first priority for the CCCS was finding ways for the Commonwealth to reach these young people.

> Sport speaks directly to the young, [said the committee] . . . Sport can provide the bridge to the classroom, acting as a very effective educational and socialising instrument . . . Through sport, for example, young children join organised and structured activities which can then bring them into educational and community social systems. . . . Sport speaks directly to the man in the street and to each and every child amongst us.[51]

Sport, went on the CCCS, contributed to individual development, national identity, economic development, and Commonwealth cohesion. In receiving the reports of the CCCS, the Chogms of the 1990s urged governments to support the Commonwealth Games Federation and treat sport assistance as part of Overseas Development Aid. The 'ABC members', along with Malaysia, Namibia and New Zealand, made grants to the Federation to enable it to acquire new office accommodation in London, professional officers for marketing and sports development and secretarial staff. New Zealand also assisted in the sports development of Pacific Island states.

*

By 1991 the Commonwealth had emerged as a forum of chief benefit to small states. Nearly half of the members (24 out of 50) had populations of less than one million. New Zealand, of course, in the not so distant past was also in the small state category and could thus relate to many of its Commonwealth partners. Reporting on the Ottawa Chogm of 1973, Frank Corner said it was a 'stimulating and impressive experience'. He testified to a relaxed atmosphere, which enabled African delegates to make jokes they would never make in the UN. He suggested that the Commonwealth provided 'as good a starting point as any for a concerted effort to solve the problems of the haves and the have-nots and the growing gap between them.'[52] Even Muldoon, who must have found Chogms a tense experience at times, returned from the Jubilee meetings which produced the Gleneagles Agreement, with 'fresh respect for the utility and vitality' of the Commonwealth. He reported to the Cabinet: 'We are not members of this Commonwealth by accident of colonial history but conviction'.[53]

By the 1990s the political Commonwealth had become less contentious because of the curing of the UDI and apartheid cancers. Britain could re-discover the Commonwealth and once again take a lead. This meant that New Zealand did not find itself engaged in a perpetual balancing act between traditional loyalties and moral principles. At the same time, the wider activities of the Peoples' Commonwealth had come to be seen as the 'real Commonwealth'. In the Vippso world many more New Zealanders came to have appreciation of, and involvement in, the affairs of the Commonwealth than the tiny body of politicians and officials who went to Chogms, SOMs, or ministerial confabulations. For many New Zealanders the Commonwealth Games ceased being the sole point of contact with the Commonwealth.

Notes

1 M. Margaret Ball, *The 'Open' Commonwealth* (Durham, N.C., 1971), pp.78–9.
2 See *New Zealand in World Affairs*, Vol.1 (Wellington, 1977), pp.78–85.
3 *The Times*, 9 February 1952.
4 Arnold Smith, with Clyde Sanger, *Stitches in Time: The Commonwealth in World Politics* (London, 1981), pp.271–3.
5 Trevor McDonald, *The Queen and the Commonwealth* (London, 1986), p.92.
6 W. David McIntyre, *The Significance of the Commonwealth 1965–1990* (London/Christchurch, 1991), pp.249–50.

7   In 1969 the communiqué began: 'Commonwealth Heads of Government met . . .' but the gathering was still titled Meeting of Commonwealth Prime Ministers. In 1971 the new title was used for the first time.
8   HGM(71) 1st mtg., 14 January 1971. MFAT PM 153/55/4, Pt.1 in ABHS 950, Box 3868. National Archives, Wellington (hereafter NANZ).
9   Smith, *Stitches in Time*, p.109–12.
10 *The Commonwealth at the Summit: Communiqués of Commonwealth Heads of Government Meetings 1944–1986* (hereafter *CW Summit*) (London, 1987), pp.156–7. My italics.
11 HGM(O)(71)8, Notified Amendments. MFAT PM 153/55/5, Pt.1 in ABHS 950, Box 3868. NANZ.
12 Smith, *Stitches in Time*, pp.272–3, 295.
13 *CW Summit*, p.167; see also Tony Garnier, Bruce Kohn and Pat Booth, *The Hunter & The Hill: New Zealand Politics & The Kirk Years* (Auckland, 1978), pp.114–22.
14 HGM(75) 5th mtg., 1 May 1975. MFAT PM 153/58/4, Pt.2. ABHS 950, Box 3872. NANZ.
15 Malcolm Templeton, *Human Rights and Sporting Contacts: New Zealand Attitudes to Race Relations in South Africa 1921–94* (Auckland, 1998), pp.148–50.
16 Templeton, *Human Rights*, p.153.
17 *CW Summit*, pp.198–9.
18 See J. Davidow, *A Peace in Southern Africa: The Lancaster House Conference on Rhodesia, 1979* (Boulder and London, 1989).
19 N. M. Green, '"A No.1 Enemy of Africa": New Zealand's reactions to the Rhodesian UDI Crisis, 1965–80' (MA thesis, Canterbury University, 1998), pp.163–4.
20 Green, 'A No.1 Enemy of Africa', pp.167–9; on New Zealand's role in the CMF see John Crawford, 'A Job Well Done: The New Zealand Army Truce Monitoring Contingent in Rhodesia 1979–80' (Ministry of Defence typescript, Wellington, 1980); David Moloney, 'Operation Midford: End of Tour Report' (Ministry of Defence typescript, Wellington, 1980); J. Crawford, 'Truce, Supervision: The Zimbabwe Model', in *New Zealand International Review* (hereafter *NZIR*), September–October 1989, pp.12–15.
21 Templeton, *Human Rights*, pp.191–2.
22 Templeton, *Human Rights*, p.199.
23 Templeton, *Human Rights*, pp.209–11.
24 *Vulnerability, Small States in the Global Society: Report of a Commonwealth Consultative Group* (London, ComSec, 1985).
25 See *Towards a New Bretton Woods – Challenges for the World Financial and Trading System: Report of a Commonwealth Study Group* (London, ComSec, 1983).
26 W. David McIntyre, 'CHOGM '87: the Commonwealth jamboree', in *NZIR*, January–February 1988, pp.2–7; *CW Summit*, pp.267–9; *The Commonwealth at the Summit, Volume 2: Communiqués of Commonwealth Heads of Government Meetings 1897–1995* (hereafter *CW Summit 2*) (London, ComSec, 1997), pp.7–12.
27 McIntyre, 'CHOGM '87', pp.8–11, 46–50.
28 McIntyre, 'End of an Era for the Commonwealth: thoughts on the Hibiscus Summit', in *NZIR*, January–February 1990, p.6.
29 McIntyre, 'End of an Era', p. 6.

30 *CW Summit 2*, p.52.
31 Private interview.
32 S. Chan, 'Actors, issues and instruments in the post-Thatcher Commonwealth', in *NZIR*, January–February 1992, p.9.
33 *CW Summit 2*, pp.82–5.
34 See A. N. Papadopoulos, *Multilateral Diplomacy within the Commonwealth: A Decade of Expansion* (The Hague, 1982).
35 See McIntyre, *Significance*, ch.9.
36 McIntyre, *Significance*, pp. 172–3.
37 *From Empire to Partnership: Report on a Seminar on the Commonwealth of Nations, 20 August 1997* (Joint Standing Committee on Foreign Affairs, Defence and Trade, Parliament of Australia, Canberra, 1997), report p.15; transcript pp.12, 20.
38 *Third Report of the Commonwealth Secretary-General* (hereafter *S-G Report*), November 1968–November 1970 (London, ComSec, 1971), pp.51, 57.
39 *S-G Report*, 1991, p.152.
40 *S-G Reports*, 1973, p.71; 1977, p.87; 1979, pp.87–8; 1981, pp.95–6; 1983, pp.93–4; 1985, pp.101–4; 1987, pp.126–7; 1991, pp.1153–155.
41 D. Mentz, 'CAB International and Developments since the 1985 Review Conference', in *Eleventh Review Conference, London, 1990: Report of Proceedings*, (Wallingford, 1990), pp.19–20.
42 *Towards a Commonwealth of Learning: A proposal to create the University of the Commonwealth for Co-operation in Distance Education* (London, 1987), p.40.
43 See John Chadwick, *The Unofficial Commonwealth: The Story of the Commonwealth Foundation 1965–1980*, (London, 1980). The Secretariat finally appointed an NGO Liaison Officer in 1993.
44 *From Governments to Grassroots: Report of the Advisory Committee on Relations between the Official and Unofficial Commonwealth* (London, ComSec, 1978).
45 C. Curtis, 'Zena Daysh: Crusader for Development', in *Human Ecology*, October 1977, pp.12–13.
46 *The Commonwealth Foundation: A Special Report 1966 to 1993*, (London, 1993), pp.4–17.
47 *Non-Governmental Organisations: Guidelines for Good Policy and Practice* (London, Commonwealth Foundation, 1995), p.18. After a review of NGO relations in 1998 it was announced that the Clus would be phased out.
48 D.A. Low, 'Commonwealth Policy Studies: Is there a case for a Centre?', in *The Round Table* 1988, No.308, p.369.
49 See C. Dheensaw, *The Commonwealth Games: the First 60 Years 1930–1990* (Auckland, 1994).
50 *CW Summit 2*, p.76.
51 HGM(91)13, Working Party on Strengthening Commonwealth Sport: Final Report July 1991 (London, ComSec, 1991), pp.1, 10, 13.
52 Report on Ottawa, October 1973. MFAT PM 153/56/4, Pt.1 in ABHS 950, Box 3869. NANZ.
53 Draft memo. for Cabinet. MFAT PM 153/60/1, Pt.1, in ABHS 950, Box 3873, NANZ.

IAN MCGIBBON

New Zealand Defence Policy from Vietnam to the Gulf[1]

NEW ZEALAND'S APPROACH TO SECURITY IN THE EARLY 1970s remained essentially unchanged from that which it had followed since the Second World War. The Cold War, which had dominated the international system for more than two decades, provided the context. The ideological conflict between the Soviet Union and its now estranged ally the People's Republic of China and the West, of which New Zealand was part, had persisted so long that it seemed to have become a permanent condition. Originating in the aftermath of the defeat of Nazi Germany, it had ensured a still continuing division of Europe. The development of thermonuclear weapons had given a new character to the confrontation. On both sides, fear of the consequences of a nuclear exchange both hardened positions and, paradoxically, pushed the contending powers together. Both blocs had an interest in the stability of the balance of power which had developed; both recognised the need to avoid any repetition of the Cuban missile crisis of 1962, when the world had seemed on the verge of a nuclear war. Confidence building and arms limitation measures had helped to reduce apprehension: of these the most important were the Anti-Ballistic Missile Treaty and the SALT (Strategic Arms Limitation Talks) agreement, both concluded in 1972. The former was designed to keep the deterrent stable by removing the danger that one side would gain a tempting degree of immunity to the other's nuclear strike, while the latter froze the numbers of intercontinental (ICBM) and submarine launched (SLBM) ballistic missiles possessed by both sides.

In the 1970s relations between the two blocs were characterised by detente. This reached its highpoint with the Final Act of the Helsinki

Conference on Security and Co-operation in Europe in 1975, which in virtually legitimising the post-war boundaries of Europe amounted to a de facto German peace settlement. The detente was also reflected in efforts to extend the SALT I agreement, which would culminate in the signature of further agreements (SALT II) in 1979. These encouraging developments notwithstanding, there remained areas of concern in the West. First, in spite of the SALT agreement, there were uncertainties concerning the all-important nuclear balance. The Soviet movement towards emulating the United States by installing multiple warheads, known as MIRVs (multiple independently-targeted re-entry vehicles) in arms control jargon, on its missiles threatened the balance, since under SALT I the Soviet Union had many more ICBMs than the United States. This offered the prospect of a huge Soviet advantage in the number of targets that could be hit. From 1976 the Soviet Union's replacement of older SS–4 and SS–5 intermediate-range (INF) missiles in Europe with more capable, longer-ranged SS–20 missiles introduced another danger while eating away at the foundations of detente.[2] In European capitals no less than in Washington, there were fears that it would undermine the basis of Western European security. Could the United States be relied upon to launch its ICBMs, and risk Soviet retaliation against American cities, if Western Europe only was attacked with these intermediate-range weapons?

The build-up of Soviet conventional weapons was a second area of concern. Proceeding apace in the 1970s, it seemed out of line with the spirit of detente. The Soviet Navy, in particular, was being hugely expanded. While not in a position to challenge the US Navy for supremacy at sea – it lacked the necessary aircraft-carriers and bases to mount such a challenge – it was becoming more visible throughout the world. In the Pacific its access to the former US naval base at Cam Ranh Bay in Vietnam, after the fall of South Vietnam in 1975, greatly extended its reach. The political impact of this development had a bearing on the third area of concern: Soviet intervention in Third World conflicts throughout the world.

Within this over-arching international context New Zealand policymakers sought to come to terms with major changes in their country's defence arrangements. Like Australia, New Zealand had been forced in the late 1960s to accept the imminent prospect of the withdrawal of the British from east of Suez. While a change of government in London led to a delay in this process, it seemed only a matter of time before Britain's one and a half centuries' presence was brought to an end (excepting temporarily in Hong Kong). Ever since the fall of Singapore in 1942, New Zealand governments had been conscious of the limitations on Britain's ability to provide the strategic basis of New Zealand's security; this recognition had underlain New Zealand's signature of a security accord, the ANZUS pact, with the United States in 1951. The British withdrawal seemed to justify the importance New Zealand, and Australia, had placed on sustaining this alliance, not least by joining the United States in the ultimately unsuccessful and unpopular effort to preserve the Republic of Vietnam. Even after the National Government of John Marshall was replaced by a Labour administration led by Norman Kirk late in 1972, there was no quarrel with the proposition advanced by senior Foreign Affairs official Ralph Mullins that New Zealand 'should retain the ANZUS Treaty as a central guarantee of our security'.[3] New Zealand derived important practical advantages from the relationship with the United States. In the defence procurement field this had become increasingly apparent in the late 1960s, and even more so during the following decade. A Memorandum of Understanding on Logistic Support Arrangements in 1982 gave New Zealand priority access to re-supply of spare parts and ammunition, the ability to slot into American production runs (thereby lessening costs), and a guarantee of re-supply in an emergency.[4] These benefits in the field of materiel were supplemented by those New Zealand gained from the flow of intelligence from American sources and from being able to send personnel to American facilities for training courses. Moreover, New Zealand secured considerable diplomatic advantages from its relationship with the West's leading power: 'ready and unrestricted access' to American policy-makers at a high level was 'one of the privileges of alliance membership', a New Zealand Chief of Defence Staff later noted.[5]

Unlike the earlier defence relationship with Britain, the New Zealand–United States alliance was not underpinned by a sense of kinship. The United States was not 'family'. New Zealand had no hope of achieving with it the comfortable link which it had, in earlier times, enjoyed with the United Kingdom. Such considerations were particularly significant for National administrations. They seemed to demand a proactive policy to ensure the continued vitality of the formal commitments contained in the ANZUS treaty. In the late 1970s Prime

Minister Robert Muldoon regarded American naval visits as providing an opportunity to bolster the alliance; he actively encouraged the American government to arrange such visits.[6] Other co-operative measures with the United States involving the armed forces included the contribution to the Israel–Egypt peace treaty monitoring organisation, the Multinational Force and Observers (MFO), in the Sinai in 1982.

Muldoon's approach to defence was backward looking, to an era of collective security within an Anglo-American framework. This was highlighted in 1982 when he offered to make available a New Zealand frigate for operations in the Indian Ocean. This would allow a British warship there to be re-deployed to the South Atlantic, where the British were mounting a major amphibious operation to regain control of the Falklands Islands which had been invaded by Argentine forces. New Zealand was the only Commonwealth country to make any military gesture of support. Not for the first time self-interest and support for Britain in strife came together to prompt a New Zealand response: apart from Muldoon's admiration for British Prime Minister Margaret Thatcher, such action probably owed much to the trade advantages which such an offer might bring, since New Zealand was embroiled in negotiations over EEC access.[7] As a result, HMNZS *Canterbury* was deployed in the Indian Ocean in May 1982, and she alternated with HMNZS *Waikato* in the role during the next 18 months.

Muldoon's ministry, from 1975 to 1984, was the last to have significant representation of Second World War veterans, for whom co-operation with Britain in strife was natural. It failed to perceive, indeed actively resisted, changing social attitudes. By the late 1970s, most New Zealanders had been born after the Second World War. They had lived in relative peace for the whole of their lives, and had never experienced a sense of direct threat akin to that which had scared their parents in the 1940s. Defence issues held little priority for them, and they were more likely than previous generations to be swayed by seductive anti-war messages. Indeed an anti-war culture had been spawned by the increasingly strident opposition to the Vietnam War. The resulting generational divide provided the setting for the demise of New Zealand's traditional approach to defence. The change was symbolised by the supersession in 1984 of 63-year-old 2NZEF veteran Muldoon by 40-year-old baby boomer David Lange. Muldoon's stubborn determination to assert the old way only strengthened the reaction to it, which increasingly focused on the issue of American nuclear-powered and armed ship visits.

In the early 1970s this had not been a matter of public controversy. Visits by American nuclear-powered warships had ceased after 1969 because of the absence of American legislation indemnifying victims of an accident involving the propulsion systems while ships were in foreign ports. By the time that the United States removed this impediment, by enacting indemnifying legislation in 1974, a Labour administration was in power in Wellington. It had no desire to promote such visits, and the United States did not press the issue. Only when Muldoon adopted a very different approach did the question of ship visits become a major public issue, as 'peace' flotillas jousted with the arriving warships between 1976 and 1984.

A pervasive anti-American feeling among New Zealanders exacerbated these developments. To be sure, such prejudice had been lessened by the 1941–45 experience among the older generation of New Zealanders, but it remained latent, and was reinvigorated by the Vietnam controversy among a significant section of the population. As Frank Corner, the Secretary of Foreign Affairs from 1973 to 1980, later reflected: 'Even as late as 1970 the general run of non-ideological New Zealanders . . . were still old-style British in their instincts. . . they shared a certain style of British superciliousness towards Americans and American culture and foreign policies; and they still tended to link their fate with that of Britain.'[8] The upshot was that the ANZUS alliance rested on relatively weak foundations, unbuttressed by sentiment or commerce in contrast to the Anglo-New Zealand relationship.

Even as New Zealand adjusted to the retraction in the British presence in Southeast Asia, another significant development was undermining the reasons for its previous focus on that region. Changes in the American approach had serious implications for the forward defence strategy upon which New Zealand had based its defence policy since the late 1950s. The United States was, in 1972, in the process of disengaging itself from South Vietnam, a process that was facilitated by a rapprochement between it and the People's Republic of China. President Richard Nixon's dramatic visit to Beijing in February underscored the changing direction of American policy. The assumption underlying Allied contingency planning in Southeast Asia – a potentially aggressive China – was shattered. This made redundant the South East Asia Treaty Organisation (SEATO), responsible over the previous 15 years for the contingency planning to which New Zealand's defence preparations had been oriented. The process of winding it up would be formally completed on 30 June 1977. The Manila Treaty of 1954, under which SEATO had emerged, was not denounced (essentially because it provided Thailand's only formal security link to the United States, which had been buttressed by the Rusk–Thanat protocol of 1962).

These developments soon affected Commonwealth defence arrangements in Singapore. The British in 1970 had agreed to leave a residual presence there as part of the ANZUK Force, in support of the Five Power Defence Arrangements (FPDA), a series of bilateral agreements negotiated in late 1971 to replace the Anglo-Malaysian Defence Agreement (AMDA). But in 1973 London decided to end even this small commitment. Awkwardly for New Zealand, Australia had also determined to remove most of its forces from Singapore as well. The New Zealand authorities were confronted with the problem of what to do with the infantry battalion which New Zealand had kept in Malaya and later Singapore since 1957. There was clearly no longer any strategic reason for its retention in Singapore. However, there were practical obstacles to its repatriation to New Zealand, not least being the lack of accommodation for it. In the event, it remained in Singapore for the time being as part of New Zealand Force South East Asia (NZFSEA), established on 1 February 1974. The continued presence was acceptable to the Singapore government; it fitted in with Norman Kirk's conception of maintaining friendly relations with Southeast Asian countries; and it seemed to offer some training and recruitment advantages for the Army, as well as facilitating New Zealand's involvement in the FPDA. Nonetheless, its anachronistic nature was fully recognised in Wellington.[9]

Meanwhile both Australia and New Zealand shifted their attention away from Southeast Asia to nearer home, Australia to its northern reaches, New Zealand to the South Pacific. This change of focus underpinned the New Zealand Defence Reviews of both 1978 and 1983. In effect New Zealand returned to its 19th-century stance, before strategic influences drew its focus out of the region. Whereas the Royal Navy had then provided the strategic basis for New Zealand's security, the United States Navy was now seen to play that role (leaving aside, of course, the ICBMs and SLBMs which provided the West's strategic deterrent). Within the framework of Western security, New Zealand had had no sense of immediate threat to its territory since 1943. Western naval supremacy made remote the possibility of the disruption of the trade routes on which New Zealand depended for its economic livelihood, or any threat to New Zealand's physical integrity. Only a major war might change this situation, as in 1939–45, but a major war was no longer considered to be the likely outcome of Cold War confrontation, if only because of nuclear deterrence. While the possibility of an accidentally triggered nuclear war could not be entirely discounted, a deliberate resort to war at this level was not anticipated because of its obviously suicidal nature. The absence, for the time being, of a significant proliferation of nuclear powers was also reassuring, the Non-Proliferation Treaty of 1968 having seemed to put the brakes on such developments (even if some powers remained outside its ambit). The upshot was that the South Pacific could confidently be predicted to remain a relatively tranquil area, where the problems were within a scale capable of being dealt with by the regional authorities.

Just as in the 19th century, the renewed regional orientation of New Zealand's defence policy encouraged cooperation with the power across the Tasman. Then New Zealand and the seven Australian colonies had joined together to help fund additional naval forces for the Southwest Pacific. For much of the 20th century, however, the defence relationship had been distant, despite several instances of close co-operation in wartime, most recently in Vietnam, where an ANZAC battalion had been established. Indifference, irritation, and sometimes suspicion marked the two countries' approaches to each other.[10] Determined to avoid big brother's domination by clinging to mother England, New Zealand had had little incentive to improve trans-Tasman defence ties until mother departed, and even then ANZUS provided an alternative external focus. The contraction of British power, the 1969 Guam (or Nixon) Doctrine – which emphasised self-help on the part of American allies – and financial constraints finally pushed New Zealand and Australia towards closer defence cooperation, paralleling a move towards closer economic ties between the two countries which would result in the Closer Economic Relations (CER) agreement in 1982. The 1944 Australia–New Zealand Agreement (or Canberra Pact), with its provisions for a zone of defence in the Southwest Pacific, received renewed attention. The absence of a formal structure of defence cooperation was highlighted. In 1972 a Joint Consultative Committee on Defence Cooperation was established. A New Zealand participant would later describe it, somewhat dismissively, as 'a relaxed and stimulating – certainly hospitable – day or two for the two chiefs [of Defence Staff] and two secretaries of defence, spent talking around the table, all skilfully disguised as a consultative council'.[11] But it set the ball rolling.

The momentum picked up after the change of government in both countries in 1975. The need for improved defence cooperation was endorsed by the two Prime Ministers at Rotorua in March 1976. This was reinforced by a meeting of the respective defence ministers in 1977, thereafter an annual event. In the same year also an Australian–New Zealand Defence Policy Group (later Defence Planning Group) of officials was also created. This was a key development: instead of the previous ad hoc consideration of issues at irregular intervals, there would be continual review of possibilities for closer cooperation.[12] Under this regime 'little happened from year to year, although there were continual incremental gains'.[13] A Defence Supply Cooperation Working Group, was established in 1977 as well, comprising Defence and Trade and Industry officials from the two countries. Meeting twice a year, it examined ways of advancing defence supply cooperation. Under a 1969 agreement, which looked to a pooling, in the long term, of the joint industrial capacities of the two countries, New Zealand manufacturers had managed to secure some contracts for supplying the Australian armed forces, but a faltering of resolve was apparent by the late 1970s. A new agreement on closer defence logistic cooperation, embodied in a memorandum of understanding signed on 2 June 1983, noted that 'the realisation of complementary logistic support capability in the two countries is itself a common strategic objective and may involve in particular cases a cost additional to the cost of procurement from a third country'.[14] The focus, then, was on greater self-sufficiency by the two South Pacific partners. These moves were complemented by a shining example of cooperation in the field: an ANZAC helicopter unit was formed for service in the MFO, which began operations on Anzac Day 1982 after the Israelis had withdrawn from the Sinai. New Zealand provided two of the unit's 10 Iroquois helicopters, along with 36 personnel.[15]

During the 1970s the armed services were also obliged to come to terms with political changes in New Zealand, as in the international sphere. Foremost of these was the advent of the third Labour Government in 1972, and its decision immediately after taking office to end the National Service scheme, under which a certain proportion of 18-year-old men each year were obliged to undergo military training and serve in the Territorial Force. This decision, which came into effect on 31 December 1972, brought to an end a system which had persisted in one form or another for more than 60 years. It 'ushered in a new era of decline' in the Army,[16] and undermined the basis of Army preparations to provide a combat brigade group and a reserve brigade group. The fact that their manpower could no longer be assured was underscored by a dramatic drop in Territorial strength. The significance of the change to a voluntary system of enlistment was lessened, however, by recognition of the need for flexibility and speed of response, neither of which could be provided by a brigade group based on part-time soldiers. The Army began to focus its attention on producing a battalion group as a ready reaction force capable primarily of dealing with contingencies in the South Pacific. This force, it was noted in 1978, would be 'readily deployable for a wide range of operational purposes – from national tasks at home, through low-key emergencies overseas in our region, to forming a national contribution alongside allied forces in an active, combat situation'.[17] It was initially intended that 1st Battalion, Royal New Zealand Infantry Regiment in Singapore would form the nucleus of this battalion group, which would include a field battery, a light armoured reconnaissance unit and sufficient supporting arms and services 'to confer operational self-sufficiency'.[18] As the concept was developed, however, it became clear that the force would need to be established in New Zealand. Accordingly 2/1 Battalion, RNZIR, at Burnham, received priority in both manpower and equipment. Between 1977 and 1983 the Army's inventory was augmented by 16 American M101A1 105mm howitzers obtained for training purposes, and 26 Scorpion fire support vehicles. Although of less significance, the Territorial Force was not completely excluded. It would provide an expansion capacity as part of a three-battalion brigade of some 3500 men, though at a state of readiness so poor as to indicate that it was more a sop to Territorials than a serious planning objective.

The emphasis on mobility and speed of deployment placed a premium on the acquisition of naval support and air transport capabilities. These presented problems for the other two services, whose attention was now focused much more clearly on meeting maritime defence requirements in the South Pacific region. The growing size of the Russian fleet, and its intrusions into the South Pacific, provided a military rationale for such an approach, which was reinforced by non-military developments in the 1970s. In particular the negotiation of the Law of the Sea Treaty, finally concluded in 1982, emphasised the importance of a reconnaissance and response capability within New Zealand's immediate vicinity. From 1977 New Zealand was responsible for an exclusive economic zone stretching 370 kilometres from land; because of the number of its island dependencies, New Zealand's zone was one of the largest in the world. The need to assist Pacific Island states with the surveillance of their zones added a further dimension to this task. There was, too, an increased focus during the 1970s on New Zealand's programmes in Antarctica, in support of which the RNZN and the RNZAF both had roles.

The RNZN had as its main striking element four frigates, including the new Leander-class *Canterbury*, commissioned in 1971. Sustaining even this force proved difficult, however, and in 1978 a three-frigate level was accepted. Two further Leanders, HMNZ *Wellington* and HMNZS *Southland*, were purchased secondhand from the Royal Navy, and arrived in New Zealand in 1982 and 1984 respectively. Nevertheless the future structure of the RNZN remained in doubt because of the capital costs involved in replacing such vessels. There was a temptation to look for alternatives. With the Royal Australian Navy seeking to replace its older submarines, the possibility of a move towards a submarine-based RNZN emerged in the early 1980s. A joint study with Australia was instituted.[19] Meanwhile the RNZAF concentrated on its ability to provide a maritime strike capability, to carry out reconnaissance in the South Pacific, and to meet air transport requirements. The strike element of the RNZAF was in a relatively satisfactory condition in the early 1970s, since 14 A–4K and TA–4K Skyhawks had been received at the beginning of the decade. In 1972 the first of 16 BAC167 Strikemasters arrived to replace the longserving Vampires in advanced training roles, and the venerable Harvards were replaced by CT/4B Airtrainers from 1976. Later in the decade the familiar Dakotas and Bristol Freighters also disappeared, replaced with secondhand Andovers from the RAF. In the early 1980s the process of modernising the A–4 Skyhawks began.

In 1984 the fleet was augmented by the acquisition of a further 10 from the RAN.

While the armed forces were concentrating on structural and equipment problems, the international situation once more began to assume a worrying complexion. A re-intensification of the Cold War was evident as detente faded in the second half of the 1970s amidst new competition between the two blocs. Disagreements over nuclear issues poisoned the atmosphere. While SALT II, which addressed the problem of MIRVs, was concluded in June 1979, it was offset by the difficulties which had arisen over INF missiles in Europe. Concern over the Soviet SS–20 deployment had led NATO to adopt a dual-track response. It resolved to deploy 464 ground launched cruise missiles and 108 Pershing II missiles (to replace older Pershings) in Western Europe, while at the same time offering to negotiate an agreement on INF missiles. The Soviet invasion of Afghanistan in December 1979, beginning a prolonged, costly and ultimately unsuccessful campaign, prompted a strong reaction in the West. It doomed the SALT II agreement: the US Senate rejected it in 1980. After Ronald Reagan assumed the Presidency in 1981, a further hardening of the American approach was apparent. Reagan took a more aggressive stance against what he termed the 'Evil Empire' and was determined to counter the 'Vietnam syndrome', the inhibition of American exercise of power because of fears of another Vietnam-like imbroglio. He sought to combat the Soviets on two levels: by building up American strength to a point where it could negotiate from a position of strength, and by vigorously contesting Soviet penetration in the Third World by supporting indigenous elements involved in conflict with Soviet-supported forces.

Reagan also hardened NATO's INF stance. When the INF talks finally got under way in November 1981, he offered the Soviets a 'zero option', under which both sides would remove all their missiles. This was rejected by Moscow, which had legitimate concerns about the intermediate-range missiles possessed by the British and French. The talks collapsed in December 1983 when the Soviets finally walked out after it had become apparent that the American missile deployment in Western Europe was going ahead. This also spelled the end of the Strategic Arms Reduction Talks, which Reagan had initiated to replace the SALT negotiations. The deployment of the American missiles proceeded against the backdrop of a determined Soviet effort to influence public opinion in the West against it. A substantial and vociferous protest movement emerged. While this effort failed to prevent the NATO deployments, it fuelled a widespread sense of unease in Europe and elsewhere about nuclear deterrence. Doomsday television documentaries on the likely effects of a nuclear war reinforced widespread fears without pointing to a practical solution to the problem presented by the vast nuclear capacity now possessed by the contending and hostile powers.

In New Zealand, far from the immediate danger, detachment lent weight to such unease. Anti-nuclear sentiment had already been fostered by environmental concern, especially over the testing of nuclear weapons. This had been given focus in the early 1970s by French atmospheric tests at Mururoa Atoll, in French Polynesia. In 1973 the Kirk government had despatched the frigate HMNZS *Otago* (later relieved by *Waikato*) to the area as a protest, and the French shortly thereafter shifted to underground testing. To environmental concern was now added fear of a breakdown of deterrence. Articulate foreign advocates, such as Helen Caldicott in April 1983, toured New Zealand expounding an anti-nuclear message. They highlighted the apparent absurdity (to the general public if not to defence analysts) and danger of the huge nuclear arsenals at the disposal of the two blocs. Among a populace little disposed to understand the arcane imperatives of nuclear deterrence, such efforts engendered a climate of fear in which the 'peace movement' was able to expand its influence.[20]

These developments provided the backdrop against which New Zealand defence strategy was thrown into disarray in 1985 as a consequence of the USS *Buchanan* affair. American nuclear ship visits had become a major issue in the late 1970s, despite the fact that there was never any pressing operational reason for them. The 1978 Defence Review had noted that ship visits and participation in combined exercises were 'an important part of the pattern of defence cooperation which gives substance to the ANZUS alliance' and that 'no needless restrictions' should be placed in the way of calls by nuclear powered vessels.[21] Visits were described as 'essential' by the ANZUS Council in 1984. In these circumstances, there was never much prospect of the David Lange-led Labour administration which took office in 1984 being allowed to let the ship visits issue slip into the background (as had occurred during the term of the previous Labour administration). There were, of course, activists who were determined to push the issue to the foreground. Labour had campaigned on a nuclear free policy, though not at the expense of ANZUS. Indeed New Zealand's continued participation in ANZUS activities after the change of government was reflected in its hosting in September–October 1984 of Exercise Triad 84, a joint combined air–land–sea exercise which was described as its 'contribution to ANZUS combined training'.[22] There was, nevertheless, a sense of unfinished business over the ship visits issue. The Reagan administration's determination to maintain a firm front to the Soviet Union left it little disposed to take a conciliatory approach to New Zealand. Behind this hard-line attitude lay a perception that some European governments were wavering in their support of the NATO missile deployment under 'peace' pressure. While New Zealand counted for little in itself – which also made it dispensable – there were fears in Washington that its actions could infect other, more important countries. The 'New Zealand disease' could not be left to incubate in the remote South Pacific.

Initially the American authorities, perhaps influenced by Lange's profession of support for ANZUS, were prepared to allow him a period of grace in which to 'educate' his party. His seeming willingness to proceed down the path of a ship visit was underscored when the Chief of Defence Staff, Air Marshal Ewan Jamieson, went to Hawaii in November 1984 'to take part in the selection of the ship to be nominated'.[23] The American authorities proposed the USS *Buchanan*, an older, conventionally powered Charles F Adams-class destroyer which was scheduled to take part in Exercise Sea Eagle with both Australian and New Zealand forces off the coast of Australia in early 1985. To this end diplomatic clearance was sought on 18 January for the *Buchanan* to make a 'routine operational visit' to Wellington in the following March.[24] The New Zealand Government baulked. When Washington rejected a request for a vessel of the Oliver Hazard Perry-class (FFG7) to be sent instead, New Zealand formally declined the *Buchanan* on 5 February 1985.

The issue upon which New Zealand focused was the ability of the vessel in question to carry nuclear weapons. The United States Navy maintained a firm stance of neither confirming nor denying the presence of such weapons, an ambiguity which had allowed countries throughout the world where governments were troubled by anti-nuclear movements to receive ship visits. It had a deterrence component as well, insofar as it was designed to leave Moscow guessing as to the exact status of particular vessels. Since the *Buchanan* was not part of the strategic nuclear forces of the US Navy – the SLBM carrying submarines – this consideration was of less relevance in New Zealand, although anti-nuclear protestors persisted in suggesting that her presence in New Zealand ports would increase the danger of a nuclear strike on New Zealand in the event of war. Air Marshal Jamieson, on 24 January, noted that the *Buchanan* carried the ASROC anti-submarine missile system, which was capable of firing a nuclear-armed missile, but that it was a 'reasonable inference' that she had no nuclear warheads aboard, given that she was a 'second-rank ship', that her current operational role did not require such armament, and that there were nuclear warheads for less than 5 per cent of the 20,000 ASROC missiles produced. Of most significance for the members of the Cabinet, however, was his admission that he could give 'no absolute guarantee that the ship does not carry any nuclear warheads' for its ASROC system.[25] Lange was out of circulation on a visit to Tokelau; by the time he returned, on 28 January, 'massive developments', within the Labour Cabinet and caucus, had virtually ruled out the acceptance of the *Buchanan*.[26]

New Zealand's action angered both its ANZUS partners. The Australian government led by Bob Hawke, sensitive to the possible impact of New Zealand anti-nuclear action on his own party, had long sought to restrain Lange. Foreign Minister Bill Hayden had, for example, made clear his belief that New Zealand was not 'behaving wisely' over the ships issue as early as December 1984.[27] The Americans were incensed by the refusal of the *Buchanan*, believing that they had been led down a garden path. New Zealand had given them the impression that a visit would be acceptable up to the moment when the application for diplomatic clearance was lodged. Once the matter became public, Washington felt the need, in the interests of the wider Western confrontation with the Soviet Union which it led, to respond firmly to New Zealand's reneging on its apparent willingness to have a visit. The Sea Eagle exercise was cancelled, and in March Australia announced that the forthcoming ANZUS Council meeting, which it was to have hosted, had been postponed. Most, but not all, American military links with New Zealand were severed: ironically, those few which survived, such as intelligence cooperation under UKUSA,[28] were later described as 'central' to New Zealand's drive for a self-reliant policy and to cooperation with Australia.[29]

Much to the New Zealand Government's relief the Americans refrained from extending the penalties beyond the political and military fields.

These measures by the United States only served to strengthen the domestic political position of Lange's government. It gleefully encouraged the perception of a little country being bullied for exercising its democratic rights, and soon made certain that a compromise would be impossible. Entering the anti-nuclear campaign in earnest, it had no difficulty, given the generally acknowledged undesirability of such weapons and the lack of a sense of direct threat to New Zealand, in fostering a climate of public opinion supportive of its stance. 'Simply by lending the authority of government to the concept of a nuclear-free defence,' Lange recalled later, 'the New Zealand administration stoked up nuclear-free sentiment.'[30] Riding the tide it had unleashed, it went further by introducing legislation which banned not only nuclear-armed but also nuclear-powered ships from entering New Zealand ports (finally enacted on 4 June 1987 as the New Zealand Nuclear Free Zone, Disarmament and Arms Control Act). The United States responded by suspending its obligations to New Zealand under the ANZUS treaty. 'So we part company as friends, but we part company', Secretary of State George Shultz put it bluntly on 27 June 1986.[31] New Zealand would henceforth be a friend rather than an ally.

From the outset of the *Buchanan* crisis Lange had professed to still support ANZUS. Throughout 1985 the Government insisted that New Zealand fully supported a conventional alliance with the United States and professed to be still firmly in the Western camp in the confrontation with the Soviet Union. Though inoperative in relation to New Zealand, the ANZUS Treaty remained in existence – in fact there was no provision for its renunciation. During 1986–87 the government began to disparage the value of the treaty, pointing, for example, to apparent loopholes in its wording which might leave New Zealand unprotected in a crisis (a legalistic approach which entirely overlooked the political significance of the treaty). This process culminated in Lange's observation during an address at Yale University in April 1989 that the security alliance was a 'dead letter' and that New Zealand should therefore consider resigning from the ANZUS Council. In the ensuing furore – his comments were reported in New Zealand on the morning of Anzac Day – even his own Cabinet, rent by divisions on economic issues, turned against him.[32] Within months he would resign.

On the wider Western front, the Labour leaders also challenged the assumptions on which Western security had rested for 40 years. Our 'whole practical policy is a repudiation of nuclear deterrence', Lange asserted in 1988.[33] Nuclear war, he declared, was the biggest threat to New Zealand security, and the nuclear ban was a way of combatting that threat. Although he claimed that New Zealand's policy was not for export, his actions spoke louder than words: in taking part in an Oxford Union debate in March 1985, he had implicitly criticised the defence policy of the British Government whilst on British soil. When 16 retired New Zealand senior officers denounced the Government's policy, asserting that nuclear deterrence had prevented nuclear war, they were savagely dismissed by Lange as 'geriatric generals' and later as 'unreconstructed military neanderthals'.[34] Nevertheless, some ambivalence in the government's ranks was noticeable: Foreign Minister Russell Marshall acknowledged in Geneva in March 1988 that deterrence was still valid for Western Europe, and necessary to keep the peace between the superpowers.[35] For his pains he was firmly rebuked by Lange.[36]

The upshot of these events was that New Zealand abandoned the defence strategy which it had followed since the Second World War. For the first time, except for the brief period from 1945 to 1951, New Zealand was not allied with the world's leading naval power. There is evidence that this outcome was not favoured by the majority of the public. Authoritative polling in 1986 indicated that 71 per cent of the population favoured maintenance of the ANZUS alliance. Awkwardly, however, a similar proportion endorsed the anti-nuclear policy which rendered that alliance impossible to sustain. The significant finding of this exercise was, however, that in 1986 a small majority of New Zealanders (52 per cent against 44 per cent) favoured maintaining ANZUS even at the expense of having nuclear ship visits.[37]

New Zealand defence strategy had hitherto been based upon the assumption of close cooperation with allies. This had been a cost-effective approach for a small country unable to develop any significant defence capability of its own. The maintenance of large stockpiles of parts and ammunition had been obviated by the ability to tap into allied logistic arrangements, first British, but increasingly from the 1960s, American. When Washington in February 1987 announced that the 1982 Memorandum of Understanding on Logistic Supply Arrangements would not be renewed,[38] the response in

Wellington was to disparage the need for such arrangements.

The Government sought to shape 'an identifiable New Zealand defence policy'[39] in a new defence review, a process in which the public was invited to participate. In late 1985, a four-person Defence Committee of Enquiry under the chairmanship of former Secretary of Foreign Affairs Frank Corner considered more than 4000 submissions. A very wide range of opinions were put before the committee, some advocating neutrality and even passive defence strategies. Although the committee's relatively restrained report urged the development of an independent defence capability, Lange was upset by its apparent support for collective security. He believed that Corner had influenced it to endorse the approach upon which ANZUS had rested: 'The committee spoke in the voice of a retired diplomat.'[40]

The Government's efforts to reconcile New Zealand's resources, public opinion in favour of collective security, and the exclusion from ANZUS were reflected in the 1987 Defence Review, which claimed to outline 'the most fundamental change in defence policies since World War II'.[41] This was in line with the Government's contention ever since taking office that New Zealand's previous defence policy had been flawed, subordinating New Zealand's real interests to those of its great power allies. 'We do not intend to shape our forces to act as an appendage to overseas forces ever ready to be deployed to wars in distant lands', Minister of Defence Frank O'Flynn had stated in 1985.[42] By 1987 the Government was insisting that New Zealand would 'not [be] a second class passenger in some global power grouping'.[43]

Despite such rhetoric the Defence Review, which was produced without recourse to the traditional inter-departmental process for such undertakings, was notable not so much for its changes as for its continuities – a reflection of New Zealand's lack of resources and, therefore, options. Neutrality, whether armed or unarmed, was rejected, and New Zealand's continued adherence to the broad Western interest was reaffirmed. The review emphasised self-reliance and a South Pacific focus, acknowledged the increased significance of the maritime environment, and pointed to the importance of closer ties with Australia in the defence field. The South Pacific orientation was not a substantial break from the previous administration's approach, for, as noted above, the South Pacific had become more important in the 1970s as the general instability there became more apparent and the Southeast Asia commitment lost salience. The difference lay in the conception that New Zealand's defence activity would henceforth be confined to this region, in essence an isolationist approach.

The possibility of developments in the region demanding a military role was highlighted in 1987, when two coups took place in Fiji, led by Lieutenant-Colonel Sitiveni Rabuka. When the first occurred, on 14 May, the frigate *Wellington* was heading for Fiji on a scheduled visit; after some hesitation she was allowed to proceed to Suva, where she docked on the 16th. As a precautionary measure *Canterbury* was later deployed from Cairns to the vicinity of Fiji. The crisis was exacerbated on 19 May by the hijacking of an Air New Zealand jumbo jet at Nadi, which led to one of the few civil–military disputes in New Zealand's history. This centred on Lange's insistence that a Special Air Service (SAS) anti-terrorist detachment be readied for immediate despatch to Fiji in a Hercules aircraft to deal with the hijacking. There was great unease among the Defence hierarchy at this proposal, especially in light of Lange's statement the previous day that he would consider transporting Fijian peacekeeping personnel back to Fiji to deal with the coup perpetrators.[44] 'In the circumstances,' Chief of Defence Staff Air Marshal David Crooks recalled later, 'to inject a military presence, no matter what shape or size, or for what purpose, seemed to me to be the height of folly.'[45] Service worries were heightened when Lange expanded the proposed mission, eventually ordering Crooks to 'despatch immediately a RNZAF C130 aircraft with sufficient military personnel aboard to act as required to protect New Zealand's interests in Fiji'.[46] These interests included the protection of the approximately 2000 New Zealanders, expatriates and tourists, then in the group. The proposed mission of the force seemed dangerously vague, in Crooks's opinion; he was not convinced that a sufficiently reliable clearance for the plane to land would be obtained from the Fijian authorities, not least because of the Government's unwillingness to deal directly with the coup plotters.[47] Although the immediate crisis was resolved when the hijacker was subdued – he was hit on the head with a whisky bottle – the reverberations of this affair could still be heard years later, as claim and counterclaim were made in the press. The mutual lack of confidence between the Government and its military advisers in the aftermath of the *Buchanan* affair was manifest. The hydrographic survey vessel HMNZS *Monowai* was sent to Suva in case the evacuation of New Zealand nationals was required; she broke down after leaving Auckland on 22 May, but finally reached Suva on the 28th. However, the situation remained calm. She would repeat this deployment in September 1987, following the second coup.

The Fiji crisis brought into stark relief the inherent instability of many of the fledgling Pacific Island states within New Zealand's region. It had three main effects. In the first place, the need for better co-ordination of New Zealand's response was evident. New procedures were introduced. These were tested successfully in 1988, when unrest developed in Vanuatu: 'it was done a hell of a lot better', Crooks's successor, Lieutenant-General John Mace, later noted.[48] Second, it gave added focus to preparations by the armed forces for rapid action in the South Pacific region. Exercise Golden Fleece, simulating 'the deployment of a brigade group to a Pacific island under threat from insurgents', in early 1989 demonstrated shortcomings in New Zealand's capabilities, particularly the need for 'a logistic support ship, more heavy transport aircraft, and light helicopters'.[49] Third, the Fijian affair had highlighted the need for better coordination of Australian and New Zealand surveillance and other efforts in the region.[50] RNZAF and RAAF Orion flights were subsequently programmed to complement each other, and attempts were made to harmonise aid programmes. In 1989 the ANZ Consultative Committee agreed to improve methods by which the two countries consulted each other in the face of further possible regional instability. This system proved useful when a further crisis erupted in 1990, this time in Bougainville, where secessionists were seeking to cut ties with Papua New Guinea. HMNZS *Endeavour, Wellington*, and *Waikato* deployed to Bougainville in July 1990 to provide a neutral venue for talks between the contending sides. Although the 'Endeavour Accord' was signed 5 August 1990, fighting later resumed.[51]

As with its emphasis on the South Pacific, the Labour Government's promotion of a close defence relationship with Australia was not a new development; rather it continued and intensified a process which had begun in the 1970s (as noted above). However much New Zealand emphasised the differing strategic outlook of the two countries, it could not avoid the logic of geography. No less than its predecessors, it accepted that New Zealand could hardly stand aside if Australia were attacked: 'The security of either New Zealand or Australia would be at severe risk if the other was seriously threatened', it noted in 1987, 'and it is inconceivable that a joint response would not be forthcoming.'[52] Some in New Zealand challenged the move towards closer ties with Australia, arguing that Australia was inherently aggressive in its regional stance.

For its part Australia, while adhering strongly to its alliance with the United States, was keen to promote continued defence capacity in its neighbour, if only to protect its southeastern flank. Should a regional crisis arise, it was recognized in Canberra, any deficiencies in New Zealand defence capabilities would have to be made good by Australian resources.[53] Combatting the perceived tendency towards non-alignment and pacifism in New Zealand became an Australian goal. Australian Minister of Defence Kim Beazley was a regular visitor to New Zealand in the aftermath of the *Buchanan* affair. His message was blunt: Australia's help in filling gaps left by the demise of New Zealand's cooperation with the United States came at a price. New Zealand must have a serious defence policy, with adequate resources devoted to it. The outcome of the Defence Review was pronounced an acceptable basis for cooperation. 'If the capabilities were less than that . . . "the whole thing would be thrown into the melting pot"', Beazley warned in March 1987.[54] The establishment of joint committees to manage the relationship in the new circumstances – an Exercise Planning Group, a Combined Communications Inter-operability Board and an Operational Logistics Working Party – gave new impetus to the process of greater formalisation of cooperation which had begun in the 1970s. All these bodies met twice a year. The concept of a Closer Defence Relationship mirroring CER came to underlie Australian–New Zealand defence cooperation in the late 1980s.

The closer relationship – and New Zealand's increased dependence on Australia (which belied the Government's rhetoric about the need for greater independence) – was particularly evident in the number of New Zealand service officers who attended courses in Australia: whereas in 1976 there had been 58 and in 1984 194, in 1986 the figure jumped to 415. Seventy per cent of New Zealand's overseas training was carried out in Australian facilities.[55] Australian forces also, at some inconvenience, met the shortfall in exercise opportunities. Out of 44 Australian exercises in 1988, New Zealand units participated in 19, all but five of which were bilateral.[56] However, New Zealand forces were not able to take part in the major Australian Exercise Kangaroo – 'the largest postwar military exercise in Australia'[57] – because of American involvement.

Similar problems were encountered regarding intelligence cooperation.[58]

Standardisation of the two defence forces' equipment was seen as valuable. It was pursued by the joint manufacture of the Steyr rifle, New Zealand's participation being described by Minister of Defence Frank O'Flynn as 'intended as a plain signal that NZ wanted cooperation with Australia'.[59] The adoption by both armies of the same light machine-gun and field guns was another step in this direction. Even if a proposal for common pilot training programmes with the RAAF did not go ahead, there was agreement in 1990 that six RNZAF A-4K Skyhawks should be stationed at Nowra in New South Wales from early 1991, to assist the RAN's anti-aircraft training – the first time New Zealand forces were stationed on a permanent basis on Australian soil.

The fourth Labour Government (1984–90) not merely changed the strategic framework within which New Zealand sought security, it also substantially changed the structure of New Zealand's defence policy-making. The new administrative orthodoxy, demanding a policy/provider split and contestable advice, was applied to the higher defence machinery. Since 1970 this had been a diarchical system in which the Secretary of Defence and the Chief of Defence Staff operated effectively in tandem, the former responsible for administrative aspects of defence provision and the latter for the forces under the Defence Council. However, a Defence Management Resource Review carried out by a former National Cabinet minister, Derek Quigley, in 1988 recommended abolishing the Council, and separating the roles of the Secretary of Defence and Chief of Defence Staff. Such an approach was seen as necessary 'because of duplications of effort within Defence Headquarters, top heavy decision making, chronic over-staffing and a confusion of policy and command'.[60] The suggested changes were made. From 1 November 1989 the Ministry of Defence and New Zealand Defence Force operated as administratively separate entities.[61] Command of the latter was vested in a Chief of Defence Force, succeeding to the Defence Council, which was formally abolished on 1 April 1990. The Ministry, which had only 72 staff in June 1990, was responsible for auditing the performance of the Defence Force, for policy and equipment procurement, and for preparing the complete Defence budget. A key task was the preparation of the annual defence assessment, a process which had started somewhat shakily with both the 1989 and 1990 assessments never being completed.

The Government had less impact in its efforts to ensure greater self-reliance of the New Zealand Defence Force. There was no significant change in the force structures of the three services. The Army's attention was re-focused on 1RNZIR, which the Government had determined should be returned to New Zealand from Singapore, where it was irrelevant to a South Pacific-oriented policy. This was achieved in 1989, after suitable accommodation had been built at Linton Camp, near Palmerston North. A small Defence Support Unit was left in Singapore to support activities associated with the FPDA, to which New Zealand continued to adhere, and bilateral training and exchange programmes.[62] The Army's task continued to be the preparation of the battalion group as the Ready Reaction Force (RRF). This entailed maintaining 1600 personnel at seven days' notice for deployment. To provide a capacity for even more rapid action if necessary, it also concentrated on providing 'a lightly equipped component within the Ready Reaction Force, based on one rifle company group comprising 120 personnel, including medical and logistic elements, maintained at 48 hours' notice to move'.[63] Under the Labour policy, the Territorial-based Infantry Brigade Group (17 units) and Force Maintenance Group (19 units) were maintained in a state capable of expansion in two years. But both the regular and Territorial components of the Army declined severely, the former because of financial restraints; the latter because of low morale arising from the Government's seeming anti-Defence approach. The main element in the RNZAF programme was the engineering refurbishment and upgrading, over three years, of the Skyhawks' navigation and weapons systems, at a cost of $140 million. A sixth Orion was also purchased,[64] and a contract for 18 Aermacchi MB339–C strike-trainers was let in May 1990.[65]

There was no significant change to the RNZN's structure. The submarine option, mooted in the 1983 review, had been rejected as early as 1984.[66] The urgent problem was to settle on replacements for the ageing frigates. It was here that the lines of the new policy intersected, and New Zealand came face to face with the implications of its new stance. Australia was keen for New Zealand to take part in a joint effort to produce frigates. Such an approach would at once ensure standardisation and help build-up defence provision resources in the region, a goal noted in the 1983 memorandum of understanding between the two countries. The Australians proposed that New Zealand replace its four existing frigates with four Anzac frigates, a procurement that would fit in with the Government's goal of closer equipment standardisation with Australia. It was also likely to have spin-offs in other areas by opening the way for manufacturers and providers in New Zealand to obtain contracts. New Zealand agreed in March 1987 to enter into planning with the Australians on 'Surface Combatants' on a joint venture basis.[67]

During the next two years the frigate question became the subject of heated public debate. Opponents complained that involvement in the programme would divert money from social objectives (even though it was intended that the Anzac frigates should be financed within existing defence allocations). Others maintained that frigates were unsuitable for the purposes required, and that their equipment with high tech gear was unnecessary (since they were really only to serve as a coastguard). Others again suggested that the Anzac frigates provided a back way into a restored ANZUS arrangement, by giving New Zealand the capability to cooperate with American forces. On the other side, it was pointed out that vessels of this size were needed for the conditions likely to be experienced in New Zealand's region of concern, that compatibility with Australian vessels was desirable, that New Zealand manufacturers could benefit substantially from the programme by participating in the whole Anzac project, and that jobs would be created for New Zealanders.[68]

The Government was confronted with the likely implications for New Zealand's relationship with Australia from any failure to take part in the project. Derek Quigley, who had been engaged to report on defence management, noted that the frigate issue was 'a litmus test of New Zealand's commitment to the trans-Tasman defence relationship'.[69] Given the greater importance of that relationship in the aftermath of the *Buchanan* affair, the Government saw no alternative to participation. As Lange later put it, 'the frigates were the price of Australian goodwill'.[70] Favourable terms were secured, which allowed a substantial New Zealand manufacturing component, and ensured numerous jobs for New Zealanders. One of the first acts of the new ministry led by Lange's successor, Geoffrey Palmer, was to announce, on 7 September 1989, that New Zealand would participate in the Anzac Frigate Project. This was formalised with the signature on 14 December 1989 of a treaty which provided for collaboration in production of eight frigates for the RAN and two, with an option for two more, for the RNZN.[71]

As these arrangements were being concluded, the whole basis of international security was undergoing a radical, and largely unforeseen, change. On 7 November 1989 East and West Berliners celebrated the demise of the Berlin Wall, the barrier which had scarred their city for 28 years and which had become a symbol of the Cold War. This dramatic event was the culmination of four years of substantial change in the Soviet Union, crucial to which was the advent in 1985 of Mikhail Gorbachev. Following a succession of old, tired men who had died in quick succession, he pointed the Soviet Union in a new, less confrontational direction. Determined to open up the system with perestroika (liberalisation) and glasnost (openness) as a means of improving economic performance, he saw the importance of easing tensions with the West. A new range of negotiations on strategic arms, intermediate-range missiles, and space weapons had begun in March 1985. These culminated in the conclusion of the Intermediate-range Nuclear Forces Treaty in 1987, a great diplomatic triumph for the United States and justification of the dual-track policy. Under its terms both the Soviet SS–20s and the NATO missiles were removed. Such measures could not, however, mask the Soviet Union's inability to compete with the United States militarily, given the parlous state of its economy. Reagan's huge build-up of the United States military drove home the point. It was reinforced by the mooted American Strategic Defense Initiative (popularly described as 'Star Wars'), a proposed space-based anti-missile system. Although the viability of such a system remained very much in doubt, it highlighted once again the technological gap which had developed between the United States and the Soviet Union. There was a loss of will in the Kremlin which would culminate in the collapse of Soviet power in Eastern Europe, and ultimately to the demise of the Soviet Union itself at the end of 1991.

These changes opened the way to new approaches to security, especially through the United Nations, long stymied by the Cold War confrontation and the veto. During the late 1980s this body, like a reawakening giant, took on a new vitality, as real and meaningful action started to emerge from its many subordinate bodies. At the highest level the Security Council began to assume the role envisaged by the drafters of the Charter. A new atmosphere of cooperation characterised relations between the all-important five permanent powers. This seemed to offer an opportunity for the Council to adopt a more active role in dealing with international crises.

For the Labour Party, the great champion of the United Nations in the 1940s, this development should have been especially welcome. During the 1980s New Zealand armed forces had responded to the changing situation by becoming increasingly involved in UN peacekeeping operations. New Zealand had been involved in such work since the 1950s in the UN Truce Supervision Organisation (UNTSO) in Palestine and the UN Military Observer Group in India and Pakistan (UNMOGIP) in Kashmir (though the commitment of a handful of officers to the latter was terminated in 1976). New Zealand contributed 10 officers (and later an Andover and 18 aircrew) to the UN Iran–Iraq Military Observer Group (UNIIMOG) monitoring the Iran–Iraq ceasefire of 20 August 1988, a commitment maintained until UNIIMOG disbanded in February 1991. Between 1989 and 1991 a five-man team served with the UN Mine Clearance Training Team, which taught mine awareness and clearance to Afghan refugees in Pakistan. In 1989–90 14 Army field engineers served with an Australian engineer unit in the UN Transitional Assistance Group in Namibia.[72] New Zealand also continued its involvement in the MFO in the Sinai even after Australia withdrew in 1986; personnel were provided for the HQ and a twelve-strong training and advisory team, later augmented by a small team of engineers and drivers, was also sent.[73]

While peacekeeping was relatively uncontroversial, it was a different story when it came to peace enforcement. The fact that the United States, as the sole remaining super-power, was the key element in enforcing the United Nations' will lessened Labour enthusiasm for such action. This became evident after 2 August 1990, when Iraq invaded its neighbour, and fellow UN member, Kuwait, citing ancient rights of hegemony as the justification for its action. At the heart of this crisis was the question of oil, not only a disputed oil field on the Iraq–Kuwait border but also Iraq's aspiration for a dominant position both in the control of Middle Eastern oil and in the Arab world generally. A possible threat to its oil supplies was bound to cause dismay in the West, so big was the threat posed to its economic well-being. But the invasion also presented a fundamental challenge to world order, akin to those which had confronted, and confounded, the League of Nations in the 1930s. The credibility of the world body was at stake.

For the second time in its history, the UN Security Council

determined upon action to enforce the peace. In contrast to the previous occasion, over Korea in 1950, the Soviet Union was present in its seat and voted in favour of successive resolutions which condemned Iraq's action and called for its withdrawal from Kuwait, imposed economic sanctions and a blockade to enforce them, and eventually the use of force to restore Kuwait's sovereignty. As in 1950 the United States was the driving force behind the UN response, and supplied the bulk of the forces that would eventually enforce its decrees, although on this occasion (unlike in Korea) a UN Command was not established. From August to December a massive build-up of forces in Saudi Arabia (Operation Desert Shield) provided immediate security to potentially threatened Saudi Arabia and the means of liberating Kuwait in due course. While the United States and Britain were the largest contributors to this build-up, there were contributions from nearly 30 other members of the United Nations.

In 1950 New Zealand's National government had been among the first to respond to the UN call for assistance in defending South Korea. This had been enthusiastically supported by the Labour Party, then led by former Prime Minister and signatory of the UN Charter Peter Fraser.[74] Forty years later there was a very different response in Wellington to Iraq's invasion of Kuwait. The Labour Cabinet dithered on a New Zealand response in August–October 1990. To be sure, it announced its intention to make a contribution if requested by the United Nations, even though other governments pointed out that no such request could be expected. When it considered options, the state of the New Zealand armed forces left it with little flexibility: their South Pacific orientation, which made a low level of technological capability tolerable, left them ill-fitted for action in a theatre like the Persian Gulf. 'New Zealand's armed forces are not currently trained or equipped to operate in the type of high intensity combat environment of the sort now being presented in the Gulf', the Ministry of Defence asserted in September 1990.[75] As in 1950, New Zealand's frigates provided the most practicable means of making a rapid contribution to the UN-endorsed naval blockade, but their lack of a close-in defence system was a problem that would first have to be surmounted.[76]

Within the Government these practical problems merely encouraged the inclination towards procrastination. Rather than urgently seeking to overcome obstacles to making a combat contribution – such as by immediately ordering the necessary close-in defence system for a frigate – the Cabinet settled for an approach based on a non-combatant contribution. This merely highlighted its unwillingness to share the risks which the successful implementation of the UN Charter peace enforcement provisions demanded. In part this was the reflection of a government in disarray: Mike Moore succeeded Geoffrey Palmer as Prime Minister on 4 September 1990. But the paralysis also had its roots in the anti-American sentiment of a significant faction within the Cabinet. As Moore would later complain, 'the old "left"' questioned the intervention: 'After advancing for a generation the proposition that the United Nations should be more proactive, they wrung their hands.'[77] Some looked to economic sanctions to force an Iraqi withdrawal, an approach which would have left Kuwait suffering under the invader's yoke for years, if not indefinitely (given the spotty record of sanctions in previous situations, such as Rhodesia). The Labour Government's action was confined to the provision of RNZAF aircraft for assistance in feeding and repatriating to their homelands refugee workers from Kuwait.[78] Impatient with this situation, Moore attempted in October to move towards making a more substantial contribution by authorising the Secretary of Foreign Affairs and Trade to sound out prospective partners and host governments on the possibility.[79] Had his party won the general election on 27 October 1990, he would presumably have sought to move in this direction.

The Jim Bolger-led National administration which took office in early November was more prepared to make a meaningful contribution than had been its predecessor. However it, too, was constrained by the practical problems, given that no steps had yet been taken to acquire the necessary equipment. With the UN Security Council on 29 November 1990 authorising members to use 'all necessary means' to ensure Iraq's withdrawal from Kuwait by 15 January 1991, time was clearly running out for a combat contribution. The Cabinet decided, therefore, to make a non-combatant contribution. Two C130s and 46 personnel (later augmented to 60) reached Saudi Arabia on 23 December 1990, and operated with RAF Hercules aircraft out of Riyadh on a variety of air transport tasks. A New Zealand Army medical team arrived in Bahrain on 19 January 1991, three days after the opening of Operation Desert Storm – the coalition's action to oust Iraq from Kuwait by force – and deployed with a US Navy fleet hospital. They were followed a fortnight later by a 20-strong tri-service team which deployed at a RAF hospital. Because of the rapid defeat of the Iraqis, and their expulsion from Kuwait (not before seriously vandalising most of its oil wells), neither of these teams handled any casualties. All the New Zealanders had returned home by the end of April 1991.[80]

Underlying the National approach was a desire to restore New Zealand's traditional approach to defence policy by reasserting its involvement in collective security arrangements with its longtime allies, especially the United States. Even before the election, however, the National Party had ensured that there would be no early resumption of the New Zealand–American defence relationship. It took power having pledged itself not to repeal the existing legislation on nuclear ships visits, the essential first step in Washington's eyes to any move towards restoring the pre-1984 arrangements. The Government had no choice, therefore, but to seek its objective by less direct means. It determined to demonstrate its credentials as a responsible and cooperative state, along the lines of its response to the Iraq–Kuwait crisis. This pointed to a continuation of the previous government's approach to peacekeeping operations, which proliferated in the early 1990s. It also set in motion a new defence review, with a view to developing a more outward looking approach than that encompassed within the South Pacific-oriented policy of its predecessor.

New Zealand, then, entered the last decade of the century in a very different position to that which had existed in 1972. The world had changed in a way that few would have predicted at that time. The international situation, long frozen in bipolar confrontation, had been transformed by the Soviet Union's effective capitulation in the Cold War. The reduction in tension opened the way to reductions in the nuclear arsenals of the United States and Russian Federation, the successor state to the Soviet Union. But it also removed constraints which had hitherto provided a degree of certainty and stability in the international system, introducing new issues for those charged with determining New Zealand's stance in the world. The seemingly stable alliance framework of 1972, buttressed by New Zealand's support for the United States in Vietnam, had by 1990 not merely been swept away; it had been rendered politically impossible of recreation. And yet, New Zealand in 1990, as for all but three of its 150 years, felt no sense of direct threat. Even without the alliance, it enjoyed the benefits of

American naval supremacy in the Pacific. Even if a threat were to develop – and this seemed unlikely in the decades immediately ahead – it lay securely behind the shield presented by the still strong United States–Australian axis. In these circumstances, defence remained in 1990 as in 1972 an area which could not be entirely ignored but did not seem to the public to require urgent attention. In that sense little had changed, or was likely to change short of a major crisis arising which threatened American power.

Notes

1. I am indebted to Frank Corner, Air Marshal David Crooks, Gerald Hensley, Dr Malcolm McKinnon, and Dr Roberto Rabel for commenting on earlier drafts of this chapter.
2. Even Soviet spokesmen would eventually admit that the Soviet Union had taken 'the initiative in some sectors of military rivalry' and had determined to produce the SS–20s 'when the strategic situation did not really necessitate their deployment on a large scale'. Yuri M. Sokolov (Soviet Ambassador in New Zealand), 'Moscow faces the world: restoring common-sense', in *New Zealand International Review* (hereafter *NZIR*), September–October 1989, p.21.
3. R.M. Mullins, 'New Zealand Defence Policy', in *New Zealand Foreign Affairs Review* (hereafter *NZFAR*), July 1972, p.33.
4. Peter Jennings, *The Armed Forces of New Zealand and the ANZUS Split: Costs and Consequences* (Wellington, 1988), p.29.
5. Ewan Jamieson, *Friend or Ally, New Zealand at Odds with its Past* (Sydney, 1990), p.viii.
6. See recollection of Anne C. Martindell (US Ambassador in Wellington 1979–81), *Evening Post* (Wellington), 23 March 1985.
7. Bruce Brown, '"Foreign Policy is Trade": Trade is Foreign Policy. Some Principal New Zealand Trade Policy Problems since the Second World War', in Ann Trotter (ed.), *Fifty Years of New Zealand Foreign Policy Making, Papers from the Twenty-eighth Foreign Policy School, 1993* (Dunedin, 1993), pp.79–80.
8. Frank Corner, 'ANZUS et cetera – June 1991', unpublished typescript, p.11 (copy in the author's possession).
9. See *Defence Review 1978* (Wellington, 1978), p.21: 'In terms of the new policy now to be implemented, or in strategic terms, . . . the continued presence of our forces in Singapore . . . is anachronistic.'
10. See Ian McGibbon, 'The Defence Relationship to 1939', in Keith Sinclair (ed.), *Tasman Relations, New Zealand and Australia, 1788–1988* (Auckland, 1988), ch.9.
11. Denis McLean, 'New Zealand's strategic position and defence policies', in Desmond Ball (ed.), *The ANZAC Connection* (Sydney, 1985), p.5.
12. Alan and Robin Burnett, *The Australian and New Zealand Nexus* (Canberra, 1978), pp.75–6.

13 Jim Rolfe, 'Closer Defence Relations, A Strategic Overview: The New Zealand Perspective', in Robert A. Hall (ed.), *Australia–New Zealand: Closer Defence Relationships* (Canberra, 1993), p.43.
14 Jennings, *ANZUS Split*, p.70.
15 John Crawford, *In the Field for Peace: New Zealand's contribution to international peace-support operations: 1950–1995* (Wellington, 1996), pp.27–9.
16 D.M. Fenton, *A False Sense of Security, The Force Structure of the New Zealand Army 1946–1978* (Wellington, 1998), p.184.
17 *Defence Review 1978*, p.33.
18 *Defence Review 1983* (Wellington, 1983), p.28.
19 *Defence Review 1983*, pp.24–5.
20 See B. J. Sinclair, 'Ideology and the ANZUS Dispute: The Legacy of the New Left and the Consequences for New Zealand's Security Policy' (DPhil thesis, University of Waikato, 1999), ch.3, for a discussion of the diverse strands which gave impetus to the 'peace movement' in this period.
21 *Defence Review 1978*, pp.54–5.
22 Secretary of Foreign Affairs to Minister of Foreign Affairs, 31 August 1984, MFAT59/206/20, Ministry of Foreign Affairs and Trade, Wellington.
23 Jamieson, p.35.
24 Aide-memoire, No.9, 18 January 1985, MFAT 59/8/5.
25 Chief of Defence Staff to Minister of Defence, 24 January 1985, MFAT 59/8/5.
26 Deputy Prime Minister to Prime Minister, nd [Sunday, 27 January 1985, 1.30 p.m.], MFAT 59/8/5.
27 Record of Conversation between Hayden and Norrish, 3 December 1984, MFAT 59/8/5.
28 The United Kingdom–United States Security Agreement of 1947, with which Australia, New Zealand, and Canada were associated.
29 See unsigned brief, nd [April 1989], MFAT156/10/2.
30 David Lange, *Nuclear Free – The New Zealand Way* (Auckland, 1990), p.156.
31 *American Foreign Policy: Current Documents 1986* (Washington, 1987), p.490.
32 *The Australian*, 26 April 1989.
33 Lange to R. Marshall, 17 May 1988, MFAT156/10/2.
34 Lange, *Nuclear Free*, pp.154–5.
35 Marshall told the Conference on Disarmament that for much of the previous 40 years 'and for both East and West, nuclear deterrence has played, and continues to play, an important role in those [collective] security arrangements and the maintenance of peace at the global level'. *NZFAR*, January–March 1988, p.23.
36 Lange to Marshall, 17 May 1988, MFAT156/10/2.
37 *Defence and Security: What New Zealanders Want, Report of the Defence Committee of Enquiry July 1986* (Wellington, 1986), pp.40, 44.
38 Jennings, *ANZUS Split*, p.29.
39 Ministry of Defence, annual report, *Appendix to the Journals of the House of Representatives* (hereafter *AJHR*), 1985, G.4, p.5.
40 Lange, *Nuclear Free*, p.159.
41 *Defence of New Zealand, Review of Defence Policy 1987* (Wellington, 1987), p.38.
42 Ministry of Defence, annual report, *AJHR*, 1985, G.4, p.5.

43 Ministry of Defence, annual report, *AJHR*, 1987, p.4.
44 See Wellington to All Posts, 23 May 1987, MFAT304/4/5. Lange stated that New Zealand would consider 'logistic support' for the return of the two Fijian battalions in the Middle East, the 47 Fijian officers in New Zealand on courses, and the commander of the Royal Fiji Military Forces, who was in Australia at the time of the coup.
45 *Evening Post*, 19 May 1992.
46 Prime Minister to Chief of Defence Staff, 19 May 1987 (copy in the author's possession).
47 The New Zealand High Commissioner in Suva, Rod Gates, did approach the Fiji Governor-General about obtaining clearance, and was requested not to raise the matter with the military authorities. The MFAT records do not indicate whether it was ever clarified that the Fijian army commander in the Nadi area had been advised of New Zealand's intention to land a Hercules there. See messages between Gates and Peter Adams, 19 May 1987, MFAT304/4/5.
48 *Evening Post*, 21 May 1992.
49 Peter Jennings, 'ANZAC defence co-operation: a question of relevance', in *NZIR*, July–August 1990, p.22.
50 See, e.g., Canberra to Wellington, 25 May 1987, MFAT304/4/5.
51 Crawford, *Field for Peace*, pp.37–8.
52 *Defence of New Zealand 1987*, p.14.
53 Jennings, 'ANZAC defence co-operation', p.24.
54 'Record of Hon. Kim Beazley's Call on Rt Hon. David Lange', 6 March 1987, MFAT156/10/2.
55 *Defence of New Zealand 1987*, p.16; James Rolfe, 'Trans-Tasman defence co-operation', in *NZIR*, September–October 1987, p.10.
56 Jennings, 'ANZAC defence co-operation', p.21.
57 Jennings, 'ANZAC defence co-operation', p.22.
58 See Canberra to Wellington, 7 March 1985, MFAT59/8/5.
59 Brief for Australia–New Zealand Consultative Committee Meeting, 9 March 1987, MFAT156/10/2.
60 James Rolfe, 'Trimming the Defence fat', in *NZIR*, July–August 1989, p.15.
61 Ministry of Defence and NZ Defence Force, annual report, *AJHR*, 1990, G.4, pp.5, 21, 35. The split was formalised by the Defence Act 1990 with effect from 1 April 1990.
62 Ministry of Defence and NZ Defence Force, annual report, *AJHR*, 1990, p.9.
63 Ministry of Defence and NZ Defence Force, annual report, *AJHR*, 1990, p.26.
64 Ministry of Defence, annual report, *AJHR*, 1986, G.4, pp.5–6.
65 Ministry of Defence and NZ Defence Force, annual report, *AJHR*, 1990, G.4, p.7.
66 Ministry of Defence, annual report, *AJHR*, 1985, G.4, p.11.
67 Brief for ANZCC, 'Anzac Ship Project', March 1988, MFAT156/10/2.
68 See *NZIR*, March–April 1989, for articles making the case both for and against the frigate project.
69 *New Zealand Defence, Resource Management Review 1988*, by Strategos Consulting Ltd (Wellington, 1988), p.234.

70 Lange, *Nuclear Free*, p.167.
71 Ministry of Defence and NZ Defence Force, annual report, *AJHR*, 1990, G.4, p.6.
72 Crawford, *Field for Peace*, pp.31–6.
73 Crawford, *Field for Peace*, pp.27–9.
74 Ian McGibbon, *New Zealand and the Korean War, Volume I, Politics and Diplomacy* (Auckland, 1992), pp.81–2.
75 'Gulf Crisis: New Zealand's Options', enclosure to Secretary of Defence to Minister of Defence, 1 September 1990, MFAT267/2/16.
76 See Memorandum for Cabinet, 'Gulf Crisis: Defence Options', nd [27 August 1990], MFAT267/2/16. The other possible combat options were six A–4 Skyhawks or an infantry battalion group. The latter would have required the acquisition of large amounts of equipment to protect New Zealand servicemen from chemical and bacteriological warfare weapons.
77 Mike Moore, 'Seeking security through inter-dependence', in *NZIR*, January–February 1998, p.21.
78 Crawford, p.39.
79 Note for File, 2 October 1990, MFAT267/2/16. It is clear that the Cabinet had not been consulted about this initiative.
80 Crawford, *Field for Peace*, p.40.

MALCOLM MCKINNON

Realignment:
New Zealand and its ANZUS Allies

IN THE YEARS 1972–1990 NEW ZEALAND'S RELATIONS WITH its allies underwent a fundamental realignment. In February 1985, the commitment of the fourth Labour Government to keeping nuclear weapons out of New Zealand ports led to a breach with the United States and difficulties in relations with Australia and, to a lesser extent, other members of the Western alliance.

On the surface the story of this realignment is a story of ships. The flotillas of small ships that sailed to Mururoa; the US naval vessels that came into New Zealand harbours between 1976 and 1984 and the yachts and kayaks that 'escorted' them. The hapless USS *Buchanan*, destined never to visit New Zealand in 1985 as planned and the even unluckier *Rainbow Warrior*, bombed and sunk in Waitemata Harbour by French secret agents, at the cost of one life, that same year. And the Australian-built frigates the Labour Government committed itself to buying in 1989. Yet beneath the surface, just as with the submarines *Haddo, Pintado*, and their brethren, are found other dimensions to the realignment.

Historiography and interpretation

What explanations have been provided to date of this change? The events of 1985, and the years preceding it, are not long ago. But they lie decisively in the past, if for no other reason than that the passage of time, with its seemingly impersonal sifting of the enduring from the ephemeral, creates a different image than that apparent at the time. In the case of the subject under review here, the years since the early 1990s have been marked by a calm, now itself nearly of a decade's duration, that is in marked contrast to the passion and the politicking that characterised the 1960s, 1970s and 1980s. This calm might seem an ideal environment for historians to go to work in, but in fact there has been little historiography of the period, if by that we mean accounts and analyses written with the object of explaining past events not present ones. Those participants who have committed their views to paper, for instance David Lange and Kevin Clements, did so close to the events described.[1] Hugh Templeton's memoir *All Honourable Men*,[2] has more of an historical perspective, but from the point of view of this chapter is limited by stopping in 1984. A biography of Muldoon is awaited; there are no historical surveys of the fourth Labour Government (or the third).

In respect of accounts written contemporary with the events, a threefold classification of the contributions can readily be made. There are those from individuals who were actively involved in the peace movement and therefore write sympathetically about the cause.[3] Then there are those from individuals who were not involved in the peace movement (some indeed held official positions) and write critically about it.[4] In the third category are those writers, often journalists or academics, who are less partisan.[5]

Recent writing on the crisis reflects the stances of the first two of these categories in being preoccupied with the 'loyalty' of either officials or activists.[6] Thus in 'Nuclear Free New Zealand' Robert White writes 'the small programme of US Navy visits to New Zealand was planned up to May/June 1985, leading up to the ANZUS Council meeting . . . This whole programme was prepared more than six months in advance, involving collaboration and possibly collusion between New Zealand, American and almost certainly Australian officials.'[7] For his part, Brian Sinclair sees the ANZUS crisis as the result of a kind of hijacking of the peace movement by a radical left movement: 'the temporary presence of anti-nuclear activists did provide radicals with a convenient cover in pursuit of their own agenda, which included opposing "American imperialism".' [8] So, in respect of the USS *Buchanan* episode, 'the peace movement's reasons for wanting a strict nuclear ship ban were as much a product of the anti-American ideology of radicals (and, to a lesser extent, of liberals) as they were a product of anti-nuclearism'.[9] Other writers describe the movement as 'isolationist'.[10]

There are problems with both these approaches. The fact that terms such as 'collaborationist', 'anti-American' and 'isolationist' can only be used negatively suggests some of their limitations for analysis.

In respect of the White argument, it is indisputable that the sentiments of some of the officials involved in the crisis were at odds with the anti-nuclear view of the peace movement and many in government. But it is also indisputable that anti-nuclearism was not the only policy which public servants were required to implement. Most particularly, maintaining good relations with allies was also a policy.

As for Sinclair's view of a peace movement with radical and anti-nuclear wings, this imputes more coherence and cohesion to the movement than it possessed. The diffuse nature of its processes was part of its essence. Peace Movement New Zealand had no agreed policy, no spokespeople, and an open mailing list. There was no nexus between ideas and power, so a free flow of ideas always obtained. At the time of the *Buchanan* episode, there were over 400 peace groups in the country; the biggest single group was Greenpeace, the biggest coalition of groups was CND, with 7 branches. For the rest, there was a great variety.[11] A bifurcation of the movement into 'liberal' and 'radical' has its place, but such a formulation misses this strong process orientation which characterised the movement. It was this that made it so different from earlier eras and forms of protest.

This chapter seeks to analyse rather than to praise or blame. Rather than attempting to evaluate the loyalty or otherwise of particular groups of New Zealanders it seems more useful to try to explain why the 'loyalties' or just plain 'outlooks' of New Zealanders through this episode became so divergent.

The argument advanced in this chapter does not depart significantly from that presented in the present writer's 1993 study.[12] There, the realignment in New Zealand foreign policy was seen to arise out of the conjunction of a protest movement with changes in New Zealand's international circumstances. The protest movement thrived as part of a widespread efflorescence of such movements in many countries from the 1960s onwards – the 'new social movements' as they have been called. The most significant changes in circumstances were that many New Zealanders ceased to feel that the country was in danger of external attack.

The combination of these developments suggests an evolutionary process and that is indeed a part of the argument. But the variant nationalisms described here as 'Anzac', 'Pintado' and 'Guamist' existed alongside each other and this coexistence is also explained.

The terms embody three distinct conceptions of New Zealand's place in the world. Anzac nationalism needs little explanation. It is rooted in the experience of the two world wars and in New Zealand's membership of first Empire and Commonwealth, later the United Nations and the Cold War Western alliance. As a hot or cold war ally, in the Commonwealth or the United Nations, New Zealand was a part of a larger whole – a vigorous part, proud indeed of its particular contributions, but still definitely a part. The differences of opinion within the wartime alliances and within the Commonwealth, were as nothing to the differences with the rest of the world. The United Nations (and before it the League of Nations), if not riven by great power rivalry, would have been, in New Zealand eyes, a Commonwealth writ large. Anzac nationalism was the dominant way in which New Zealanders looked out at the world until the 1960s and retained a lot of vitality after that date. 'Pintado' and 'Guam' are both phenomena of the later 1960s onwards. The former takes its name from the US nuclear powered submarine which visited Auckland in January 1978. 'Pintado nationalism' pits itself against rather than with erstwhile allies, the 'pitting' in this story being against nuclear weapons and associated aspects of military and naval power. This did not make it a purely nationalist movement, indeed internationalism is a crucial part of the Pintado outlook, but in this story it is this new attitude to close allies that is most distinctive. 'Guam' is named for the Guam Doctrine announced by US President Richard Nixon in the middle of 1969, when he indicated the intention of the United States to see the countries of Asia and the western Pacific do more for their own security. It stands here for somewhat more than that, for what Secretary of Foreign Affairs George Laking called the 'chill wind of loneliness' that, understood more broadly, looked back to the attack on Pearl Harbor and the fall of Singapore in 1941–42, and also to Britain's economic retreat from empire.[13] For 'Guamists', in other words, New Zealand was 'on its own'.[14] In this account the transition from ANZAC to 'Pintado' is key, but 'Guamist' operates in a kind of counterpoint to 'Pintado', as will be demonstrated.

Speaking institutionally, the defence forces remained predominantly 'ANZAC nationalist' in outlook, 'Guamists' were particularly to be found in the Ministry of Foreign Affairs, and 'Pintadoans' in the protest movements. Politicians and journalists could be found in all three camps. No one in the 1970s or 1980s used these terms: it remains for the reader to judge whether the introduction of them here is helpful, and the concepts underpinning them are convincing.

1972–1979: the environmental campaign against nuclear power and nuclear weapons testing

Environmental concerns revolving around nuclear power and atmospheric nuclear weapons testing had been preoccupations in the South Pacific since the late 1950s and the testing by the United States and Britain. The New Zealand campaign for nuclear disarmament (CND) began a campaign for a Southern Hemisphere Nuclear Free Zone (extending the 1959 Antarctic Treaty's ambit to the equator) with the slogan, 'No Bombs South of the Line'. With the partial test ban treaty of 1963 the United States, Great Britain and the Soviet Union ended their atmospheric nuclear weapons testing. But in 1962, with Algerian independence, France had decided to relocate its nuclear weapons testing programme from that country to its Polynesian territories. This produced an outcry in New Zealand and the petition that CND organised got 80,000 signatures.[15] France began testing at Mururoa in 1966 and the New Zealand Government at that time did make formal protests. However, occurring as they did at the height of the United States–Vietnam war, in which New Zealand was involved as an ally of the United States, not as much attention was paid to the tests as might have expected from the outcry in 1963. Renewed action against French nuclear weapons testing gathered momentum again in 1972 – the first year for some time in which controversy about Vietnam had been off the front pages and TV news.[16] In that and the two subsequent years, protest yachts sailed to Mururoa to demonstrate against the tests. In 1973 the Labour Government deployed a frigate in support of the protest fleet. France stopped *atmospheric* nuclear testing in 1974 – an action that was widely seen as a victory for New Zealand, Australian and South Pacific protest, and for their taking of France to the International Court of Justice. Subsequent phases of underground testing came to elicit just as much protest however.

The campaign against French testing had established certain characteristics that remained noticeable in the way the peace movement evolved. A wide spectrum of public opinion was critical of French testing: in Auckland, for instance, the Mayor handed out medals to some of those embarking for the test zone during the 1973 protest. The

Marlborough Express of 19 July noted that 'ordinary New Zealanders are showing immense interest in the saga of Mururoa. Support for the decision of the Government to send a frigate into the area has been widespread.'[17] Further, the issue set New Zealand not against an historic or ideological adversary but against a long-term ally, and it did so over a cause that was principled but also 'local'. In this pattern lay the beginnings of 'Pintado' nationalism. What would happen if the actions of much closer allies, for instance Australia, Britain or the United States, aroused similar concerns?

The other dimension of environmental activism was the campaign to keep nuclear powered vessels out of ports. In 1971 the National Government had told the United States it would not accept visits by nuclear-powered vessels until the United States agreed to accept liability in the event of accident and/or widespread contamination. Under new Congressional legislation passed in 1974 the US Government accepted liability in the event of accident and/or widespread contamination. But the Labour Government deferred taking any decision to invite such vessels into New Zealand waters.[18]

This caution was related to differences between New Zealand and the United States on a broader issue. Both the campaign against French testing and that against visits by nuclear powered ships were part of a larger cause – that of making the South Pacific (a pragmatic refinement of 'south of the line') entirely 'nuclear free'. Following the July 1975 South Pacific Forum, the New Zealand and Fiji Governments lobbied for the inscription of an item on the United Nations agenda, 'establishment of a nuclear weapons free zone [SPNWFZ] in the South Pacific'.[19]

The debate about 'nuclear ships' and the campaign for a SPNWFZ also overlapped with a wider debate about New Zealand's alliance relations that had been triggered by the country's involvement in the Vietnam War. Many in the Labour party, keen to 'kill off' SEATO, the alliance under which New Zealand had been formally drawn into Vietnam, did not see why ANZUS needed to survive either. The Labour leadership was more cautious. ANZUS – the alliance between New Zealand, Australia and the United States, dating from 1951 – was widely seen in New Zealand as crucial to the country's security from attack. It was also integral to the world view of ANZAC nationalism – the idea that New Zealand's international relations were a matter of cooperation with like-minded countries in a common cause. Accordingly Norman

Kirk himself carefully distinguished his call for new policies towards Asia and the world at large from any idea of dismantling ANZUS.[20] His successor as Prime Minister, Bill Rowling, was equally careful: 'the defensive alliance formed with Australia and the United States through the ANZUS Treaty will be maintained' said the party's 1975 election manifesto.[21] But the very need for political leaders to make such statements was evidence that a debate had been joined.

Labour lost power at the election in November 1975 and the new National Government, under Prime Minister Robert Muldoon, brought a quite different approach to these issues. The resolution on a SPNWFZ was voted on at the General Assembly after the change of government, but at the 1976 South Pacific Forum (held in Rotorua) the communiqué stated that any zone established must be 'compatible with existing security arrangements'.[22]

Further, with Labour debating the merits of whether or not to admit nuclear powered naval vessels and whether to stay in ANZUS, Muldoon had sensed the possibility of exploiting the politics of the issue. New Zealanders, he (correctly) gauged, would be reluctant to see ANZUS jeopardised. In 1976 not only over 76 per cent of National voters, but nearly 66 per cent of Labour voters wanted ANZUS to continue.[23] Anzac nationalism, in other words, was alive and well. So Muldoon was on firm electoral ground when he stated shortly after taking office: 'it would be fair to say that we have gone through in the last six months perhaps a period of slight – and I emphasise slight – uneasiness as far as the United States was concerned. . . . I think we are past that now because publicly and officially we've made it clear to the Americans that we want ANZUS to continue in the fullest possible respect.'[24]

The most public and official way this was expressed was – within six weeks of the election – through Muldooon's announcing an end to any ban on nuclear warships visiting New Zealand ports. The USS *Truxtun* visited Wellington in August 1976 and the USS *Long Beach* Auckland in October. And while the polls could not tell whether New Zealanders wanted visits by such vessels, they certainly tell us that most accepted them: in 1976, 53.35 per cent of those polled agreed that New Zealand should give permission for American nuclear-powered ships to visit its ports, whilst 37.7 per cent were opposed.[25] The anti-nuclear movement was thus an established but a minority movement. Labour took issue with the view that a readiness to accept the entry of nuclear powered ships was implicit in support for the ANZUS treaty. It was unclear therefore just what stance Labour would take in government if the United States rejected such an interpretation, but it would have been aware that even on the anti-nuclear issue (let alone ANZUS), majority public opinion was not with it.

Having said that, this did not mean that ANZUS was immune, or likely to stay immune, to political developments in the 1970s. Indeed we can posit a kind of 'hollowing out' process, that, while it left the outer shell of the relationship intact, was weakening its core. This was a process mostly occurring in New Zealand but it is pertinent to recall that United States attitudes and interests were changing too. The new Carter administration in Washington took a more phlegmatic view of America's Cold War alliances than had any administration since 1948. Economic issues loomed large both in the United States and in New Zealand: 'it is . . . probable that security matters will simply cease to loom as large in [either] country's consciousness as economic issues assume a dominant role in relationships between them'.[26]

For foreign policy practitioners, in particular, this phase of American strategy was in essence a reinforcement of a trend that had been observable since 1969 and the formulation of the Guam Doctrine. It might not be life without ANZUS but it was life without some of the comfortable assumptions of the recent past. Such practitioners, like it or not, were being drawn out of the comfortable world of Anzac nationalism to something considerably more bracing. It was not so much that cooperation with familiar friends had become impracticable, more that it had become less relevant.[27]

'Hollowing out' could also be discerned in the disagreement over whether or not New Zealand was in any way endangered by a foreign power. Muldoon argued yes: in 1976 particularly, his speeches were replete with references to Soviet naval expansionism in the Pacific and Indian Ocean and the possibility of Soviet missiles reaching New Zealand. Yet it seemed that not even many in his own party, nor even the Americans, took this too seriously.[28]

Did Muldoon therefore misjudge the public mood about ship visits much as Labour activists were tempted to about ANZUS? There was massive public support for the SPNWFZ, 84 per cent support amongst Labour voters in 1978, but even 57 per cent support amongst National voters.[29] The 'Campaign Half Million' presented a petition to Parliament seeking to stop for all time any nuclear presence in New Zealand.³⁰ Opposition to port visits may not have been so pervasive – 38.75 per cent in 1978³¹ – but even so it reached into 'middle New Zealand' with support from groups neither directly involved in the flotillas, nor usually identified as protest organisations, such as the Auckland Chamber of Commerce and the Business and Professional Women's Clubs.³²

And the visits did offer perfect opportunities for the protest movement to promote its cause through a kind of political theatre:

> The January 1979 visit of the *Haddo* provided the spectacle activists sought. Police efforts to break up the protest fleet resulted in collisions; the submarine was hit with paint-bombs thrown from kayaks; some boats were capsized by the *Haddo*'s bow wave; and one man managed to board the submarine and posture defiantly. This last act proved a media bonus for the Peace Squadron as it again emphasised the romantic image of human against the machine, and the patriotic image of Kiwi against invader.³³

Correspondence about the actions of protestors in respect of the *Pintado* makes that submarine's name the apt one to describe this outlook. The father of one Chris Baker, who had been criticised for paddling his surfboard in front of the *Pintado* wrote that:

> his mother and I are worried about his action . . , taking those risks. In the same way my grandparents worried about my father joining up in World War I, and my parents worried about me in the RNZAF in World War II . . . . Kiwis have a long history of the defiance of two-fingered bullies, both military and political. For me it was a world free of Nazis, for Chris it is a nuclear weapon free Southern Hemisphere.³⁴

In 1978 this was far from a widespread view, but it had put down roots. As one peace activist later commented, a 'wise American military strategist looking back would be bound to wish that these nuclear-powered warships had never been sent to New Zealand.'³⁵ After the *Haddo* visit, no American nuclear ships visited the Waitemata until the middle of 1983 and this may have been a backhanded compliment to the peace squadron's activities.

1979–1984: The Campaign Against Nuclear Weapons

The anti-nuclear campaign of the 1970s was strongly grounded in environmental concerns and even the anxieties of the campaigners about nuclear weapons were partly environmental.[36] The campaign in the 1980s had a more anti-militarist character, it resembled more an actual peace movement. In this respect it drew on the burgeoning anti-nuclear movements in Europe and the United States, to which we will shortly return. But in the period 1979–80 the escalation of Cold War tensions in an arc stretching from the South China Sea to the Middle East triggered not so much a peace movement as a Vietnam War style critique of American foreign policy. In these years American foreign policy dramatically 'hardened', in contrast to the first two years of the Carter administration. The Vietnamese attack on and occupation of Cambodia, the Iranian revolution and subsequent oil shock and hostage crisis for the United States, and the Soviet intervention in Afghanistan at the beginning of 1980 all contributed to this hardening and provoked a renewed American interest in the role of ANZUS in its global strategy:

> more and more we see the Pacific Ocean and the Indian Ocean as closely connected strategic zones; in which, as far as the Pacific is concerned, we are linked in the North with Japan, in the centre with the Philippines ... ASEAN ... Thailand ... and then in the South with Australia and New Zealand.[37]

'Washington officials', wrote another commentator, 'believe the ANZUS alliance can be refocussed towards the Indian Ocean despite the language of the treaty which locates its members' obligations in "the Pacific area" '.[38]

This pressure was not calculated to endear ANZUS to the Labour Party and there was a renewed conference call in 1980 (the first since 1977) for New Zealand's withdrawal, and criticism of the Muldoon government for acquiescing in the US interest in expanding ANZUS into the Indian Ocean.[39]

In fact Muldoon was fairly adept at 'ducking out from under'. Thus, although New Zealand supported the de facto expansion of ANZUS into the Indian Ocean, and planned equipment spending was brought forward, other initiatives were more limited. Actions such as cutting the Soviet fishing quota, suspending scientific and other exchanges did not affect New Zealand exports to the Soviet Union. Moreover the quota cutback, according to fishing industry sources, had been planned before the Afghanistan crisis. And when Muldoon talked of helping the United States in the Gulf, he meant primarily providing naval and air staging facilities – and even then he recognised that it was more likely that Australian facilities would be used. Foreign Minister Brian Talboys got the 1980 ANZUS communiqué toned down to an 'as resources permit' in respect of participation in the Indian Ocean. The Government also discouraged, rather than embargoed, New Zealand participation in the 1980 Moscow Olympic Games.[40]

United States pressure over Indian Ocean issues did not intensify in the early 1980s, perhaps because it quickly became evident that the Afghanistan crisis was going to be a 'Vietnam' not for the United States but for the Soviet Union. In contrast, anxiety about the global nuclear weapons contest was escalating in the Western alliance, including New Zealand, triggered in particular by events within NATO: 'the movements of the 1980s are closely related to a single political decision: the dual-track decision of NATO in December 1979 to deploy medium-range missiles in Europe in 1983 if negotiations with the Soviet Union to limit this type of weapons system were not successful.'[41] In Britain, a country where developments had a particular influence on New Zealand, END, a European nuclear disarmament movement was launched in April 1980, with much encouragement from prominent historian E. P. Thompson. In the United States, the nuclear freeze campaign was a comparable cause. The intensity of discussion about the anti-nuclear issue was evidenced by the substantial sales of Jonathan Schell's *The Fate of the Earth*; the broadcast by the ABC network of 'The Day After' – an exploration of what the world might be like after a nuclear exchange; and the publication by Catholic bishops in May 1983 of a pastoral letter, which evidenced an unprecedented dissent from United States foreign policy.[42] Aware of the early developments, an umbrella group, Peace Movement New Zealand (later Aotearoa) had formed in 1981.[43]

There was other emulation too. From 1980 many Labour party-controlled councils in Britain had declared themselves nuclear-free – some 155 by October 1983.[44] A New Zealand Nuclear Free Zone committee was formed in 1981.[45] Peace campaigner Larry Ross was particularly active in promoting the cause. Between March 1981 and March 1982 three other municipalities joined the Auckland suburb of Devonport (the first) in declaring themselves nuclear-free; by October/November 1983 there were some 33 more.[46]

Again, in Britain, after a series of demonstrations, a permanent protest camp was established outside the missile base at Greenham

Common, England. A small number of women stayed at the camp permanently but on certain occasions very large numbers were present; for instance in December 1982 30,000 attended and 'embraced the camp'.[47] Equally, in New Zealand there was a 'burst of support', wrote one journalist

> this year [1983] for the anti-nuclear and disarmament movement. Some say this is attributable to [Australian-American activist] Helen Caldicott's visit, others say it is merely our usual time-lag in cottoning on to what is happening in the rest of the world.[48]

For New Zealand nonetheless, one focus of the protest remained distinctive – the issue of port visits by nuclear powered or nuclear armed warships. The *Truxtun* had visited Wellington in 1980 and again in 1982, and both the USS *Texas* and the Royal Navy's *Invincible* Wellington and Auckland in 1983. Auckland was also visited by the submarines *Phoenix* and *Queenfish* in November 1983 and March 1984 respectively. There were protests on all these occasions.[49] Polling had showed 31.5 per cent opposition to ships with nuclear weapons visiting New Zealand ports in 1978: this figure had risen to 72.4 per cent opposition in 1984[50] (in contrast, concern about nuclear power seems to have declined – a poll in October 1984 recorded 58 per cent opposition to nuclear armed craft but only 29 per cent to nuclear powered but not armed craft[51]).

Assessment

The burgeoning of the peace movement in the early 1980s had taken it into the mainstream of New Zealand politics, with dissent seemingly becoming orthodoxy. By 1984 three of the four main political parties had virtually interchangeable anti-nuclear stances. Of those parties, neither Social Credit, a populist party, nor the New Zealand Party, a National splinter group led by maverick Wellington real estate tycoon Robert Jones, was left wing. Further, Muldoon called an early election in 1984 because National (government) MP Marilyn Waring decided to vote for an anti-nuclear bill introduced by Labour. This 'crossover' dimension to the anti-nuclear movement was very significant and will be commented on further below.

What then about the other underlying factors discussed in respect of the 1970s?

Firstly, it might have been thought that the collapse of detente at the end of the 1970s would complicate the ability of the peace movement to avoid being targeted as 'pro-Soviet'. Certainly the Soviet intervention in Afghanistan and the crackdown on Solidarity in Poland had hardly been good for the Soviet image in the West. Yet in New Zealand, redbaiting of the peace movement, that is, the tagging of protest movements as communist or left wing in an effort to discredit them with the wider public, was tried but proved seemingly ineffectual.[52] Given the rapid expansion of numbers of individuals supporting the movement it is difficult to imagine it growing faster under any circumstances. It may indeed be that the redbaiting encouraged some otherwise apathetic people, although this can only be a supposition. Equally it may have been that ordinary citizens listened to US President Reagan's rhetoric and were made as apprehensive by that as they were by pondering the motives and actions of the geriatric leaders of the Soviet Union.

Secondly, and likely to be more significant in the event of a change of government, was the waning of any belief, despite the collapse of detente, that New Zealand itself was threatened by the Soviet Union, or, indeed by anyone or thing save the nuclear weapons of its allies. The communiqué of the 1982 ANZUS Council, in which the National Government participated, referred to Soviet ambitions, whilst in 1984 Jim McLay, the National Party's deputy leader, talked of the Soviet reach into Pacific waters.[53] But were others convinced? In 1980 one retired US diplomat noted that 'there are certain tendencies in New Zealand . . . to think of this country as singularly blessed as indeed it is, by its physical circumstances, its location and the character of its people. But because of this, to think also that New Zealand could escape the troubles of the world were it not with its connection with the United States, which . . . is some times seen, even in New Zealand, as adding to its dangers.'[54] And this indeed was at least the Labour view. As Lange was to say later, 'I didn't consider we were in danger. Cam Ranh Bay [a Vietnam naval base available to the Soviet Union] was closer to Paris than it was to Wellington.'[55] Labour Party president Margaret Wilson saw the major threat to world peace not as one particular country, but 'the existence of nuclear weapons themselves.'[56] And such views did also spread beyond Labour. Robert Jones, the leader of the New Zealand Party, asked why the Russians would invade New Zealand given that they could buy its butter at below world market prices.[57] In the 1985 survey of public opinion, only 31% of New Zealanders identified the Soviet Union as a potential military threat over the next five years, 1% fewer than thought there were no such threats.[58]

It cannot be proved, but it seems likely, that the 'crossover' dimension to the anti-nuclear movement – its spread across the political spectrum from its point of origin on the left – was influenced by this low level of threat perception. That in turn meant that the 'flavour' of New Zealand's alignment with the United States differed from those of other allies, for instance, Norway, the Netherlands and Denmark. Thus, Norway had developed a strong anti-nuclear movement but there was also acceptance, rooted in Norway's experience of German invasion in World War II and the fact that it shared a land border with the Soviet Union, that it had to be able to allow its allies' navies access to its waters. Denmark had somewhat similar experiences; thus the Danish island of Bornholm had been occupied by the Soviet Union briefly after the war. The governments of these nations did not challenge the refusal of the United States to neither confirm nor deny whether any particular naval vessel or aircraft was carrying nuclear weapons. They trusted to the United States to observe the restrictions they placed on the peacetime deployment of such weapons.[59]

Did it distinguish New Zealand from Australia? Debate about ANZUS had been as vigorous, if not more vigorous, in Australia than in New Zealand since the election of the Labor government in that country in March 1983: it was Australia which had driven the review of ANZUS at the ANZUS Council meeting in July 1983. But by the time of the election of the New Zealand Labour Government a year later, the Hawke Labor Government had professed itself satisfied with the review which had been carried out. Did this outcome reflect Hawke's skill in outmanoeuvering ANZUS critics both in and out of the Australian Labor Party? Or did national security, of the traditional kind, remain more of a preoccupation in Australia than in New Zealand? 1984 polls on whether or not the country was threatened recorded a 33.4 per cent 'yes' (likely threat) in New Zealand but a 43 per cent 'yes' in Australia.[60] The fact that, while New Zealand opinion regarded Australia as the most important country to New Zealand, Australians accorded that status to the United States, may have contributed to reducing the salience of ANZUS – seen primarily as an alliance with the United States – in New Zealand.[61]

Thus ANZUS was, as it were, further hollowed out, and through the early 1980s there was vigorous debate amongst commentators about its future.[62] And that very debate itself chipped away at unquestioning acceptance of the alliance as a 'fact of life'. Yet the sentiment was still there, the longstanding familiarity with the idea that ANZUS represented far more (or less) than a guarantee of security and/or an obligation to collaborate and that vigorous argument about nuclear weapons operated for most New Zealanders within that framework not outside it – in a word, Anzac nationalism. It would therefore appear to be political suicide for a government to be seen to be undermining ANZUS, despite – or perhaps because – of the feelings of the New Zealand public on the port visits issue.[63]

Accordingly, just as in the 1970s, the Labour leadership was concerned to reconcile anti-nuclear sentiment with ANZUS, not to junk the latter along with former. In the 1981 election campaign, Labour welcomed conventional but not nuclear powered vessels: its support for an effective SPNWFZ would have precluded it.[64] The 1983 conference took place after Australian Labor had taken office. At that conference a resolution on withdrawal from ANZUS was modified (with great reluctance on the part of the conference floor) to become a call for:

i   an unconditional anti-nuclear stance;
ii the active promotion of the SPNWFZ;
iii in respect of ANZUS, the acceptance of an absolutely equal partnership on all issues handled within the terms of the agreement, and unanimous agreement on all decisions taken under those terms;
iv an absolute guarantee of the complete integrity of New Zealand's sovereignty.[65]

Was this compromise between what activists and what the electorate wanted a stable one? Time would tell. Certainly Labour's leadership was far from sure. Commentators noted during the 1984 election campaign that Lange got 'jittery' when ANZUS was mentioned, the debate within Labour being far from over.[66]

The crisis: 1984–1985

The crisis can be said to have commenced with the election of a Labour government on July 14, 1984, now committed to a policy which the

United States had already made clear would make it impossible for it to maintain an alliance relationship with New Zealand. At the ANZUS Council meeting, held in Wellington in the immediate aftermath of the (snap) election, an odd situation supervened. The outgoing Foreign Minister, Warren Cooper, met his Australian and American counterparts, despite the fact that he was unable to offer commitments in respect of the incoming government's policy. The incoming (but not yet in office) Prime Minister, David Lange, met US Secretary of State Shultz. To Lange, writing some years later, 'if Shultz had it in mind at that meeting that New Zealand would eventually change its anti-nuclear policy, the thought hung in the air unspoken.'[67]

Through the next six months the ministers in the new Labour Government most involved in the issue, the Prime Minister and Minister of Foreign Affairs, David Lange, and the Minister of Defence and Deputy Minister of Foreign Affairs, Frank O'Flynn, endeavoured to reconcile what was now policy – no nuclear weapons or nuclear powered vessels in New Zealand ports – within the framework of existing relations with the United States (and in particular with the United States refusal to neither confirm nor deny the presence of nuclear weapons on particular aircraft or ships). ANZUS in their view, in other words, could be – was – a non-nuclear alliance. The energies of the Ministries of Foreign Affairs and Defence were directed to this end.[68] So indeed were those of significant elements in the United States administration.[69] The political instinct of the party's leadership – as distinct from the activist members – undoubtedly told them that Labour would be vulnerable to National if it pursued the more radical course of withdrawing from ANZUS.[70] But it was one thing to assert that ANZUS was non-nuclear, another thing to demonstrate it when confronted with an action – a nuclear powered and possibly armed ship entering New Zealand waters – which challenged that view.

The defining moment was always likely to be a ship visit, but issues to do with aircraft had also to be addressed. The government agreed, on the recommendation of the Secretary of Foreign Affairs, Merwyn Norrish, to give clearance for visits by aircraft for the ANZUS military exercise Triad 84, which took place for three weeks from 23 September. Doubtless anticipating questions, the Secretary of Foreign Affairs noted that

Mr Doug Kidd, MP, has now stated that the F16s taking part are nuclear capable and has attempted to suggest that the Government is being inconsistent in its policies toward ships as contrasted with aircraft. . . . The fact is that the situation of aircraft is different from that of their ships: since aircraft are seldom more than a few hours' flying time from their bases there is no requirement – unlike ships – for them to carry their nuclear armament with them on routine exercises. . . . In any event the concept of 'nuclear capability' is rather meaningless – a Wadestown bus . . . is theoretically nuclear capable.[71]

Lange wrote boldly across the bottom of the memorandum, 'I concur'. And the Triad exercise went ahead as planned. When it came to a ship, a similar stance would be taken, that is the government would have to make its own determination. Given that the United States was not prepared to bend its 'neither confirm nor deny' stance in respect of the presence or otherwise of nuclear weapons on its craft, it would be up to the New Zealand Government to make the determination, on the evidence that they had to hand. In November 1984 Chief of Defence Staff Ewan Jamieson met US officals in Hawaii. It seems reasonable to assume that at this time the choice of a craft which just might carry nuclear weapons but was highly unlikely to, was made.[72] In other words attempts were being made in both the United States and New Zealand to reconcile the two policies. Back home, government spokespeople stressed not the virtues of the new policy so much as as the right of the government to have such a policy, any policy, presumably a way of both signalling to the United States and to peace activists in New Zealand the government's determination. Thus, speech notes for the Prime Minister drafted in December 1984 emphasised that the government would ensure

> as it promised in the election, . . . that ships that do come into our ports meet *our* criteria. That means that we will make our own assessment of the characteristics and mission of each ship . . . . The United States makes no exception to [its] policy . . . . But equally clearly, *we* make no exception to *our* nuclear policy.[73]

The USS *Buchanan* 'fitted the bill'. In being asked to report on the acceptability of the request in terms of New Zealand's anti-nuclear policy, the Chief of Defence Staff reported that:

> Like almost all other anti-submarine warships in the USN the USS *Buchanan* is fitted with ASROC [anti-submarine rocket], which is its only weapon system capable of being nuclear-armed. I can give no absolute guarantee that the ship does not carry any nuclear warheads for that purpose but after careful consideration . . . I believe it most unlikely.[74]

The two principal reasons which Jamieson advanced were that, firstly, while over 20,000 ASROC missiles had been produced, no more than 850 nuclear warheads existed and secondly, that the *Buchanan* was a relatively old ship (1962) which had been excluded from the list of those of its class which were to be substantially modified.[75]

Officials therefore prepared for a visit, but opposition mounted in the party and amongst extra-parliamentary groups. It was known by the middle of January that a request had been received from the United States. Acting Prime Minister Geoffrey Palmer (Lange was incommunicado in Tokelau) released a statement stressing the Government's determination both to maintain its anti-nuclear policy *and* its commitment to ANZUS.[76] But the party political pressure was now intense. On 27 January Palmer noted in a memorandum to Lange that he had had conversation with several members 'who are afraid we will let the ship in. Anderton says he will break with us if we do not follow our policy on this. Some marginal members have legitimate and real concerns. Anne Fraser told me on Sunday she would lose her activists if we let the ship in. The Peace groups are still with us but will demonstrate if we let the ship in'.[77]

Over the weekend supporters of peace organisations throughout the country were being contacted to make known their opposition to any dilution of the nuclear free policy. Access to a phone with discounted toll charges helped Wellington activists in the task, which produced a mass of telegrams at Parliament when Cabinet met on the Monday morning.[78] 'If in doubt, keep them out' distilled the outlook of the movement into one pithy phrase. This was an issue on which many activists both in the peace movement and in the Labour Party had been lobbying for over a decade. It was a policy which the previous National Government had vigorously opposed. If now, with Labour in government, the policy ended up being effectively the same as before, what was the point of being in office?

Under the circumstances it was almost a foregone conclusion that the Government would return to the Americans explaining that it did not feel that it had 'enough information available' to be certain that a visit from the *Buchanan* would not breach the anti-nuclear policy and therefore proposed instead a visit from a more modest craft, the non-nuclear weapons carrying capacity of which would be unquestioned and which would, the Prime Minister assured the United States, 'be received very warmly by my Government and by the New Zealand people'.[79]

If in Wellington the numbers meant that the *Buchanan* would be turned down, in Washington they would mean that New Zealand would be 'turned out' and this was conveyed by the US Ambassador to Lange on 3 February: 'a denial of port access to a US Navy ship contributing to the common defense of the alliance would be a matter of grave concern that would go to the core of our mutual obligation as allies.' The leak of the New Zealand request for the sending of a different kind of ship, seemingly as a way of putting pressure on the US Administration to compromise, had just the opposite effect.[80]

Three weeks later the Administration conveyed to the New Zealand Government the nature of the measures it was taking in response to what it saw as the failure of an ally to assume the responsibilities of an ally.[81] These included the curtailment of intelligence, of any participation in military exercises in which New Zealand was involved, and the opportunity to talk about substantive issues to senior officials in the State Department and the Pentagon.[82]

Assessment

The proximate cause of the crisis was clearly the failure to reconcile two policies – the claims of the ANZUS alliance, i.e. of New Zealand's allies, and the anti-nuclear policy. A central strand in Anzac nationalism was that, while there might be disagreements with your allies, they would both be tolerated, and be subsumed for the greater good when required.

Much of the development of the anti-nuclear movement could be fitted within an Anzac context – the debates over values, the changing formulations of interest were both familiar aspects of such an outlook. But as was evident at the time of the *Pintado* and other such visits, the material existed for something more.

In 1985 differences were neither tolerated nor subsumed and this in itself fuelled 'Pintado' nationalism. It was most in evidence when the pressure was most overt. In January, the substance of a letter from Prime

Minister Bob Hawke of Australia to Lange, addressing the importance of ensuring there were no obstacles to US Navy ship visits to New Zealand, was leaked. It was also widely understood that Secretary of State Shultz had written to Lange on similar lines, at about the same time.[83] Palmer regretted that 'the substance of the letter by the Australian Prime Minister to the New Zealand Prime Minister has been released. I regret it because it appears to place public pressure on the New Zealand Government.'[84]

Results from two contrasting poll questions are suggestive. In 1984 58.7 per cent and in 1985 59 per cent of those polled agreed that 'the New Zealand government should give permission for American nuclear-powered (but not nuclear-armed) ships to visit New Zealand ports; in 1984 45.4 per cent of those polled approved of the 'Labour Government policy' of banning nuclear-powered vessels from New Zealand ports, and in 1985 this had risen to 52.3 per cent.[85]

Such nationalism could only be reinforced when, later in the year, the Greenpeace vessel, *Rainbow Warrior*, in Auckland preparatory to voyaging to the French nuclear weapons testing zone, was sunk by French agents at the wharfside with the loss of one life.[86] The arrest of two French secret agents in New Zealand sheeted home the responsibility for the incident firmly to the French Government, but France was slow to admit remorse and only the two agents arrested in New Zealand were ever held accountable.

Yet for all this, Anzac nationalism was far from expiring. One metropolitan paper ran a banner headline on the results of a public opinion poll, 'Poll calls for vote on ship rejection'. The story identified the major findings of the poll as strong support for continued membership of ANZUS (78 per cent), and an 'overwhelming demand' for a referendum (83 per cent). The poll result of 56 per cent opposition to nuclear armed warships visiting New Zealand was relegated to the next paragraph.[87] Letters to the editor of another metropolitan paper in early February, which had 'poured in', it said, were 'about evenly divided with anti-ANZUS correspondents supporting the Government's ban on American ship visits and pro-ANZUS writers fearing that opting out of the alliance would be a betrayal of freedom and would leave us defenceless.'[88] Polls showed continued, if non-specific, support for ANZUS, whilst Dr Jim Sprott led the Peace Through Security movement, which gathered signatures for a referendum on the anti-nuclear policy.[89] Later in the year 15 former heads of the army, navy and air force publicly ptotested Labour's policy.[90]

As for the practitioners of diplomacy, it was ironic but true that the experience of the ANZUS crisis created a novel kind of 'on our own' outlook, it being the officials rather than the protest movement which bore the direct brunt of American displeasure.[91] While diplomats might be unsettled by the displeasure of allies, they were also prepared to respond robustly to what they felt was intemperate comment on the part of those allies:

> The Americans are acting as if one of their firmest allies has turned against them. If you're not with us in every particular you must be against us. That's ... nonsense.[92]

Equally, the way that France was able to exercise pressure on New Zealand to secure the return of its secret agents was a vivid demonstration of how 'on its own' New Zealand was. Support from New Zealand's allies – Britain and the United States – who were also allies of France, was conspicuous by its absence.[93]

Would realignment survive? 1985–1990

Despite the enthusiasm of many supporters of the anti-nuclear policy for taking more steps, the Government held to the view that its quarrel was not with ANZUS or its allies, but with the question of whether or not the alliance could be nuclear free. Thus, general approval was given to United States Deep Freeze aircraft visits within days of the crisis 'breaking'.[94] Much play was made of New Zealand's contribution to Western interests in the South Pacific. There was some irony in this, given that Labour spokespeople had rejected the idea of a Soviet threat. But (fortuitously?) the South Pacific was in the early to mid 1980s a zone of what might be called 'post-colonial' instability in Vanuatu and Fiji, and independence movements in French territories.

For its part, the United States did not seek to extend – or seek to resolve – the dispute by extending it into the economic sphere. For the United States economic and defence relations were habitually compartmentalised and the scale of this dispute was not sufficient to override that. As one American official had made clear back in 1980, 'if New Zealand for reasons of its own, were to follow a neutral course', it might affect . . . the atmosphere in which we in the Washington bureaucracy deal with trading issues, but I think that even there it would not affect the atmosphere in a decisive sort of way.[95]

And this indeed proved to be the case. For all this, the breach remained. At the 1986 South Pacific Forum member countries signed the Treaty of Rarotonga, finally establishing the long-awaited South Pacific Nuclear Weapons Free Zone. Shultz and Lange met in Manila in July of that year, but found no common ground on the central issue, that of reconciling the United States 'neither confirm nor deny' policy with New Zealand's anti-nuclear stance. At an Australian–United States meeting in San Francisco shortly afterwards, the United States announced that it was suspending its security obligations to New Zealand. New Zealand was now not an 'ally' but a 'friend'. While the personal chemistry between Lange and the Americans was not good, the fact that the Labour Government had made it clear it intended to proceed with anti-nuclear legislation was a more fundamental obstacle.[96]

The legislation passed into law in June 1987 during the last parliamentary session before the September general election. From then until the election, the peace movement's energies focused on securing the return of the Labour Government to office, as National's policy, while anti-nuclear, would have operated on what leader Jim Bolger called a 'trust me' principle, which would not therefore breach the US neither confirm nor deny principle. In the final weeks of the campaign, both Labour and National exploited the anti-nuclear issue, but National did so by comparing Lange with third world leaders like Libya's Colonel Gaddafi.[97] This suggested that National did still reckon that there might be electoral disadvantage for Labour in the policy – but the Labour victory, although it probably owed more to economic factors (the election was held at what proved to be the height of a stock market boom) was not evidently undercut by the anti-nuclear policy.[98]

For the Government itself, therefore, the course of its second term (1987–90) was not marked by the same effervescence over the anti-nuclear issue of the first three years. There was no immediate likelihood of a thaw in relations with the United States. On the New Zealand side the policy had ceased to be negotiable. The waning of Cold War tensions did no harm to Labour's stance and the issue in fact had now become one for National to grapple with rather than Labour, although one episode in 1989 suggested otherwise.

On 24 April of that year Lange, in a speech at Yale University, suggested that New Zealand and the United States would be better able to repair their relationship if they put ANZUS behind them, and that, accordingly, it might make sense for New Zealand to withdraw from the ANZUS Council, of which it had not been an effective member since 1985. New Zealand had not been an active member of ANZUS for over four years, but the suggestion elicited a sharp rebuttal from the Cabinet in New Zealand that such a position was in any way agreed policy. The timing of the news of the address – Anzac day morning, a day above all others when Anzac nationalism was at the centre of events – was curious. Lange found himself isolated on this as on economic issues, (or isolated on this because of his position on economic issues) and resigned the prime ministership in August with deputy Geoffrey Palmer succeeding him.[99]

Yet in respect of the ANZUS/anti-nuclear conundrum itself, a poll taken nearly two months after Lange's speech, asking questions which had last been asked in 1985, showed a strengthening of support for the anti-nuclear policy. Asked if the choice were between breaking ties with the United States and allowing ships that could be nuclear armed into New Zealand ports, 52 per cent said they would rather break defence ties, a seeming strengthening compared with 1985.[100]

By 1989, therefore, New Zealand had undergone a significant realignment in its foreign relations. The United States relationship had been central in this process because the United States was the only nuclear power with which New Zealand had a substantial relationship – the other allied nuclear power, Britain, had no strategic presence in the Pacific. But other nations were also involved, in particular Australia, the other ANZUS partner. What would be the nature of the relationship with Australia in the aftermath of the ANZUS crisis? The Australian Government had regarded New Zealand, not the United States, as responsible for the breach. The Hawke Government had not pursued the anti-nuclear cause as vigorously as it had been in New Zealand and was therefore additionally cautious about New Zealand's stance. As has been noted, the suspicion that there had been Australian pressure on New Zealand in January 1985 had an adverse effect on New Zealand public opinion.

But at a more general level, opinion in New Zealand remained favourable to cooperation with Australia in defence as in other spheres.

A 1986 poll showed that 81 per cent of New Zealanders thought a great effort should be made to get on with Australia, compared with only 63 per cent for the United States. In this poll Australia also ranked highest (68 per cent, compared with the US 52 per cent) as the country with which it was important that an alliance should be made.[101]

It did seem therefore that while realignment might be cutting a new perceptual boundary between New Zealand and the United States, something more like Anzac nationalism still applied in respect of the 'deep structure' of New Zealand relations with Australia. And indeed, Australia was, of course, the country for which the word Anzac was most appropriate as a shorthand expression. Further, in other spheres – family relations, common labour market, common trade area, common sports – there was far more contact with Australia than with the United States. The recurrent sporting competitions were indeed the classic exemplars of Anzac nationalism, where the very competitions, with their rules and agreed outcomes, provided the overarching structures within which the contests were played out.

So could there possibly be any disruption in the elaboration of 'closer defence relations' – CDR?[102] The answer turned out to be yes, the proximate cause being the campaign waged by members of the peace movement against the scheme for New Zealand to replace its old navy frigates with new ones purpose built, in conjunction with an Australian frigate-building programme, primarily in Australian shipyards.

The campaign was most marked through 1988 and into 1989. A decision in principle had been taken in March 1987, but only after the election did the specifics trigger restlessness in the peace movement. The anti-frigate campaign thus found fertile party political soil.[103] The pre-1987 unity and vitality of the Labour Government had vanished into a maelstrom of ideological argument about economic policy. At the end of 1988, two right wing ministers, Roger Douglas and Richard Prebble, were sacked, and early in 1989 Jim Anderton, former President of the party and now an MP, took the left wing away to a 'New Labour' party.

The relationship of the campaign to formulations of values and interests was also revealing. Anti-militarists suggested that the project only helped maintain the 'Anglo-Saxon club . . . consisting of us and the Australians patrolling the boundaries of the South Pacific ready to deal with anyone United States thinks is out of line.'[104]

More generally, New Zealanders had become anti-militarist. A 1989 poll showed only 38 per cent of New Zealanders prepared to take up arms in defence of their country, compared with 77 per cent of Americans polled and 60 per cent of Australians. Only seven countries participating in the world-wide survey, including defeated Germany, Austria, Italy and Japan, had lower figures.[105]

As with the 'hollowing out' of ANZUS in the early 1980s, interest arguments seem likely to have at least fostered this outlook. The divergence of New Zealand from Australian interest was expressed over both strategy and over cost: 'the simple truth is that New Zealand neither needs nor can afford these frigates.'[106]

The argument over the former exposed the different conceptions of national security which, as we have already seen, may have influenced the differing outcomes of debates over ANZUS in 1983–84 in the two countries. It reverberated sufficiently in 1988 for Lange to both acknowledge and then refute it. 'Our interests [with Australia]', he argued in August 1988, were not

> identical – our geographical outlook is different, we have our own regional priorities and you will be aware that we have important differences on the specific question of nuclear ship visits. But the scope of our shared strategic interests is wide. And just as it is impossible for us to limit our Pacific horizon to the Kermadecs we cannot regard our interest in Australia's security as confined to this side of the Blue Mountains.[107]

But it was over the cost of the frigates that the anti-frigate campaign most effectively mobilised New Zealand public opinion: '. . . the prime simple reason why the Australian frigates [sic] can and must be stopped is the impossibly high cost'.[108] And it was such arguments which took the campaign into the conservative camp, just as had the anti-nuclear campaign in the early 1980s, eliciting a very different kind of conservatism than that identified with the armed forces and the National Party. Thus, in a letter to the *Bulletin* addressing points made by columnist Laurie Oakes, former New Zealand Party leader Bob Jones argued that, with no threat, what was the point of spending the money on frigates?[109] Similarly Roger Douglas, who at the end of 1988 had lost his job as Minister of Finance, was reported as saying that

> the cost of the Anzac frigate project could not be met within the existing defence budget. . . . he did not think New Zealand should join the project

for four frigate warships, expected to cost about $2.16 billion . . . This was in direct conflict with an earlier statement by Defence Minister Bob Tizard.[110]

The debate might have remained a purely domestic one if it had not been that the advocate and prime mover of the frigate building programme was Australia. Defence Minister Kim Beazley came to Wellington in December 1988 and February 1989 for talks with his New Zealand counterparts. He was a blunt speaker and Foreign Minister Russell Marshall's claim that there was 'no pressure, no arm twisting from Australia, whatever the imaginative posters that now decorate our streets whenever Kim Beazley pays us a visit these days may imply'[111] rang rather hollow. Even from the other side of the Tasman, it could look like undue pressure. Beazley was, one journalist said,

> assuming the role of neighbourhood bully in the eyes of the New Zealand peace movement. He wants New Zealand to buy four . . . ANZAC class frigates, which Australia is also acquiring. . . . There is a mood of resentment among many New Zealanders that Australia is telling them what sort of navy they should have.[112]

As in 1985 therefore, outside pressure fed nationalist sentiment. Polls indicated that 'solid majorities opposed the project not just on cost grounds during conditions of economic difficulty but in retaliation against perceived Australian pressure.'[113]

The officials and the politicians stood between this new wave of 'Pintado' nationalism and the Australians. Indeed one of the primary reasons for participating in the project was to strengthen the overall relationship with Australia. As an in-house memorandum put it in July 1989, 'if we were to take a narrow New Zealand approach and setting aside trans-Tasman factors we would want to look more closely at cheaper ships. The other side of the coin is that we are in the Anzac project precisely because of the special value we attach to working with Australia on defence.'[114]

It was not a comfortable place to be and must have heightened, as had the ANZUS crisis, a 'Guamist' sense of being 'on our own'. But the difference from the 1985 ANZUS crisis was equally marked. The reconstructed Labour Government of August 1989, with Deputy Geoffrey Palmer as the new Prime Minister, did sign an agreement – although for two not for four frigates – in September. Thus the further stage that unfolded in relations with the United States after the refusal to admit the *Buchanan*, did not occur in relations with Australia. It is unprofitable to speculate what might have happened if the Government had decided not to sign up. It would have been a further triumph for 'Pintado' nationalism but it might not have led to a fundamental breach with Australia; it could be presumed that, as with the ANZUS crisis, diplomatic energies would have been directed to damage limitation exercises and efforts to strengthen common ground with Australia in other spheres.

But the fact that the frigate agreement was made suggested that, despite the realignment, there was vitality in the Anzac as well as in the Pintado outlook. Where would the balance come to rest? Through 1989 National continued to adhere to its 'trust me' formula but its stance was weakened, not just by the strengthening of anti-nuclear sentiment at home, but by the Palmer Government's own pursuit of a diplomatic rapprochement with the new Bush Administration in the United States, facilitated possibly by Lange's resignation. Over the year's end the United States invaded Panama and removed the Panamanian leader Manuel Noriega, arresting him and imprisoning him in the mainland United States. At the United Nations New Zealand was among only a small minority of countries that supported this action,[115] which was widely regarded, irrespective of the validity of the claims that Noriega was a collaborator with drug cartels, as an example of old fashioned US imperialism in Latin America. In early March Mike Moore, Minister of Foreign Affairs and Trade, met Secretary of State James Baker at the State Department. After the meeting Mr Moore said that New Zealand and the United States would now cooperate in all areas except the 'quarantined' defence relationship.[116]

If Labour could succeed in such an endeavour, whilst keeping the anti-nuclear legislation, National had lost the remaining electoral card in this area – that only it could ensure a resumption of normal relations with the United States. Only days later, the National Party caucus decided to abandon its opposition to the anti-nuclear policy. This precipitated the resignation of Don McKinnon from the position of defence spokesperson, but successfully ensured that the issue could not be used to National's disadvantage in the forthcoming election. The anti-nuclear policy had become bipartisan, ANZUS or no ANZUS, although the advent of a National government did provoke some further politicking.[117]

The realignment of New Zealand's foreign relations in the 1980s arose out of a shift in the circumstances and values shaping those relations. The possibility of realignment seemed in the 1970s to arise at least partly because of the retreat by the powers from New Zealand's part of the world, but the more powerful trigger proved to be the anti-nuclear movement which accomplished a change in policy placing New Zealand in a distinctly different position vis a vis the Western world than it had occupied prior to 1984. It produced too a new kind of nationalism, one that was forged in 'combat' with friends rather than foes. This did not altogether displace the older nationalism, but provided a vigorous alternative to it both at the time and into the 1990s.

Notes

1   David Lange, *Nuclear Free – The New Zealand Way* (Auckland, 1990).
    Kevin Clements, *Back from the Brink: The Creation of a Nuclear-Free New Zealand* (Wellington, 1988).
2   Hugh Templeton, *All Honourable Men: Inside the Muldoon Cabinet, 1975–1984*, (Auckland, 1995).
3   For the pre-1985 period, Roderic Alley (ed.), *Alternatives to ANZUS*, Vol. 2 (second revised edition, Wellington, 1984); John Henderson, 'The Burdens of ANZUS', in *New Zealand International Review* (hereafter *NZIR*), May–June 1980; Tom Newnham, *Peace Squadron: The Sharp End of Nuclear Protest in New Zealand* (Auckland, 1986). For the post-1985 period, Clements, *Back from the Brink*; E. Grebenschikov, 'ANZUS: The Labyrinths and Deadlocks of the Bloc Policy', in *Far Eastern Affairs* No.2, 1985; E. Hodges, 'David and Goliath in the Ocean of Peace: Case Studies of "Nuclearism", "Nuclear Allergy" and "The Kiwi Disease"', Ph.D thesis, University of California, San Diego, 1990; Lange, *Nuclear Free*; Margaret Wilson, *Labour in Government, 1984–1987* (Wellington, 1989), especially pp.55–67.
4   For the pre-1985 period, Henry Albinski, 'American Perspectives on the ANZUS Alliance', in *Australian Outlook*, Vol.32 No.2, August 1978; R. D. Muldoon, *Muldoon* (Wellington, 1977); R. D. Muldoon, *My Way* (Auckland, 1981). For the post-1985 period, Dora Alves, *Anti-Nuclear Attitudes in Australia and New Zealand* (Washington, 1985); Ewan Jamieson, *Friend or Ally? New Zealand at Odds with its Past* (Sydney, 1990); Peter Jennings, *The Armed Forces of New Zealand: the ANZUS Split: Costs and Consequences* (Wellington, 1988); Denis McLean, *New Zealand: Isolation and Foreign Policy* (Sydney, 1990); Ramesh Thakur, *In Defence of New Zealand: Foreign Policy Choices in the Nuclear Age* (Boulder Col., 1986).

5   For the broader context, Roderic Alley, 'ANZUS and the Nuclear Issue', in Jonathan Boston and Martin Holland (eds.), *The Fourth Labour Government: Radical Politics in New Zealand* (Auckland, 1987); Bryce Harland, *On Our Own: New Zealand in the Emerging Tripolar World* (Wellington, 1992); John Henderson, Richard Kennaway and Keith Jackson, *Beyond New Zealand* (Auckland, 1980); Colin James, *The Quiet Revolution* (Wellington, 1986); Paul Landais-Stamp and Paul Rogers, *Rocking the Boat: New Zealand, the United States and the Nuclear-Free Zone Controversy in the 1980s* (Berg, Oxford, London & Munich, 1989), see especially pp.157–9; Stuart McMillan, *Neither Confirm Nor Deny* (Wellington, 1987); Michael Pugh, *The ANZUS Crisis, Nuclear Visiting and Deterrence* (Cambridge, 1989); Malcolm Templeton, *Defence and Security: What New Zealand Needs* (Wellington, 1986).

6   Brian Sinclair, 'Ideology and the ANZUS Dispute: the Legacy of the New Left and the Consequences for New Zealand's Security Policy' (D.Phil in Political Science, University of Waikato, 1998); Nicky Hager, 'The Peace Movement Origin of the Nuclear Free Legislation', in 'A Celebration: 10 Years of Nuclear Free Legislation', Working Paper No.6, University of Auckland, Centre for Peace Studies, 1997; Richard Northey, 'What the 1984–1990 Labour Government Thought It Was Doing' in 'A Celebration'; Robert E. White, 'Nuclear Free New Zealand: 1984 – New Zealand Becomes Nuclear Free', Working Paper No.7, University of Auckland, Centre of Peace Studies, 1997. The present writer is indebted to the Sinclair thesis for some bibliographical references.

7   White, 'Nuclear Free', p.30.
8   Sinclair, 'Ideology and the ANZUS Dispute', pp.125–6.
9   Sinclair, 'Ideology and the ANZUS Dispute', p.273.
10 Thus McLean, *Isolation and Foreign Policy*.
11 Interview with Kevin Hackwell, 8 April 1999.
12 *Independence and Foreign Policy: New Zealand in the World Since 1935* (Auckland, 1993).
13 *External Affairs Review*, August 1969, p.17.
14 As Harland, *On Our Own*.
15 Hager, 'Peace Movement Origin', p.2, *Independence and Foreign Policy*, p.187.
16 *Independence and Foreign Policy*, pp.187, 189–90.
17 *Independence and Foreign Policy*, p.189.
18 Clements, *Back from the Brink*, p.84; *New Zealand Foreign Affairs Review* (hereafter *NZFAR*), May 1975, pp.79–80. For an upbeat account of the advent of nuclear-powered warships see Nathaniel Kenny, 'Mighty *Enterprise*, World's Largest Ship' and Adm. George Anderson, 'Our Nuclear Navy', in *National Geographic* 123/3 (March 1963). Both stress the operational advantages of nuclear-powered ships (no need to refuel), whilst Kenny mentions in passing that *Enterprise* 'is equipped to carry both nuclear and conventional weapons. Compared to the cataclysmic blast of all this carrier's capability, the combined explosion of every World War II bomb would seem a feeble firecracker' (p.434).
19 *Independence and Foreign Policy*, p.190.
20 For Kirk support of ANZUS see *NZFAR*, June 1973, p.11; December 1973, p.39. The communique of the February 1974 ANZUS meeting made no reference to

nuclear weapons or the South Pacific Nuclear Weapons Free Zone, *NZFAR*, February 1974, pp.6–8.
21 Stephen Levine, 'Public Opinion and the ANZUS Treaty', *NZIR*, May–June 1976, p. 16.
22 *NZFAR*, November 1975, p.54, December 1975, p.46, January 1976 p.42, March 1976, p.29.
23 Levine, 'Public Opinion and the ANZUS Treaty', p.17.
24 *NZFAR*, March 1976, p.20.
25 David Campbell, 'The Domestic Sources of New Zealand Foreign Policy in Comparative Perspective', Working Paper No.16, Peace Research Centre, Australian National University, 1977, p.62.
26 Malcolm McKinnon, 'Costs and Continuity: New Zealand's Security and the United States', in *Political Science*, July 1978, p.43. See also *Independence and Foreign Policy*, pp.199–200, 219–21.
27 See, for instance, Secretary of External Affairs George Laking's comments in the late 1960s, cited in *Independence and Foreign Policy*, pp.182–4.
28 *Independence and Foreign Policy*, pp. 197–8.
29 Stephen Levine, 'Public Opinion and Foreign Policy', in *NZIR*, March 1980, p.20.
30 *AJHR* 1977 I1, p.4, petition of Raewyn McKenzie and 333,087 others; see also *AJHR* 1978 H4, 'Nuclear Power Generation in New Zealand', report of the Royal Commission of Enquiry, p.171.
31 Campbell, 'Domestic Sources', p.62.
32 *New Zealand Herald*, 4 November 1977.
33 Sinclair, 'Ideology and the ANZUS Dispute', p.131. See also Newnham, *Peace Squadron*, pp.35–47.
34 22 April 1978, reproduced in Newnham, *Peace Squadron*, p.33.
35 Hager, p.2. Comments that there were no strategic reason for American ships to visit regularly 'surfaced' only to be as regularly discounted by American officialdom. See, for example, 'ANZUS: A Dialogue', in *NZIR*, November–December 1980, p.6; Jennifer Hellen, 'Turning the Nuclear Tide', in *New Outlook*, October–November 1983, pp.17–18. White notes that Ministry files 'show no evidence to support claims that Muldoon invited specific nuclear warships to visit', but also notes an episode in 1983 where Muldoon 'gave the nod' to a proposed visit by USS *Texas* ahead of the formal request for diplomatic clearance from the US embassy. See Robert E. White, 'Nuclear Free New Zealand: 1984: New Zealand Becomes Nuclear Free', University of Auckland, Centre of Peace Studies, Working Paper No.7, 1997, p.17.
36 See abridged version of Auckland Peace Squadron policy statement of December 1976 in Newnham, *Peace Squadron*, pp.20–1.
37 Evelyn Colbert (recently retired State Dept officer) commenting in 'The Alliance: A Dialogue', in *NZIR*, November–December 1980, p.7.
38 Bruce Wallace, 'Which Way the Alliance?' in *NZIR*, November–December 1980, p.10.
39 *Independence and Foreign Policy*, pp.204–5; *Auckland Star*, 23 August 1980.
40 *Independence and Foreign Policy*, pp.201–3. Muldoon's personal dislike of Carter

may also have been a factor, see *New Zealand Listener*, 15 October 1977.
41 Werner Kaltefleiter, 'Introduction', in W.Kaltefleiter and Robert L. Pfaltzgraff (eds.), *Peace Movements in Europe and the United States* (London, 1985), p.1.
42 James Finn, 'The Peace Movement in the United States' in Kaltefleiter and Pfaltzgraff, *Peace Movements*, pp.168–70; Jacqulyn K. Davis, 'The US Nuclear Freeze Campaign, Facts and Fallacies', in Kaltfleiter and Pfaltzgraff, *Peace Movements*, pp.173, 175; Jonathan Schell, *The Fate of the Earth* (New York, 1982).
43 *Rocking the Boat*, pp. 20–1
44 Paul Byrd, 'The Development of the Peace Movement in Britain', in Kaltefleiter and Pfaltzgraff, p.72.
45 Landais-Stamp and Rogers, *Rocking the Boat*, pp.20–1.
46 *New Outlook*, October–November 1983, p.16.
47 Byrd, 'Development of the Peace Movement', p.72.
48 *New Outlook*, August/September 1983, p.23
49 Newnham, *Peace Squadron*, pp.48–54. *New Zealand Herald*, 6 August 1983 records march numbers against the *Texas* visit in Auckland on 5 August at between 15,000 and 30,000; *Dominion*, 11 August 1983 between 7000 and 10,000 in Wellington.
50 Campbell, 'Domestic Sources', p.63; Charles Crothers and Georgina Murray, 'Auckland Attitudes on International Peace Issues' (New Zealand Political Studies Association, 1985).
51 *Press*, 6 October 1984, on MFAT 59/206/20.
52 Thus, in 1982 Labour leader Rowling rejecting Cooper's claim that New Zealand was likely to become an ally of the Soviet Union: Labour had always been opposed to Communism. Lange rejected similar charges by Cooper at the time of the 1983 ANZUS Council meeting, *Dominion*, 19 July 1983.
53 *NZFAR*, April–June 1982, pp.26–30; *New Zealand Times*, 14 March 1984.
54 Evelyn Colbert, 'The Alliance: Common Interests', in *NZIR*, November–December 1980, pp.7–8.
55 David Lange, *Nuclear Free*, p.40.
56 Margaret Wilson, *Labour in Government, 1984–1987* (Wellington, 1989), p.56. Wilson was president of the Labour Party, 1984 to 1987.
57 Interview with Kevin Hackwell, Wellington, 8 April 1999. For further criticism of the idea of a Soviet threat see Ray Galvin, *Living Without ANZUS* (Auckland, 1984), pp.17–22. Galvin was a young Auckland Presbyterian minister.
58 Campbell, 'Domestic Sources', p.53, citing the *Annex to the Defence Committee of Enquiry: Public Opinion Poll on Defence and Security: What New Zealanders Think* (Wellington, 1986), p.18.
59 *Evening Post*, 5 June 1986; for further discussion of European NATO members see MFAT 59/8/5 Pt. 3, memorandum prepared for Deputy Minister of Foreign Affairs, February 1985; NZ embassy, the Hague to SFA, Wellington, 24 May 1985, re Norway.
60 Campbell, 'Domestic Sources', p.52; William Watts, 'Australia, New Zealand and the United States: Mutual Perceptions' in Richard Baker (ed.), *Australia, New Zealand and the United States: Internal Change and Alliance Relations in the ANZUS States* (New York, 1991), p.152. Space does not permit extended discussion of the Australian experience. Further, see Joseph Camilleri, *ANZUS: Australia's*

Predicament in the Nuclear Age (Melbourne, 1987), espeically pp.102–11; Watts, 'Mutual Perceptions', pp.144–52.
61 For polling data see Watts, 'Mutual Perceptions', pp.144–5.
62 *Independence and Foreign Policy*, pp.204–6.
63 A McNair 1985 poll found 78 per cent support for New Zealand membership of ANZUS in response to an open question ('do you favour New Zealand being a member of ANZUS?'). A more focused question in asked by NRB 'Do you wish New Zealand to remain a member of the ANZUS military alliance?' with a larger sample attracted 66 per cent support in 1984, 71 per cent support in 1985; Campbell, 'Domestic Sources', p.56. See also Lange, *Nuclear Free*, p.60.
64 'ANZUS: A Dialogue', in *NZIR*, November–December 1980, p.6, *New Zealand Herald*, 25 September 1981.
65 Wilson, *Labour in Government*, pp.62–3; Lange, *Nuclear Free*, pp.34–5.
66 'Lange will be weakened by port visit issue, cuts little ice with New Zealand electorate', *Australian Financial Review*, editorial, 18 June 1984; see also *Auckland Star*, 29 June 1984, 'Muldoon accusing Lange of being weak on ANZUS, unable to resist left and SUP influence'; *Auckland Star*, 7 July 1984.
67 Lange, *Nuclear Free*, p.58.
68 Throughout the months preceding the breaking of the crisis, calendars had been drawn up envisaging a graduated sequence of events which would lead to a reconciliation of the anti-nuclear policy with continued participation in ANZUS. See MFAT 59/8/5 Pt.2. See also Lange, *Nuclear Free*, pp.65–8.
69 'Mr Shultz [US Secretary of State] has made it clear that the United States is not going to force the issue of nuclear powered or equipped platforms before early 1985'. SFA to MFA 31 August 1984, MFAT 59/206/20. See also Lange, *Nuclear Free*, pp.104–5.
70 'I thought that if I kept stressing the government's intention to take an active part in ANZUS at the level of conventional armaments then I had fair chance of winning the battle for public opinion inside New Zealand'. Lange, *Nuclear Free*, p.60.
71 SFA to MFA 31 Aug 1984, 59/206/20.
72 See, for example, reference in Wood to Norrish (NZ embassy Washington to Wellington), tgm no 5386 (p.4), 17 December 1984, MFAT 59/8/5 Pt.2.
73 SFA to PM 20 December 1984, attached speech notes, p.1, MFAT 59/8/5. Similarly, Palmer, Acting PM, press statement 21 January 1985: 'Where we receive a request for the visit of a naval vessel of any nation we will make our own independent assessment to ensure they comply with our nuclear policy.'
74 CDS to Minister of Defence, 24 January 1985, MFAT 59/8/2.
75 CDS to Minister of Defence, 24 January 1985. Whereas a critical commentator argued that 'this was still the Cold War era, and there is not good reason to assume that a nuclear capable US Navy Ship would undertake a cruise of this duration away from nuclear weapons storage bases without its own supply of nuclear weapons'. See White, 'Nuclear Free New Zealand', p.35.
76 Statement of 22 January 1985 is on MFAT 59/8/5 Pt.2.
77 MFAT 59/8/5 Pt.2; see also letter, Gen. Sec. of Labour Party to Dep. PM, 25 Jan 1985, expressing wish to ensure that there was no deviation from the anti-nuclear

policy. 10,000 demonstrated in Auckland within two day of the news of a possible *Buchanan* visit.
78 Interview with Kevin Hackwell, Wellington, 8 April 1999.
79 PM to US Ambassador, 31 January 1985. The proposed alternative was an FFG 7.
80 Wood to Francis/Norrish, Washington to Wellington No.527, 30 January 1985, 59/8/5 Pt.2; US Ambassador to PM, 3 February 1985; PM to US Ambassador, 4 February 1985, MFAT 59/8/5 Pt.3; Lange, *Nuclear Free*, pp.88–9.
81 Washington to Wellington, 26 February 1985, No.1116, MFAT 59/8/5.
82 Washington to Wellington, 27 February 1985, No.1137, MFAT 59/8/5; Lange, *Nuclear Free*, pp.99–100.
83 Correctly. For the original texts of the letters see MFAT 59/8/5 Pt.2. Notes from Lange's meeting with the American ambassador on 29 January record him saying that the Hawke letter, being published, has 'aroused nationalism and anti Australian, anti American policy'
84 MFAT 59/8/5, statement of 25 January 1985. Notes on this file suggest that the leaks came from Australian sources in Washington.
85 Campbell, 'Domestic Sources', p.62. The first two polls were NRB ones, the other two Heylen ones.
86 See Michael King, *Death of the Rainbow Warrior* (Auckland, 1986); Lange, *Nuclear Free*, pp.120–7.
87 *Dominion*, 18 February 1985.
88 *Evening Post*, 16 February 1985; see also 28 February 1985, 16 March 1985.
89 *Evening Post*, 14 March 1985, 'Sprott aims for million in nuke poll bid'. A 70,000 name petition calling for a referendum was in due course presented to Parliament but no referendum was held. *Evening Post*, 5 June 1986. Sprott was quoted as saying 'most people are delighted to see those ships here. Suddenly they feel naked and insecure and they don't like it.'
90 *Evening Post*, 11 December 1985.
91 For one example see Wood to Norrish, tgm no 5386, 17 December 1984 which details the reactions of State Dept. officials to some particular statements by Lange. The telegram refers to reported 'violent' reaction (from other agencies), that the officials spoken to 'appeared shaken', that for one of them, one comment in particular 'really socked me'.
92 SFA, Merwyn Norrish, 'World Understanding and the National Interest', *NZFAR*, January–March 1985, p.30.
93 King, *Death of the Rainbow Warrior*, p.194.
94 SFA to MFA 21 February 1985, MFAT 59/206/20.
95 Colbert, 'The alliance: a dialogue', in *NZIR*, November–December 1980, p.7.
96 Lange, *Nuclar Free*, pp.135–48.
97 Interview with Kevin Hackwell, Wellington, 8 April 1999.
98 Further, see Jack Vowles, 'Nuclear Free New Zealand and Rogernomics: the Survival of a Labour Government', paper presented to the NZ Political Studies Assn. Conference, Wellington, May 1989.
99 Lange's account is in *Nuclear Free*, pp.200–7; see also *New Zealand Herald*, 26, 27, 28 April 1989.
100 From transcript of Radio New Zealand News 15 June 1989, on MFAT 156/10/2.

The poll cites a figure of 44 per cent in 1985; this would appear to refer to the 16 per cent who, when first asked, opted for taking New Zealand out of ANZUS and not having any ship visits *plus* the more than half of the 44 per cent who wanted to stay in ANZUS without nuclear ship visits but who, when 'pushed to the wall' opted to leave ANZUS. See 'Defence and Security: What New Zealanders Want: Report of the Defence Committe of Enquiry', Wellington, 1986, pp.62–4; *Annex to the Defence Committee of Enquiry : Public Opinion Poll on Defence and Security: What New Zealanders Think* (Wellington, 1986), pp.76–8.
101 Campbell, 'Domestic Sources', pp.51, 54.
102 Analogously with CER, closer economic relations.
103 *Dominion*, 10 Febrary 1989.
104 *Dominion*, 28 February 1989.
105 *Dominion*, 28 August 1989.
106 Nicky Hager, *The Case Against New Frigates* (Wellington, 1988), p.1.
107 Speech notes for address to Wellington branch, NZIIA, 10 August 1988.
108 Hager, *Case Against*, p.6.
109 *Bulletin*, 7 March 1989, p.14. The relevant Oakes column appeared on 21 February.
110 *Dominion*, 16 December 1988.
111 *Dominion*, 12 April 1989.
112 Transcript from ABC Four Corners, 22 May 1989, MFAT 156/10/2.
113 See Roderic Alley, 'The Public Dimension', pp.295–317 below.
114 Notes for PM meeting with Australian Prime Minister Hawke, c. July 1989, MFAT 156/10/2/1.
115 Referred to in *Dominion*, 2 March 1990; see also Lange, *Dominion*, 19 March 1991 on criticism by US embassy of his stance on the Noriega issue – he had argued that the 'debased' nature of the Noriega regime would not in itself justify violating Panama's integrity.
116 *Independence and Foreign Policy*, pp.284–5.
117 Interview with Kevin Hackwell, 8 April 1999.

STEPHEN HOADLEY

Trans-Tasman Relations: CER and CDR

TO A DISTANT OBSERVER, CLOSE TRANS-TASMAN RELATIONS may seem unremarkable. The convergence of New Zealand and Australia's interests, and co-operation by their governments in pursuit of those interests, appear as natural as their geographic proximity. The forging of extensive and deep economic, political, and military ties, culminating in the world's most comprehensive bilateral free trade arrangement and intimate defence cooperation, might be judged from afar as not only inevitable but also essential if these two relatively small English-speaking states are to survive and prosper in the turbulent Asia-Pacific environment.

Sovereign States, Distinct Economies

Yet, the two states remain sovereign, their economies distinctive in structure and orientation, their politics patriotic, and their peoples proud of their own histories and protective of their countries' unique values and interests. The relationship has a chequered history, one that displays not only convergence but also divergence and even acrimony at times. Convergence of policy, when it occurred, did not take place naturally, easily, or quickly, but was fashioned by the visions and commitments of leaders who negotiated patiently to make it happen. And it did not always last. Of particular relevance here is the observation that trade negotiations in the period 1960–1992 succeeded only after serious disagreements were faced and difficult compromises hammered out.

This chapter focuses on how New Zealand and Australian leaders negotiated economic and defence cooperation agreements in the 1970s and 1980s, known collectively by the acronyms CER (Closer Economic

Relations) and CDR (Closer Defence Relations). It directs attention to the process of negotiation and explores how differences were resolved, bargains made, and new arrangements created to bring mutual benefit to the negotiating states. It may be read as an account of why the New Zealand and Australian governments have initiated negotiations, how they have conceived the issues and pursued their interests, and what they have given up and gained in order to reach a remarkable series of agreements.

The 1960s

For most of the 20th century until the 1960s, with the notable exception of World War II, Australia did not figure prominently on New Zealand's horizon, and even less did New Zealand appear on Australia's. Diplomacy was conducted through high commissions in each other's capitals, in occasional ministerial and high-level officials' meetings, and at multilateral forums. Government-to-government relations proceeded in a friendly fashion, but without urgency, mostly concerned with harmonising policies in the South Pacific. Military cooperation after the Second World War was cordial but neither deep nor extensive, mostly concerned with consulting with the United States in the annual ANZUS meetings of defence and foreign ministers.

In the 19th century Australia had been New Zealand's biggest market but with the development of refrigeration in the 1880s and steadily improved shipping services, New Zealand's trade turned decisively to Britain. The trans-Tasman trade relationship remained mutually advantageous but not close. The two countries' leaders had discussed economic cooperation sporadically since the 1880s, signed trade agreements in 1922 and 1933 extending British preferential tariff rates to each other, and negotiated a Trade Understanding to grant special import licenses in 1956.[1] But in 1960 only 4 per cent of New Zealand exports went to Australia and a similar proportion of Australia's exports to New Zealand. Bruce Brown pithily summed up the trans-Tasman relationship as it had existed throughout much of the century: the two countries sat 'back to back in the Pacific', New Zealand trading through Panama, Australia through Suez.[2]

The mutual aloofness was soon to change. In 1961 Britain declared its intent to seek membership in the European Economic Community (EEC). This jeopardised New Zealand's Commonwealth Preference tariff and privileged access to the British market. At the same time, world prices for bulk agricultural commodities were declining as other countries became self-sufficient and began supplying world markets. New Zealand's and Australia's export growth slowed and by the later 1960s, as the countries continued importing to support their high standards of living, their balance of payments fell deeper into deficit.

Britain's EEC membership application precipitated a trade policy reorientation in Wellington, for New Zealand's export industries, producing a substantial volume of pastoral and forest products, had to either find new outlets or enlarge traditional ones. Similar impulses were felt in Canberra.

Faced with these prospects, the governments of New Zealand and Australia began to take a renewed interest in each other's markets.[3] The attractions were several; they included proximity, familiarity, cultural, legal, and monetary similarity, an unrestricted and common labour market, and substantial interpenetration of private sector activity – for example in manufacturing, banking, finance, and insurance. New Zealand traders were attracted by the potential of the Australian market to absorb dairy products facing exclusion from the British market. Conversely, New Zealand had become the largest market for Australian manufactures and was seen also as a proving ground and a stepping stone to markets farther afield, a view soon to be adopted by New Zealand as well.

At that point, too, the New Zealand forest products industry was looking for a profitable way to use maturing stands of exotic timber (Monterey or radiata pine) planted in the inter-war period, noted that Australian demand for pulp and newsprint was growing, and estimated that New Zealand could sell these products more cheaply than current Australian producers. This trade would also alleviate the four-to-one trade imbalance New Zealand faced with Australia.

The Australian forestry producers, too, saw an opportunity to rationalise the industry on a trans-Tasman basis, in which New Zealand would concentrate on pulp, newsprint, and tissues while Australia would concentrate on fine papers and more intensely processed products, with each selling its speciality to the other. This intra-industry arrangement proved viable, and rationalisation did occur, producing greater efficiency for both sides. More importantly, this example quickly led Australian industry and political opinion leaders to the conclusion that free trade with New Zealand would not only open and secure trans-Tasman markets, but also prepare Australian industry for competition in wider markets such as Asia.

The NAFTA Experiment 1965–1978

Converging interests stimulated the political leaders, notably trade ministers John Marshall in New Zealand and John ('Black Jack') McEwan in Australia, to spearhead a five-year negotiating effort, beginning in 1960. The specific objective was to liberalise bilateral trade in forest products, but selected manufactures were also included for consideration. The result of the subsequent negotiations and compromises was the New Zealand Australia Free Trade Agreement of 1965, popularly known as NAFTA.[4] The heart of NAFTA was a list of products that would be traded freely, without tariffs or quotas, between the partners. This list was to be expanded by semi-annual meetings by representatives of the two governments.

Despite the hopes of the negotiators, NAFTA soon bogged down and became increasingly an institution of managed trade. Industry lobbies used their veto power to delay additions to the free trade list. While the number of items enjoying free trade had risen from approximately 1000 at the inception of the Agreement in 1965 to 1,760 by 1974, this still represented only 37 per cent of the items on the New Zealand Customs Tariff list.[5] Many of the additions were of little trade value or were not competitive. Using import licences and quotas, New Zealand was particularly prone to protect motor vehicles and parts and steel products, items Australia was particularly keen to export.

The year 1978 proved to be a turning point for Australian trade officials. Australian negotiators demanded more liberal granting of import licences in return for better access for New Zealand apparel, but later constricted New Zealand's access, whereupon New Zealand unilaterally raised tariffs against Australian apparel. In April 1978 New Zealand wool carpet exports met restrictions, and to secure their access New Zealand officials were obliged to allow more Australian synthetic carpet into their market, over the objections of New Zealand manufacturers. Leaders of the Confederation of Australian Industries made veiled threats to pull out of NAFTA altogether and concentrate on Asian markets unless New Zealand granted Australian products better access.

Inordinate time and effort were spent by negotiators for small gains, particularly by Australia. Professor Sir Frank Holmes summed up the impasse at the time,

> surely our Government is as sick as the Australian ministers and officials are of devoting their valuable time to haggling over peas and beans or whether things like horseshoes, heraldic badges, and non-electric gongs of base metal should be added to Schedule A [the free trade list].[6]

Journalist Colin James later wrote that by 1978 many Australian leaders and officials were ready to abandon NAFTA as more trouble than it was worth and 'NAFTA began to look in serious danger of collapsing'.[7] Australia's aloofness was compounded by the inability of Prime Minister Malcolm Fraser to warm to his New Zealand counterpart, Prime Minister Robert Muldoon.

Negotiating CER 1978–1983

By 1978 the trade ministers of the two governments were well aware that NAFTA could no longer serve the two countries' maturing economic interests. Yet, neither country wished to move back to the pre-1965 relationship, for each had a stake in the other, not only in interpenetration of capital and free interchange of labour but also in political consultation, defence co-operation, and cultural exchange. As political leaders and officials repeated at every occasion, each country was the other's largest market for manufactured goods. This was a base worth developing jointly as a springboard to the burgeoning Asia-Pacific markets.

Furthermore, the failure of the GATT Tokyo Round to reduce the subsidisation of European and American agricultural exports stimulated in New Zealand and Australia a defensive reaction on the one hand, and on the other a determination to set up a reformed and liberalised market regime to exemplify what GATT should be. These impulses converged on the conclusion that NAFTA had to be drastically reformed or superseded altogether by a new trans-Tasman trade regime. New Zealand political leaders initially were inclined to reform NAFTA, while Australian leaders were beginning to conceive more bold innovations.

In September 1977 New Zealand Deputy Prime Minister Brian Talboys had acknowledged that 'our relationship with Australia is more important to us than our links with any other country in the world'.[8]

Talboys put his sentiments into action by making a three-week visit to Australian Commonwealth and State ministers, officials, and industry leaders in March 1978. His tour was a personal and diplomatic success, and Talboys proved able to engage Australia's prime minister in a way that always eluded Muldoon. The result was a joint statement – the Nareen Declaration – with Prime Minister Malcolm Fraser pledging renewed efforts to liberalise trans-Tasman trade not only for bilateral benefit but also for 'the development of efficient industries that can meet international competition and provide increasing employment opportunities'. The two leaders encouraged the formation of the Australia-New Zealand Business Council as a stimulant 'to promote trade and to assist the development of *close economic relations* between the two countries'.[9]

The Nareen Declaration was followed by a meeting of trade and industry ministers in April 1979 to review progress. The ministers concluded that 'the institutional framework of NAFTA in today's circumstances is limited' and agreed 'to look to the newly formed Australia-New Zealand Business Council and others to probe and study how commercial activity between the two countries can be further extended'.[10] This was followed up by invitations to private sector business leaders to work with government officials to reach consensus on mutually beneficial modes and pace of liberalisation. A multi-faceted consultative process between the two governments and the principal producer associations thus gathered momentum that was to prepare political and business opinion for a substantial trade policy change with minimum political backlash, a circumstance unprecedented in the trans-Tasman relationship in 150 years.

However, as thinking and consulting raced ahead, the NAFTA relationship deteriorated. At the April 1979 NAFTA meeting, Australian ministers refused New Zealand requests for better access for whiteware appliances, carpets, forest products, and beans unless they got relief from import licensing, which New Zealand was reluctant to grant except on a token, case-by-case basis. Australia's Minister of Trade and Resources Doug Anthony is reported to have said, in exasperation, that he was no longer prepared to deal with the minutiae of peas and beans, horseshoes and harness bells.[11]

In New Zealand the political initiative was seized by Minister of Customs Hugh Templeton. In June 1979 Templeton gave a speech to the Wellington Chamber of Commerce in which he stressed the global context of New Zealand's trade. He pointed out the need to devise a new trans-Tasman trade arrangement culminating in a full free trade area, and pledged 'I have made it a personal priority to help break the impasse'.[12] This speech and Templeton's subsequent efforts are credited with creating a climate of opinion that moved New Zealand leaders to accept the nascent Closer Economic Relations concept.

Another boost was the meeting of Prime Ministers Muldoon and Fraser at Lusaka in August 1979. Their deliberations progressed beyond the issue of reciprocal trade access to encompass 'broad areas of economic cooperation', indicating Muldoon's acceptance of a wider focus. Their communiqué mandated a round of joint studies and meetings by officials in preparation for serious ministerial-level talks.[13] Nevertheless Muldoon, personally wary about closer ties with Australia, was much more cautious than Templeton, and in his Lusaka statement he hedged his approval of cooperation with Australia by stressing the necessarily long-term and gradual nature of any structural changes that might be set in motion thereby. As late as February 1981 he was still pessimistic about a new agreement, saying 'there is a slightly less than 50 per cent chance that this thing can be brought together'.[14]

In the bilateral negotiations that ensued, the Australians were prepared to move faster and farther than the New Zealanders. In New Zealand, Templeton urged rapid and radical progress, but Muldoon clung to reforming NAFTA, with Deputy Prime Minister Talboys and others agreeing with Templeton's long-term vision but echoing Muldoon's caution for the near term. Officials, likewise, displayed different emphases. Treasury and Reserve Bank officers were attracted to a comprehensive free trade arrangement consistent with their growing disenchantment with the interventionist and protectionist policies of the Muldoon Government, while Department of Trade and Industry officers were inclined to negotiate liberalisation on a sector-by-sector basis, consistent with their proposals to reform NAFTA from within.[15]

Industry leaders initially were cautious, particularly towards any weakening of import licensing or diminution of export incentives. But over time specific industries and specific firms began to take distinctive positions. Modern, export-oriented firms such as Fisher and Paykel, Feltex, and the Dairy Board eventually declared themselves in favour of CER. However, older textile and footwear firms, enterprises such as

Atlas and Holeproof and the electronics subsidiaries Thorn EMI and Autocrat were reliant on border controls to secure their market share domestically, and consequently resisted liberalisation.[16] Federated Farmers and the Bureau of Exporters and Importers favoured liberalisation, whereas in contrast the New Zealand Plastics Institute, the Pharmaceutical Manufacturers Association, the Textile and Garment Manufacturers Federation, and the Wine Institute opposed it. Over time the New Zealand Manufacturers Federation divided, with its Trade Group led by Ian Douglas favouring CER, and its regional affiliate, the Auckland Manufacturers Association, remaining sceptical.[17]

After the Muldoon–Fraser meeting at Lusaka in August 1979 each government had set up formal interdepartmental working parties on trans-Tasman economic cooperation. By the time the prime ministers next met in March 1980, the officials had worked out a set of principles to guide their negotiation on a 'closer economic relationship'.[18] These principles were: the freest possible movement of goods; an outward looking approach to trade; favourable treatment of each other's citizens; consideration of each other's interests; and frequent consultation.

The annex to the communiqué contained the essence of the nascent agreement: 'progressive liberalisation of trade across the Tasman'. Liberalisation was to be effected by making *all* goods duty free (some immediately, some after five years) except those on a deferred list, which was to be kept 'as short as possible'. This turned NAFTA's free-trade-list approach on its head by putting the burden of proof on any exception to the overarching principle of duty-free access. Also, the prime ministers reiterated that they were 'especially concerned' to make New Zealand-Australia cooperation 'provide a stronger base for the expansion of their economic and trade links with other countries'.

Six Difficult Issues

By the end of 1980 six issue-clusters preoccupied the negotiators. They may be summarised, with indications of how they were resolved, as follows.[19]

1 Tariff Reduction

Tariff schedules differed considerably, so the two parties decided to harmonise tariffs in three phases to protect vulnerable industries. First, all tariffs were to be reduced immediately to a maximum of 25 percent.

Second, tariffs were then to be reduced by five percentage points per year so that most tradeables would be duty free in five years. Third, products to be protected were to be put on a deferral list for further negotiations.

2   The Deferral List

Each side was tempted to defer tariff cuts as long as possible. The New Zealand negotiators assembled a lengthy list of sensitive products, one that initially included automobile and steel products, wines, agricultural chemicals, teas, wool grease and woollen yarn products, pineapples, aerated waters, and prepared vegetables.[20] The Australians submitted a shorter list in which dairy, horticulture, textile, plastic, and whiteware products predominated. Attention then shifted to when the deferral period should end, with Australia calling for 1992 and New Zealand holding out for an indefinite period for sensitive industries. They eventually converged on 1995.

3   Access

The Australian negotiators' prime objective was to gain better access for their manufactured exports to the New Zealand market; it was equally evident that New Zealand manufacturing leaders were reluctant to allow liberalised access lest their smaller firms be rendered unprofitable. Thus officials invested much negotiating effort in finding a way to satisfy Australian exporters and New Zealand manufacturers simultaneously.

4   Subsidies and Monopolies

New Zealand was committed to export incentives, including subsidies, but Australia objected strenuously to them. Agricultural support or stabilisation schemes that might produce distortions of trans-Tasman trade were also tackled by the negotiators. The New Zealand side was worried about subsidies, rebates, or price supports of Australian wheat, wine, tobacco, sugar, and canned fruit, whereas the Australian side was concerned about New Zealand's statutory monopoly marketing of dairy products (the Dairy Board), wheat (the Wheat Board), tropical fruits and grapes (Fruit Distributors Ltd), vegetables, and berryfruit. Eventually both subsidies and monopolies were surrendered.

5   Government Purchasing

New Zealand wanted to be included in the 'buy Australia' policies of the federal and state governments, administered through a complex system of rates of preference. While the Australian Federal Government proved sympathetic to New Zealand's position and speedily adjusted federal preferences so as not to discriminate against New Zealand suppliers, it was powerless to change state governments' purchasing policies. Despite persistent representations by New Zealand, this issue was not resolved until 1989.

6 Intermediate Goods

'Buy Australia' policies and higher tariffs encouraged Australian manufacturers to use materials and components ('intermediate goods') from Australian suppliers whose prices tended to be higher than world market prices. New Zealand manufacturers, by contrast, purchased intermediate goods from world markets at the cheapest available prices, so the final products tended to be less expensive than the Australian equivalent, and had potential to capture larger market shares if traded freely. Australian negotiators urged New Zealand to allow a compensation for this structural advantage, and used this rationale to defer tariff freeing of several sensitive products.

Negotiations Pause and Industries Adjust

In spite of substantial progress on the above issues by negotiators, in early 1981 the pace slowed. The reasons included Muldoon's distraction by the controversial South African rugby tour; his solicitousness of the Auckland Manufacturers Association's special pleading;[21] the general election in October 1981 which left the National Party with a majority of only one seat in Parliament; and the preoccupation of Australian ministers with elections in the key manufacturing and agricultural states of New South Wales, Victoria, and Tasmania.

Also governments were obliged to pause to give industry associations time to voice their anxieties, and adjust to the prospect of trade liberalisation. This was an astute move, and subsequently many industries began to play a creative role in the negotiations. In late 1981 and early 1982 the carpet, wine, dairy, and steel industry associations met with their trans-Tasman counterparts to draft industry agreements. These were essentially intra-industry orderly marketing arrangements brokered and later underwritten by the governments. The carpet agreement set up a 10-year phase-in schedule for Australian synthetic carpet access to the New Zealand market, thereby allowing the New Zealand carpet industry time to adjust and compensating it by allowing immediate free access for wool carpet to the Australian market. The wine agreement of 11 February 1982 was negotiated by the Wine Institute of New Zealand and the Australian Wine and Brandy Corporation; it eased New Zealand's adjustment by delaying the commencement of the tariff reduction schedule until 1986.

The dairy industry agreement of 13 April 1982 was worked out by a Joint Dairy Industry Consultative Committee representing the New Zealand Dairy Board, the Australian Dairy Corporation, the Australian Dairy Farmers Federation, and the Australian Dairy Products Federation and then embodied in a memorandum of understanding between the governments. The Committee pledged to consult in order to avoid undermining the returns or price structures of the industries, to avoid dumping or unfair trading practices, and to cooperate in international markets. New Zealand was to restrain its exports of cheddar to a pace no faster than total market growth in Australia and to avoid exporting milk or cream except in the event of a shortfall in Australia. Steel was dealt with in an Attachment noting that trade in deferred iron and steel products would be made compatible with CER 'as soon as practicable'.[22] These intra-industry arrangements, although less visible than the government-to-government negotiations, proved essential to making CER work.

The Remaining CER Issues Resolved

The two notable improvements the CER negotiators made over their NAFTA predecessors were first, to adopt the principle of free trade and second, to commit their nascent agreement to a timetable. All goods were to be traded duty-free unless explicitly excepted, and the exceptions in the deferral list were progressively to be eliminated. This reversed the NAFTA approach of excluding tradeables unless they were explicitly added to a duty-free list.

The major items that ended up on the deferral list were wine, wood products, carpet, iron and steel, whitegoods, furniture, and motor vehicles. In addition, Australia got interim protection from New Zealand fruit and sugar products while New Zealand was allowed interim protection from Australian wheat, wheat flour and wine. The New Zealand Government revoked the Wheat Board's monopoly in 1987 and deregulated the wheat market but Australia was slow to reciprocate in fruit and sugar. While this was irritating to New Zealand officials, Australian officials pointed out they were conceding access for New Zealand potatoes, textiles, and footwear, items previously blocked under NAFTA and earlier agreements. Trade in dairy products, a major concern of Australian dairy farmers, was addressed by a memorandum of understanding under which dairy trade was to be 'liberalised progressively under the CER in such as way as not to result in unfair competition between industries or disruption to industries of either country'.[23]

Worked out between officials in consultation with industry leaders, the procedure of setting sensitive products aside in the deferral list or dealing with them through side protocols and intra-industry agreements gave confidence to the negotiators that the essence of an agreement was within reach. In February 1982 Templeton visited Canberra to confer with Australian Federal ministers. This visit reinforced the position of Anthony, who by mid-May persuaded his Cabinet colleagues to back him. In July 1982 Anthony then travelled to Wellington where he and Muldoon announced they had reached broad agreement.[24]

A final flurry of negotiation took place in October 1982. A 'Heads of Agreement' was signed on 14 December 1982 and CER was brought into operation on the first day of 1983. The impending Australian election delayed the signing of a complete final agreement until 28 March 1983.[25] In Opposition Bob Hawke, a former trade union leader, had expressed doubts about trade liberalisation, and by implication, about CER. The delay in signing the final agreement allowed Hawke, who became Prime Minister in early March 1983, to reconsider the Agreement, which he did to his satisfaction. Hawke subsequently honoured CER, and presided over the 1988 review, but his enthusiasm never equalled that of his predecessor.

The 1988 CER Review

The 1984 general election that brought David Lange's Labour Government to power also brought Roger Douglas to the Finance portfolio and Mike Moore to the Foreign Affairs and Overseas Trade portfolios. Douglas subsequently initiated a radical economic reform programme characterised by sweeping deregulation and privatisation, and Moore backed the liberalisation of imports of goods, capital, and entrepreneurial expertise. Their policies bore fruit inasmuch as many New Zealand firms, now weaned from subsidies and thus increasingly competitive, gained market share in Australia. They decided to push CER further, to achieve full free trade in goods as soon as possible, to eliminate non-tariff and qualitative barriers and 'behind-the-border' trade distortions, and to extend free trade practices to new areas such as services.

The focal point for these innovations was the 1988 review, as provided for in the 1983 CER agreement. As the review date approached, New Zealand officials led by Mike Moore began clarifying their objectives, choosing focal issues, and sounding out their Australian counterparts. In November 1987 Prime Ministers David Lange and Bob Hawke met in the Bay of Islands, agreed on an agenda and timetable, and gave officials a mandate to commence negotiations. New Zealand's goals (set out in Table 1) were more numerous and ambitious than those of Australia, and New Zealand took the initiative in review negotiations, in contrast to the period 1978–82 when Australia took the initiative.

Table 1: New Zealand's initial goals for the 1988 CER review

- Extension of CER to meet New Zealand's free trade objectives.
- Consideration of how goods deferred in 1983 could be included.
- Removal of Australian bounties and subsidies that distorted trade.
- Harmonisation of laws, standards and regulations of laws.
- Widening of CER to include services, especially investment.
- Removal of anti-dumping provisions.
- Removal of the Memorandum of Understanding on dairy products.
- Joining the Australian states' National Preference Agreement at a rate of zero preference.
- The establishment of a formal body for managing disputes.

The Review Negotiations

Leaders and officials met with increasing frequency throughout late 1987 and into 1988. The conduct of the review required a year of intensive inter-departmental preparatory work, five rounds of negotiation between officials, a round of ministerial negotiation, and a final exchange of concessions prior to its signing. There were also extensive consultations with private sector interest groups.

Following the 1978-82 precedent, the negotiators started with a goal of complete liberalisation, then concentrated on isolating and minimising those issues that proved sensitive to either side. The technique of non-reciprocal concessions was employed, which differed from trade-offs because they were not synchronised one-for-one deals but rather concessions made by each side at varying times to keep the negotiation moving closer to the liberal ideal. The concessions made by each side are summarised in Table 2.[26]

However, not all of New Zealand's goals were achieved. In deference to Australia the review took the form not of a consolidated negotiation but a series of separate negotiations that eventually manifested themselves as three protocols, three exchanges of letters, two memoranda of understanding, two agreed minutes, and one communiqué.[27] Agreements on investment and a number of services sectors were not among them. On investment, Canberra argued that under the Nara Treaty with Japan, Australia could give no special access to New Zealand without giving it to Japan and other countries, which it was not inclined to do. On services, despite early assurances that initial exclusions were listed only *pro forma* pending consultation with state governments, the final Australian exclusion list remained longer than New Zealand's and included key sectors such as banking and insurance as well as air services and consultancy. New Zealand had to be content with securing a commitment to a review of the exclusions in 1990 in the hope of removing some of them at that time. Memoranda of understanding were signed to reduce technical barriers to trade and harmonise quarantine, customs and business laws.

While some last-minute concessions by New Zealand left the impression that Australia had gained the most, as one would predict of a more powerful negotiator facing a less powerful one, the comparison of Australia's concessions to those of New Zealand in Table 2 shows a fairly even exchange. And a comparison of outcomes with New Zealand's initial objectives listed in Table 1 shows a high rate of achievement. One may conclude that the New Zealand negotiators' strategies of clarifying their goals and principles and linking the key issues were effective. Goals, principles, and linkages were emphasised consistently and persistently, persuading Australian negotiators of their importance to New Zealand, and moving Australia to make concessions not earlier contemplated. As Australia's High Commissioner to New Zealand

Table 2: Concessions by New Zealand and Australia in the 1988 CER review negotiation

Concessions by New Zealand

- New Zealand agreed to removal of import monopolies.
- New Zealand agreed to a long list of Australian exceptions from the services liberalisation protocol.
- New Zealand agreed that its Export Market Development Tax Incentive would not apply to exports to Australia from 1 July 1990, and to phase out its non-performance export incentives.
- New Zealand signed a Record of Understanding that the New Zealand Dairy Board would act in relation to sales in Australia as it did in relation to sales in the New Zealand domestic market.
- New Zealand dropped its demand for a disputes settlement mechanism.
- New Zealand agreed to conclude the 1988 Review with a collection of declarations, protocols, and memoranda reflecting the diversity of the two sides' positions rather than a consolidated document reflecting the linkages New Zealand sought at the outset.

Concessions by Australia

- Australia agreed to the removal of anti-dumping provisions in the CER agreement, and to let domestic competition laws deal with any complaints regarding unfair competition.
- Australia agreed to remove two export subsidy programmes for goods exported to New Zealand and committed themselves to further discussion of motor vehicles.
- Australia agreed that bounties paid directly for exports to New Zealand would be removed by 1 July 1990.
- Australia agreed to long-term disciplines and consultations for industry assistance policies.
- Australia agreed to conclude a services protocol.
- The Australian Federal Government agreed to support the New Zealand bid to enter the National Preference Agreement at zero preference.

recently reflected, 'We have long been impressed by the sense of purpose and clear goals which New Zealand negotiators bring to all their bilateral exchanges with us'.[28] On the other hand, New Zealand negotiators proved flexible at the end of the negotiation process and conceded some issues of particular sensitivity to Australia, and thereby kept the negotiation moving forward to an outcome favourable to New Zealand on balance.

The Consolidation of CER

Deputy Prime Minister Geoffrey Palmer had taken the lead for New Zealand in the 1988 review negotiations, and when he succeeded David Lange as Prime Minister in 1989 he backed New Zealand's participation in the Australian ANZAC frigate programme. These initiatives, and Palmer's more sober personality in contrast to Lange's flamboyance, smoothed the way for rapid implementation of the 1988 review. Labour's days were numbered, and in October 1990 the National Party led by Jim Bolger won power. Nevertheless Bolger's government maintained the momentum and led CER past several milestones.

In 1989 the two governments freed all services trade not on the 1988 review exemption list. New Zealand subsequently freed trade in domestic air services, postal services, radio and television broadcasting, shortwave and satellite broadcasting, and stevedoring, while Australia freed banking, postal services, and construction, engineering, and general consultancy. New Zealand gained the benefit of equal treatment in bidding for contracts under the Australian states' National Preference Agreement, which was subsequently renamed the Government Procurement Agreement.

In 1990 full free trade in goods was achieved, five years ahead of schedule, and Prime Ministers Hawke and Palmer pledged to work for free trade in services by 1995. The two governments abolished antidumping measures, signed a draft Agreement on Standards, Accreditation, and Quality to make the certifications, credentials, and quality standards of each country acceptable to the other, and set in motion negotiations to harmonise business laws. Australia abolished export incentives and bounties applying to trans-Tasman trade, and in its turn New Zealand abolished import monopolies on apples, pears, and bananas.

In 1991 the governments agreed to set up a Joint Accreditation System to raise their quality management systems to international standards and provide for mutual recognition of each other's certifications of them. In 1992 the governments signed a Memorandum of Understanding to make progress towards a single trans-Tasman aviation market; this foreshadowed the freeing of trade in aviation services, a major sector still on the exemption list, by 1994.

During this period business laws were further harmonised by New Zealand legislation including the Reciprocal Enforcement of Judgements Amendment Act, the Securities Act, the Consumer Guarantees Act, and the Financial Reporting Act, each with its Australian counterpart, and by accession, along with Australia, to the international Patent Co-operation Treaty and the Convention on the Settlement of Investment Disputes.[29]

To this list of economic cooperation measures must be added one distinct from but often associated with CER: the Trans-Tasman Travel Arrangement. This agreement, formalised by the prime ministers in 1973, extended generous visiting, residence, and work privileges by the two governments to citizens of the other and thereby institutionalised a common labour market that had been evolving since the earliest days of European settlement. Analysts observed that by 1992 the array of CER and related agreements gave New Zealand and Australia the most comprehensive free trade area in the world, deeper and more extensive than the existing Canada-US or (then) prospective North American free trade areas.[30]

The 1992 Review of CER

It was in this buoyant context that the two governments undertook a third round of CER negotiations in 1992. The incontrovertible success of CER notwithstanding, the governments still wished to finish the job they had begun and to dismantle the 'second generation' barriers to free trade that had proved politically intractable during the first two rounds of 1978–82 and 1988. Urged by academic economists, free trade enthusiasts, and manufacturing, finance, and exporting association leaders such as those participating in the Australia-New Zealand Business Council and the New Zealand Business Roundtable, the governments decided to tackle these second generation issues.[31]

Moreover, there was uneasiness in New Zealand that the momentum of trans-Tasman economic cooperation would slow if Australian leaders, perceiving they were gaining less from CER than New Zealand, were to lose interest and turn increasingly to Asia. There were also concerns that reform-fatigued political leaders in both countries would succumb to rising electoral demands for welfare policies that might have protectionist or trade distorting consequences.[32] The obverse of this view was that governments had to take initiatives not only to complete the original CER agenda but also to project a vision for more ambitious cooperation, a vision that, for some commentators, should extend to a customs and monetary union in the longer term.[33] Paradoxically, it was not the failure of CER but its success and the ambition to achieve more that brought the two governments to the negotiating table in 1992.

It took 15 months of negotiations at officials and ministers levels to conclude the review in October 1992. The outcome was unspectacular but substantial. Three agreements were reached, on (1) rules of origin, (2) industry assistance, and (3) technical barriers to trade.[34] A fourth agreement was concluded the previous month, wherein each country's airlines were to be allowed after 1994 to compete in the other's domestic air services market. As Ansett already flew in New Zealand, this would bring symmetry to the aviation relationship.

Evidence of CER Achievements

By the early 1990s, with Closer Economic Relations having been in effect for nearly a decade, trade relations between New Zealand and Australia were enjoying vigorous and sustained growth. As a proportion of total trade, New Zealand's merchandise trade with Australia grew from an average of 13.9 per cent in the 1970s to 18.2 per cent in the period 1985–1993; Australia's trade with New Zealand grew from 4.1 per cent to 7.1 per cent in the same interval.[35] New Zealand did especially well; its merchandise exports to Australia rose steadily from NZ$1,037 million in 1983 to NZ$3,355 million in 1992. Australia's importance as a market rose from 13 percent to 20 percent of New Zealand's total exports, and the trade ratio improved from 2 to 1 in Australia's favour to near parity during the first decade of CER.[36] Australia became New Zealand's best trading partner, New Zealand became Australia's third best trading partner, and each strengthened its position as the other's best customer for manufactured goods.

In parallel developments, trans-Tasman investment grew nine-fold, from NZ$2 billion to NZ$18 billion during the period 1983 to 1991;

and intra-industry trade, inter-corporate alliances, trade in services, and movement of tourists and migrants also registered increases in the 1980s over corresponding figures for the 1970s, increases attributed directly or indirectly to CER.[37]

Diplomatic and Political Relations

Trans-Tasman diplomacy, if less visible than trade, was nonetheless substantial and a vital element of the relationship. The leaders had met at Imperial conferences, and consultation during World War II was close. The Canberra Pact of 1944 symbolised convergence of interests, and the two governments worked together to help draft the Charter and shape the new institutions of the United Nations. New Zealand's formal links with Australia were established in 1905 but remained at consular level until 1943 when the New Zealand High Commission was established in Canberra. Thereafter New Zealand's representation gradually increased to handle frequent consultations on a wide range of matters of joint concern, and by the late 1980s more New Zealand officials were based in Australia (47) than in the United States (36) or in Britain (33).[38]

By that time New Zealand and Australia had decades of experience in consulting closely on a wide variety of matters of common interest such as bilateral, regional, and global trade liberalisation, negotiations in the GATT, military deployments to Korea, Malaya, and Vietnam, participation in ANZUS, SEATO, United Nations and Commonwealth institutions, donation of economic aid through the Colombo Plan, and assistance to Pacific island countries through the South Pacific Commission and South Pacific Forum-affiliated agencies. The Ministry of Foreign Affairs Annual Report for 1985–86 stated 'New Zealand's single most important bilateral relationship is its relationship with Australia'.[39]

Relations between top leaders were not always warm. The differences in style, disagreement on policies, and raw personality clashes between Muldoon and Fraser, and between Hawke and Lange, were discussed openly in the media. For example, Hawke's view of New Zealand was coloured by the nuclear-free policy proclaimed by the Labour Government elected in July 1984, and by the personality of David Lange, the new Prime Minister, which he found erratic and shallow. 'I am unimpressed with the [nuclear-free] policy and with Lange', Hawke wrote of the time.⁴⁰ His January 1985 letter to Lange trying to dissuade him from the nuclear-free policy was leaked to the press and provoked a sharp retort as it was seen to interfere. Relations between the prime ministers were subsequently correct but never cordial, and it was not until Geoffrey Palmer became Prime Minister in 1989 and facilitated New Zealand's participation in the Australian Anzac frigate programme that relations between leaders began to warm.

Nevertheless converging interests transcended personalities, and fostered a growing number of meetings, made possible by frequent air services, of counterpart ministers, parliamentarians, officials, administrators, and specialists, who consulted by phone and fax between meetings. The prime ministers pledged to meet annually and in fact met seven times in the 18 months prior to April 1995. Foreign ministers met twice annually. In 1994 47 meetings of ministers and 59 meetings of high-ranking officials were convened.⁴¹ New Zealand ministers were invited to join their Australian federal and state counterparts in 26 different councils of ministers concerned with specialised topics ranging 'from cultural affairs to construction standards'.⁴² Members of select committees of the two national parliaments and the six state parliaments and officers of semi-governmental and autonomous agencies met periodically. Contacts have been institutionalised among private sector groups such as the Australia-New Zealand Business Council and the trade union councils, cultural associations including the Australia-New Zealand Foundation, and a host of professional and scientific bodies.⁴³

Defence Cooperation

The catalyst for closer trans-Tasman defence policy coordination was the decision by Britain in the late 1960s to initiate a withdrawal of most of its forces from theatres 'East of Suez'. This dire prospect cast in a new light New Zealand's and Australia's common experience in Malaya and Vietnam, their growing equipment compatibility, and Australia's ambition to develop a defence industry in which New Zealand was a potential participant. This had led the two Ministers of Defence in 1969 to negotiate a Memorandum of Understanding on Co-operation in Defence Supply.⁴⁴ The Memorandum first looked back to reaffirm the principles of the Canberra Pact of 1944⁴⁵, then pledged their (belated) implementation. The two governments agreed to improve information exchange; policy coordination; and standardisation, reciprocity, and mutual help in defence purchases and logistics. This was to be accomplished by periodic meetings of relevant ministers and officials and the co-opting of counterpart representatives in official committees. In 1970 the two prime ministers met and agreed that 'the co-ordination of effort in areas such as planning, purchasing, standardisation of equipment, training and operational procedures should be regarded as the first priority by the armed services of both countries'.[46]

In the later 1970s Cold War tensions increased, Soviet naval deployments in the Pacific escalated, and Soviet diplomatic and economic penetration of the South Pacific was attempted. As in the 19th century and again in the 1940s, the common threat drew Australia and New Zealand closer together. In 1976 the two prime ministers declared the need to improve defence cooperation. In 1977 the defence ministers resolved to revitalise the Australia-New Zealand Consultative Committee on Defence Co-operation (comprised of secretaries of defence and chiefs of staff), set up an Australia-New Zealand Defence Policy Group of officials, and hold regular ministerial meetings. New Zealand's 1978 *Defence Review* decried the fact that the two forces 'had developed in parallel but not always in a coordinated way'. Its drafters recalled that a framework for cooperation existed, noted that defence cooperation was a vital element of overall relations between the two countries, and forthrightly stated that 'the New Zealand relationship with Australia [is] the single most important strand in our international network'.[47]

This theme was echoed in the 1983 *Defence Review*, which was based on the concept that New Zealand and Australia constituted a single strategic entity, and was given weight by the negotiation of a new, more extensive Memorandum of Understanding on Closer Defence Logistic Co-operation that same year.[48] An inter-governmental Defence Supply Co-operation Working Group was established.

In 1985 the Labour Government's nuclear-capable ship ban provoked the United States to end military cooperation with New Zealand. While Australia's Prime Minister Bob Hawke deeply disapproved of the nuclear-free policy, and had a low opinion of David Lange's leadership ability, he lobbied United States leaders to avoid imposing economic sanctions. And he resolved to step up defence cooperation with New Zealand to compensate to some degree for the cut-off of US cooperation.[49] New Zealand responded to the opportunity and turned increasingly to

Australia for planning, exercises, training, and intelligence exchanges, and the presumption grew that New Zealand armed forces should buy Australian-made weapons and materiel. This was encouraged by Australia, which was willing to bear the bulk of the development costs in the interest of securing longer production runs, joint training and maintenance savings, and interoperability.

In the mid-1980s New Zealand purchased British light artillery pieces and Austrian assault rifles made under licence in Australia, and was engaged in joint procurement of a defence communications network. By the late 1980s the two governments had signed a total of 20 bilateral defence cooperation agreements. As well, New Zealand and Australia worked together in seven multilateral agreements on intelligence, maritime surveillance, exercises, defence science, and standardisation of equipment and operational procedures.[50]

Anzac Frigate Collaboration

In 1987 New Zealand joined an Australian feasibility study of a new class of light frigates, to be built in Australia. The projected cost of four ships for New Zealand – over NZ$2000 million – generated public, peace movement, and Labour Party opposition.[51] The Labour Government countered that major components of the total of 12 ships would be built in New Zealand, generating substantial income and jobs and transferring skills. Also, the Government made it plain that joint construction, equipping, training, and operating activities would reinforce New Zealand's economic, political, and defence ties with Australia. Defence and strategic arguments for acquiring new frigates to replace the four old ones were cited by the Government (and disputed by its opponents) but the economic and political arguments – jobs, technology transfer, CER, good relations with Australia, international credibility – were just as important in convincing sceptics in the government caucus that ultimately had to make the decision.

Australian leaders, particularly Minister of Defence Kim Beazley, echoed these arguments and, when New Zealand's participation appeared shaky, hinted that failure to participate would jeopardise CER. A sweetener was then offered in the form of substantial concessions on price and an invitation to bid for Australian defence contracts. In late 1989 the New Zealand Government, now led by Geoffrey Palmer, agreed to purchase two frigates with an option on two more at a price 30 per cent less than Australia's first estimate in 1986. In essence, Australia was to bear all design, development, and setting-up costs, and New Zealand had to pay only for the material and work on the two ships. In addition, the Australian prime contractor was required to contract out 20 per cent of the work to New Zealand-based firms, valued at over NZ$500 million, and to double that amount if New Zealand purchased the second two frigates. New Zealand also got access to valuable technology and defence contracting opportunities in Australia.

As David Lange later revealed, maintaining the special relationship – economic and political as well as defence – with Australia was uppermost in the minds of New Zealand Labour ministers when they decided to go ahead against considerable domestic political opposition. Since then sceptical queries raised by the Parliamentary Select Committee on Foreign Affairs and Defence have been answered satisfactorily as New Zealand firms, because of their lower costs, have been able to win Anzac Frigate contracts well in excess of the agreed minimum, and the project has given a visible boost to the engineering industry and the economy of the port city of Whangarei.[52]

Closer Defence Relations (CDR) 1991

By 1991 trans-Tasman defence co-operation had progressed well, and New Zealand's new Prime Minister Jim Bolger had established a close rapport with Prime Minister Bob Hawke. The annual meeting of the Australia-New Zealand Defence Consultative Council became the occasion to deepen further the defence relationship. After a review of existing and potential links, New Zealand Minister of Defence Warren Cooper, at the suggestion of Secretary of Defence Gerald Hensley, proposed a defence counterpart to CER, to be called Closer Defence Relations or CDR. That term was accepted by Australian Minister of Defence Robert Ray.[53] The objective of CDR was to maximise the combined efficiency and effectiveness of the defence forces of the two countries. This was to be accomplished by the following six means: institutionalised consultations on strategy and capabilities; development of complementary force structures; enhancement of interoperability; coordination and consultation on procurement, resources, and contingency plans; cooperation on training, base and infrastructure support; and establishment of a common methodology for costing CDR arrangements.[54]

In 1992 a working committee appointed to refine the CDR concept reported that the two governments were already conducting 137 joint defence and military activities, ranging from the Anzac Frigate Project and the long-term deployment of New Zealand A-4 Skyhawks to the Australian base at Nowra, to a host of consultations on technical matters. In 1992 the defence establishments negotiated eight further initiatives to the CDR list, including new planning, administration, training, and deployment activities[55] and in 1994 discussed how New Zealand forces could be used in the event of an attack on the continent of Australia.[56]

With the exception of the debate over acquisition of the Anzac frigates, and objections by groups opposed to armed forces on general grounds, CDR has not been controversial. The Defence Committee of Enquiry poll of 1986 found that 68 per cent of New Zealanders favoured an alliance with Australia (52 per cent favoured an alliance with the United States, and only 35 per cent with Britain).[57] The same poll found 70 per cent supported defence cooperation with Australia 'in all circumstances' and an additional 25 per cent supported it 'in some circumstances'. Queried about the nature of that cooperation, 63 per cent wanted New Zealand forces to be independent but compatible, and 26 per cent favoured complete integration with Australia's defence arrangements. Finally, 81 per cent believed New Zealand should assist Australia in 'all' or 'most' circumstances if Australia were attacked. In 1991, 75 per cent of New Zealanders were confident that Australia would help if New Zealand were threatened.[58]

Conclusion

By the 1990s a relationship that had been marked by mutual disregard in the earlier part of the century had been converted into one of the closest in the world. Building on NAFTA's modest beginnings in 1965, and proceeding through the CER agreement of 1983 and the two reviews of 1988 and 1992, the two governments had succeeded in liberalising and deepening bilateral economic linkages to a degree their predecessors could hardly have imagined. At present they preside over a vibrant trans-Tasman intercourse that includes not only free trade in goods but also unimpeded exchanges in services and labour, in which the two countries are increasingly viewed as a single market. Although Australia refused to enter into a formal agreement freeing investment, in practice it has encouraged capital from New Zealand, and few practical barriers exist.

Political ties have perforce become more intimate, with joint meetings of ministers initially in the economic sectors, and subsequently in all policy sectors, becoming the norm. Defence ties have widened and deepened correspondingly, symbolised by the Closer Defence Relations announcement of 1991 and manifested even before that date by frequent consultations, joint weapons purchases, and long-term deployments of personnel and units to each other's territory.

Nevertheless merger, whether of currencies, political institutions, or armed forces, is not currently on the agenda of either government. There is no question of one country submerging its culture, identity, or way of life in the other. The future of the trans-Tasman relationship may be summed up by the word 'harmonisation'. That is, the governments and leading associations of each country are committed increasingly to making their laws, policies, procedures and practices harmonious with those of the other even as they continue to differ in title, idiom, and detail. Guided by its own distinctive traditions, institutions, and icons, each country will evolve towards its own destiny. But the evolution of each will be shaped in part by the other.

Notes

1. Alan and Robin Burnett, *The Australian and New Zealand Nexus* (Canberra, 1978), p.112–14.
2. Bruce Brown, '"Foreign Policy is Trade": Trade is Foreign Policy. Some principal New Zealand trade policy problems since the Second World War', Ann Trotter (ed.), *Fifty Years of New Zealand Foreign Policy Making: Papers from the 28th Foreign Policy School, 1993* (Dunedin, 1993), p.85.
3. The following passage draws from Burnett, *Australia and New Zealand Nexus*, ch.4.
4. Burnett, *Australia and New Zealand Nexus*, ch.4, provides a thorough and detailed account of NAFTA.
5. P. J. Lloyd, *Economic Relationships between Australia and New Zealand* (Canberra, 1976), p.81.
6. Sir Frank Holmes, 'Australia–New Zealand Relations: Time for a Commitment to Progress', in *New Zealand Foreign Affairs Review* (hereafter *NZFAR*), July–December 1979, p.28.
7. Colin James, *A New Path: The Tasman Connection* (Wellington, 1982), p.42.
8. 'New Zealand in a Changing World – The Regional Scene', in *NZFAR*, July–September 1977, p.28.
9. Text of the Nareen Declaration of 19 March 1978 is found in *NZFAR*, January–March 1978, pp.27–9. The emphasis on *close economic relations* is mine.

10 *NZFAR*, January–June 1979, p.18.
11 Brown, 'Foreign Policy is Trade', p.87.
12 James, *A New Path*, p.44.
13 *NZFAR*, July–December 1979, p.49.
14 *New Zealand Herald*, 10 March 1981.
15 Ted Woodfield, Assistant Secretary of Trade and Industry from 1979, and later High Commissioner to Australia, recalls that Trade and Industry was not averse to trade liberalisation. Five years previously its officials had proposed putting all goods save exceptions in Schedule A (freely traded). Interview and written communication, February, March 1995.
16 Industry opinions are charted in Christopher Bruce Cronin, *Close Encounters Over C.E.R.: Auckland Manufacturers and Government at the End of the Seventies* (MA thesis, University of Auckland, 1986).
17 *Auckland Star*, 4 December 1979 and *New Zealand Herald*, 28 December 1979.
18 *NZFAR*, January–March 1980, p.16.
19 Ministry of Foreign Affairs, 'A/NZ CER: Joint Working Party Meeting: Wellington 7–10 October 1980: Overview Paper', 3 October 1980, MFAT 40/4/1 Pt.30, and *Australia/New Zealand Closer Economic Relations: Report by Joint Working Parties* (Canberra, 26 November 1980).
20 Cabinet Economic Committee Minutes, 3 October 1980, and Annex 1, MFAT 40/4/1, Pt.31.
21 Hugh Templeton believes that if it had not been for Muldoon's conservatism, oversensitivity to sectoral interests, and distraction by political events of the day, ANZCERTA could have been completed in two or three years instead of four. Personal communication 7 April 1995. Also see Templeton's *All Honourable Men: Inside the Muldoon Cabinet 1975–84* (Auckland, 1995), ch.13.
22 Texts of the carpet, wine, dairy and steel agreements may be found in *Proposed Arrangements for a Closer Economic Relationship between Australia and New Zealand June 1982* (Wellington, 1982), pp.28–36 and annexes to *New Zealand Australia Closer Economic Relations Trade Agreement (with Exchange of Letters)* Canberra, 28 March 1983 [in force 1 January 1983], New Zealand Treaty Series 1983, No.1, Ministry of Foreign Affairs, Wellington, 1983.
23 Peter J. Lloyd, 'Australia-New Zealand Trade Relations: NAFTA to CER', in Keith Sinclair (ed.), *Tasman Relations: New Zealand and Australia 1788–1988* (Auckland, 1987), p.157.
24 *NZFAR*, July–September 1982, p.24.
25 *NZFAR*, April–June 1983, p.41.
26 Officials involved were reluctant to see the negotiations in terms of concessions traded, preferring to see them as adaptations in response to reasoned arguments.
27 These agreements are listed in Steve Hoadley, *New Zealand and Australia: Negotiating Closer Economic Relations* (Wellington, 1995), p.80.
28 HE R. J.Greet, 'Australia and New Zealand Economic Relations: A Current Perspective', talk to the Prudential Breakfast, Wellington, 5 April 1995, p.12 of speech notes.
29 'Progress in Harmonisation of Trans-Tasman Business Law: Joint Statement on 1 September by the Australian Attorney-General and the New Zealand Minister of

Justice', in *Ministry of External Relations and Trade Record*, September 1992, p.40.
30 For a comparison of CER to the Canadian–US Free Trade Agreement see Ramesh Thakur, 'Bilateral Trade in Services', in *Australian Journal of International Affairs*, November 1991. The European Union was more comprehensive but not comparable to the trans-Tasman arrangement because it was a customs union partially governed by supra-national institutions.
31 'A Long Term Strategy for the New Zealand Australia Economic and Trade Relationship', Australia–New Zealand Business Council discussion paper, Wellington, 1991.
32 Chris Eichbaum and Rolf Gerritsen, 'The Impossible Politics of CER: The Prospects for the ANZ Closer Economic Relations Agreement in 1993 and Beyond', in *Australian Outlook*, August 1993; Ted Woodfield, 'A Trans-Tasman Community?', in *New Zealand International Review* (hereafter *NZIR*), July–August 1994, pp.18–21.
33 Peter J. Lloyd, *The Future of CER: A Single Market for Australia and New Zealand* (Wellington, 1991).
34 For details see Hoadley, *New Zealand and Australia*, pp.86–7. For a consolidated list and discussion of CER agreements see *A Guide to CER* (Wellington, 1995) and *Closer Economic Relations* (Canberra, 1997).
35 Stephen Edwards and Sir Frank Holmes, *CER: Economic Trends and Linkages* (Wellington, 1994), p.150.
36 *New Zealand and Australia: Closer Economic Relations*, Ministry of External Relations and Trade Information Bulletin No.42, Wellington, May 1993, p.9; Edwards and Holmes, *CER*, p.150.
37 Edwards and Holmes, *CER*, pp.138, 146, 148; 'Trans-Tasman Trade in Services 1982–1992' and 'Trans-Tasman Total Direct Investment Stock 1987–1993', Ministry of Foreign Affairs and Trade, MFAT Australia Division, information sheets, Wellington, August 1994). Also on achievements of CER see Sir Frank Holmes, *The Trans-Tasman Relationship* (Wellington, 1996) and *Impact of the CER Trade Agreement*, Bureau of Industry Economics Report 95/17, Canberra, September 1995.
38 *New Zealand Representatives Overseas*, Wellington, July 1988.
39 *Report of the Ministry of Foreign Affairs for the Year Ended 31 March 1986* (Wellington, 1986), p.6.
40 Bob Hawke, *The Hawke Memoirs* (Port Melbourne, 1994), p.265; also see pp.279–86.
41 Figures compiled from *The Digger's Diary: A Calendar of ANZAC Events*, MFAT, Wellington, monthly issues for 1994.
42 PM Geoffrey Palmer, 'New Zealand and Australia: Beyond CER', in *NZIR*, July–August 1990, p.4.
43 *The ANZAC Connection: Australia New Zealand Foundation* (Canberra, 1980).
44 The text of the Memorandum, and discussion of other aspects of Australian–New Zealand military cooperation, is found in Desmond Ball (ed.), *The ANZAC Connection* (Sydney, 1985). Also see Burnett, *Australia and New Zealand Nexus*, ch.3.
45 The Canberra Pact 1944 pledged trans-Tasman defence consultation and

cooperation, particularly in the South Pacific. For details see Hoadley, *New Zealand and Australia*, pp.109–10. For text see *New Zealand Foreign Policy Statements and Documents 1943–1957* (Wellington, 1972).
46 *Australian Defence Report 1970* (Canberra, 1970), p.13.
47 *Defence Review 1978*, p.17.
48 Text in Ball (ed.), *ANZAC Connection*, pp.137–9.
49 Hawke, *Hawke Memoirs*, pp.284–5.
50 Agreements listed and discussed by Alan Burnett, *The A-NZ-US Triangle* (Canberra, 1988).
51 The following passages on the ANZAC Frigate issue draw on Alan Burnett and Peter Jennings, 'The Future of Australia/New Zealand Relations' in *The Australian Quarterly*, Autumn 1989, pp.33–49; Peter Jennings, 'Australia, New Zealand and the ANZAC Ship Project', unpublished paper presented to the New Zealand Political Studies Association Conference, Dunedin, May 1990; Stephen Keys, *The ANZAC Ship Project in New Zealand* (MA thesis, University of Auckland, 1990); and articles in *NZIR*, issues of January–February and March–April 1989.
52 Report of the Foreign Affairs and Defence Committee on the Inquiry into the Policies Related to the Execution of the ANZAC Ship Project, House of Representatives, Second Session, Forty-third Parliament, Wellington, 1992.
53 'Presentation to CASEM 92: Closer Defence Relations' (unpublished Ministry of Defence briefing paper); Minister of Defence Warren Cooper, 'Current Issues in the Defence of New Zealand' (Speech to RNZAF Command and Staff College, 3 October 1991); Ramesh Thakur, 'Closer Defence Relations: Costs and Benefits to New Zealand', in Robert A. Hall (ed.), *Australia New Zealand Closer Defence Relations* (Canberra, 1993), pp.110–11. Also see articles in Hall by Stuart Woodman, p.9, and remarks by Air Vice Marshal Robin Klitscher, p.144.
54 'Presentation to CASEM 92: Closer Defence Relations' and other briefing papers and press releases kindly made available by New Zealand Ministry of Defence. Also see Thakur, 'Bilateral Trade', pp.107–8.
55 Ministry of Defence briefing papers; also see Thakur, 'Bilateral Trade', pp.113–14 and Peter Jennings, 'Achieving Closer Defence Relations with New Zealand', in Hall, *Australia New Zealand*, p.58.
56 'NZ Strengthens Defence Link with Australia', in *New Zealand Herald*, 30 July 1994.
57 *Defence and Security: What New Zealanders Want*, Defence Committee of Enquiry Report, Wellington, July 1986, p.41.
58 *The Bulletin*, 27 August 1991, p.19. Only 25 percent of Australians were confident that New Zealand would come to their help.

ANN TROTTER

An Evolving Relationship: New Zealand and Japan

'THERE IS NO COUNTRY IN ASIA WITH WHICH NEW ZEALAND has wider contacts than Japan' was the official claim in 1968.[1] It was a claim which was equally valid in 1990. By that time, however, the nature and quality of the relationship between New Zealand and Japan had changed. A new maturity, due in part to the fact that the relationship had been subjected to tensions in the 1970s and 1980s, was evident. The relationship was also affected by changes in the world scene over the period 1972–1990. These altered the balance between Europe, the United States and countries in the Asia-Pacific region. Japan was the so-called 'engine of growth' in the Asia-Pacific and as such was of vital importance to New Zealand.

Notwithstanding New Zealand's claim of 'wide contacts' with Japan, trade was at the heart of the relationship in 1972. Such interests as New Zealand and Japan shared in the political field, even the fact that both countries were allies of the United States, appeared unremarkable and were unlikely to penetrate the consciousness of the New Zealand and Japanese publics. Events in the mid 1970s and late 1980s demonstrated, not surprisingly, that New Zealand was without a constituency in Japan and had no leverage with the Japanese Government. This was a lesson for New Zealand politicians in particular and the New Zealand public in general. Clearly, if the relationship was to develop, New Zealand politicians, businessmen and the public had to learn how to communicate effectively with Japan and the Japanese people. The 1970s and 1980s were, as a result, marked by efforts in both the public and private sector in New Zealand to increase people to people contacts, promote understanding of one another's culture, build a constituency and broaden the basis of New Zealand's contacts with Japan.

As New Zealand sought to broaden the basis of the bilateral relationship in the 1980s, changes in the balance of power were taking place as the United States looked to reduce its responsibilities in the western Pacific. The political and economic environment in the Asian-Pacific region was changing and Japan was taking a crucial part in the promotion of these changes. The concept of a Pacific Basin Community was one which had had advocates in Japan since the 1960s. Set up in 1967 the Pacific Basin Economic Cooperation Committee (to be renamed the Pacific Basin Economic Council [PBEC] in 1971) was driven as a result of the initiative of Japanese and Australian businessmen. New Zealand business gave the organisation 'most favourable support'.[2] In 1972 Sir Keith Holyoake, then Minister of Foreign Affairs, speaking in Tokyo noted the importance of the Pacific Basin and the opportunities it presented. 'It is a setting,' he said, ' in which Japan, New Zealand and their friends must consider what they can do together and with others'.[3] The government was not involved in PBEC but the 1980s saw the development of a number of similar organisations through which a greater sense of community between governments, officials, businessmen and academics of the region was promoted. By 1990 New Zealand had become a keen advocate of greater cooperation between countries in the region. New Zealand was aware of the importance of Japan's role as a major economic force, as a supporter of the Pacific Basin Community concept and as the power whose importance to the United States would ensure American interest and participation in these developments. In 1990 Japan had become a global player which gave New Zealand's diplomatic relations with it a significance beyond questions of bilateral trade and a complexity and maturity not evident in 1972.

Diplomatic style

New Zealand had practised the techniques of 'patient diplomacy' in its relations with Japan in the 1960s. New Zealand officials were aware that no 'sanctions and baits' at New Zealand's disposal were sufficient to push Japan into a politically drastic alteration of policy, particularly that protectionist agricultural policy which was of special interest to New Zealand. It was recognised that New Zealand was most likely to obtain concessions in the wake of heavy-weight pressure on Japan from the United States. Up to the mid 1970s a policy of patient pressure on

Japan suited the style of New Zealand governments, both National and Labour. When Japanese Prime Minister Tanaka visited New Zealand in October 1974, the first Japanese Prime Minister to visit since 1967, the Labour Prime Minister, Bill Rowling, stressed that New Zealand looked to Japan as a natural, a growing and a permanent market for New Zealand products and referred to the ready understanding which had developed at the governmental and official levels. In their joint statement the Prime Ministers expressed satisfaction in the 'close and rewarding relationship' between their two countries.[4]

The even tenor of the relationship was, however, disturbed in that year. Japan banned all beef imports. It was a move designed to protect prices received by Japanese beef producers. New Zealand had never been more than a residual supplier of beef to Japan, the major suppliers being the United States and Australia, but the total ban on beef coincided with a drop in mutton and lamb sales and in the sale of wool and timber. This downturn was the result of the effects of the 1973 'oil shock' in Japan. In the financial year 1974–75 New Zealand had a balance of payments deficit with Japan.

In October 1975 Robert Muldoon, previously Minister of Finance, became Prime Minister (and remained Minister of Finance). He claimed a particular interest in international finance and trade and considered a direct style particularly appropriate in dealing with these matters. As Minister of Finance in the 1960s he had experience of working with Japanese officials in setting up the Asian Development Bank and believed that he understood the Japanese negotiating style. His unsubstantiated claim was that while his hardline 'point blank' approach might not be 'the Japanese way' it had worked in the past, specifically in the case of the negotiations relating to the establishment of an aluminium smelter at Bluff in which the Japanese had invested in 1968.[5] Muldoon's outspoken style was to make a distinctive imprint on New Zealand foreign policy in general and on New Zealand-Japanese relations in particular. This was demonstrated most forcibly in the period 1976-1978 over the question of access to New Zealand's Exclusive Economic Zone (EEZ).

In 1976, following decisions taken at the Law of the Sea Conference, it was decided that New Zealand would extend its Exclusive Economic Zone to 200 miles. The New Zealand fishing industry could not exploit this resource fully and the government was prepared to assign the surplus to states, such as Japan, which had been fishing in New Zealand waters. In New Zealand access to the EEZ was now seen as a negotiating card by which the total economic relationship with Japan might be improved. Prime Minister Muldoon visited Japan in 1976 and sought 'overall economic cooperation' and a cessation of the 'arbitrary exclusions' which were causing New Zealand so much difficulty. Muldoon warned that without long-term import agreements Japan would not be assured of access to the EEZ after 1977. What followed became known as the 'fish-for-beef' controversy although New Zealand's interest was always in 'steady and predictable access' for all its agricultural exports to Japan.[6]

Muldoon's tough talk in Japan won support in New Zealand where the idea of linking fishing access to agricultural exports as a lever to open the Japanese market appealed. But through 1976 and 1977 both the Prime Minister's 'hardline' approach and combative posturing, and the more diplomatic lobbying of the Minister of Foreign Affairs and his officials, failed to persuade Japanese officials into the negotiating arena. Japan would not recognise 'linkage' between Japanese agricultural import policies and access to New Zealand's economic zone.

In the long run, the Japanese market for New Zealand fish was more important than was the right to fish in New Zealand waters to Japan. In July 1978 New Zealand and Japanese officials developed a formula by which New Zealand gave Japan fishing access and Japan agreed to take account of 'New Zealand's interests'. There was no specific reference to improving the level of access to the Japanese market for New Zealand agricultural products which the Prime Minister had demanded. Face was saved, however, when, following approval of a joint communiqué, a New Zealand statement was issued implying that the Prime Minister's intervention had resulted in an improved agreement. The New Zealand–Japanese Fisheries agreement was signed on 18 August 1978. Japan had secured fishing access, New Zealand had received no assurances for an improved 'overall economic relationship'. Nevertheless New Zealand's ambassador in Japan concluded that the episode had stimulated Tokyo's awareness of a small partner's trading interests.[7] From 1978 annual consultations between officials on fisheries and on beef, and six monthly dairy supply issues consultations began to be held.

This episode was not a happy one for New Zealand but, apart from being an educative experience for both parties, at a practical level its outcome was not unimportant since it brought another dimension to contacts taking place at officials level. Foreign Ministry officals had been involved in annual talks on political matters since 1967. Talks about fish, beef and dairy exports and access had now been added. In 1980 annual talks on international economic questions were instituted,[8] and from 1986, regular talks on issues likely to arise at the United Nations General Assembly took place. From 1987, to these talks was added annual consultation on regional overseas development aid (ODA) questions.[9] The result was that by 1990 New Zealand had an unusual and, for a small country, remarkable consultative network with Japan, a global economic power.

Towards better understanding

Though tensions were to recur over particular issues in the late 1980s, the fish-for-beef controversy was the most spectacular. In general New Zealand governments were at pains to promote the relationship and accepted that ministers and officials had to go to Japan saying the same kinds of thing about New Zealand's desire for better access for its agricultural products every time. On the occasion of Japanese Prime Minister Nakasone's visit to New Zealand in 1985 the New Zealand Prime Minister, David Lange, spoke in terms designed to show friendship and win cooperation. He told Mr Nakasone:

> You are our biggest customer for exports and Japan is also the major source of our imports. . . . In short we like doing business with you . . . New Zealand and Japan share many common interests internationally and in the Asian and Pacific regions.[10]

While it is true that New Zealand and Japan share 'common interests internationally', their perception of the relative importance of these interests inevitably was and is different. New Zealand's focus on the importance of its trade with Japan tended to blind the politicians and the public to wider issues affecting the New Zealand–Japan relationship and to the impact which New Zealand policy in relation to a third country might have on its relationship with Japan. Two episodes in the late 1980s demonstrated that, in spite of progress in understanding undoubtedly made in the previous two decades, there were still areas of common interest internationally where more effective communication between New Zealand and Japan was necessary.

In both New Zealand and Japan there existed active anti-nuclear and environmental lobbies. Governments in both New Zealand and Japan were aware that they must take account of the interests of these lobbies but the influence accorded them by their respective governments was quite different. After the fence-mending exercises of the early 1980s New Zealand's anti-nuclear policy and concern for environmental issues related to fishing were to cause unlooked-for tension between New Zealand and Japan.

Among New Zealand officials, New Zealand's relationship with the United States through ANZUS was recognised as a link which might help increase New Zealand's standing in Japanese eyes. Japan and New Zealand had both signed treaties with the United States and therefore had an ally in common.[11] Alliance with the United States was felt to enhance New Zealand's status as an advanced Pacific country to be consulted by Japan in matters relating to regional organisation. When Japanese Prime Minister Ohira visited New Zealand in 1980 the concept of Pacific Basin Community, then in its infancy, was discussed. In 1980 Japanese Maritime Self Defence Forces participated in the naval exercise, RIMPAC 80, with United States, Australian, New Zealand and Canadian vessels. In some circles the suggestion of a JANZUS alliance was made.[12]

In 1985 the New Zealand Government adopted a nuclear free policy. It rejected the American policy to 'neither confirm nor deny' the nuclear status of its vessels and refused to grant access to New Zealand ports to American warships on that basis. This made for strained relations between New Zealand and the United States. The United States declared that ANZUS was 'inoperable'. This had its effects on New Zealand's relations with Japan where the government had to take account of the domestic anti-nuclear lobby. Nuclear questions and the access of United States vessels to Japanese ports were sensitive political issues. But while Japanese governments had to be aware of their anti-nuclear lobby, they had also to be aware of the sensitivities of their most important ally and trading partner, the United States. The Japanese Government did not welcome attention drawn to New Zealand's anti-nuclear policies and was careful to distance itself from New Zealand on these questions at that time.

On the other hand as the American presence was reduced in the South Pacific, Japan – in response to the rather delicate situation, and with United States concurrence – became increasingly active in the area. In particular, increasing amounts of Japanese development aid became available to the small island states whose welfare had always been regarded of concern to New Zealand. In 1987 the so-called Kuranari doctrine set out the framework for Japanese foreign policy in the South Pacific and served notice that the Japanese Government wished to increase its political, diplomatic and economic presence in partnership with the countries of the area. New Zealand responded positively to these developments, Prime Minister David Lange stating that the Government 'welcomed' Japan's intention to play a greater role in the region. He offered New Zealand's cooperation in exploring constructive avenues.[13] Annual consultations between New Zealand and Japan on overseas development aid questions were established.

The environmental issue of the late 1980s concerned driftnet fishing by distant water fishing nations in southern oceans. This method of fishing, which involved setting a long net to drift with the currents of the ocean, was seen in New Zealand as especially destructive. Tighter restrictions in the northern fishing waters had, however, forced vessels south to target southern albacore tuna and threatened fisheries in 200 mile zones in the South Pacific. This issue was really one for the South Pacific as a whole and was a general economic and environmental issue but New Zealand and Japan were the main players. When agreement between the affected coastal states and the distant water fishing nations could not be reached, New Zealand, to the irritation of the Japanese who considered New Zealand was sacrificing bilateral relations for domestic political considerations, publicised and politicised the issue in an address by the Prime Minister, Geoffrey Palmer, to the General Assembly of the United Nations. This move, in October 1989, was an effective ploy by New Zealand in its own interests and on behalf of small island nations. It was strongly supported by the United States. A UN resolution, of which New Zealand and the United States were the principal sponsors, provided for a moratorium on all driftnet fishing by 1992. Japan announced in July 1990 that it would comply by 1991.[14] This was seen in New Zealand as a major concession and, in recognition of the fact that more frequent and better consultation between the two governments might have avoided or ameliorated the tension in the relationship caused by this issue, efforts were made to re-establish the relationship on a firm footing. Prime Minister Palmer visited Japan in

July 1990 and an agreement was reached for more frequent ministerial consultations and for the initiation of a number of projects in the environmental research area.[15]

Trade Development

By 1990 Japan was taking 18 per cent of New Zealand's exports, was providing 18 per cent of its imports and had become New Zealand's second trading partner after Australia. The two-way trade was worth more than NZ$5 billion.[16] The rising importance of Japan to the New Zealand economy owed much to the improved access to the Japanese market for New Zealand products which began in 1985. Then, in response to external pressure to liberalise its markets, the Japanese government announced a comprehensive series of market-opening measures. Tariffs were reduced on a few products of some interest to New Zealand – sphagnum moss, casein glues, prepared crustaceans and molluscs, and wine – but not New Zealand's major agricultural exports. Some import procedures were also simplified. A review of building procedures that year approved radiata pine for construction framing, a development for which New Zealand had long been lobbying.[17]

As members of the General Agreement on Tarriffs and Trade (GATT) Japan and New Zealand were committed to tariff reduction and New Zealand's particular interest was of course in improved access for its agricultural exports to Japan and elsewhere. In 1986 the Uruguay Round of Multilateral Trade Negotiations was launched. This became a major platform for New Zealand to make its case. With other GATT members Japan agreed to address the issue of its import controls on agricultural products. But the resistance of the powerful rural lobby in Japan meant that this politically sensitive question could not be addressed easily or comprehensively. Though access had improved for radiata pine, certain horticultural products, fish and dairy products by 1990, restrictions remained. Furthermore, competition from Chile in areas such as kiwifruit and other fruits and from dumping of subsidised dairy products (notably cheese by the EEC) meant that New Zealand could not take the more open Japanese market for granted.[18]

All the same, in this period rising affluence and changing tastes in Japan created new opportunities for New Zealand to exploit. Tourism became an important source of both foreign exchange and people to people contact. Between 1980 and 1987 New Zealand as a destination grew rapidly in popularity among Japanese tourists. The range of Japanese tourists diversified and came to include honeymooners, young single women and older retired travellers – the latter the so-called 'silver' market. By 1990 Japan had become New Zealand's third biggest tourist market with 108,000 Japanese entering New Zealand – 92,000 on holiday, the rest on business or to visit family and friends. Spending on average approximately $400 per day, these were New Zealand's most valuable tourists.[19] One result of this was to encourage Japanese investment in tourist-related enterprises such as hotels, restaurants and golf courses.[20] Both tourism and trade were boosted by the growth in direct air services between the two countries. The first air agreement was signed in 1980 and by 1990 there were seven direct flights per week.

From the mid 70s the New Zealand–Japan trade was usually in New Zealand's favour. New Zealand's principal export earners in 1990 were aluminium ingots, fish, wool and kiwi fruit. Japan also took logs, paper pulp, beef, sheepmeat, dairy produce, iron ore, fresh fruit, vegetables, flowers and, for the first time, ice cream. From Japan, New Zealand took motor vehicles, machinery, communications and electrical equipment.

Investment and Business

The United Kingdom finally having entered the European Economic Community on 1 January 1973, New Zealand businesses were more than ever anxious to establish contacts in Japan. In 1974 the Japan–New Zealand Business Council (JNZBC) was established and the first New Zealand–Japanese businessmen's conference was held in Tokyo that year. Thereafter meetings were held annually, alternately in New Zealand and Japan. The aim of the Council in New Zealand was to educate New Zealand businessmen, politicians and organisations about the benefits of doing business with Japan. The Council tried to ensure that businessmen and politicians had adequate briefings when they visited Japan on investment and business missions, sought to encourage investment by equity participation or joint venture, and became a useful forum for airing issues in the bilateral relationship as well as exploring areas for cooperation outside two-way trade. In 1974 the large Japanese companies, accustomed to international trade, were looking for investments through which they might gain competitive advantage. Their overseas investment was resource-oriented. The small and medium sized companies, whose often innovative technology might have been valuable to New Zealand, were not attuned to foreign trade at that time.[21]

In 1974 Japanese companies had already invested in New Zealand in aluminium production (the Bluff smelter) and forestry. Beyond this, these large companies were not interested in investing in New Zealand partly because of the tight government policies on overseas investment in both New Zealand and Japan. In the next decade regulations in Japan were relaxed but the New Zealand Government maintained a protectionist stance and Japanese investment largely remained limited to a few resource-based joint ventures, which now included iron sands, fishing and wool processing.[22] The exception was the case of car assembly for which New Zealand's protectionist policy had the effect of promoting investment. In the 1970s, existing Toyota and Nissan car assembly plants were expanded and several new assembly plants were established in response to government policy to protect the domestic car-related industry.[23]

In 1979, under the auspices of the JNZBC, a Japanese mission was sent to New Zealand to inspect various investment opportunities. That year the New Zealand Government announced a liberalisation of its protectionist policy and exchange controls.[24] In the next five years Japanese investments in New Zealand increased slightly in numbers and the actual amounts invested grew. But in terms of the global expansion of Japanese investments the New Zealand figure remained low.[25] This remained a matter of concern to the JNZBC. At the annual conferences in the 1980s the New Zealand side was keen to provide information on investment opportunities in a wide range of industries.[26] In 1982 the JNZBC organised a fact-finding mission to Japan on investment, with the aim of discovering the reasons for Japan's apparent hesitancy in directing investment to New Zealand. The mission hoped to promote a better understanding of New Zealand's investment criteria and climate, and to convince Japanese at the highest level of the value of strengthening economic ties through capital or equity investment participation in New Zealand.[27] Among its conclusions the mission found that a principal reason for the relatively small Japanese involvement was generally lack of knowledge or even awareness of New Zealand.[28] Part of the problem was also the asymmetry between the large Japanese enterprises and New Zealand's companies, even the largest of which were small in Japanese terms. A recommendation by the JNZBC for the development of a national strategy for attracting Japanese investment to New Zealand failed to influence the government at that time. The positive achievement of this mission was in leaving more detailed and complete information on New Zealand available in key places in Japan.[29]

In 1985 the Japanese Government moved to encourage foreign investment by Japanese companies. Japanese investment in New Zealand increased thereafter but proportionately more slowly than the global amount invested by Japan. It might have been expected that the greater the proportion of a country's trade with Japan, the greater the level of investment. But this was not the experience in New Zealand's case. Yet as the JNZBC recognised, trade without the support of investment could not be expected to grow rapidly.[30]

From 1985 to 1988 the New Zealand Government moved to make New Zealand a more attractive investment destination by liberalising overseas investment regulations and foreign exchange control regulations, and reducing corporate tax and tariff rates.[31] Reflecting the change in government policy the New Zealand Prime Minister, David Lange, told Japan's Prime Minister Nakasone, when he visited New Zealand in 1985, 'We welcome investment from Japan particularly because we know your people value stability and like to make investment decisions on a long-term basis.'[32] The Finance Minister, Roger Douglas, visited Japan in 1986 and 1988 to promote New Zealand's changed economic policies and opportunities for investment. In 1990 Prime Minister Geoffrey Palmer, on a visit to Japan, also made the case for increased Japanese investment in New Zealand. This lobbying had limited results. Japanese investments increased in number and capital amounts, and the areas in which investment was made became more diversified. But investment was not in proportion to the expansion of Japanese investment globally and it continued to increase at a rate lower than that of New Zealand's trade with Japan.

From the 1970s, Japan had been an important source of borrowing for the New Zealand government and by the 1980s a considerable proportion of government borrowing was designated in yen. In 1989 the collapse of the Development Finance Corporation (DFC), in which a substantial majority of the debt was held by Japanese banks and financial institutions, revealed a gap in understanding between New

Zealand and Japanese business outlooks. The Japanese creditors found it hard to believe the New Zealand Government would allow a major financial institution, at the time the seventh largest in New Zealand, to fail. Moreover the statutory management procedure which the DFC was required to follow was not well understood in Japan. The situation had the potential to damage New Zealand's financial reputation. In the end a restructuring package which offered the creditors a substantially higher return than had been anticipated was negotiated and agreed by October 1990. While the outcome was better than expected, fundamental differences between the Japanese and New Zealand ways of doing business had been revealed again and in the short term led to the blocking of a proposed New Zealand Government bond issue in Japan in 1989.[33]

Over 100 senior representatives of major banks and other businesses in Japan attended the 16th joint meeting of the JNZBC in Auckland in October 1989. This was especially pleasing to New Zealand businessmen at that time. It was accepted that New Zealand had to gain a keener appreciation of the motives of potential investors and to work harder on restoring investor trust, and that this was particularly important following the collapse of the Development Finance Corporation.[34] The episode led to a tightening of banking supervision and reform of companies and securities law in New Zealand and underlined once again the importance of effective communication with Japan.

In 1990 the JNZBC established an Investment Task Force which reported at the JNZBC meeting in October of that year. The report identified a number of constraints to increased Japanese investment – the small size of the economy, lack of cost competitiveness, changeable government policy, lack of investment incentives, and absence of government involvement in attracting investment. It recognised that its efforts had not been sufficient to raise the New Zealand profile in Japan and concluded the there must be 'strenuous efforts' to improve New Zealand's competitiveness and to present an image based on purpose and direction.[35]

By 1990 Japanese companies had invested in a diverse number of enterprises in New Zealand including hotels, restaurants, commercial buildings, golf courses and ski fields as well as motor vehicle assembly plants, fishing, forests and aluminium production, but generally the Japanese had not shown much enthusiasm for major investment in New

Zealand. New Zealand's share of Japanese total foreign investment was a mere 0.3 per cent. On the New Zealand side by 1990, in contrast to 1972, there was undoubtedly greater awareness of the importance of doing business with Japan and the protocols attached thereto. Much of this was a result of efforts of JNZBC which in 1990 was calling for a long-term strategic approach to the future development of trade with, and investment from, Japan. (See Tables 1 and 2 below.)

Table 1: Japanese Investment (US$millions)

	1986	1987	1988	1989
NZ	93	121	117	101
Australia	881	1222	2413	4256
USA	10,165	14,704	21,701	35,540
Britain	984	2473	3956	5239
Canada	276	653	626	1362
Ireland	72	58	42	133

Source: *New Zealand International Review*, May–June 1991.

Table 2: Areas of Japanese Investment

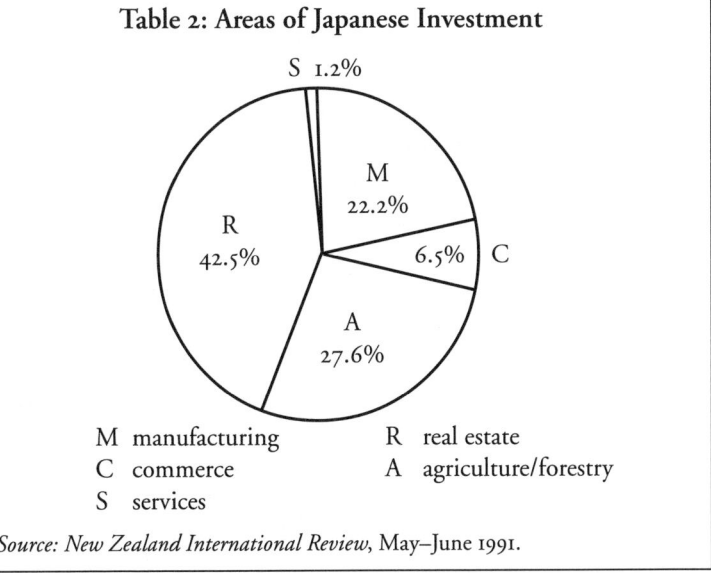

- S 1.2%
- M 22.2%
- R 42.5%
- C 6.5%
- A 27.6%

M manufacturing R real estate
C commerce A agriculture/forestry
S services

Source: *New Zealand International Review*, May–June 1991.

Mutual Understanding

Efforts to promote a New Zealand constituency in Japan and greater understanding of Japan and Japanese culture in New Zealand were not confined to the JNZBC through the 1970s and 1980s. A variety of organisations – semi-official, sporting and cultural – established in this period brought new groups of people into contact with Japan and the Japanese.

The Japan Advisory Committee, later known as the Japan Advisory Council (JAC) was formed in 1976 to bring together people from the private sector, universities and government to foster, by a variety of means, the relationship with Japan. The Council was active in its early years in promoting seminars and publications and acting as a channel of communication, but much of its work had been overtaken by 1990 by more specialised organisations such as the JNZBC, Japan Societies and Sister Cities.[36]

In 1973 the first sister city link was established between Christchurch in New Zealand and Kurashiki in Japan. Thereafter similar sister city links were formed, especially after the establishment of a direct air route in 1980. By 1990 there were 17 such relationships. While the linkages varied in the enthusiasm with which they were pursued, exchanges of local body officials, exchange visits of school students, participation in local events and festivals in both countries helped destroy stereotypes and for many ordinary New Zealanders gave an insight into Japanese culture and a human face to a relationship the official promotion of which had been biased towards trade. At the same time, through the 1970s and 1980s, Japan Societies were established in most regions and in Christchurch, a Japan Centre was set up. These organisations published newsletters and held meetings where information on travels in Japan was exchanged and Japanese guests entertained. By 1990 it could be claimed with some justification that, as a result of the work of these organisations, the average New Zealand citizen was now better informed about Japan and Japanese culture of which many had some direct experience in New Zealand or Japan.[37]

In 1977 the Japan-New Zealand Dietmembers Friendship League was established. The aim was to assist and promote among New Zealand members of Parliament the importance of New Zealand's bilateral relations with Japan. It also aimed to strengthen New Zealand's connections with the Japanese political world and particularly with influential policy-makers involved in areas of greatest importance to New Zealand. In Japan senior and influential members of the Japanese Diet were active in support of this organisation which was valuable not only for the insights it was able to give to New Zealand politicians but for the constituency-building work of the New Zealand Embassy in Tokyo. It was one means of contacting high-ranking Diet members. Through the 1980s a number of delegations travelled from both countries and in 1990 New Zealand established a Prime Minister's Visiting Fellowship to bring an up-and-coming Japanese politician on a study tour of New Zealand every year. As with the sister cities this organisation depended for its success on the enthusiasm and drive of a few individuals in both the New Zealand Parliament and the Japanese Diet. The degree of support in New Zealand fluctuated according to changes in the political scene which from time to time removed the enthusiasts from Parliament.[38]

The Government as a whole was, however, conscious of the need to raise the level of understanding of the New Zealand public about the characteristics of Japanese society and culture. The emphasis was on the education of youth. In 1974 the Government put aside funds for a programme of cultural exchanges with Asian countries including Japan and an agreement with Japan to introduce exchange programmes in educational and cultural fields was signed.[39] Exchange programmes between New Zealand and Jaapanese students of all ages were encouraged. In 1979 the New Zealand and Japanese Education Departments signed an agreement for the direct exchange of secondary teachers.[40] The New Zealand–Japan Foundation established by the New Zealand Government in 1980 to mark the visit of Japanese Prime Minister Ohira supported educational and cultural activities designed to promote greater understanding of Japan by New Zealanders and to inform the Japanese about New Zealand. It sponsored a bi-annual lecturership in New Zealand studies at the University of Tokyo, Komaba, in 1988.[41]

Japanese language study had been introduced at the Universities of Auckland, Canterbury and Massey in the late 1960s and from the mid 1970s, the Ministry of Education encouraged the teaching of Japanese language in secondary schools. As the focus of New Zealand's trade and tourist traffic increasingly centred on Japan, the popularity of Japanese language as a school subject increased through the 1980s. By 1990, Japanese was second only to French in terms of the number of students learning the language with 12,442 students in 145 secondary schools involved. This helped promote Japanese studies at the universities where Japanese language was available which, by 1990, included Victoria University of Wellington. The New Zealand Centre for Japanese Studies was established at Massey University to mark the visit of Prime Minister Nakasone in 1985. It became operational in 1987, funded from Japanese sources and Massey University and, for a limited period, by the New Zealand-Japan Foundation. It seeks to foster greater knowledge and expertise in the broad field of Japanese studies throughout the country and to focus attention on the significance of Japan for New Zealand. In its early years it was particularly concerned with raising the standard of the teaching of the Japanese language in schools.[42]

In 1986 the Japanese Government introduced the Japanese Educational Programme (JET) to New Zealand by which New Zealand graduates were recruited for twelve months to teach English in Japanese secondary schools. By 1990 about 100 teachers were being recruited under this scheme. In addition a New Zealand-Japan Working Holiday Scheme was introduced in 1986. This is a reciprocal agreement aimed at encouraging young adults to visit each other's country. At the same time a six month visa-free period for New Zealand and Japanese holidaymakers was introduced to facilitate this and other tourist traffic between the two countries. In 1990, 600 young New Zealanders went to Japan and 950 young Japanese visited New Zealand.[43]

Outside these government and local-body sponsored programmes there were a number of other activities which took enthusiastic individuals and teams to Japan. Rugby teams from New Zealand universities visited Japan, carrying on a practice first begun in 1936. A Japanese rugby team toured New Zealand in 1974 and an All Black team went to Japan in 1987. In the athletics field, runners, both men and women, participated in marathons in Japan as they had since 1960 and in the 1980s had considerable success. New Zealand potters, flower arrangers and proponents of martial arts continued to seek inspiration from their Japanese counterparts. At a number of different levels, Japan was becoming better known to New Zealanders.

Beyond a Bilateral Relationship

In 1980 when Japanese Prime Minister Ohira visited New Zealand the idea of a Pacific Basin Community was being promoted in both Japan and Australia. New Zealand's support for the concept was at that time cautious. The initial idea was seen by New Zealand as favouring, and more attractive to, highly industrialised nations. There were fears about possible Japanese or Japanese–American domination and concern about a lack of provision for participation of small Pacific Island states. These island states made it clear that they resented not being consulted and, given its political and economic ties with them and New Zealand's perception of itself as as a spokesman for small states, New Zealand could not ignore this reaction.[44] Nevertheless New Zealand took part in the conference held in Canberra in September 1980 . This was attended by academics, businessmen and government officials in their private capacity from Japan, the United States, Australia, New Zealand, Korea and the ASEAN countries. The conference recommended the setting up of the Pacific Cooperation Committee. New Zealand and Japan became founder members of the Pacific Economic Cooperation Conference (PECC) in which government, private sector and academic representatives are all involved. Conferences held in member countries throughout the 1980s provided another forum in which New Zealand and Japanese officials, academics and businessmen could exchange ideas. The committee considering regional trade in agricultural products was one in which New Zealand could air its problems with agricultural protectionism in Japan and elsewhere in the region.[45]

New Zealand's enthusiam for the idea of a Pacific community had grown considerably by 1989 as a result of the expansion and diversification of New Zealand's trade in the Asia–Pacific region, and the increase in diplomatic relationships this involved. The success of Closer Economic Relations (CER) with Australia, New Zealand's trading problems with the European Union and moves for the development of a North American free trade area also led to further consideration of the merits and perils for New Zealand of regional organisations.[46] Therefore Australian Prime Minister Bob Hawke's proposal in 1989 for an Asia Pacific Economic Cooperation (APEC) initiative was received with approval. For New Zealand, Japan's membership of and support for this grouping was fundamental. Not all Southeast Asian countries, notably Malaysia, saw New Zealand and Australia as legitimate members of a predominantly Asian grouping, and the suggestion of an economic bloc of East Asian countries exclusively was one which might have been inimical to New Zealand's interests. In the 1970s and 1980s Japan had become a pivot of economic relationships around the Pacific. Thus so long as Japan supported the concept of APEC and remained immune to feelers for an exclusively East Asian economic bloc, the logic of the claim for a broad Asia–Pacific group of which New Zealand and Australia were members was unlikely to be challenged. For New Zealand, by 1990, considerations such as the increasing globalisation of the post-Cold War world's economy, of which APEC was in part a reflection, gave a broader and more complex political dimension to the New Zealand-Japan bilateral relationship.

Conclusion

In 1990 Japan remained the Asian country with which New Zealand had widest contacts and there was no doubt that these had multiplied in the preceding two decades. Perhaps for this reason New Zealanders readily recognised Japan as different from other Asian countries although they were less able to recognise the diversity of the countries of the rest of Asia. With Japan there had been regular growth in visible trade; Japanese tourist numbers had increased; Japanese investment, while still undesirably small, had increased; communications between the two countries had improved; there was a wide range of people to people contacts and on the official level too contacts had increased. A stable relationship in which there would be no unpleasant surprises on either side appeared to be established.

While this gave cause for satisfaction there could be no complacency on the New Zealand side. At this time New Zealand was experiencing the effects of radical reforms introduced since 1984 and was undergoing rapid change. For many New Zealanders it was a time of uncertainty. In this climate, when many New Zealanders felt threatened by change, it became clear that all prejudice against Japan had not disappeared. The death of Emperor Hirohito in 1989 revealed that among some returned servicemen and others of their generation, hostile attitudes remained.[47] In 1990 the sale of a golf course at Wairakei to a Japanese company was held up after protests by Maori and other interests. This postponement was denounced by business interests such as the JNZBC and ultimately was overturned by a new government in November 1990.[48] Not all the reaction to the Wairakei sale was fuelled by racism, but the incident demonstrated that for all the efforts of the past two decades there was still work to be done before it could be said with confidence that the importance of the New Zealand-Japan relationship was understood by New Zealanders and the stability of the relationship was assured. It was clear in 1990 that the Japanese market and Japanese culture would continue to present opportunities and to provide a challenge to the abilities, initiative and sensitivity of all New Zealanders in the decades to come.

Notes

1 New Zealand Japanese relations (Brief for Muldoon) 31 August 1968, MFAT 40/12/1.
2 Esme Marris and Malcolm Overland, *The History of the Pacific Basin Economic Council 1967–1997* (Wellington and Honolulu, 1997), p.6.
3 'New Zealand Japan Relations', in *New Zealand Foreign Affairs Review* (hereafter *NZFAR*), June 1972, p.40.
4 'Visit of Prime Minister of Japan', in *NZFAR*, November 1974, p.5.
5 John Henderson, 'Muldoon: New Zealand and the World'(interview with PM Muldoon), in *New Zealand International Review* (hereafter *NZIR*), May–June 1977, p.10.
6 'The Prime Minister's address on Foreign Affairs and Overseas Trade', in *NZFAR*, April–June 1976, pp.9, 29. The most detailed account of this controversy is by Steve Hoadley, *Negotiating with Japan, Lessons from the Fish-for Beef Dispute 1976–1978* (Palmerston North, 1993). The following section owes much to Hoadley's analysis.
7 See Hoadley, *Negotiating with Japan,*pp.38–45 for details of these negotiations.
8 'Asian Visitors to New Zealand', in *NZFAR*, January–March 1980, p.23.
9 'Mr Palmer Visits China, Japan', in *NZFAR*, January–March 1987, p.21.
10 'Asia. Ties with Japan Reinforced', in *NZFAR*, January–March 1985, p.42.
11 R. H. Wade to PM, 3 December 1971, MFAT 40/12/1.
12 Akio Watanabe, 'A Tale of Two Island Countries: The New Zealand–Japan Relationship', in T. J. Hearn (ed.), *New Zealand and Japan, Papers of the Sixteenth Foreign Policy School University of Otago* (Dunedin, 1981), p.85. Watanabe cites Edward. A. Olsen, 'Adding a J to Anzus', in the *New York Times*, 13 May 1981, in support of this idea.
13 'Brief Visit by Japanese Ministers', in *NZFAR* , January–March 1987, p.22.
14 See Ian Kennedy, *Japan and New Zealand: Adding Value* (Wellington, 1992), ch.12, pp.80–4 for a detailed discussion of this issue.
15 'Prime Minister's Visit to Japan', in *New Zealand External Relations Review* (hereafter *NZER*), July–September 1990, p.8; Don McKinnon, 'A Vital Link for

the Future', in *NZIR*, May–June 1991, p.7.
16 Speech by Graham Ansell to JNZBC, 17 October 1990.
17 Maarten Wevers, *Japan, Its Future and New Zealand* (Wellington, 1988), p.128.
18 Wevers, *Japan*, p.128.
19 Takeo Iguchi (Japanese ambassador to New Zealand), 'A Growing Partnership', in *NZIR*, May–June 1991, p.5; Yoshihiro Nigo, 'Japanese Investment in New Zealand 1958–1990', (M.Lit. thesis, University of Auckland, 1993),ch.5, pp.161–2.
20 Nigo, 'Japanese Investment', ch.5 pp.161–98; Philip Burdon, 'Exploiting Opportunities', in *NZIR*, May–June 1991, p.26.
21 Interview wth Esme Marris, formerly Director-General, NZ Committee of JNZBC, 29 May 1998.
22 Nigo, 'Japanese Investment', pp.36–41.
23 Nigo, 'Japanese Investment', pp.103–44.
24 Reserve Bank of New Zealand, 'Foreign investments in New Zealand', supplement to Reserve Bank Bulletin, November 1979, pp.5–6.
25 Nigo, 'Japanese Investment', pp.41–9; Andrew Meehan, 'Attracting the Yen: the Investment Picture', *NZIR*, May–June 1991, p.28.
26 JNZBC group A,B,C papers 1982–84 quoted by Nigo, 'Japanese Investment', p.45.
27 JNZBC, *Report of Fact Finding Mission to Japan on Investment*, 1982, p.1; Nigo, 'Japanese Investment', p.46.
28 JNZBC, *Report of Fact Finding Mission*, p.22. See also Nigo, 'Japanese Investment', pp.45–7.
29 This was the view of Esme Marris quoted by Nigo, 'Japanese Investment', p.48.
30 Meehan, 'Attracting the Yen', pp.27–8.
31 Exchange Control Regulations (1985); The Overseas Investment Regulations 1985. Amendment No.1, 1987/69 pp.271–2, Amendment No.2, 1989.
32 'Japan May Help New Zealand Trade Deals', in *New Zealand Herald*, 21 January 1985.
33 See Kennedy, *Japan and New Zealand*, ch.11, pp.74–9 for a more detailed discussion of this crisis.
34 *NZER*, October–December 1989, p.20.
35 Meehan, 'Attracting the Yen', p.28; JNZBC, *Task Force Report*, 'Japanese Direct Investment in New Zealand', 1990, pp.27–35; See Nigo, 'Japanese Investment', Appendix 5, pp.307–9 for an analysis of the 1990 Task Force report.
36 'Japan Advisory Council', August 1990, attachment *to New Zealand Centre for Japanese Studies Newsletter*, August 1990.
37 Iguchi, 'A Growing Partnership', p.5; MFAT 58/268/9/15 Vol.2,(Sister City Relationships) 58/268/4 (Japan Societies of New Zealand).
38 MFAT 58/268/1/1 Pt.1 (New Zealand/Japan Dietmen's League).
39 *NZFAR*, July 1974, p.15; *New Zealand–Japan Exchange Programme*, Department of Education 1985, p.1 (Pamphlet in MFAT 58/268/9/7 Pt.3).
40 MFAT 58/268/7/6 Pt.2.
41 Tokyo to Wellington, 25 July 1989, MFAT 58/268/9 Pt.6.
42 Iguchi, 'A Growing Partnership', p.4; MFAT 58/268/7/6 Pt.2.
43 Iguchi, 'A Growing Partnership', pp.4–5.

44 A. Haas, 'Development the Pacific Way', in *NZIR*, July–August 1980 p.18; Ann Trotter, 'The Pacific Community – A View from New Zealand', in John Chapman (ed.), *Proceedings of the British Association for Japanese Studies*, Vol.6 Pt.1, 1981 p.134.
45 Ann Trotter, 'Quest for Interdependence', in *NZIR*, January–February 1985, pp.8–11.
46 This was especially relevant given the realignments following the end of the Cold War. See Bryce Harland, *On Our Own: New Zealand in the Emerging Tripolar World* (Wellington, 1992); Sir Frank Holmes and Crawford Falconer, *Open Regionalism? NAFTA, CER, and a Pacific Basin Initiative* (Wellington, 1992).
47 *The Press*, 10, 14, 17, January, 1989.
48 *New Zealand Herald*, 27, 28, July; 28 September; 1, 12 October; 24 November 1990

JOHN MCKINNON

Breaking the Mould:
New Zealand's Relations with China[1]

The context

The period set for the studies in this volume has a logic derived from New Zealand's political history, spanning as it does two Labour Governments and the intervening National administration. It is easy to devise patterns out of this history, whether that is by way of contrast between two reforming governments and a conservative party only grudgingly coming to terms with some of the most explosive international issues of the day; or alternatively a treatment which stresses elements of continuity in New Zealand's foreign policy – a close regard for economic welfare, combined with a dissenting sometimes quixotic and reformist approach to international issues, and the opportunity, with the onset of detente, to bring these impulses to bear on relations with the communist Government of China.

For China it so happens that this period of time almost exactly equates to a phase of China's external relations which has a distinct character. On 15 July 1971 United States President Richard Nixon revealed that his administration had been engaged in secret discussions with communist China and that as a result he would be visiting Beijing in 1972, thus abandoning the policy of isolating China which the US had held to since 1949. China, for its part, moved to a warmer relationship with the United States than with its fellow communist former ally, the Soviet Union. Later that year the Government of the People's Republic was seated in the United Nations by vote of the General Assembly. At the other end of the period under review, 1990 came one year after civil unrest in China had culminated in Chinese forces imposing their will on their own people – a commonplace of Chinese political experience, but on this occasion executed in full view of the rest of the world. Western reaction to Tiananmen, as these events became known, was immediate, strong and critical. With the fall of the Berlin Wall later that year, China was no longer so necessary to the United States as a strategic partner; indeed it had become, by default, the most powerful country in the world which did not subscribe to core American values.

In China's external relations then, 1972 and 1989 set the limits of the period when China, without surrendering its independence of action, found common cause with the United States in opposition to the Soviet Union. Whatever New Zealand's motives were in developing relations with China, for China itself this ingredient is fundamental. It coloured many aspects of China's external policy over those years; and it is scarcely surprising that relations with New Zealand could not escape that frame of reference.[2]

In terms of China's internal development the period is not such a good fit. Major change came to China not in 1972 but in 1978, when the third plenum of the 11th central committee of the ruling Chinese Communist Party (CCP) launched China on its current path of economic liberalisation. And Tiananmen did not bring about a change in this general direction, although the events surrounding it cost the incumbent general secretary his office. Yet though neither year is a beginning or ending, there is a common thread, for this was the era in which Deng Xiaoping was in fact if not in name the ruler of China. Deng's policies made a major contribution to improving the welfare of the Chinese people. This endeavour shaped a large part of what New Zealand encountered in China in the 1970s and 1980s.

In 1972 that was in the future. What was significant in 1972 was that the two countries had been apart since the communist takeover of China in 1949. Moreover, two of the principal links between them before 1949 – the missionaries, and New Zealand's own Chinese community – were not and could not be prominent in the new relationship. Perhaps more surprisingly the party-to-party relations that the Chinese Communist Party had nurtured in New Zealand before 1972 were of little use. These withered once direct contact between governments was established.[3] There were links which straddled the great divide. A number of old China hands – Ron Howell, Ramon La Varis, Vic Percival, Warren Freer MP – used their familiarity with People's China to the benefit of

New Zealand. The New Zealand–China Society did likewise. And New Zealand did have a presence in China: Rewi Alley, the New Zealander who had been in the country since 1927, and who had cast his lot with the communists, was a prominent Western 'friend' of China and well placed to welcome his compatriots to his adopted country.[4] But for the handful of individuals who were politically, professionally or personally committed to building a relationship between China and New Zealand, novelty was the major key.

Breaking the mould?

New Zealand had acquired international personality within the British Empire and Commonwealth, and its diplomatic instincts were still marked by that heritage. In 1972, on the eve of Britain joining the European Economic Community, New Zealand's diplomatic representation was focussed on fellow members of the Commonwealth and on allies in Asia or Europe.

In a short space of time the newly elected Labour Government of Norman Kirk extended New Zealand's diplomatic horizons to four new parts of the world – the Middle East, the Soviet Union and its sphere of influence, Latin America, and of course China. In each case there was a mix, but a varied mix, of political and economic motives.

With respect to China, New Zealand's reasons for establishing formal relations were couched in terms of the need for New Zealand to be able to deal directly and non-confrontationally with all the four great powers involved in the affairs of Asia and the Pacific – the United States, Japan, China and the Soviet Union.[5] New Zealand was an ally of the United States and had a close relationship with Japan. While it had no resident mission in Moscow, it did have diplomatic relations with the Soviet Union. China was the obvious gap.[6] The quest for new markets provided an additional motive. China, the most populous country in the world, might prove to be one.[7]

But there was a complication with China which did not apply to the Middle East, Latin America and the Soviet Union. New Zealand did already have a diplomatic relationship with 'China' – with the government of the 'Republic of China' which had taken refuge in Taiwan after 1949. How could it establish a relationship with the People's Republic without jettisoning Taiwan, as required by the People's Republic?

New Zealand was not the first country to grapple with this problem. Canada had recognised China and severed its official relationship with Taiwan in October 1970; Japan in September 1972. The joint Japan-China communiqué was printed in full in the New Zealand Foreign Affairs Review.[8] This development had been guardedly welcomed by Prime Minister Marshall[9] but the National Government was still concerned not to sacrifice relations with Taiwan, and took no action on the issue before it lost office in the general election of November 1972. It was thus left to the incoming Labour Government headed by Norman Kirk to cut the gordian knot. By this time many had followed in Canada's footsteps: New Zealand, on 22 December 1972, became the 38th country to recognise the People's Republic since Canada had done so.[10]

Thus New Zealand was not breaking new ground, and the shift in recognition from Taipei to Beijing could be presented as unexceptional.[11] Yet within the New Zealand context the move was significant and is still regarded as one of the noteworthy achievements of the Kirk Government. Why? On the positive side because China and its people were at this time a cause which was popular with those who supported the new government. This was a government which was demonstrating its independence of action from traditional allies, amongst other things by embracing former adversaries.

But the action was also significant because it was not entirely cost-free. The Government had to confront two widespread and related sentiments – loyalty to Taiwan, and continued suspicion of communism. Kirk, in his 1971 NZIIA pamphlet on New Zealand and its neighbours,[12] while acknowledging and welcoming changes in the Asian environment, did not explicitly suggest that New Zealand should recognise the People's Republic. And when in other speeches he did, Kirk commented that an exchange of representatives might be further into the future.[13] The New Zealand Labour Party had supported Taiwan's political rights up until the party conference in May 1972. The 'Republic of China' ambassador, Konsin Shah, was a popular figure in Wellington, and Kirk disliked having to break the news to him.[14] When officials suggested that New Zealand should recognise China, Kirk's initial response was that that would be something for the second term.[15] It was Australia's decision to switch recognition to Beijing that precipitated New Zealand into action.[16] Yet even after this step was taken Kirk did not regard the sending of a goodwill mission as a matter of urgency.[17] Views fed to him by new

Labour MPs in marginal electorates may also have played a cautionary role.[18]

Even so the recognition was criticised on two related grounds by the new Opposition: that its language was tougher on the status of Taiwan than that secured by the Canadians, and that Taiwan was unnecessarily and brutally sacrificed. On both points the Government rejected the charges, arguing in a paper circulated to MPs that if New Zealand had had to concede language less satisfactory than that in the Canadian communiqué, it was only because the previous government had left this move so long. On Taiwan the government took refuge in the agreement that 'private' relations with Taiwan could continue unhampered.[19]

If the Opposition was critical, the New Zealand–China Society, which had held the banner for relations with China over many years, was pleased. Its president wrote to Kirk on New Year's Day 1973, congratulating him on this event.[20]

China had a different starting point. Even before the cultural revolution, China's contacts with the developed world had been constrained by the reach of US power, by continuing support for Taiwan, by China's own fiercely independent policy, and by its support for revolutionary movements. For China, sending diplomats, students and traders to Western countries carried risks which had to be carefully balanced against the strategic benefits. If there was a model for China's dealings with non-threatening capitalist states it derived from China's experience with the smaller powers of Europe – Sweden, Denmark – with which it had established official links in the 1950s.[21] In many respects New Zealand and Australia were similar to Scandinavia, but they also made their own contribution to China's expanding horizons. They were part of the English-speaking world but without the history of intervention in Chinese affairs which coloured China's attitudes to the United Kingdom and the United States. Unlike the Europeans, they were located in the Asia-Pacific region. The establishment of relations with them represented a breach in the anti-communist, pro-Taiwan wall with which China saw itself surrounded and additional opportunities to counter Soviet influence.[22] These features did much to determine the value of what China saw in its relations with these two South Pacific democracies.[23]

The pattern of contact between China and New Zealand over the succeeding 18 years reveals three major ways in which the distance between the two countries was narrowed and relations between them fostered – political, economic and cultural.[24] On the political side the principal manifestation was high level visits, a custom to which both sides gave almost equal weight. On the economic side we see the steady development of trade and investment, from virtually zero, until by 1990, China was at the top of the second tier of New Zealand's trading partners. On the cultural front, despite entirely different structures and philosophies on the two sides, we see the use of students, cultural groups, teachers, as vehicles for building what were described as people-to-people contacts.

The real measure of what the two countries achieved in those 18 years can be judged either by comparing the New Zealand-China relationship with China's relations with other countries similarly placed, or against New Zealand's efforts to develop links with other parts of the world. The former is the more elusive as the 'special relationship' haunts descriptions of relations between China and its new partners, a testimony to the skill of Chinese diplomacy.[25] The latter will be touched on in the course of this chapter.

On the way

Giving effect to the establishment of diplomatic relations took some months. Pressure to move quickly came from a number of quarters.

Rewi Alley was in New Zealand in February 1973 and reported some concern amongst mid-level officials in Beijing that New Zealand was moving rather slowly.[26] A further point was made delicately by Alley: New Zealand was not the only new player in town and if it were to get anywhere in its relations with China it had to attract attention: to this end high-level visits were highly desirable.[27] The authority for this view was questioned[28] but used by officials to prod ministers into actions.[29]

Pressure also came from those lured, as generations of foreigners had been before them, by the untold riches believed to lie behind the 'bamboo curtain'. A number of traders who had had longstanding relations with China lobbied government ministers in the first months of 1973.[30]

Kirk had no wish to go to China himself, fearing that he would be tagged as soft on communism.[31] So it was decided that Overseas Trade Minister and Associate Foreign Minister Joe Walding[32] should make a first official visit to China in March, and that the plans to open an embassy in Beijing sometime in 1974[33] would be brought forward. Kirk made an announcement to this effect on 7 March 1973.[34] In a neat move the first staff of the Chinese embassy in Wellington arrived in the capital on 26 March 1973, the day before Walding and his party set foot in China.[35] The first ambassador from the People's Republic, Pei Jianzhang, presented his credentials on 16 May 1973. In six years in Wellington, he and his wife did much to overcome the barriers of ignorance and suspicion which surrounded the new China.

The decision to send a ministerial-led mission had been taken on the grounds that only at that level could New Zealand begin the process of hearing Chinese views and presenting New Zealand's views to the Chinese leadership, and only in that context could all other contacts with China take place.

The context within which China viewed this new relationship could be inferred from the speech of welcome to Walding given by Vice-Foreign Minister Qiao Guanhua. Acknowledging the 'new independent foreign policy' expounded by Kirk, Qiao described the Pacific as not living up to its name, under the manipulation of expansionist forces and an arena of rivalry between the super powers. He pledged to work with New Zealand to safeguard the independence and sovereignty of all countries in the Pacific region.[36] It did not take New Zealand long to interpret the code: China was totally preoccupied with the Soviet Union, and its fear of that country shaped all aspects of its foreign policy. So New Zealand's relations with the US, its membership of SEATO and ASPAC, even its continuing (quiet) links with Taiwan, did not elicit any adverse comment from the Chinese side.[37]

Also evident from the preliminary discussion of a trade mission was that China saw the establishment of a political relationship as the foundation on which all else was based. Commercial and cultural contacts were seen as an expression of and a consequence of that basic fact, not necessarily as things to be pursued for their own sake.[38]

New Zealand's perspectives reflected its own historical experience, as did China's. Perhaps the most striking, evident in the speech that Walding gave during his first visit, was the emphasis that New Zealand gave to social and economic welfare. Grasping at what could link two such obviously different countries as New Zealand and China, Walding said that the most important thing that the two countries had in common was a striving for human equality. Walding said that New Zealand's goals for peace and progress derived from the nature of its society – and of its interests as a country which relied heavily on international trade.[39]

But there were issues on which the two countries took different views throughout the period under review, amongst them nuclear testing and China's policy in Southeast Asia. Both topics were touched on in the first visit. Walding expressed doubts about China's support for communist insurgency in Southeast Asia. Qiao distanced China from these movements, saying that ideas could not be spread by force and if people in Southeast Asia did not want revolution it could not be imposed on them. Zhou Enlai, whom Walding also met, argued that the Chinese in Southeast Asia should merge with their host populations.[40] While not evident at the time, these proved to be signs that China was coming to the view that support for Communist insurgencies in Southeast Asia was inimical to its larger strategic goal of opposing the Soviet Union.

The other issue, nuclear testing, was less easily resolved, and remained in some degree in contention between the two countries until China signed the Comprehensive Test Ban Treaty (CTBT) in 1997. At the time of the Walding visit it was dealt with quite straightforwardly: 'there was some discussion between the two sides on the question of disarmament and nuclear testing. Each side restated its known views expressed at various UN meetings and on other occasions'.[41] This was the year when the Labour Government impressed its anti-nuclear credentials on the world by bringing a case in the World Court against France for its atmospheric nuclear testing and by sending a frigate to French Polynesia to protest the tests. On 27 June 1973 China did conduct an atmospheric test and New Zealand did protest,[42] but perforce had to observe that while it would similarly have made a case against China in the World Court, it could not, because China had not accepted the compulsory jurisdiction of the Court. New Zealand did take every opportunity to register its views on nuclear testing with the Chinese – including on occasions which some might regard as inappropriate – such as when the new ambassador presented his credentials.[43] Yet in New Zealand, China never incurred the opprobrium for its testing that France did and the exchange of protests did not damage the burgeoning relationship. This was perhaps less because China's testing was regarded as more acceptable than France's, than because France's was regarded as uniquely unacceptable, taking place in a region a world away from metropolitan France and in the face of opposition from the states and territories of that region.

But these differences did not impede and indeed scarcely clouded the step-by-step establishment of the formalities of diplomatic relations. Following the first ministerial visit an advance team for the embassy established itself in Beijing in July 1973. New Zealand's first ambassador to China, career diplomat Bryce Harland, arrived in Beijing on 16 September and presented his credentials to the then head of state of the People's Republic, Acting Chairman Dong Biwu, on 20 September 1973. He was received by Premier Zhou Enlai soon afterwards.[44]

Labour to National

Labour inaugurated the relationship with China. The further development of that relationship fell to the National Government of Robert Muldoon, elected to office in November 1975. Norman Kirk had died on 31 August 1974. His successor, Bill Rowling, had publicly expressed interest in visiting China,[45] but was unable to do this before his government went out of office. So the honour of being the first New Zealand leader to visit China, and the only New Zealand politician to meet Mao Zedong, fell to Muldoon.

There were two respects in which National's policy towards China differed from Labour's: National was more concerned to sustain links with Taiwan, and National was more publicly and directly critical of the Soviet Union than Labour. From China's point of view, the latter attribute far outweighed any difficulties with the former, especially as National did not reverse the basic commitment to recognise only one China.

In respect of Taiwan a slight shift in policy became evident in relation to the visit of a Taiwan softball team. Shortly after the change of government Muldoon received a letter from the New Zealand Softball Association about the prospective visit of a team from Taiwan to participate in an international competition in New Zealand in January 1976. Officials took the view that if a team came under the name of 'Republic of China' China would have no option but to break off diplomatic relations.[46] As National had a policy platform which forbade interference with sporting links,[47] the new Government was not prepared to dictate to the Softball Association who should or should not attend its meeting. Instead Cabinet agreed that on such occasions the Government would request sports bodies to refrain from flying the 'ROC' flag; that it would be entirely divorced from any occasion where the flag was displayed and that there would be no ministerial hospitality which would involve Taiwan sports teams.[48] When the Chinese ambassador called on the Prime Minister the issue of sporting contacts was touched on but the Prime Minister subsequently observed that the ambassador had spoken mainly about the Soviet Union.[49]

To avoid any ambiguity, Muldoon was careful in his public utterances not to give undue comfort to supporters of Taiwan. In a wide-ranging address on international affairs in Auckland on 7 April, he stressed that New Zealand wanted friendship with China. He questioned the previous Government's handling of Taiwan but made it clear that the break with Taiwan was an egg 'which could not be unscrambled'. In phrases redolent of China's approach, Muldoon said that New Zealand wished to maintain a state of peace and friendship with all the countries of the world and that arising from that relationship it would hope that not only trade, but the exchange of cultural visits and people could continue.[50] But what would have given even more comfort to China was Muldoon's ringing condemnation of the Soviet Union – its actions, he said, pointed not to defence but to imperialism and aggression. Indeed, at a meeting a few days previously, Zhang Qunqiao had told Ambassador Atkins that China appreciated the comments Muldoon had been making about the actions of the Soviet Union.[51]

Meanwhile dramatic events had taken place in China. Premier Zhou Enlai had died on 8 January 1976. In April demonstrations in support of him had taken place in Beijing. By the time Muldoon arrived in Beijing, in late April, Deng Xiaoping had been ousted from government and Hua Guofeng had been confirmed as premier. Access to the ailing Mao Zedong was jealously guarded, but Muldoon was given the privilege of a brief meeting with him in the leadership compound at Zhongnanhai on 30 April 1976. The conversation lasted only 10 to 15 minutes, and despite Mao's frail condition Muldoon was convinced that he was having a conversation with Mao, and that his remarks were not simply being invented by his female interpreters.[52] Certainly to the extent that Mao's utterances were interpreted to the New Zealanders, the threat from 'Russia' was what was dominant in Mao's mind. When Muldoon exited

China through Hong Kong, his candid comments on the state of health of the leader whose nominal hospitality he had just enjoyed attracted international attention.[53] What struck the New Zealanders as much as Mao's physical weakness was the evident affection towards him of his colleagues and attendants. Muldoon also met Mao's wife, Jiang Qing, whom he later described as a very dynamic character. In fact Muldoon met all the leading figures in the drama that was unfolding in China as Mao's life slipped away, and confessed that the country was the most fascinating of all those he had visited over the years, if only because of the isolation it had experienced to date.[54]

While entirely satisfactory on the political front, Muldoon had been advised by officials that any further expansion of trade was likely to be more gradual. He was also briefed to intimate to the Chinese that the 'present high level of cultural exchanges, at least from the New Zealand end, cannot be maintained under present economic circumstances'.[55]

The visit indicated that the two governments could deal with each other and find points of common ground but that did not mean that there were no differences. China continued its regular programme of testing nuclear weapons, and New Zealand continued to protest. An atmospheric test took place not long after Mao died – on 26 September 1976. An underground test followed in October. Thereafter there was generally one test a year, sometimes two, some underground, and some in the atmosphere. From the 1980s underground testing became the rule, even though China did not officially forswear atmospheric testing.

Another point of difference arose over China's reaction to the Vietnamese invasion of Cambodia in December 1978. Fearful of this outright aggression by a client of the Soviet Union, China decided to 'teach Vietnam a lesson.' What it received was a bloody nose. New Zealand regarded China's action as no more justifiable than Vietnam's original invasion of Cambodia, and called on China to withdraw.[56] The rapidity of China's withdrawal alleviated the tension. New Zealand and China were able to find more common ground in the approach to developments in Cambodia itself, although here too there was a difference in the two countries' respective approach to the evicted government of Cambodia, the Khmer Rouge, which persisted for many years.

Muldoon was one of the last foreign leaders to meet Mao.[57] 1976 continued to be a dramatic year for China. On 28 July a massive earthquake struck northern China. Mao died on 9 September. Three weeks later Mao's widow, Jiang Qing, and three of her closest allies were arrested by Hua Guofeng. For some time the direction of policy in China was uncertain. But in 1977 Deng Xiaoping was rehabilitated. And in December 1978 the third plenum of the eleventh central committee of the Communist Party set China on the path of the 'four modernisations'. The opening up of China by Deng would in due course change much of the character of China's interaction with all countries, including New Zealand.

Visits

For both sides the flow of ministers to and fro was a measure of the progress achieved in the relationship, and it was the exchange of high level visits which marked the point that relationship had reached. It was not necessarily the case that such visits were directed to a specific objective, although normally there were a range of agreements and announcements which accompanied them. It was the fact of them taking place which was significant. And recalling that it was not in the tradition of Chinese statecraft that Chinese leaders travelled abroad, such visits were a measure of how willing China now was reach out to the world.[58]

China did not rush to impose this practice on its new diplomatic partner. The first member of the Politburo to visit New Zealand was a vice-chairman of the National People's Congress (NPC), Ulanfu, who led an NPC delegation to New Zealand in September 1977.[59] An alternate member of the Politburo, Chen Muhua followed in 1979; Vice-Premier Li Xiannian in May 1980.[60]

Thereafter New Zealand was regularly on the circuit of visits undertaken by China's leaders: Premier Zhao Ziyang visited in April 1983, General Secretary Hu Yaobang in April 1985, and Premier Li Peng in November 1988. For each of these leaders the visit to New Zealand (always coupled with a visit to Australia) was the first to a developed country. Australia and New Zealand were reaping the benefit of their co-location with China in the Asia-Pacific region – and New Zealand the benefit of its proximity to Australia. There was also a sense that New Zealand and Australia were favoured as destinations – because of their somewhat easier ambience – before the Chinese leadership ventured to the larger Western countries.[61]

Li's visit coincided with one event in which China showed a less than assured touch in its relations with the South Pacific. In May 1980

China fired a missile into waters west of Tuvalu, but failed to give any notice to the countries closest to the target zone. Others such as Japan were advised – but asked to say nothing publicly in advance of the event.[62] Faithfully anti-Soviet, Muldoon explained that New Zealand understood the circumstances which had led China to take this action, but New Zealand's concern was demonstrated by the despatch of the unarmed naval survey ship, HMNZS *Monowai*, to the impact area.[63]

Li's visit to New Zealand had made it feasible for Muldoon to return to China: the visit ledger was in balance. On this occasion, September 1980, Muldoon met the new leaders of China – Deng Xiaoping, who had been in disgrace four years before, and Zhao Ziyang, who had just been appointed premier in place of Muldoon's host on his previous visit, Hua Guofeng. Hua was still in office as chairman of the party, but, as Muldoon observed, in explaining his change in role he seemed like a man speaking his own obituary.[64] Muldoon was impressed by both Deng and Zhao, and his reception in China was no doubt enhanced by the strong anti-Soviet line he continued to espouse. Muldoon, who had expelled the Soviet ambassador from New Zealand earlier in the year, not long after the Soviet Union had invaded Afghanistan, told Deng that China need have no fear about New Zealand's attitude to Soviet expansionism.[65] A shared concern about Soviet aggression also allowed China and New Zealand to find common ground on policy in the South Pacific, where Soviet overtures, even to conservative states such as Tonga, were worrying New Zealand and Australia. Muldoon told Hua Guofeng that it was very important for China to take account of the South Pacific Forum member states because the Forum was a valuable vehicle for regional cohesion and political stability and observed that any backing (political or economic) that China could give the Forum island countries could only help to secure regional political stability.[66] Recognising the difficulties China's missile test had created in the South Pacific, both Zhao and Hua expressed their regrets that it had happened in that way, and gave thanks to New Zealand for its counsel.[67]

Muldoon found that China's other major international concern was as strong. The United States presidential election campaign which would bring Ronald Reagan to the White House was in full swing, but Deng told Muldoon that it would be sheer daydreaming to think that China would swallow its attitude to Taiwan to ensure a tough anti-Soviet position in Washington.[68]

Outside Beijing, Muldoon was struck by the distance that China would have to travel to achieve the 'four modernisations'.[69] Muldoon and his party were the first Western visitors to the coastal province of Fujian, long off-limits because of its location just across the straits from Taiwan. This visit gave them the opportunity to meet Li Lairong, a botanist who had worked with New Zealand's DSIR during the 1940s.[70] Another consequence of this tour was that the Governor of Fujian paid a return visit to New Zealand in February 1981.[71] It was one of the outcomes of the devolution of economic power promoted by Deng and Zhao that provinces in China were permitted some autonomy in their external relations.

Muldoon was invited by Zhao to return to China in five years time. That did not occur but Zhao himself did visit New Zealand, in April 1983. Solidarity against the Soviet Union was still in evidence but Muldoon had added another string to his bow – his concern that the international trade and payments system needed to be reformed. Muldoon wrote to Zhao on this subject in February 1983, and Warren Cooper, who led a trade mission to China that same month, told Zhao that Muldoon wanted to discuss the topic when Zhao was in Wellington.[72] Zhao was polite but non-committal: when in Wellington he said that Muldoon's proposal for reforming the international trade and payments system was an important initiative 'which should be given attention and serious consideration'. Welcoming Zhao to New Zealand, Muldoon described the visit as the 'culmination of the exploratory stage' of the relationship.

This visit revealed another theme in relations between the two countries – New Zealand's support for China's entry into international organisations. On this occasion New Zealand was promoting China's membership of the International Labour Organisation (the ILO) and the Asian Development Bank (the ADB). Here it was the smaller country which was in a position to help the larger. Muldoon believed the full participation of all great powers enhanced the strength of international organisations. New Zealand similarly welcomed China's accession to the Antarctic Treaty in June 1983.[73]

Labour back in office

In mid-1984 Labour was back in government with David Lange as Prime Minister. Labour had won office conclusively after Muldoon called the election ahead of time. Lange had already paid two trips to China – the second just a few months earlier in 1984 – and the Chinese authorities could see which way the wind was blowing. The New Zealand embassy reported that, judging from experience in observing other visits of foreign dignitaries to Beijing, Lange was received exceptionally warmly and was given access to an unusual number of senior people.[74]

To Premier Zhao Ziyang, Lange stated the importance of China to New Zealand and to the Labour Party. China was a major power of great importance to New Zealand with regard to both commerce and trade and because of China's strategic position. Lange's interlocutors emphasised strategic concerns. Zhao told Lange that China sided neither with the USA nor the USSR, but nor did it pursue a single 'equidistant' policy. Foreign minister Wu Xueqian amplified this: the Pacific region was becoming a centre for superpower rivalry in addition to Europe.

In office Lange was confronted with the exceptionally difficult task of bridging the gap between his party's anti-nuclear policy and his country's security alliance with the United States. Perhaps mindful of what lay ahead, he had taken the trouble when in Beijing to ascertain China's views on ANZUS. He told Wu Xueqian that the impression he had gained during his previous visit was that China seemed to approve of New Zealand's membership of ANZUS. Wu replied that the position had not changed – and that it was quite understandable that to protect their security Australia and New Zealand had joined in an alliance with the United States.[75] In the event, when New Zealand's anti-nuclear policy precipitated a breach in the ANZUS alliance, official opinion in China, despite its own nuclear status, did evince sympathy for New Zealand. While a strong ANZUS could be seen as important in restricting Soviet expansionism,[76] to support the United States in this matter would have been at odds with China's more deepseated interest in restraining both superpowers. Thus the official organ of the Communist party argued that New Zealand's decision in banning visits by nuclear armed warships was a sign of the greater difficulties encountered by the superpowers in trying to control their allies, whether through alliances or compulsion.[77]

In April 1985 Lange hosted a visit by the most senior Chinese leader yet to visit New Zealand – Hu Yaobang, leader of the Communist Party since 1981.[78] The public statements and speeches contained the now expected references to the excellent relationship, the growth of trade, the diversity of people-to-people contacts and the many issues on which the two sides shared a common view, even if there were a few on which they did not. Given that this visit occurred at the height of controversy over New Zealand's anti-nuclear policy, Hu's support for New Zealand was welcome, although the latter was concerned to stress that its anti-nuclear policy was not for export and did not mean that New Zealand was distancing itself from the West. Hu said that New Zealand upheld peace and opposed war, and was a major stabilising factor in the South Pacific. Hu commended New Zealand for playing a peace role.[79]

China's support for New Zealand extended to a welcoming attitude to the revived initiative to create a South Pacific nuclear free zone. Hu Yaobang said that China fully supported that proposal.[80] And at a later date China signed the protocols to the treaty establishing the zone, at a time when France, the United Kingdom and the United States refused to do so.[81]

A few weeks before Hu's visit Tony Small, the New Zealand ambassador in Beijing, penning his farewell despatch, pondered the favoured status New Zealand seemed to have achieved in its relations with China, noting that New Zealand was the first Western country visited by both Zhao Ziyang and Hu Yaobang. But Small injected two cautionary notes: there was little room for complacency, and one should not indulge in undue expectations that the adoption of Western fashions and styles meant that China was converging 'asymptotically' to the values of the West.[82]

China's focus on modernisation began to bear fruit in the mid-1980s. The country's annual rate of economic growth exceeded 10 per cent. All countries engaged in relations with China found that their resources were scarcely sufficient to cope with the immense explosion of China's interaction with the rest of the world.

In order to keep some handle on the multifarious activities that now linked China and New Zealand an interdepartmental committee was formed in Wellington late in 1984. Its first task was to survey the whole field of official and officially-sponsored links with China. A year later it was noted that the task of keeping the Chinese in touch with New Zealand's interests could become more challenging and complex as China's own global interests grew. The need for a strategy was grounded in the judgment that, despite the changes that had occurred in China, the political relationship remained the foundation of all other contact, and that to achieve the economic benefits which New Zealand prized, a broadly-based coordinated approach to China was required.[83]

The fruit of this was a much enhanced programme of governmental exchanges, officially named the China Coordinated Programme. There was a substantial increase in the funding available – from $198,000 to $600,000, although mainly through the allocation of separate departmental funds to the one item.[84] The objective for New Zealand was clear: public sector scientific and technical cooperation, as well as academic, cultural and other contacts should be structured in such a way as to support, in particular, the efforts of the private sector to penetrate the Chinese market.[85]

At the beginning of 1986, prompted by the same sense that developments in China were moving at a pace beyond New Zealand's ability to cope, the Foreign Affairs and Defence Committee of Parliament, under the chairmanship of then backbencher Helen Clark, undertook a wide-ranging review of New Zealand's relations with China, one of the most comprehensive studies ever undertaken by the Committee. Like the ambassador a year before, the Committee tried to explain why it was New Zealand seemed to enjoy an especially favourable relationship with China. The reasons it identified varied between the self-evident (trade, taking care with relations with Taiwan), to the less so (a country in which China could test Western opinion) to ones which might seem optimistic (shared views on international issues). Some factors which clearly were important to China – such as attitudes towards the Soviet Union – were not explicitly mentioned.[86] Nor did the Committee contemplate whether China's relations with countries other than New Zealand might be equally 'special'. The Committee's conclusion was that the two countries had indeed achieved a unique association, and that this was an example of cooperation between two different societies. But the Committee cautioned that New Zealand could not afford to coast on past successes nor on the efforts of a small number of those dedicated to extending relations, such as Rewi Alley.[87]

China was also the focus of the 1986 Otago University Foreign Policy School. Held in May, the two day conference provided a view of New Zealand's relations from many perspectives – the historian's, the trader's, the MP's – as well as a number of academic presentations on aspects of contemporary China.[88]

The sequence of high level visits was maintained with David Lange's tour of China in March 1986, his first to that country as Prime Minister.

Lange was able to congratulate China on its decision to cease nuclear testing in the atmosphere and to express the hope that it would cease underground testing before too long. The two sides decided to pursue agreements on double taxation, investment, and science and technology.[89]

The most photogenic event of the visit, featured on the first illustrated cover of New Zealand's official foreign affairs journal, was Lange's meeting with Rewi Alley. In these last years of his life Alley's star had never shone brighter in both his native and his adopted lands. A Rewi Alley scholarship in agricultural science had been instituted in 1985.[90] In 1987 New Zealand made a grant of $180,000 to the Bailie school in Shandan in Gansu, with which Alley had been associated throughout his years in China.[91] That same year the 60th anniversary of Alley's arrival in China was commemorated with a special function in the Great Hall of the People in Tiananmen Square.[92] When Alley died, on 27 December 1987, at the age of 90, the sense of loss in his homeland was more widespread than Alley could ever have conceived when he embarked on his journey with China in 1927. In commenting on his death Lange acknowledged that there were times when Alley's commitment to China put him in opposition to many of his compatriots. But Lange drew attention to the central fact of Alley's life – that his commitment to China was for better and for worse. During the cultural revolution he suffered with his adopted family and with his friends, never contemplating abandoning the country that had become his second home. Many outsiders, said Lange, had been fascinated by China, but only a handful had committed their whole lives to the country.[93]

The cycle of visits continued, with Vice-Premier Wan Li visiting New Zealand in October 1986, Deputy Prime Minister Geoffrey Palmer reciprocating in March 1987 and state councillor Gu Mu coming to New Zealand in November 1987.[94] The expression of sentiments during these visits was uniformly positive, so much so that there may have been moments when the imagination of the speech and communiqué writers deserted them. How else to explain the comment in November 1987 that the two sides confirmed 'a remarkable congruity of views on the kinds of economic structures desirable in both countries'?

New strands were woven into the relationship in 1987 with the establishment of a dialogue between foreign ministry officials in April[95] and with the visits of the frigates *Southland* and *Canterbury* in July. This was the first ever visit by the Royal New Zealand Navy to Shanghai[96] and the first substantial defence contact between the two countries.

The final head of government visit of this period took place in November 1988, when China's new premier, Li Peng, toured New Zealand. It was his first overseas trip since assuming that office and took him also to Australia and Thailand. Li was accompanied by three ministers, and the themes which had characterised relations between China and New Zealand – animal husbandry, the South Pacific nuclear free zone, investment protection (an agreement was signed) – were repeated with varying emphases. Lange said that it was difficult to imagine anything less than the present full and friendly relationship between the two countries. Unfortunately the events of the following year were to prove him wrong.[97]

Trade and economic relations

The maintenance of a satisfactory political relationship was a primary objective for both countries, but the economic benefits that could accrue from an expanded trading relationship lay not far behind, especially for New Zealand.[98] The lure of the huge Chinese market was as seductive for New Zealand as for other nations.[99] Responding to this interest, the first ministerial visit to New Zealand from China was undertaken in July 1973 by the Minister of Foreign Trade, Bai Xiangguo. Hugh Watt, then Acting Prime Minister, said that he was pleased that Bai had come to talk about something that New Zealand was always keen to discuss, namely trade. Bai made plain that it was the establishment of diplomatic relations which allowed the potential for bilateral trade to be brought into play, and that that potential would be handled by 'trading bodies' on both sides.[100] In October Joe Walding paid his second visit to China, this time wearing his hat as Minister of Overseas Trade, and accompanied by a large trade mission. A basic trade agreement was signed on 9 October 1973. Each country granted the other most favoured nation (MFN) status and a joint trade commission (JTC), in the style of centrally planned economies, was established to provide a vehicle for reviewing and fostering trade. By the end of the year Kirk was able to say that New Zealand exporters had won more than $10 million worth of orders,[101] although the smallness of the absolute quantities was readily acknowledged.[102]

The JTC first met in Wellington in April 1975 and thereafter usually annually, and alternately in the two countries.[103] A number of other agreements supplemented or amplified the scope of the original trade agreement, extending to technical aspects of agricultural trade and to tax and investment.[104]

The Chinese market grew steadily in the period under review, and the range of products traded expanded also. But the pattern was similar to that which had prevailed, albeit at low levels, from the very earliest trading days of New Zealand.[105] China looked to New Zealand as a source of raw materials and commodities for its industrial processing – wool, tallow, milk powder, butter, sausage casings, hides and skins. New Zealand's forests made a significant contribution. Whether in the form of pulp or as logs, wood products were the second largest category exported to China, and New Zealand Forest Products maintained direct representation in China. The natural resources of New Zealand went, as they had done for a century, into the factories of the northern hemisphere. From China came a vast array of manufactured goods. But there was one significant difference from those earlier days. In the past the trade had generally been in China's favour. That was no longer the case. One of the regular issues raised at successive JTCs was that New Zealand did not do sufficient to balance the trade – which was from 1975-76 increasingly and substantially in New Zealand's favour.[106]

New Zealand did take a number of steps to meet this concern. New Zealand granted China developing country status in 1978 (the first country to do so), with the result that 70 per cent of China's imports to New Zealand received a margin of preference. The main import items were textiles, yarns, tea, chemicals, animal bristles and the like. Special exhibition licences for trade fairs were one way in which New Zealand encouraged China to probe the New Zealand market, as were licences under the developing country handicraft scheme, and some special licences for handknotted carpets and instore promotions. China also benefited when import licenses were phased out and tariff levels reduced. But there were structural features which impeded the growth of China's trade into New Zealand: sometimes even the minimum orders processed by Chinese producers were larger than the New Zealand market could absorb. Moreover China serviced its largest markets (Japan, North America and the European Community) first.[107]

China's external trade policy framework was not static. In expanding its trade to China, New Zealand was, as were many other countries, a beneficiary of China's decision to open up to the world. A range of new approaches to foreign trade was developed in China from 1978, such as the decentralisation of foreign trade administration through the formation of new export and import corporations, the establishment of special economic zones in the coastal provinces of Guangdong and Fujian (both provinces with extensive links with overseas Chinese communities), and the institution of the China International Trust and Investment Corporation as the equivalent of a merchant bank. The combined effect of these and other measures was that China's total trade increased by 72 per cent between 1980 and 1985. The New Zealand-China trade took its slice of this, more than doubling during these years.[108] The annual value of New Zealand's exports to China reached $538 million in the last full year of the period (July 1988–June 1989).[109]

China's increasing integration with the rest of the world was also reflected by its participation in international organisations. China had taken Taiwan's place in the IMF and the World Bank in 1980. China joined the ADB in 1986 and sought GATT membership in the same year, having become an observer of the GATT textile commission in 1981, and of the GATT Council in 1985. New Zealand assisted by providing training for Chinese officials on the GATT process.[110] New Zealand welcomed these steps. It was not in the business of extracting strategic leverage out of China's interest in joining these bodies.

It would have been remarkable if New Zealand's trade with China had not been able to grow in those years. And it did grow faster than that with New Zealand's other trading partners.[111] Yet the speed of the change and the potential size of the Chinese market so dazzled New Zealanders that comment about trade with China, while never factually incorrect, often lacked proportion. Thus in 1983 China was billed as New Zealand's seventh largest market, but as such it was only taking 2.2 per cent of the country's total exports;[112] similarly in 1984–85 China was New Zealand's sixth largest market, taking $298 million of New Zealand's exports, amounting to 2.6 per cent of the total export trade. At the end of the period China was, and was described as, New Zealand's fifth largest export market. Yet while taking 3.6 per cent of the country's exports it was nowhere near comparable in value as an export market to the four majors – Australia, Japan, the United States and the European Community.[113] And New Zealand's exports did not grow as rapidly as those of some of China's other trading partners, hardly making a dent in the pattern of China's imports.[114]

Yet it was also true that amongst the emerging markets which New Zealand was exploring, China proved to be the tortoise which outran the hares. In a field which also included the Soviet Union, Latin America, Eastern Europe and the Middle East, China was the steady and ultimately winning performer. It provided almost a model of how at a government-to-government level mutually beneficial trade could develop between two very differently organised economies. And not only did China perform well. Its style of trade negotiations proved rather more congenial to New Zealand than that of some of its rivals. China was far from being a self-centred and arrogant 'middle kingdom'. In commerce China was meticulous in observing both the letter and spirit of equality. Warm relationships developed amongst trade officials on both sides, not out of a grudging respect from having worsted or bested one another in a bitter negotiation, but as a personal expression of sharing in a common enterprise.[115]

Traders themselves did not always find it so easy to develop business in China. The Chinese method of business, the importance of friendship as a prerequisite to the closing of a deal, the isolation experienced by those required to spend extended periods of time in China, all contributed to this.[116] These difficulties were acknowledged in parliamentary scrutiny of New Zealand's relations with China[117] and helped tilt the China trade towards a few major commodities, of which the most important by far was wool. China had an interest in New Zealand's cross-bred wools for carpets and for knitting yarns. While there were market, currency and price driven fluctuations in what China bought, wool regularly constituted the largest single New Zealand export to China, and that market took a sizeable amount of New Zealand's wool clip. In 1984–85 China was the largest market by value for New Zealand wool. At the peak in the mid-late 80s, 80 per cent of New Zealands's exports to China were wool and as much as 30 per cent of New Zealand's exported wool was sold to China.[118] The growth in the mid-80s was a direct consequence of China expansionary economic policies. Equally the market could contract suddenly when the brake was put on, as occurred in 1988–89: in the year ending December 1988 only 7 per cent of New Zealand's wool was sold to China.[119]

One feature of trade with China, as with other emerging markets, was the effort made to provide some foundation for commercial enterprise through joint ventures, investment and technical assistance. For China New Zealand was a modern, English-speaking source of technical knowledge which could itself help China modernise. Chinese officials quickly defined the fields of activity in which New Zealand could be deemed to be of interest to China. They were animal husbandry,[120] geothermal energy and forestry.[121]

But moving beyond trade was not always easy. The New Zealand Wool Board invested in a plant in Nantong in Jiangsu province with a view to equipping the factory to handle scoured wool and machine knitwear, and coupled that with a seven year agreement to buy specified volumes of scoured wool from New Zealand. But this agreement fell over when under a regulatory change the plant had to become self-funding.[122] A similar fate befell a Chinese investment with a New Zealand wool cooperative in a scouring plant in Washdyke, South Canterbury when the central authorities baulked at the autonomous importing of scoured wool.[123]

Investment associated with pastoral farming was more successful. In the early years of the relationship China, faithful to the principles guiding its centrally planned economy, preferred dealing with only one representative of a New Zealand sector. Anxious that the several firms with interests in this business not cut each other's throat, the New Zealand Government encouraged the formation of a commercial consortium under the name of China-New Zealand Agricultural Consultants Ltd – CHNZAGCO. The major ventures of CHNZAGCO were model farms in the southern provinces of Guizhou and Guangxi. A first team travelled to Guangxi in June 1979 to evaluate specific sites for a farm.[124]

It was in the nature of emerging markets that government involvement went beyond the practices which governed business with New Zealand's established trading partners. The formation of CHNZAGCO was just one instance. The trade promotion activities of the appropriately named Export-Import Corporation were directed towards China, with the establishment of an office in Xiamen in December 1986. Another feature of trade with China was the large mission, in which a minister would travel to China accompanied by selected business executives and managers. The practice, embraced by both parties of government in New Zealand, was set with the first such visit by Joe Walding in October

1973. The National Government followed suit with Brian Talboys leading missions in 1977 and 1979 and Warren Cooper in 1983. Mike Moore took the trade portfolio when Labour returned to government in July 1984. Later that same year he visited China with 40 accompanying businessmen. The benefit of these missions was hard to gauge. They could not relieve the firms of the need to follow up on many subsequent occasions with their Chinese partners. But in giving a kick start to business ventures, in raising the profile of China as a market in New Zealand, in exploiting the undoubted fact that ministers had an entree where business did not, the missions almost certainly earned their keep.

The traders also helped themselves. A New Zealand–China Trade Association was formed in 1980 by Ron Howell and other China traders. In 1986 the Association had 90 member companies and had sent three missions to China at the invitation of the China Council for the Promotion of International Trade.[125]

Cultural exchanges

For New Zealand an entirely novel feature of the developing relationship with China was the role accorded 'cultural exchanges'. New Zealand governments, because of parsimony, and because of the nature of New Zealand society, had rarely utilised what may loosely be defined as cultural instruments as part of its diplomatic effort. Many countries did, and as the British Council or the Goethe Institute demonstrated, it was certainly not a phenomenon confined to communist countries. But there was a particular way in which communist countries handled such exchanges, and it is not surprising therefore that China set the pace on cultural exchanges, while New Zealand struggled to find sufficient money to reciprocate and had to invent an appropriate institutional structure – the 'China Exchange Programme' (CHEP) – to deal with this aspect of the relationship.[126]

It was, in fact, the visit of a ping pong troupe to New Zealand in July 1972, as in the United States, which was a harbinger of the establishment of diplomatic relations. But in one respect that visit was quite unrepresentative of what was to follow, for sport featured very little in the officially sanctioned programme of exchanges which took place after 1972. This may have been in part a consequence of how the bureaucratic lines were drawn in Beijing. The fact that the most popular sports in the China and New Zealand were not the same was also relevant.

In 1973 one of China's renowned acrobatic troupes – from Guangzhou – made the first post-recognition visit. New Zealand's response was to send a group of potters, who also visited Korea and Japan.[127] A visit by New Zealand's national youth orchestra followed, and was reciprocated by the Shanghai Philharmonic. China's Minister of Culture Huang Zhen visited New Zealand in May 1981; Allan Highet as Minister for the Arts was deemed to be New Zealand's minister of culture and he paid a return visit to China in September 1981. Further visits at ministerial level were exchanged in 1988–89.

The world of the Maori was brought to the attention of China. In 1978 a Maori carver demonstrated his art to admiring crowds in the Forbidden City[129] and in 1979 a Maori performing group held concerts in Guilin, Guangzhou and Beijing. In the south they were brought alongside some of China's minority nationalities, which to the Chinese enjoyed a status similar to that they perceived Maori to have in New Zealand.[130]

Exchanges of this kind had some impact on knowledge of each country in the other, but educational exchanges were far more significant. In this sphere self-interest, especially in language learning, was to the fore on both sides. One of New Zealand's attractions for China was that it was English-speaking. China was quick to identify ways of utilising this. At an early stage New Zealand teachers were recruited to teach in China while a steady stream of Chinese students came to study the English language in New Zealand. In the other direction the New Zealand Government, as part of the China Exchange Programme, selected New Zealanders, mostly university students, to study the Chinese language in China for one to two years. The investment in Chinese language acquisition paid off, with many students subsequently employed in the public or private sectors dealing with China.[131]

There was another reason why this commitment from the New Zealand side was significant. The Chinese Government was still reacting against the years in which foreign powers had exploited and plundered China. Anything which smacked of this, such as foreign development assistance, was unacceptable to the Chinese authorities. Education was the closest New Zealand came to offering 'aid' to China in those early years of the relationship. Chinese support for New Zealand students in China helped make it clear that this was an exchange, not aid.

China changed its policy in the 1980s and was prepared to accept foreign development assistance. In June 1981 both the New Zealand embassy in Beijing and the Chinese embassy in New Zealand were exploring with Wellington the boundaries of New Zealand's aid policy.[132] The issue was not only of interest to managers of the relationship. New Zealand businesses often felt themselves disadvantaged in the highly competitive Chinese market because their government did not ease their path with soft loans, aid and the like.[133] In fact it was not until 1986 that official development assistance to China did commence, with the allocation of $250,000 for a programme for China. In 1989/90 this reached $750,000. In support of New Zealand's commercial objectives, the expenditure was targeted to grasslands.[134]

China had long done its own recruiting of experts. The commonest task foreign experts from countries such as New Zealand were asked to perform was the 'polishing' of English translations of Chinese publications. Many journalists and teachers spent one or two years, mostly in Beijing, engaged in such tasks.[135] China also had an interest in other skills available in New Zealand, such as medicine, nursing, tourism, information technology, agriculture and management.[136]

Treated as part of the cultural exchange programme by China, but seen as supporting trade and commercial objectives by New Zealand, scientific exchanges partook of the character of both. The Chinese took them seriously: a small but senior delegation from the Royal Society of New Zealand was received by Deng Xiaoping when it visited China in 1975. Agreements for scientific and technological exchange were a staple of centrally planned economies. When a mission of senior DSIR officials led by the Minister of Science and Technology visited China in 1984, they signed a joint technology agreement with China's State Science and Technology Commission which identified six areas of major interest to both countries: horticulture, storage of food, hill country grasslands, geothermal energy, earthquake engineering, and industrial processing. The weighting to New Zealand's economic interests is obvious. A fully fledged intergovernmental science and technology agreement was signed in 1987. The range of exchanges was remarkable, and included the replenishment of New Zealand kiwifruit with root stock from its Chinese relative.[138]

Over time the range of areas in which official exchanges took place steadily widened, even to areas such as banking and law, in which it might be thought, given the divergent nature of the societies, that there would be little in common between the two countries.[139]

The exchanges and contacts which were undertaken by the governments were amplified and extended by an even larger range of people-to-people contacts. Local authorities in New Zealand developed 'sister city' links with Chinese counterparts. This was a familiar concept in other parts of the world. In China it developed as a degree of autonomy was devolved to provinces and major cities in their dealings with the outside world. The first such exchange was established in March 1981 between Hastings in Hawke's Bay and Guilin in Guangxi, and was promoted by a New Zealand scientist who had built up contacts with the Chinese horticulture institute in Guilin. By 1996 there were 11. The matches were sometimes rather curious, but no more so than others elsewhere in the world. While such relationships sometimes had a deserved reputation for being little more than an excuse for intercontinental junketing, with China such bonds were one of the few ways durable links could be established outside the central authorities.[140]

Despite the general success of people-to-people exchanges, there were some mixed experiences. During his visit to New Zealand in 1985 Hu Yaobang invited a group of young people to visit China. A delegation was duly organised, led by Richard Northey and Katherine O'Regan, two of the younger MPs, one Labour and one National. The delegation was an eclectic group, so much so that its members spent more time in China quarrelling amongst themselves, with scant regard for the embarrassment this behaviour caused the Chinese hosts.[141] Notwithstanding, at least some were prepared to host the return visit from China in 1986.[142]

The New Zealand–China Friendship Society continued to foster links through its network, and for some years remained the principal way by which travellers other than those associated with an official exchange could visit China. This role diminished with the opening up of China to a variety of modes of travel from 1979 on. The Society's role in New Zealand was matched by a much larger number of official and quasi-official organisations in China – the counterpart Chinese People's Association for Friendship with Foreign Countries, and others such as the People's Institute of Foreign Affairs, which hosted two visits from the New Zealand Institute of International Affairs during this period.[143]

Tiananmen

The steady development of relations between China and New Zealand was interrupted in June 1989, when Chinese troops forcefully suppressed student demonstrations in the heart of the Chinese capital – Tiananmen Square. Along with other Western countries New Zealand's reaction was immediate and sharp. An internal foreign ministry analysis of these events noted that China would be disposed to press ahead with 'business as usual', that Western countries would not find this very easy to reciprocate in the immediate aftermath of Tiananmen, but that given the interests at stake in China, any prolonged shunning of China was unlikely, if only because it might be perceived as giving an advantage to the Soviet Union.[144] The steps taken by New Zealand were carefully calibrated to this analysis, demonstrating in a number of formal and symbolic ways the government's outrage but not ceasing support for people-to-people contacts or business dealings. Crucially there was to be no embargo on trade. High-profile bilateral activities that could be seen to lend an appearance of endorsement of the events of 3-4 June were eschewed.[145] A formal protest was made, the forthcoming visit of the Minister of Police, Peter Tapsell, was cancelled, and a review of future ministerial level exchanges was undertaken. Maximum advantage was taken of the delays which often attended the setting up of exchanges; other initiatives were put on the 'back burner' rather than cancelled outright.[146] Social contact at ministerial and permanent head level was suspended. And the Government officially expressed concern that a relationship on which New Zealand was coming to place increasing reliance might be less predictable than was once thought.[147]

The actions in Tiananmen Square did expose serious tensions in the New Zealand and general Western view of China. The Chinese Government had not itself changed its mode of dealing with dissent. What had changed was Western engagement with China, and Western expectations that China would move towards Western political standards, as it was moving towards Western economic models. What had also changed was the ability of electronic media – present in force in China because of the visit of President Gorbachev – to transmit images of what happened in Tiananmen Square around the world.[148] In explaining to China why New Zealand had reacted in the way it had, New Zealand ministers and officials were obliged to lay stress on those points on which the two countries differed, aspects which, while never denied, had never been highlighted in the standard presentations on the relations between the two countries. Foreign Minister Russell Marshall told the Chinese ambassador that the two countries had different systems and attitudes, and that New Zealand could not share China's view that the events of June and their aftermath were solely an internal matter for China.[149]

Yet while the West had misinterpreted China, in another respect it had not. China had changed. Ironically China was by almost every definition a more liberal society in 1989, when Westerners were shocked by what happened in Tiananmen Square, than in the early 1970s, when they embraced Mao and explained away the cultural revolution, something even the Chinese themselves gave up doing some years later. It seemed always China's fate to be the subject of debate within the West. One of the significant consequences of Tiananmen was that the political Left, which had given China the benefit of the doubt in the 1970s and 1980s, ceased to do so.

In the aftermath of Tiananmen, the New Zealand Government sought to strike a balance between popular shock at the abuse of human rights in China, and a continuing recognition that China remained an important partner for New Zealand in the Asia-Pacific region. Government replies to letters from concerned citizens expressed shared concern at the horror of the events of early June while registering that China remained a country with which New Zealand would need to continue to be in contact.[150] On 24 August 1989 it was announced that there would not yet be a renewal of contacts at a ministerial level – violations of human rights could not be regarded as simply an internal affair. But New Zealand would encourage the participation of China in the GATT, would promote people-to-people contact and business dealings; exchanges would take place 'where appropriate' and support for high-level bilateral activities would be considered on a 'case-by-case' basis.[151] A number of bilateral visits did take place later in the year; in featuring them under the general heading of 'North Asia – a booming trade relationship' in the Foreign Affairs Review there was not a single reference to Tiananmen.[152]

One of the trickiest issues confronting the Government was the future of Chinese students and other Chinese nationals who happened to be in New Zealand in June 1989 and did not wish to return to China.

Despite assurances from Premier Li Peng that no returning student would be adversely treated, the Government moved with care, and allowed extension of visas to take place as a matter of course, while the tenor of events became clearer.

A further easing of the relationship was announced by Foreign Affairs and Trade Minister Mike Moore on 5 March 1990: officials would travel to Beijing for official consultations with Chinese authorities and ministerial visits would resume soon. The shift in policy was anchored to a number of elements – there had been no recurrence of major violence; martial law had been lifted; detainees had been released; and New Zealand's concerns had been made known to the Chinese Government.

Secretary of Foreign Affairs Graham Ansell led a delegation to the first official consultations with China since Tiananmen in Beijing in April 1990. The visit was described as a further step in the evolution of the New Zealand-China relationship. While Ansell reported that trade had dropped off, he noted that this was related to the state of the Chinese economy – not to reverberations from Tiananmen.[153]

The next relaxation came in August, over a year after Tiananmen. Under the heading 'New Zealand/China: Revitalising the Relationship' the New Zealand Foreign Affairs Review reported that the Government had begun to take steps to 'revitalise' the relationship. The Government's response was described as a measured one: the level of contact had been raised again. The first visits under the new dispensation were by Vice Foreign Minister Liu Huaqiu in August 1990 to New Zealand and Minister of Forestry Jim Sutton in September 1990 to China. Sutton was the first ministerial visitor from a Western country to visit China since the events of June 1989. New Zealand's willingness to give an early sign that it could look ahead as well as back in its relationship with China was duly acknowledged: Sutton was received by Premier Li Peng. Sutton's message that New Zealand wanted to cooperate with China in areas of mutual benefit was carefully balanced with an expression of the continuing concern of New Zealanders and their government about the human rights situation in China.[154] When therefore Labour handed over the reins of government to National in November 1990, the relationship with China was back on an even keel, although specific issues, such as the fate of students in New Zealand at the time of Tiananmen, were unresolved.

Conclusion

Eighteen years is not a long period of time, but it was a period in which New Zealand and China had to compensate for the previous 23 years of separation. If that was the fundamental objective on both sides, then it was accomplished. If in 1972 New Zealand had sought primarily a dialogue with China then that had been achieved. While the era of multilateral engagement with China lay ahead, the practice of exchanging views on key international issues had become well-established, if at times ritualistic. There had not been such high expectations on the economic front, but China proved to be a solid and at times substantial addition to New Zealand's markets.

Each side had become familiar with the other's mode of doing business. Chinese visiting New Zealand were struck by the informality, the wealth, the lack of people and the sparkling nature of the country. New Zealanders in China became accustomed to the ritual of the Chinese banquet, the enticement to drink toasts in fiery maotai, the formal exchange of compliments and titles, in general to the customs of a venerable civilisation. At times New Zealanders were frustrated by the rigidity in the patterns of doing business in China. And the many New Zealanders who participated in people-to-people contacts, while enjoying them for their own sake, were often puzzled, and sometimes disturbed, by the political overlay that was an invariable accompaniment of such encounters. But more often those visiting China were fascinated and intrigued with what they saw and, at least before June 1989, willing to give China and its people the benefit of the doubt.

Yet throughout the two countries diverged in the way they viewed the international system and their place in it. Without a revolutionary past of its own, New Zealand had no great quarrel with the way the world was ordered – although it could see many ways in which that order could be improved, particularly to make the fortunes of small countries more dependent on the rule of law than the exercise of power. China was not so content. Apart from its own revolutionary temper, China was preoccupied with two large unresolved and related issues – its independence, limited as it saw it by one hegemon after another (the European powers, Japan, the United States and now the Soviet Union), and its reunification. For China, being a strong and powerful country was the only way to ensure that its interests were respected by those who had hitherto trampled over them.

Anything which China felt challenged it on these two key issues could do great damage to the links between the two countries. Conversely 'recognition' in several senses was the key which unlocked the relationship. Treating China with respect, according its interests legitimacy – matters on which New Zealand had no reason to be grudging – helped build confidence in the relationship. And the handling of relations with Taiwan was a fundamental test for China of the sincerity with which New Zealand approached its relations with China. It was also a challenge. For if New Zealanders tended to underestimate the political context in which most contact with China took place, China tended to overestimate the political significance of actions by New Zealanders.

The professional managers of the relationship in New Zealand were well aware of Chinese sensitivities, and generally successful in calculating to a nicety the relative benefit to New Zealand of any course of action, particularly one involving Taiwan. But to the New Zealander in the street these matters were of little moment. The practical benefits of relations with China were thought to be at the centre of New Zealand's interests. If commercial returns from China were thin or difficult to achieve, interest waned, and acceptance of the peculiar way in which New Zealand had to deal with Taiwan became less automatic. Events such as Tiananmen played to this sentiment.

Yet the conclusion from the record of these years is that differences of perspective, policy and practice did not impede the establishment and management of a relationship from which both could benefit. If there is a message to be drawn from New Zealand's resumed encounter with China it is not that the two countries enjoyed a uniquely special relationship, but that despite being so different they could still find a sure foundation on which to engage with each other.

Notes

1 I should record that the views expressed in this chapter are entirely my own and do not represent any official viewpoint. My thanks to Ken Ross, and to other present and former colleagues in the External Assessments Bureau and in the Ministry of Foreign Affairs and Trade who either commented on a draft of this paper or helped me track down information. Following the convention adopted by China in 1979, Chinese personal and place names are spelt in pinyin, even when they were familiar in other transliterations before that date: thus Zhou

Enlai instead of Chou En-lai and Beijing instead of Peking. The *New Zealand Foreign Affairs Review* (hereafter *NZFAR*) followed suit almost immediately, although it did not switch from 'Peking' to 'Beijing' until 1985. 'Beijing' was not officially adopted as the designation of the embassy until 1990.

2   Zhang Beihua argues that the frame of reference into which China fitted its relations with New Zealand was the theory of the three worlds, in which the first world was the competing superpowers (the United States and the Soviet Union), the second world the other developed countries (including Australia and New Zealand) and the third world the developing world. China saw itself as resisting the hegemonic tendencies of both superpowers and enlisting the support of both the second and third worlds in that mission. See his 'Sino-New Zealand Relations: Political, Economic and Cultural Development to the 1980s' (M.Phil thesis, University of Waikato, 1988) pp.43–7. While this theory was undoubtedly the formal organising principle of China's external policy, what is evident and noteworthy during the period under review is the extent to which China saw the Soviet Union as the primary threat to the world, and on this basis found common ground with the United States – and other countries, including New Zealand. But the tension between theory and practice explains *inter alia* why China could at one moment support New Zealand's membership of ANZUS while at another favour New Zealand's anti-nuclear policy. See pp.239–41. See also K. Janaki 'China's Search for Allies', in *New Zealand International Review* (hereafter *NZIR*), May–June 1979, pp.19–21.

3   The New Zealand Communist Party (CPNZ) had been one of the few in the world to support the Chinese Communist Party not the Communist Party of the Soviet Union at the time of the Sino-Soviet split, and had reaped Chinese gratitude accordingly. Party leaders regularly visited Beijing. At the time of the first ministerial visit to China (see pp.231–2), CPNZ general secretary Vic Wilcox was also in Beijing. The Renmin Ribao carried photos of Wilcox meeting Premier Zhou Enlai on the front page and of Walding meeting Qiao Guanhua inside. But by the end of the year the embassy was reporting that references to the CPNZ in the official Chinese media had fallen away: MFAT 58/264/1 New Zealand Embassy Beijing to Ministry of Foreign Affairs (hereafter MFA) 27 December 1973.

4   Rewi Alley's role in New Zealand's relations with China cannot be dealt with appropriately within the confines of this article. See Geoff Chapple, *Rewi Alley of China* (Auckland, 1980); and Rewi Alley, *Rewi Alley: An Autobiography* (Beijing/Auckland, 1987), with a catalogue of his writings pp.329–31. A critical view of Rewi Alley, including of the New Zealand Government's interactions with him after 1972, is in Anne-Marie Brady, 'Man to Myth: Rewi Alley of China' (MA thesis, University of Auckland, 1994). A collection of Rewi Alley papers has been donated by the Chinese People's Friendship Association to the Alexander Turnbull Library Wellington and was deposited in the Library in April 1999.

5   See Prime Minister Norman Kirk in *NZFAR*, December 1972, p.14 and the Annual Report of the Ministry of Foreign Affairs for the year ended 31 March 1973 in *NZFAR*, June 1973, p.9.

6   The lead up to New Zealand's recognition of the People's Republic is covered by John Scott, 'Recognising China', in the previous volume of *New Zealand in World Affairs*, Vol.II (Wellington, 1991) pp.227–52.

7   Although the prospects of trade growth with China were not rated highly by the government's economic advisers, *source:* W. B. Harland.
8   September 1972, pp.44–8.
9   *NZFAR*, September 1972, p.70.
10 Scott, 'Recognising China', p.250.
11 'It is logical . . .; there is no point in delaying about such a fundamental issue", in *NZFAR*, December 1972, p.14.
12 Wellington, 1971; see also M. McKinnon, *Independence and Foreign Policy* (Auckland, 1993) p.173.
13 D.J. McCraw, 'Objectives and Priorities in New Zealand's Foreign Policy in Asia 1949–75: a study of the recognition of the People's Republic of China and of Security policies in South-east Asia' (Ph.D thesis, University of Otago, 1978), p.272.
14 McCraw, 'Objectives and Priorities', pp.275, 259, 280; Margaret Hayward, *Diary of the Kirk Years* (Wellington, 1981) p.107.
15 Scott, 'Recognising China', p.249; on Kirk's caution see also Steve Hoadley, in *New Zealand and Taiwan: The Policy and Practice of Quasi-Diplomacy* (Wellington, 1993), p.8 and n.10.
16 Scott, 'Recognising China', pp.249–50.
17 Telegram from MFA to New Zealand High Commission Canberra 23 January 1973, MFAT 58/264/1 Pt.3.
18 See Kirk's careful reply to Trevor Davey, the new MP for the marginal electorate of Gisborne, where maize growers felt particularly disadvantaged by the severing of relations with Taiwan, MFAT 58/264/1 Pt.3, 2 February 1973.
19 Letter of 12 March 1973, MFAT 58/264/1 Pt.3. There was some subsequent scrutiny of the English and Chinese texts of the communiqué, as attention had been drawn to different formulations used in respect of the Chinese position on Taiwan. In the communiqué recording the establishment of diplomatic relations between Canada and China in October 1970 Canada 'takes note' (zhuyi dao) of the Chinese position. The United Kingdom, upgrading its relations in March 1972, 'acknowledges' (chengren) the Chinese position, and this became known as the British formula. Japan, in September 1972, 'fully understands and respects' (chongfen lijie he zunzhong) the Chinese position. Australia and New Zealand in December 1972 followed the 'British' formula ie acknowledge/chengren, as did the the United States in December 1978. See also Scott, 'Recognising China', p.250. Hoadley provides a detailed survey of New Zealand's relations with Taiwan after 1972.
20 MFAT 58/264/1 Pt.3.
21 Zhang, 'Sino-New Zealand Relations', p.21. China's second ambassador in New Zealand, Qin Lizhen, had previously served in Norway.
22 Until 1972 China had no diplomatic missions in non-communist Asia east of Burma.
23 Cf. Lindsay Watt, *New Zealand and China Towards 2000* (Wellington, 1992) p.29.
24 Zhang uses this tripartite approach to the relationship.
25 See reflections on Canada's 'special relationship' with China in terms which could be applied *mutatis mutandis* to New Zealand in B. Michael Frolic, 'The Trudeau Initiative', in Paul M. Evans and B. Michael Frolic (eds.), *Reluctant Adversaries:*

Canada and the People's Republic of China, 1949–1970 (Toronto, 1991), pp.212–13.
26 Report of meeting with MFA officials on 6 February 1973, MFAT 58/264/1 Pt.3; *Christchurch Star*, 9 February 1973.
27 Alley to MFA officials 6 February 1973, MFAT 58/264/1 Pt.3.
28 See comment from the Chinese Permanent Mission to the United Nations in New York reported by the New Zealand Mission to MFA on 20 March 1973, MFAT 58/264/1 Pt.3.
29 Submission to the Prime Minister 8 February 1973, MFAT 58/264/1 Pt.3.
30 Hardware importer J. C. Lawford of C. E. Lawford Ltd met Associate Minister of Foreign Affairs and Minister of Overseas Trade Joe Walding on 8 February 1973, MFAT 58/264/1 Pt. 3. Ron Howell of Vadco Traders referred to in submission to the PM of 8 February 1973, MFAT 58/264/1 Pt.3.
31 Tony Garnier, Bruce Kohn and Pat Booth, *The Hunter and the Hill* (Auckland, 1978), p.124,
32 The Foreign Affairs portfolio itself was held by PM Kirk.
33 For this timing see reference in submission of 8 February 1973 to PM, MFAT 58/264/1 Pt.3.
34 *NZFAR*, March 1973, p.32.
35 Successive Chinese ambassadors to New Zealand in this period were:
    1973   Pei Jianzhang
    1979   Qin Lizhen
    1984   Zhang Longhai
    1987   Ni Zhengjian.
36 *NZFAR*, April 1973, p.6.
37 Draft report by W. B. Harland on the Walding visit 7 May 1973, MFAT 58/264/1 Pt.4.
38 Draft report by W. B. Harland 7 May 1973, MFAT 58/264/1 Pt.4.
39 *NZFAR*, April 1973, pp.7–8. See also Zhang, 'Sino–New Zealand Relations', p.52, noting the extent to which Walding listed the differences between the two countries. Perhaps it was the same imperative to find points in common that had New Zealand subscribing to opposition to 'hegemony' – in the press communique issued at the conclusion of the visit, *NZFAR*, April 1973, p.9.
40 Draft report by W. B. Harland 7 May 1973, MFAT 58/264/1 Pt.4.
41 *NZFAR*, April 1973, p.9.
42 See Kirk's comment in his speech to the NZIIA 25 August 1973 in *NZFAR*, August 1973, p.10. It so happened that this was the very day that the advance party for the New Zealand Embassy in Beijing entered China, and found itself grounded in Guangzhou because of the associated closure of Chinese air space.
43 Ambassador Harland's report on his first week, MFAT 58/264/1 Pt.4, 24 September 1973.
44 Successive New Zealand ambassadors to China in this period were:
    1973   W. B. Harland
    1975   R. B. Atkins
    1979   H. Freeman-Greene
    1982   F. A. Small
    1985   L. J. Watt
    1990   M. J. Powles.

45 *NZFAR*, August 1975, p.55. He did visit as Leader of the Opposition in September 1976, just after Mao's death, and met a Hua Guofeng confident that he was to be Mao's successor. John Henderson, *Rowling: The Man and the Myth* (Auckland, 1981), pp.156–7.
46 Norrish record of conversation with Muldoon, 3 December 1975, MFAT 58/264/1 Pt.5.
47 W. David McIntyre, 'From Singapore to Harare', pp.92–6 above.
48 MFAT 58/264/1 Pt.5, 22 December 1975.
49 R .D. Muldoon, *Muldoon* (Wellington, 1977), p.197.
50 *NZFAR*, April–June 1976, p.10.
51 NZ Embassy Beijing to MFA, 6 April 1976, MFAT 58/264/1 Pt.6. Kennaway, 'The Great Power Context', in John Henderson, Keith Jackson and Richard Kennaway (eds.), *Beyond New Zealand: The Foreign Policy of a Small State* (Auckland, 1980), p.27 notes the widespread view that Muldoon's early stress on the Soviet threat was related to his wish to be assured a favourable reception during his visit to China. See also McKinnon, *Independence and Foreign Policy*, p.197.
52 Muldoon, *Muldoon*, p.128.
53 NZ Embassy Washington to MFA, 24 May 1976 in MFAT 58/264/1 Pt.6, enclosing amongst other reports an article from *The Washington Post* of 9 May 1976.
54 Muldoon, *Muldoon*, p.182.
55 Corner to Muldoon, 7 April 1976, MFAT 58/264/1 Pt.6.
56 *NZFAR*, January–June 1979, p.27; see also Rod Alley, 'Another Vietnam?', in *NZIR*, April 1979, p.25
57 He was followed by Lee Kuan Yew of Singapore on 12 May and last of all by Bhutto of Pakistan on 27 May, *China Quarterly*, July–September 1976, pp.683, 685.
58 When Chairman Hua Guofeng visited North Korea in May 1978 it was the first visit to any foreign country by China's most senior leader in 21 years – since Mao went to Moscow in 1957.
59 *NZFAR*, July–September 1977, pp.22–3.
60 *NZFAR*, April–June 1980, p.39.
61 Because of the changing structures of the Chinese government and party it is not a straightforward matter to determine what, in Chinese terms, is a high-level visit. If we define head of government in China to include the General Secretary of the party as well as the Premier, then there were three visits each way in the period: Zhao, Hu and Li from China and Muldoon (twice) and Lange (once) to China. China had its own challenge in interpreting official protocol in New Zealand, duly according high ranking to visits by the Chief Justice and by Speakers of the House because of their place in New Zealand's official order of precedence.
62 Telegram NZ Commission Hong Kong to MFA, Wellington, 22 May 1980, MFAT 58/264/1 Pt.10.
63 *NZFAR*, April–June 1980, p. 39.
64 R. D. Muldoon, *My Way* (Wellington, 1981), p.154.
65 Telegram NZ Embassy Beijing to MFA, 14 September 1980, MFAT 58/264/1 Pt.10.
66 China opened embassies in Apia and Suva in 1976 and in Port Moresby in 1980.

Missions in Tarawa and Vila were added in the 1980s. See K. Ross, *Regional Security in the South Pacific: the Quarter-Century 1970–95* (Canberra, 1993), p.63.
67 Telegrams NZ Embassy Beijing to MFA 14 September 1980, MFAT 58/264/1 Pt.10.
68 Telegrams NZ Embassy Beijing to MFA 14 September 1980, MFAT 58/264/1 Pt.10; and Muldoon, *My Way*, pp.154–5.
69 *Source:* Simon Murdoch (then attached to the PM's office).
70 *NZFAR*, July–September 1980, p.8. Li was returning to China from the United States in 1941 when his ship was diverted to New Zealand. Contact between Li and his former colleagues in New Zealand was re-established when Li sent a small box of kiwifruit seeds to the New Zealand Embassy in Beijing.
71 *NZFAR*, January–March 1981, p.29.
72 Muldoon to Zhao, 24 February 1983 and telegram NZ Embassy Beijing to MFA 8 March 1983, MFAT 58/264/1 Pt.12; see also *NZFAR*, No.1, 1983, pp.14–15.
73 China acceded to the Antarctic Treaty on 8 June 1983. It sent a large expedition to the Antarctic peninsula area in the 1984–85 season to establish a base and conduct research. Having done this China was admitted to consultative status in the treaty in September 1985: Report of the Foreign Affairs and Defence Committee On the Inquiry into the New Zealand-China Relationship 1987 (hereafter FADC Report), p.84.
74 NZ Embassy Beijing to MFA 23 February 1984, MFAT 58/264/1 Pt.12.
75 NZ Embassy Beijing to MFA 23 February 1984, MFAT 58/264/1 Pt.12.
76 Zhang, 'Sino–New Zealand Relations', p.74.
77 Article in *Renmin Ribao*, 31 January 1985, cited in *The China Quarterly* 102, p.381. See also the comments supportive of Labour policy by Rewi Alley in his autobiography, pp.268–9.
78 Initially as Chairman and then, under the new party constitution adopted in September 1982, as General Secretary. Although as such he had no rank in the state hierarchy, New Zealand had no difficulty in treating him as a head of government: Zhang, 'Sino–New Zealand Relations', p.78.
79 Zhang, 'Sino–New Zealand Relations', p.72, citing *Beijing Review*, 24 March 1986 p.12 [sic]. Of incidental interest is that during this visit Hu announced significant – and subsequently controversial – reductions in the levels of China's armed forces.
80 *NZFAR*, April–June 1985, p.43.
81 China signed the South Pacific Nuclear Free Zone protocols on 10 February 1987; they entered into force for China on 21 October 1988. [The Soviet Union had been the first nuclear weapon state to sign the protocols – in December 1986].
82 Ambassador Beijing to MFA, 26 February 1985, MFAT 58/264/1 Pt.14.
83 Submission December 1985, MFAT 58/264/1 Pt.15. See also on same file Pt.14 exchange of messages between Embassy Beijing and MFA 30 August, 2 and 18 October and strategy paper October 1985.
84 Although it was noted that achievement of that figure was still dependent on MFA being able to spring the funds: MFA to New Zealand Embassy Beijing 5 February 1986, MFAT 58/264/1 Pt.15.
85 Submission 21 January 1986 and minutes of interdepartmental committee 4 February 1986, MFAT 58/264/1 Pt.15; E. A. Woodfield, 'The New Zealand-China Trade Relationship', in Ann Trotter (ed.), *New Zealand and China* (Dunedin, 1986), pp.109–10.

86 There is speculation p.16 that China's interest in the South Pacific may be directed at countering Soviet activity.
87 FADC Report, pp.17, 60.
88 The proceedings were published: see Trotter, *New Zealand and China*.
89 *NZFAR*, January–March 1986, p.6; Zhang, 'Sino–New Zealand Relations', pp.79–80. China had last tested in the atmosphere in 1980.
90 Other scholarships honouring Rewi Alley were established by the University of Waikato in 1977 and by Christchurch City Council in 1986: Brady, 'Man to Myth', pp.104–5.
91 *NZFAR*, January–March 1987, p.22. $150,000 was a grant for the capital construction; $30,000 a subsidy to the New Zealand-China Friendship Society.
92 *NZFAR*, April–June 1987, pp.25–6.
93 *NZFAR*, October–December 1987, pp.30–1. In April 1988 a number of commemorative meetings were held in honour of Alley at the scenes of his labours in China – Shandan, Lanzhou and Beijing. Associate MFA Fran Wilde represented New Zealand. See also Zhang, 'Sino–New Zealand Relations', pp.155–9.
94 *NZFAR*, July–September 1986, p.28; January–March 1987, p.21; No.1, 1988, p.31.
95 SFA Merwyn Norrish visited China. His host on that occasion, Vice Foreign Minister Zhu Qizhen, returned the visit in April 1988: *NZFAR*, April–June 1987, p.25 and April–June 1988, p.32.
96 *NZFAR*, October–December 1987, p.29.
97 *NZFAR*, 1989, No.1, pp.37–8.
98 See generally C. B. Stanworth, 'China's trade doors are open', in *NZIR*, January–February 1980, pp.28–9; Warren Cooper speech 23 August 1983 on 'New Zealand's Trading Relationship with China', in *NZFAR*, July–September 1983, pp.8–11; Woodfield, 'Trade Relationship'; FADC Report, pp.23–39; Frances Lee, 'Trading with China', in *NZIR*, January–February 1987, pp.17–22; Zhang, *Sino–New Zealand Relations*, ch.5 'Economic Relations', pp.85–125; Barbara G. Sutton, 'New Zealand–China Trade Relations in the Eighties' (post-graduate diploma thesis, University of Otago, 1989); Tim Beal, 'New Zealand and Greater China', in Tim Beal and Yongjin Zhang (eds.), *New Zealand and China: Present and Future Issues in NZ–China Relations* (Wellington, 1996), pp.85–133; Yongjin Zhang, 'New Zealand Trade with China in the 1990s', in Beal and Zhang, *New Zealand and China*, pp.135–56; Kang Yuanfei, 'New Zealand Trade with China', in Beal and Zhang, *New Zealand and China*, pp.157–64.
99 The cliché 'if I could sell just one widget to every person in China . . .' was exemplified in New Zealand by the post-war commentator who argued that 'if every Chinese was to require one pound of butter a year, China would be able to dispose of New Zealand's entire export of the stuff'. Philip Mathews, *China and New Zealand* (Auckland, 1949) p.6, cited by Zhang, 'Sino-New Zealand Relations', p.99.
100 *NZFAR*, July 1973, pp.3–6.
101 *NZFAR*, December 1973, p.30.
102 Rowling in FAR February 1975 p.10: only 0.96 per cent of New Zealand's total exports.
103 *NZFAR*, April 1975, p.30. The final JTC for this period was the 13th, held in Beijing in April 1990.

104 Including trademarks (June 1975), extending MFN to shipping (May 1976); conditions of entry for bovine semen (October 1984), live cattle and sheep (March 1985), and pipfruit (April 1985); cooperation in forestry and wool/textiles; double taxation (September 1986), scientific and technical cooperation (March 1987), plant quarantine (June 1988) and investment protection (November 1988): Woodfield, 'Trade Relationship', pp.1–2; Lee, 'Trading with China', p.17; Sutton, *New Zealand–China Trade*, pp.10–12.

105 C. J. Elder and M. F. Green, 'New Zealand and China 1792-1972', in Ann Trotter (ed.), pp.16–17, 23–4, 28–31, 43–4, 54–6.

106 See e.g. *NZFAR*, November 1983, p.28; *NZFAR*, 1988, No.1, p.31.

107 Woodfield, 'Trade Relationship', p.106; Lee, 'Trading with China', p.19; Zhang, *Sino–New Zealand Relations*, p.104.

108 Woodfield, 'Trade Relationship', p.110 notes that whereas China's total imports were estimated to be up to 70 per cent in 1985, New Zealand's exports [only] expanded by 40 per cent from 1983 to 1985.

109 Beal, 'New Zealand and Greater China', p.124.

110 Lee, 'Trading with China', p.18.

111 Kang, 'Trade with China', pp.157–8.

112 *NZFAR*, July–September 1983, pp.8–10.

113 Cf. Darryl Walker and John Henderson, 'China: A Study in Changed Perceptions', in Henderson, Jackson and Kennaway, *Beyond New Zealand*, p.197.

114 Between 1986 and 1994 the annual growth rate of United States exports to China was 21 per cent, of New Zealand 9 per cent: Kang p.160. In the late 1980s New Zealand supplied only 0.70 per cent of China's imports: Watt, *New Zealand and China*, p.11.

115 Zhu Youlan, the long serving official of the Ministry of Foreign Trade who dealt with New Zealand, became a close friend of senior trade official Harry Clark and his wife.

116 Spelt out in great detail by Howard Scott at the 1986 Otago Foreign Policy School: Trotter, *New Zealand and China*, pp.113–23.

117 FADC Report, pp.31–2.

118 Roger Buchanan, 'Chasing the Dragon', in *Wool Report New Zealand* 4/88 p.7; Watt, *New Zealand and China*, pp.10–11.

119 *Source:* Roger Buchanan, NZ Wool Group. Thus the collapse of exports in 1989-1990 was not a consequence of Tiananmen as suggested by Zhang, 'New Zealand Trade with China', p.141. See below n.153.

120 Usage in the Chinese language draws a clear distinction between agriculture – nongye – and animal husbandry or pastoral farming – xumuye. New Zealanders tend to refer indiscriminately to 'agriculture' but by that mean predominantly sheep and cattle raising.

121 For just one example of the citation of these areas see the report of the visit of Vice-Premier Li Xiannian in May 1980, *NZFAR*, April–June 1980, p.39.

122 *Source:* Roger Buchanan, NZ Wool Group. See also *NZFAR*, October–December 1980, p.42.

123 *Source:* Roger Buchanan, NZ Wool Group. See also *NZFAR*, October–December 1985, p.30. Towards the end of the period there were a number of joint ventures in both countries. In China these ranged across sectors as various as livestock

feed meal processing (Shandong), printed circuit board manufacture (Shenzhen), textile quilts, small air compressors (Fujian), and processing/repackaging of fish (Zhuhai). None were large investments: Sutton, 'New Zealand–China Trade', p.37. See lists in A.E. Bollard, 'A Note on Chinese–New Zealand Economic Relations in the Year of the Sheep', Working Paper 91/6, NZ Institute of Economic Research, Wellington, 1991, pp.12–13.

124 *NZFAR*, January–June 1979, p.28. Both Guizhou and Guangxi were poor provinces, not frequented by Westerners at this time. One of the consequences was that New Zealand visitors regularly came into contact with senior provincial officials – including Hu Jintao, then party secretary in Guizhou, now (1999) vice-president of China.

125 Victor Percival, 'China-New Zealand Trade: Difficulties and Successes as viewed from the perspective of the old China hand', in Trotter, *New Zealand and China*, p.124.

126 Cf. generally FADC Report, pp.35–56, 108–11; Zhang, 'Sino-New Zealand Relations', ch.6, pp.126–65. New Zealand studies programmes were established in a number of tertiary institutions in China in this period – in Hefei (Anhui), Nanchong (Sichuan) and Shanghai: Wang Xiaoning, 'New Zealand Studies in China's Higher Institutions', in Beal and Zhang, *New Zealand and China*, pp.21–6. As events turned out, one of New Zealand's greatest cultural attractions – the work of Katherine Mansfield – cost nothing to publicise in China, as the Chinese at an early stage showed an interest in her writing – though not necessarily always acknowledging her identity as a New Zealander. Certainly by the mid-1980s Chinese translations of Mansfield's short stories, many by Xiao Qian, were appearing in popular journals, and at least one collection was published in paperback – adorned with a portrait of Mansfield. *Source:* F. A. Small and L. J. Watt. A photo exhibiton and seminar in memory of the centenary of Mansfield's birth was held by the Shanghai International Studies University in 1989: Wang, 'New Zealand Studies', in Beal and Zhang, p.24.

127 *NZFAR*, September 1974, p.26.

128 Michael Bassett visited China in 1988 and Wang Meng returned the visit in March 1989: *NZFAR*, January–March 1989, pp.28–9.

129 English was dispensed with, and Maori was translated directly into Chinese.

130 The Maori dimension in New Zealand life was reflected in other ways: a comment by ambassador's wife Beryl Small to a visiting Maori group led to the establishment of a Maori room, He Pakiaka, in the offices of the New Zealand Embassy in Beijing in March 1986. FADC Report, p.41.

131 Chinese was not regularly taught in New Zealand at either a secondary or tertiary level. Unable to rely on graduates qualified in Chinese arriving on its doorstep, the Ministry of Foreign Affairs had gone offshore to train diplomatic officers in Chinese. The first, with some prescience on the part of the Ministry, was sent to the RAAF language school in Point Cook out of Melbourne in early 1972, with the expectation that he would be posted to the New Zealand Commission in Hong Kong, *source:* C. J. Elder. In 1986 it was noted that Chinese was a minor language in New Zealand schools and universities, lagging well behind Japanese in this respect, FADC Report, pp.51–3.

132 NZ Embassy Beijing to MFA, 9 June 1981 and MFA to Chinese Embassy

Wellington, 25 June 1981, MFAT 58/264/1 Pt.10.
133 See exchange of correspondence with CHNZAGCO, 12 January and 10 February 1986, MFAT 58/264/1 Pt.15.
134 Ministry of Foreign Affairs Review of New Zealand Official Development Assistance: 1985; New Zealand Bilateral Assistance Programme Project Profiles 1986–87, 1988/89 and 1989/90.
135 There is an entertaining account of such an experience by *New Zealand Herald* journalist Mervyn Cull, *The Foreign Expert* (Christchurch, 1997).
136 Zhang, *Sino–New Zealand Relations*, p.147.
137 Zhang, *Sino–New Zealand Relations*, pp.149–50; *NZFAR*, April–June 1984, p.34.
138 Kiwifruit (*Actinidia deliciosa*) used to be known in New Zealand, in testimony to its origins, as the Chinese gooseberry. The Chinese name is mihoutao – literally 'monkey peach'.
139 New Zealand's Minister of Health visited China in April 1980; bankers and lawyers from China visited New Zealand in October 1983: *NZFAR*, October–December 1983, p.28.
140 Zhang, *Sino–New Zealand Relations*, pp.153–5; *NZFAR*, January–March 1981, p.30; Lorraine Brill, 'Sister Cities', in Beal and Zhang, *New Zealand and China*, pp.27–32; Mary Gray, 'More than forty years of New Zealand-China Friendship', in Beal and Zhang, *New Zealand and China*, pp.37, 42.
141 Helen Clark to PM Lange, 7 March 1986, MFAT 58/264/1 Pt.15; FADC Report, pp.31, 46–7.
142 FADC Report, p.47.
143 Zhang, *Sino–New Zealand Relations*, pp.160–2; on the NZIIA visits see Colin Aikman's report in *NZIR*, September–October 1980, pp.27–8; and John Scott's in *NZIR*, January–February 1987, pp.2–6.
144 MFA, 19 June 1989, MFAT 58/264/1 Pt.22.
145 MFA, draft 2 August 1989, MFAT 58/264/1 Pt.23.
146 Telegram MFA to NZ Embassy Beijing, 29 June 1989, MFAT 58/264/1 Pt.22.
147 *NZFAR*, April–June 1989, pp.53–5.
148 For a comment on the different perspective in ASEAN see *Evening Post*, 17 July 1989 reporting MFA Russell Marshall on his return from an ASEAN PMC meeting.
149 Telegram MFA to NZ Embassy Beijing, 22 August 1989, MFAT 58/264/1 Pt.23.
150 See numerous letters on MFAT 58/264/1, Pt.22.
151 *NZFAR*, July–September 1989, pp.20–2.
152 *NZFAR*, October–December 1989, pp.19–21.
153 *NZFAR*, January–March 1990, pp.25–6. This statement is supported by the statistics: thus the wool trade had already fallen away before June 1989. Bollard, p.7 notes that post-Tiananmen restrictions on foreign exchange and the requirement for direct purchasing did hit New Zealand hard as most New Zealand exports were semi-processed material for light industry.
154 *NZFAR*, July–September 1990, p.24; source: M. J. Powles.

JOHN HENDERSON

New Zealand and Oceania

THE PERIOD COVERED BY THIS CHAPTER BEGINS AND ENDS with leading New Zealand politicians declaring New Zealand's emerging identity with the other island nations of the South Pacific. In July 1972 Brian Talboys, then Minister of Overseas Trade in a National Government (and later also Foreign Minister from 1975 to 1984), reflected on what he referred to as a swing in the pendulum of New Zealanders' perception of their place in the world, and proclaimed: 'if we had a British past we certainly have a Pacific future'. He stressed the importance of the countries of the region 'working together as a South Pacific community'.[1] The theme was enthusiastically taken up the following year by the newly elected Labour Prime Minister, Norman Kirk, as part of his 'regional', 'moral' and more independent foreign policy. 'We are no longer "Europeans", we are New Zealanders and as such are now attuned to the reality of our geographic situation.'[2] On a further occasion he called for the building of 'a real community in the South Pacific and partnership of independent countries who deal with each other on the basis of equality.'[3] Labour lost office in 1975, but National Prime Minister Rob (later Sir Robert) Muldoon who prided himself on being a tough realist in foreign affairs, nevertheless had a 'soft spot' for his South Pacific neighbours. On a visit to Fiji in 1976 he declared: 'Today New Zealanders share a strong sense of belonging to the South Pacific ... It is our region. We cannot change our geography or our history."[4] In the late 1980s Labour Prime Minister David Lange confidently asserted: 'We now not only accept but celebrate what the map tells us – that we are a South Pacific nation'.[5] His successor, Geoffrey Palmer, used part of his brief period as Prime Minister to commission a comprehensive report on the New Zealand – Pacific Island relationship which concluded that New Zealand should take its place as a constructive member of the Pacific Island community.[6] The period ends with the 1991 definitive statement on regional identity by the National Government's Deputy Prime Minister and Minister for External Relations and Trade, Don McKinnon: '. . . the debate over whether New Zealand is a South Pacific nation is over. This is home.'[7]

This chapter will assess the degree to which during the two decades of the 1970s and 1980s New Zealand moved in real terms – as opposed to political rhetoric – towards identifying with the Pacific Island region's political, strategic, economic and environmental challenges. The key question was summed up in the title in an article written in 1985 by a close observer of Pacific affairs, Tony Haas: 'Pacific Island or Metropolitan Power?'[8] An answer was provided by the title of Ron Crocombe's book – which provides the most comprehensive survey of New Zealand-Pacific Island relations: *Pacific Neighbours: New Zealand's Relations with Other Pacific Islands*.[9] But this chapter will suggest that as New Zealand entered the last decade of the century the journey 'home' to the Pacific still had some way to go.

But first it is necessary to define the region, which is referred to in a number of ways: the South Pacific, Oceania, Australasia and the Pacific Islands. This chapter prefers the terms Oceania or Pacific Island Countries (PICs). The term South Pacific became inappropriate in the late 1980s as Micronesian states north of the equator gained independence and joined the regional organisations. The term 'Oceania' has the advantage of capturing the main physical characteristic of the region – vast expanses of ocean – and linking the Pacific Island states to both New Zealand and Australia, as well as increasingly with Asia and the wider Pacific basin and Pacific rim states.

Polynesian links

What makes New Zealand's relationship with the Pacific Island region quite different from that with any other part of the world is the large number of Pacific Islanders from Polynesia who have in recent times followed in the tracks of New Zealand's indigenous Maori people. Most of the recent Polynesian migration to New Zealand occurred in the late 1950s and throughout the 1960s when New Zealand experienced a severe labour shortage – especially for the factories in Auckland. The new arrivals took on the jobs New Zealanders were generally reluctant to work at. By 1971, the beginning of the period covered by this chapter, there were 43,700 Pacific Islanders living in New Zealand. Over the next decade the Pacific Island population more than doubled to over 94,000 in 1981. At the time of the 1991 census the number identifying as Pacific Islanders had risen to 167,000. The population was set for a further rapid expansion as there was a heavy concentration in the younger age group. The 1991 census revealed that 38.7 per cent of that population was under the age of 15, compared with 23.2 per cent of the overall population.[10]

The result was an increasing Polynesian character to the New Zealand population. The Pacific Island Polynesian people in 1991 made up nearly 5 per cent of New Zealanders. More than half (58 per cent) were New Zealand born. When combined with the indigenous Maori population – which in 1991 made up about 13 per cent of the total population – the result is that nearly a fifth of the population identified themselves as Polynesians.[11] The proportion continued to grow, and significantly influence New Zealand's relations with the Pacific Island region, and especially the Polynesian states.

The 170,000 Pacific Islanders living in New Zealand in the early 1990s made it the fourth most populous Pacific Island state – after Papua New Guinea, Fiji and the Solomon Islands. When the 1991 Maori population of 434,847 is added, New Zealand's Polynesian population was nearly equal to the total population of Fiji. The Pacific Island population concentrated mainly in Auckland, which even by 1972 could confidently lay claim to being the capital of Polynesia as it was by far the world's largest Polynesian city.

The overwhelming majority (around 98 per cent) of New Zealand's Pacific Island population came from just four Pacific Island states: Samoa (50 per cent), Cook Islands (23 per cent), Tonga (16 per cent) and Niue (9 per cent). Most of the people from these states (with the partial exception of Tonga) have relatives living in New Zealand. The explanation lies in New Zealand's historical ties with its Polynesian neighbourhood and most significantly its rule of Samoa, the Cook Islands, and Niue for much of the 20th century. By the early 1970s the decolonisation of New Zealand's Pacific Island Territories was almost complete. In 1962 Western Samoa, which New Zealand had ruled since World War I as a League of Nations Mandate and then a United Nations Trust Territory, became the first Pacific Island state to gain its independence. (Tonga, never a colony, ended its status as a British protectorate in 1970.) The Cook Islands, which New Zealand had ruled (along with Niue) since 1901, became self-governing in free association with New Zealand in 1965. Niue achieved a similar status in 1974. This left Tokelau, which had in 1990 a population of just 1,600, the sole remaining New Zealand territory.

The constitutional ties with the Cook Islands, Niue and Tokelau continued to give their people free right of entry as New Zealand citizens. The result has been that by 1990 most of these countries' populations lived in New Zealand. The 1991 census revealed that there were 47,019 Cook Islanders in New Zealand – which was nearly three times the population of the Cook Islands. The proportions were much greater in the case of Niue. The 18,477 Niueans living in New Zealand were nearly eight times the population of Niue. Tokelau's New Zealand population of 4,917 was about three times the number living on the three atolls that make up Tokelau.[12]

These population statistics provide the reason why all three Island states showed no desire to sever constitutional links with New Zealand. Although both the Cook Islands and Niue were fully self-governing they did not seek to assert their right to assume full sovereignty because of fears that this might jeopardize their citizens right of free entry to New Zealand. The economies of both countries also remained heavily dependent on New Zealand aid and the money (remittances) sent home by those who have made the move to New Zealand. In the case of Niue the decline of population threatened the continued viability of the state. In the period 1974–1991 its population dropped from 4,600 to around 2,200. The trend of Niueans' voting with their feet – or rather air tickets – was clearly towards an effective re-integration with New Zealand, an option rejected when self-government was achieved in 1974.

Had Western Samoa and Tonga enjoyed the same right of entry to New Zealand similar population declines are likely to have occurred. Western Samoa came close when in 1982 the Privy Council in London ruled on an immigration case that all Samoans born between 1924 and 1949 were British subjects, and therefore New Zealanders. The ruling would have given around 60 per cent of Samoans the right to live to New Zealand, but was negated by special legislation following urgent talks between the New Zealand and Samoan Governments. The New Zealand Government was concerned about the impact of a wave of

Samoan immigrants on rising levels of unemployment in New Zealand, while the Samoan Government wished to avoid losing a significant proportion of its population. But Samoan people were given special treatment under an annual quota allowing around 1,100 Samoans to emigrate to New Zealand.[13] No other Pacific Island gained a similar arrangement, or indeed Treaty of Friendship with New Zealand to which the immigration issue is linked.

The ability of Polynesians to migrate to New Zealand remained vital for both economic and social reasons. Remittances made a very significant contribution to the economies of Polynesian countries. In the case of Tonga, and to a lesser extent Samoa, emigration also reduced pressures on land and other scarce resources, and provided a safety valve for those frustrated with social and political systems still heavily dominated by traditional authority. It is for these reasons that immigration has been the single most important issue in New Zealand's relations with Polynesia.

While Pacific Island immigration provided the links that bound New Zealand to its neighbourhood, it has also became the most divisive issue in bilateral and regional relations. The Pacific Island population which had been actively sought during times of labour shortages was later quite unjustifiably blamed for rising levels of unemployment during harsher economic times. An unusual – for New Zealand – element of racism was drawn into in the 1975 election campaign. The National Party television election advertisements featured fuzzy headed cartoon characters as the reason why New Zealanders could not get jobs, houses or hospital beds. This formed a backdrop for the newly elected National Government's crackdown on illegal immigrants – the so-called 'overstayers'. These were mainly Polynesians from Samoa and Tonga who had remained in New Zealand illegally after their temporary work permits had expired. Nevertheless Polynesian New Zealanders were understandably incensed that they were subject to random police checks on their citizenship. Police and Immigration officials' tactics – and especially dawn raids – were sharply criticised. A senior Samoan politician told the author that the really lasting insult was the use of police dogs to round up his people. The accusations of racism were substantiated by statistics revealing that while 86 per cent of those prosecuted for overstaying were from the Pacific Islands, they made up only one third of the overstayers.[14] The whole sorry affair was a low point in New Zealand's relations with its island neighbours.

In an effort to correct the harm created by the overstayer crisis, the National Government's Foreign Minister, and Deputy Prime Minister, Brian Talboys, undertook an unprecedented three week tour of the region early in 1977 (which must still stand as the longest Pacific Island tour by any senior minister). He returned from visiting Western Samoa, Tonga, Cook Islands, Fiji and Niue and declared that the overstayer issue 'was no longer a matter of contention' but added: 'No one disguised the fact that it left scars.'[15] These scars were apparent more than a decade later in 1987 when a visa-free scheme was quickly cancelled following an influx of 'visitors' from Fiji, Western Samoa and Tonga.

As a largely unskilled workforce concentrated in the manufacturing sector, Pacific Islanders were once again particularly hard hit by the decade of economic restructuring which began a decade later in the mid 1980s. Unemployment rates for Pacific Islanders were double that of the total New Zealand work force. (The Pacific Island unemployment rate rose from 12 per cent in 1986 to 28 per cent in 1991.) Income levels for Pacific Islanders were only around two thirds that of the rest of New Zealand. Education and health levels were also significantly lower, and crime rates much higher.[16]

This underclass status for the Pacific Island population affected and reinforced the attitudes of the majority culture and called into question the rhetoric about New Zealand's Pacific identity. A 1986 survey asked respondents how they got on with people from other countries. Twice as many people considered they 'got on well' with people from Australia (46 per cent) and the United Kingdom (43 per cent) compared with Pacific Island peoples (22 per cent). When asked about how much effort New Zealanders should make to be on good terms with people from other countries, those favouring a 'great deal' of effort (multiple choices were permitted) – while high for the Pacific (64 per cent) – were still below Australia (81 per cent) and the United Kingdom (69 per cent).[17] The results would appear to confirm the conclusion of the historian, Malcolm McKinnon, that the majority of New Zealanders' identity is Anglo-Celtic, not Polynesian.[18] But a 1990 poll did show a yearning for a national identity. Over 70 per cent of respondents in a nation-wide poll agreed with the proposition that New Zealand should place more stress on its own culture and identity and less on its British past.[19] On the other hand more recent polls have shown a general hostility to more immigration from both Asia and the Pacific Islands.[20]

There were, and remain, serious foreign as well as domestic policy consequences for New Zealand in the disturbing correlations between race and economic status. New Zealand could not credibly promote its Pacific identity and heritage when its own Polynesian people were disadvantaged. How a country organises itself at home will inevitably reflect on its image abroad. Foreign Minister Brian Talboys recognised this following the lengthy 1977 trip he made through the South Pacific. 'Our ability to influence developments in the region depends as much on our responsiveness to the needs of the island communities within New Zealand as on our readiness to assist these communities in the island countries themselves."[21] Mary Boyd, a long time observer of New Zealand's relations with the Pacific, has concluded that while New Zealand could 'legitimately claim to be a Pacific nation . . . social policy lagged behind foreign policy', and that New Zealanders 'still had to come to grips with the Pacific Island Polynesian communities in their midst . . .'[22]

Political Links

The remaining constitutional ties New Zealand maintained with the Cook Islands, Niue and Tokelau formed the strongest political links with the region during the period. It was these links, and especially the movement of island people to New Zealand, which made New Zealand part of the region rather than an outside power. The rights and obligations regarding the Cook Islands' relationship was spelt out in a 1973 exchange of letters between the Heads of Government, Norman Kirk and Premier Albert Henry, which spoke of a 'partnership freely entered into and freely maintained' leaving the Cooks 'free to pursue their own policies and interests'. Kirk added that the nature of the relationship 'also creates an expectation that the Cook Islands will uphold in their laws and policies, a standard of values generally acceptable to New Zealanders'.[23] The nature of the relationship was put under severe strain in 1978 when the New Zealand High Court Judge Gavin Donne, who was also Acting Head of State, disallowed the results of the General Election. He found long serving Premier Albert Henry had acted corruptly in flying in supporters from New Zealand to vote for him. Some New Zealand police took a well-timed 'holiday' in the Cook Islands, and some extra police were sworn in, but were not required as a peaceful change of government took place, with Tom Davis as the new Premier.

Nevertheless the genuinely 'free' nature of the association is underlined by the fact that the Cook Islands (and Niue) could, at a time of their choosing, end the relationship and become fully sovereign states. In the case of foreign affairs and defence matters, for which New Zealand retained constitutional responsibility, New Zealand was by 1990 acting on the requests of the Cook Islands and Niue, and did not seek to direct them. Indeed, during the period of the Lange Labour Government in New Zealand, the Cook Islands let it be known that they would permit visits by nuclear ships. The true objective, no doubt, was to demonstrate the Cook's 'independence'.

The Kirk Labour Government expanded New Zealand's Pacific Island concerns well beyond the countries with which it had historical links. In mid-1973 Kirk announced a 'comprehensive' review of South Pacific policy, and declared: 'New Zealand has special concern and acknowledges a special responsibility to assist and cooperate with its neighbours in the South Pacific.'[24]

Successive governments accepted this commitment. In the 1970s and 1980s New Zealand developed comprehensive diplomatic links throughout Oceania. In 1972 there were just five posts. By 1990 this had expanded to 10 as more island states gained independence. This represented more than a fifth of New Zealand's overseas posts, and more than any other region. Indeed, the region became by far the largest commitment of the Ministry of External Relations and Trade – absorbing 43 per cent of its expenditure in the 1988–89 financial year.[25]

But an internal 1989 management audit called into question whether New Zealand was gaining value for money. The report bluntly stated: 'There is a degree of complacency in the Ministry about our ability to deal successfully with the South Pacific. We need to recognise our ignorance' – which was attributed mainly to a lack of experience.[26] At the time of the audit no one working in the South Pacific division in Wellington had served in the region; only three of the Heads of Mission had previous experience in a Pacific Island post, and all but two were on their first posting as a Head of Mission. There was also a lack of training in the Pacific Island languages, cultures, and history, which called into question the prevailing assumption that New Zealand had special knowledge of the region.[27] The 1990 Government policy review made similar comments (although in milder terms). It noted the need to encourage diplomatic staff to specialise in Pacific affairs, and that the region should not be 'regarded as some enforced system of "country service" en route to a choice post in Europe and North America'.[28]

The 1990 policy review also pointed to the important gaps in New Zealand's diplomatic representation. No country maintained a diplomatic post in the Polynesian state of Tuvalu (which New Zealand covered from Fiji). While New Zealand maintained a modest post in the French territory of New Caledonia, there was no representation in the vast territory of French Polynesia, or the U.S. State of Hawaii. The biggest gaps were in Micronesia. New Zealand had no representation in Nauru (which was also covered from Fiji). The tiny two person post in Kiribati faced the daunting task of covering (in addition to Kiribati) the former US territories of the Federated States of Micronesia, Marshall Islands and (from 1993) Palau.

Regionalism

Support for regional cooperation has been an important part of the recent history of New Zealand's political relationship with Pacific Island states. In 1972 the South Pacific Commission (SPC) celebrated its 25th anniversary. It began life as a grouping of the colonial powers with possessions in the region, with New Zealand as a founder member. Its membership expanded to include Pacific Island states as they gained independence, as well as the remaining dependencies, and in 1990 numbered 27.

But the SPC was handicapped by the location of its headquarters in the French territory of New Caledonia, and its inability to discuss political issues of major concern to the newly independent or self-governing states. In August 1971 – which had been designated 'South Pacific Year' – New Zealand played a major role in meeting demands, especially from newly independent Fiji, for a political body to represent the region by hosting a Wellington meeting of Heads of Government from Nauru, Western Samoa, Tonga, Fiji and the Cook Islands as well as the Australian Minister for External Territories. This gathering set the foundations for the region's most important grouping, the South Pacific Forum, which has met at the Head of Government level every year since. Its membership expanded as more Pacific Island states gained independence or self government, and in 1990 totalled 15 – double the number of founder members.

The Wellington meeting set the tone for the annual meetings – informality. It reflected the 'island style' of discussion – with the 'Pacific way' as a new concept of regional collaboration. But while the early description of the Forum as having no constitution, no agenda and no formality, no longer applies (although the organisation still exists without a constitution), the spirit of consultation and compromise continued. Muldoon – who was proud of the fact that he never missed a Forum during his nine years as Prime Minister – provided the following description: 'The tradition is that you do a little talking and a lot of listening. Then, after long silences in the Polynesian way, people at the extremes are expected to move towards the centre.'[29]

New Zealand backed the creation in 1972 of the South Pacific Bureau for Economic Cooperation to provide advice to the Forum. Its name reflected the Forum's main concern – economic development – and the related topics of aid, trade, and transport. But its role was wider, and in 1988 the organisation was renamed the Forum Secretariat. New Zealand agreed to meet a third of the Secretariat's costs – with Australia making a similar contribution, and the remaining third paid by the Pacific Island states. But while a necessary part of any effective regional organisation, the Secretariat came at the cost of changing the previous informal process.

New Zealand also supported the establishment of other key regional agencies, which reported annually to the Heads of Government meeting. Amongst the most important of these was the Forum Fisheries Agency (FFA) established in 1978 with its headquarters in Honiara, Solomon Islands. The FFA proved itself a regional success story in the sustainable management of a vital resource. New Zealand contributed both financial assistance and practical support through RNZAF surveillance flights. The FFA played a major role in brokering the 1986 U.S. multilateral fisheries agreement which resolved a bitter dispute with the U.S. over tuna fishing.

Transport of freight has long been a key concern of Pacific Island states given the vast distances and small volumes involved. In 1973 Norman Kirk hosted a Pacific Island shipping conference at Waitangi. National Prime Minister Sir Robert Muldoon played a major role in establishing a regional shipping line, the Pacific Forum line, in 1977.

New Zealand also supported the establishment in the late 1960s of the University of the South Pacific in Suva, which was established as a regional university on a former New Zealand air force base at Lauthala Bay.

In contrast to these successes, proposals to enhance political cooperation between parliamentarians failed to take root. This was despite encouragement from New Zealand. When he was Leader of the Opposition Labour leader Norman Kirk called for the establishment of a Pacific Council made up of representatives of the parliaments of the region.[30] As Prime Minister, Kirk repeated his call for a Pacific Council to give parliamentarians a more direct and effective voice in regional affairs.[31] But Kirk's untimely death prevented him from carrying the initiative further. Although the 1974 Forum agreed to give the proposal 'careful consideration', no further action was taken. An opportunity to develop a sense of regional consciousness and shared views on common problems was lost. Mike Moore – Minister of Overseas Trade and Marketing and briefly (in 1990) Prime Minister – also promoted the establishment of a Pacific parliament.[32] A major 1990 review of New Zealand's relations with the region suggested that New Zealand should take the lead in promoting a regional parliamentary association.[33] But, as with the earlier proposals, no formal moves to link the region's parliaments followed. The Commonwealth countries actively participated in the activities of the Commonwealth Parliamentary Association, which included regional meetings and seminars. However the former U.S. territories in Micronesia were not members, and participated in their own sub-regional gatherings.

Strategic Concerns

Questions raised at a 1970 Canberra conference on the foreign relations of the Asia-Pacific region revealed a high level of pessimism about the future of Pacific islands which had gained, or were soon to achieve, independence. It was observed that the Westminster/Washington model of democratic government had broken down in many parts of Asia, Africa and Latin America. Viewed in this wider comparative perspective, the small emerging Pacific Island states were considered even less viable entities. This seemed to point to an era of instability, political coups, which might be exploited by the Soviet Union, and perhaps eventually to a Pacific 'Cuba'.[34]

With the benefit of hindsight it can be seen that these assessments were too pessimistic. With the partial exception of Vanuatu, the transition to independence proved to be a generally peaceful and orderly process for Pacific Island states. It was not until May 1987 that the region experienced its first (and bloodless) military coup in Fiji. No other Pacific Island country was subject to a military takeover,[35] which was in stark contrast to other third world regions.

Nevertheless for the Pacific Island governments of the day, which had assumed tranquillity was the normal state of affairs, the mid to late 1980s seemed particularly unstable. For a time it appeared that problems that had besieged small states in the Caribbean and Indian Ocean were now about to confront Oceania. The Commonwealth took a particular interest in the 'vulnerability' of small states.[36] For New Zealand the peaceful isolation of its South Pacific location exploded when French agents in 1985 sank the Greenpeace anti-nuclear protest vessel *Rainbow Warrior* in Auckland harbour. The same year the region was shocked by its first political assassination, of Palau leader Haruo Remeliik. Intrigue was further heightened in 1988 when his successor, Lazarus Sali, committed suicide. In 1987 concern about Libya's involvement in Melanesia was followed by the two coups (May and September) in Fiji. The following year riots took place in the Vanuatu capital of Port Vila, followed by an attempted 'constitutional' coup when the President illegally sought to appoint a new Prime Minister. Violence also erupted in the French territory of New Caledonia, and in 1989 the independence leaders were assassinated. The increasingly troubled decade also included concern about tension along the Papua New Guinea–Indonesian border, and concluded with violence breaking out on Bougainville as the island sought to secede from Papua New Guinea.

New Zealand's response to these regional 'crises' must be considered against the background of the Cold War. The 1978 Defence Review noted increased Russian and Chinese interest in the region and warned: 'The South Pacific is no longer insulated against outside pressures.' The Review added that the 'goodwill and cooperation' of the Pacific Islands was 'essential for our security'.[37] Both New Zealand and Australia pursued throughout the Cold War period a policy of strategic denial – of seeking to prevent a potentially hostile power, and particularly the Soviet Union – from establishing itself, or gaining influence, in the region. It was not, in hindsight, a difficult policy to implement, as there were few such challenges. The region remained, for the most part, outside the concerns of the principal Cold War protagonists.

The few tentative and low level approaches to the region by the Soviet Union provoked what now seem a massive over-reaction from both New Zealand and Australia. In April 1976 Tonga effectively played the 'Russian' card, by establishing diplomatic relations with the Soviet Union and entering talks about economic assistance in return for a Soviet fisheries deal. Counter-offers of large increases in 'Western' aid from New Zealand, Australia and Britain succeeded in preventing any deal being completed.

The Tongan Soviet initiative had the effect of causing both New Zealand and Australia to take the region seriously in security terms. References to security issues in Oceania began to appear in the annual ANZUS communiqués. But these 'red' scare tactics were resented by some Pacific Island states. The outspoken condemnation of the Soviet–Tongan overtures from New Zealand Prime Minister Robert Muldoon earned the mild but justifiable rebuke from the Tongan Foreign Ministry: 'Tonga has many friends, all we ask of them is that they don't choose our enemies for us.'[38] Nevertheless Foreign Minister Brian Talboys expressed his belief (or hope?) that Tonga and Western Samoa 'would prefer to go on looking to their traditional friends, rather than turning to new and possibly dangerous sources of help'.[39] The decision to establish a New Zealand High Commission in Tonga was evidence that New Zealand realised it needed to work harder to understand regional developments.

A decade later similarly modest Soviet approaches for fishing deals again produced a very hostile response from New Zealand. Kiribati nevertheless did enter into – but did not renew – a one year fishing licence agreement with the Soviet Union in 1985. A similar 1987 deal with Vanuatu also soon lapsed – but was regarded as particularly significant as it provided for port access. There was, as Thakur has rightly observed, 'more than a degree of hypocrisy in New Zealand's opposition, as it was at the same time benefiting from the fishing deals it had signed with the Soviet Union'.[40]

In July 1986 Soviet President Gorbachev's speech in Vladivostok created further concern as it seemed to signal a renewed Soviet interest in the wider Pacific. But although there was some increase in the number of visits by diplomats and delegations passing through the region, there was in practice little change to past Soviet indifference towards the South Pacific.

The Soviet 'threat' was always exaggerated – although more by the news media than by assessments of professional diplomats. The conservative and Christian nature of most Pacific Island states made them unlikely breeding grounds for communist subversion. Only Vanuatu deviated slightly from the Western camp by participating in the conferences of the non-aligned movement and establishing relations with Cuba in 1983. It was not until 1990 that the Soviets opened an embassy in the region – in Port Moresby, Papua New Guinea. (It proved to be short-lived, and closed in 1992.) The predicted correlation between vulnerability and Soviet meddling did not seem to apply to Oceania. As a 1994 assessment reflected, fears of 'political hot spots' in the region in the 1970s and 1980s tended not to materialise.[41] Nevertheless, as has been noted, New Zealand throughout the Cold War period continued to take a hard line anti-Soviet attitude. The position did not change when the Labour Government came to power in 1984. If anything, its strong opposition to nuclear weapons (to be covered later in this chapter) required it to take an even harder anti-Soviet line to prove its policy was anti-nuclear, not anti-American. The limited nature of the Soviet Union's activities in Oceania meant that the ending of the Cold War had less impact on this region than in other parts of the world.

The outside power that provoked the strongest response from Australia, and to a lesser extent New Zealand, was an unlikely one: Libya. Again, as in the case of the Soviet Union, the alarmist response was not justified. The Third World radicalism professed by Libya's leader Colonel Gaddafi was unlikely to take root in the Pacific Islands, and in practice does not seem to have extended beyond inviting a limited number of Melanesians to Tripoli for 'training'. What particularly concerned Australia were plans to establish a Libyan 'People's Bureau' in Port Vila, and the scope this would provide for meddling in the politically unstable politics of Vanuatu. On 1 May 1987 Australian Foreign Minister Bill Hayden made a dramatic early morning trans-Tasman dash for talks at Ohakea airforce base with New Zealand Prime Minister, David Lange. The visit was shrouded in secrecy – which caused Lange (who considered the Australians were grossly over-reacting) to joke that the talks were so secret that he was not told in advance what they were about. He added that the secrets were safe, as after the meeting was over he was no wiser. As it turned out there was little substance to Australian concerns. Vanuatu considered its links with Libya (and Cuba) to be consistent with its status as a non-aligned state, and saw the Ohakea meeting, which (despite the secrecy) attracted massive media coverage, as an attempt by Australia and New Zealand to intervene in its affairs. It nevertheless asked the Libyan representatives to leave. Australia closed the Libyan People's Bureau in Canberra, and Libya's already minimal presence in the region disappeared.

In view of the high level of concern about the Soviet Union and Libya, the more relaxed response to China's activity in the region is surprising, particularly as it was of a more extensive and permanent nature. In the 1975–80 period China established embassies in Western Samoa, Fiji, Papua New Guinea and later in Vanuatu, Kiribati, Marshall Islands and the Federated States of Micronesia. Part of the reason for the lack of concern about China was the assumption that it related more to its rivalry with Taiwan than hostility towards the West. Four of the Forum states chose to recognise Taiwan: Nauru, the Solomon Islands, Tonga and Tuvalu. In return they received generous development assistance. While containing Taiwan's influence was clearly a major factor behind China's interest in the region, it is likely to also have related to longer term strategic considerations.

To some Pacific Island states there seemed to be a contradiction between New Zealand's (and especially David Lange's) strong hostility to any Soviet overtures, and a determination to hold fast to an anti-nuclear foreign and defence policy, even when this was at the cost of New Zealand's active participation in the ANZUS alliance. But while there was some unease that the region as a whole was less secure as a result of the weakening of the ANZUS alliance, generally New Zealand's opposition to nuclear weapons had strong support from other Pacific Island states. This was because of the deep distaste for nuclear weapons which had developed as a result of the extensive testing of nuclear weapons in the region by the United States and United Kingdom in the 1950s, and by France from the mid-1960s onwards.

In 1973 New Zealand and Australia, with the backing of the South Pacific Forum, took action against French nuclear testing at the International Court of Justice (ICJ). France had commenced atmospheric testing at Mururoa in French Polynesia in 1966 and immediately faced growing opposition from New Zealand and the other South Pacific

Forum states. In 1973, in a highly symbolic move, New Zealand Prime Minister, Norman Kirk, with Forum backing, despatched the frigate HMNZS *Otago*, with Cabinet Minister Fraser Coleman aboard, to the vicinity of the testing area as a symbol of the opposition of New Zealand and its neighbours. The action succeeded beyond expectations in its main objective of attracting the attention of the world's news media. As Kirk observed: 'it established our identity and its value went far beyond nuclear testing'.[42] Although France refused to recognise the ICJ ruling, in 1974 it moved its testing from the atmosphere to underground.

In August 1975 New Zealand and Fiji placed a proposal for a South Pacific Nuclear Weapon Free Zone on the United Nations agenda. Labour Prime Minister Bill Rowling argued the move was necessary to ensure 'our area, the South Pacific region – does not get caught up in this mad arms race . . .' and 'to tell the nuclear powers that it's hands off as far as our region is concerned'.[43] The move was not supported by the National Party opposition, which was concerned about undermining the ANZUS alliance. In an ironic twist the UN General Assembly adopted the NWFZ proposal in December 1975 – after Labour had been defeated at the polls.

The re-election of a Labour Government in 1984 gave renewed impetus to the NWFZ proposal. The 1985 Forum meeting in the Cook Islands adopted the Treaty of Rarotonga which prohibited the testing, manufacture, acquisition and stationing of nuclear weapons, or dumping of nuclear material, in the region as defined. But, largely as a result of Australia's insistence, the treaty protected US interests by allowing for the transit of nuclear ships through the region, and permitting port visits. Vanuatu considered the Treaty too weak, and Tonga too strong, and neither signed. China and the Soviet Union signed the protocols in 1987 and 1986 respectively, but the US and United Kingdom withheld their support. Not surprisingly, so did France – until it had completed its series of testing in 1996.

New Zealand took a leading role in opposing French nuclear testing. As has been noted, in 1985 it paid a heavy price when the Greenpeace anti-nuclear protest vessel *Rainbow Warrior* was sunk by French agents while berthed in Auckland harbour. Although the world-wide publicity surrounding the sinking and the detention of two French agents increased New Zealand's anti-nuclear credentials in the region and around the world, it also highlighted the problem New Zealand had when its economic interests in Europe clashed with political requirements at home and regionally. France made it clear that the continued detention of the French agents would be at the cost of New Zealand trade not just with France, but to Europe generally. The result was victory for economic reality over moral outrage. The French agents were transferred from a New Zealand jail first to Hao atoll in French Polynesia to supposedly serve out a reduced sentence, but were soon being given a heroes' welcome in France.

The issue was complicated by the extensive French possessions in the South Pacific. French territories stretch in a giant arc to New Zealand's north – from New Caledonia in the west, through Wallis and Futuna to the widely scattered islands of French Polynesia, the site of the nuclear tests. The official line generally preferred by the Ministry of Foreign Affairs has been to recognise the reality of France's presence in the region, and acknowledge its constructive role as an aid donor. But the testing of nuclear weapons clearly called into question the legitimacy of France's continued presence as a colonial power, long after colonialism had been deemed unacceptable in other parts of the world. Labour Prime Minister David Lange raised the issue in 1986 over moves to reinscribe New Caledonia on the United Nations list of colonial territories whose progress towards self government would be monitored.

Fiji Coups

The 1987 Fiji coups challenged past assumptions about the benign nature of the Pacific Island region which seemed to have escaped the turbulence of other areas of the world. Professor Ramesh Thakur considers the coups presented 'the most complex challenge ever to New Zealand foreign policy in the South Pacific'.[44] The historian Malcolm McKinnon agreed the coups "transformed the framework of New Zealand-Pacific relations'.[45] The fact that it was not predicted called into question the extent to which New Zealand knew its neighbourhood. As an 1990 official review of policy observed, the failure of intelligence agencies to predict the coup demonstrated that 'a greater effort was needed for New Zealand to know and better understand the dynamics and evolving shape of political systems in the Pacific Island region'.[46] An internal 1989 Ministry (MERT) audit was more blunt, and called into question New Zealand's ability to effectively monitor Fiji politics. The audit asked the blunt question: 'Were we so preoccupied with dealing (very effectively) with the Westminster style apparatus that was in place in Fiji that we failed to see or fully understand the real underpinnings of power?'[47]

New Zealand's response to the coups has also been subject to sharp criticism. One of the most extraordinary claims is that New Zealand (and Australia) contemplated military action against Fiji. The former long-serving Fiji Prime Minister, Ratu Sir Kamisese Mara (who was effectively restored to power by the May coup led by Lieutenant–Colonel Sitiveni Rabuka) has claimed that the threat posed by Australia and New Zealand to Fiji following the coup was one of the reasons he agreed to serve in the post-coup administration: 'Had they had the means they would have taken over . . .'[48] He has also claimed that ANZAC forces would have invaded 'if they had not been dissuaded by the Island governments'.[49] These accusations were given some credence by some extraordinary assertions by the then Chief of Defence Staff, Air Marshal David Crooks, who claimed that the actions contemplated by Prime Minister Lange could have put New Zealand and Fiji forces into conflict.[50] National Party Prime Minister Jim Bolger considered it 'appalling that it was even suggested that New Zealand defence forces would be there in live combat against Fijians'.[51] He ordered an inquiry by his Department, but later stated that it was 'not in New Zealand's interests' to release the report.[52]

The author of this chapter was head of Prime Minister Lange's office at the time, and strongly refutes these allegations that New Zealand contemplated a military assault against Fiji. Lange has repeatedly stressed that he never considered military intervention to restore the elected Fiji Government.[53] The reasons were a rejection of what Lange referred to as 'gunboat diplomacy', and his assessment that 'our Armed Forces were quite incapable of defeating the more numerous and well-trained Fiji army in open combat'.[54] Lange, unwisely, did say he would 'consider' a request to help transport loyal Fijian forces back from the Middle East peacekeeping duties to restore constitutional government. But no request was forthcoming, and he quickly dropped the idea in recognition of the need to avoid a civil war situation.[55] In fact the coup received wide support from the indigenous Fijian people – and most Pacific Island states (which rated indigenous rights ahead of democratic rights).

There were three specific circumstances which caused the Lange government to contemplate military action – but in each case this would have been carried out with the agreement and cooperation of the Fiji authorities. The first was the protection of New Zealand citizens in Fiji. The second was provision of security for the New Zealand High Commission and its staff – who were in some potential jeopardy because a number of key figures associated with the deposed regime were being sheltered. The third was the hijacking of an Air New Zealand aircraft at Nadi five days after the coup. New Zealand naval vessels were given clearances by the Fiji Governor General to help meet the first two needs, and clearance was obtained to fly in SAS special forces to end the hijacking. The latter force was not required as a member of the crew overpowered the hijacker, and evacuation of New Zealand citizens and diplomats did not prove necessary. Because of the damaging long term implications for New Zealand foreign policy of the claims that New Zealand contemplated playing 'regional policemen' by intervening, it is important to repeat: the envisaged use of the military was confined to limited and specific roles agreed upon with the Fiji authorities. No military intervention to reverse the coup was planned, or even contemplated.

In September 1987 Rabuka launched a second coup when he again seized control and declared Fiji to be a republic. Fiji's membership of the Commonwealth was then deemed by the Commonwealth Heads of Government meeting in Vancouver, Canada, to have lapsed. Lange attended the meeting, but did not play a major role in initiating the expulsion of Fiji. Although New Zealand (and Australian) forces were again put on various stages of alert in order to help with the evacuation of New Zealand nationals, they were not required.

In the two years following the Fiji coups the question of the use of New Zealand military forces in the region was considered on two occasions relating to Vanuatu and Bougainville. In May 1988 Vanuatu Prime Minister Walter Lini sought New Zealand (and Australian) assistance to contain rioting in the capital, Port Vila. A power struggle between Prime Minister Lini and his Party leader, Barak Sope, lay behind the troubles, and New Zealand was reluctant to intervene in internal domestic political strife. The assistance was restricted to riot equipment.

The issue of Bougainville's secession from Papua New Guinea, which was to emerge as the regions' most serious security issue, flared up in 1989. Bougainville had unilaterally declared its independence in the weeks before Papua New Guinea's independence in 1975, but eventually agreed to remain within a provincial system of government. Disputes over the land and royalties associated with the Panguna mine became violent in 1988 and in May 1990 the Bougainville Revolutionary Army (BRA) declared the Island independent. The response of the Papua New Guinea government was to dispatch first police, then military forces, and finally to impose a blockade on the island.

In an attempt to end the bloodshed, the New Zealand Government agreed in mid-1990 to make available naval vessels to provide a neutral base on which peace talks could take place. But although the latter did result in the Endeavour Accord (named after the New Zealand naval supply ship, HMNZS *Endeavour*) it was not able to be effectively implemented, and the fighting resumed.

By the late 1980s New Zealand defence policy was firmly focussed on its own region in Oceania. While critics portrayed this as isolationist, Labour's 1987 Defence Review pointed out the vastness of the area, stretching from the Antarctic to the equator and encompassing some 16 per cent of the globe.[56] Although National's return to power in 1990 restored the rhetoric of a wider role supporting Western alliance interests, in practice the strong strategic regional focus remained.

Economic Issues

During the 1970s and 80s the Pacific Islands region was an important, but not major, region for New Zealand trade. The percentage of exports to the region averaged about 3 per cent – declining from 3.5 per cent in 1979 to 2.8 per cent in 1989. The balance of trade remained heavily in New Zealand's favour – with the region taking 10.6 per cent of its imports from New Zealand in the 1979–87 period. Most – around two thirds – of the trade has been with Polynesia, followed by Melanesia, and a very small amount with Micronesia.[57]

Nevertheless, while the total amount of trade was relatively small, particular markets were important. In 1989 exports to Fiji – which was New Zealand's largest Pacific Island market – totalled $150 million. This exceeded exports to Singapore, Indonesia, Thailand or Saudi Arabia for the same year. Two way trade with Fiji was greater than that with Iran. Exports to Papua New Guinea were greater than to Eastern Europe, excluding the Soviet Union. The French territories of New Caledonia and French Polynesia were further important markets – taking more New Zealand exports than Switzerland, Sweden or Egypt. The region provided a particularly useful market for manufactured exports.[58]

At the 1980 Forum in Kiribati an important regional economic step was taken with the establishment of SPARTECA – the South Pacific Regional Trade and Economic Cooperation Agreement. This arrangement allowed for the unrestricted duty free access of products from Forum island countries to Australia and New Zealand. But SPARTECA brought only limited gains, mainly to the larger states of Fiji and Papua New Guinea. This was because the problems for most Forum island states, and particularly the very small, was not access, but rather the ability to generate export products, and the cost and provision of transportation.

The late 1980s saw a generally diminishing commercial role for New Zealand in the region. Like New Zealand, the Pacific Island states were increasingly looking to Asia for their economic futures. While demand for New Zealand engineering, construction and consulting services remained strong, banking and insurance services were significantly reduced. In 1990 the Bank of New Zealand sold its banking interests in Fiji and Western Samoa.

Aid

A 1989 audit report of MERT identified foreign aid as a 'principal tool in our foreign policy' in the South Pacific. It noted the importance of aid for providing access to key decision makers at both the political and official levels. While the report also emphasised the role of aid in developing island state economies, it linked this to reducing the scope for outside 'undesirable influences' to meddle in the region.[59] The rationale related (as has been noted) principally to the Cold War, and was spelt out in 1983 by Malcolm Templeton, a Deputy Secretary of Foreign Affairs: 'Our interests coincide with those of our island neighbours. They do not want to be obliged to seek aid from outside powers at the price of political interference ... We do not want that to happen.'[60]

The point being made is an important one: that in the 1970s and 1980s aid was principally given for political not development reasons. Political outcomes were more important than the economic and humanitarian reasons for providing the aid. Aid was an important instrument of foreign policy. As the 1990 policy review put it: 'Our mana as a people of the Pacific is maintained through our ODA because it gives substance to our relationships.'[61]

It is essentially for these political reasons that the South Pacific became the increasing focus of New Zealand aid. In 1971–72 44 per cent of New Zealand's aid went to the Pacific Islands. By 1979 this had increased to 69 per cent, and a decade later had risen further to an estimated 80 per cent of bilateral aid.[62] This concentration took place despite the fact that the Oceania region was relatively well off when compared with other areas of developing countries, both in terms of standard of living and aid levels. If New Zealand had been concerned mainly with meeting human needs – such as hunger, shelter, and education – the aid would have been directed towards Africa rather than the Pacific Islands, which were amongst the world's highest aid recipients on a per capita basis.

Even within the Pacific Island region the aid was further concentrated on four relatively well-off Polynesian states closely associated with New Zealand – Western Samoa, Cook Islands, Niue and Tokelau – which received around 50 per cent of New Zealand's Pacific Island aid. Much of this was for budgetary assistance, and not for economic development. All enjoyed high rates of literacy, compared with just 50 per cent literacy rates in large parts of Melanesia. A country such as the Solomon Islands, where the need was great, received very little aid from New Zealand.

It can nevertheless be argued that New Zealand had a special responsibility to those countries it had helped give birth to. In the case of Niue, this obligation was written into the constitution where it was stated (section 7): 'It shall be the continuing responsibility of the Government of New Zealand to provide necessary economic and administrative assistance to Niue.' But in terms of aid outcomes, it can be argued that the high levels of aid made the states more, not less, dependent. The budgets of the Cook Islands, and Niue became heavily dependent on New Zealand, and through aid the states became net importers of food. Despite the aid, emigration to New Zealand remained at high levels while living standards declined.

But while concentrated to benefit a relatively small number of countries, the overall amount of aid declined. This was despite the idealistic goal of 1 per cent GNP for total resource transfer set by Labour Prime Minister Norman Kirk, which included the recognised target of 0.7 per cent of GNP for development assistance. It also far exceeded New Zealand's contribution at the time – just 0.28 per cent of GNP.

The Kirk government did succeed in doubling this to 0.51 per cent in 1975, but it then was allowed to gradually decline to just 0.21 per cent in 1991.[63] This led to the admission by Foreign Minister Don McKinnon that any further reduction would 'destroy our credibility as a donor nation'.[64] The decline was even worse than these figures suggest, as by 1990 New Zealand had withdrawn a number of services previously provided free – such as airport calibration and meteorological assistance.

By 1990 New Zealand contributed less than 10 per cent of the region's aid, and was far behind relative newcomers to Pacific aid, such as Japan. With the declining levels of aid came the risk of a loss of influence. The 1990 policy review noted the concern of a number of New Zealand Heads of Mission throughout the region that in relation to aid New Zealand 'was living on a reservoir of goodwill that is running dry'.[65]

The nature of aid also changed in the 1970s and 80s from a focus on budgetary assistance and infrastructure to human resource development (particularly education), and fostering the private sector. In 1976 the Pacific Islands Industrial Development Scheme (PIIDS) was launched in an effort to promote employment opportunities. The scheme provided incentives for New Zealand companies to establish business enterprises in the island states, thereby helping to provide job opportunities and economic self reliance in the islands. The scheme was open to the criticism that it was aiding New Zealand business as much as Pacific Island countries. So too was the overall programme, as approximately 70 per cent of the aid was spent on New Zealand services.[66]

Environmental issues

It was, for the most part, not until the 1980s that New Zealand began to take regional environment issues seriously. The clear exception to this statement was the strong opposition to French nuclear testing, which is covered in an earlier part of this chapter. The 1980s brought about a recognition of how vital the environment was to a region comprised largely of ocean. The 1982 United Nations Convention on the Law of the Sea opened up the prospects of the island states being able to benefit from their massive maritime exclusive economic zones. What were small dots on the map were now linked together by these zones, which covered much of the world's largest ocean. Indeed, the vastness of the maritime economic zones rendered the term 'small states' no longer appropriate.

The region recognised the importance of environmental issues with the establishment of the South Pacific Regional Environment Programme (SPREP) in 1986. The goal was to promote the new catch cry – sustainable development. Initially SPREP operated as part of the South Pacific Commission (SPC) programme, but in 1990, with the help of a special grant from New Zealand, it became established as an autonomous regional organisation.

In the late 1980s New Zealand – at times in marked contrast to Australia – identified with, and worked to help resolve a number of serious threats to the region's environment. These issues included driftnet fishing, the disposal of chemical weaponry on Johnston Island, and climate change. New Zealand's increased concern about these issues was in part a result of the interest shown by Labour Prime Minister Geoffrey Palmer, who held office in 1989-90 following Lange's resignation. It is significant that Palmer also held the environment portfolio.

New Zealand took a leading role in seeking to ban driftnet fishing, which became a central issue at the 1989 Tarawa Forum. A follow up meeting took place in Wellington later in the year which agreed to the Convention for the Prohibition of Fishing with Long Driftnets. New Zealand then worked with the United States in the United Nations General Assembly to obtain a United Nations resolution to end drift netting on the high seas.

But on a further issue New Zealand joined the rest of the region – with the notable exception of Australia – in opposing the use by the United States of Johnston Island for the destruction by furnace of US chemical weaponry removed from Europe. The same facility had been used to destroy the chemical Agent Orange following the end of the Vietnam War. To much of the region it appeared to be a repeat of the nuclear testing issue – the use of the central Pacific to carry out activities that would not be acceptable in the metropolitan territories. The issue dominated the 1990 Forum in Port Vila, with Australian Prime Minister Bob Hawke arguing a lonely defence of the US case, while Palmer was sympathetic to the position of the Pacific Islands.

Potentially the most serious environmental issue which began to emerge in the 1980s was concern over climate change, and the effect on sea levels. The worst case scenario predicted a rise in sea levels which might render atoll states uninhabitable. It was pointed out that countries such as Kiribati, Tuvalu, and the Marshall Islands rose only 1.5 metres above sea level. The issue was a particular concern of the 1989 Tarawa Forum, and at a follow up meeting in Majuro in the Marshall Islands. There was a deep feeling of resentment from the Forum states that they were being presented with a potentially catastrophic problem not of their making. New Zealand listened sympathetically, Australia less so.

Conclusion

An Australian authority on the international relations of Oceania, Stephen Henningham, has argued that neither New Zealand nor Australia 'has compelling economic or strategic interests in the region'. Both countries, he maintains, 'are regarded by the island governments as being closely associated with but not of the island region'. [67] However, a further leading Australian regional specialist, political scientist Richard Herr, after reflecting on the greater knowledge and interest in Pacific Island affairs in New Zealand compared with Australia, concluded: 'Given New Zealand's history, geography and demography, I find it difficult to imagine a New Zealand foreign policy which did not identify closely with the South Pacific region.'[68]

This chapter's survey of the 1970s and 1980s lends support to Herr's conclusion, and highlights the differences between New Zealand and Australian attitudes towards their region of Oceania. While it is true that New Zealand's economic stake in the region remained relatively small when compared with the major markets for New Zealand produce in Australia, Asia, North America and Europe, it nevertheless remained the region through which trade must pass on its way to these larger markets. Furthermore, to a much greater degree than for Australia, the Pacific Island region provided a useful market for New Zealand, especially for manufactured goods. Again, the major environmental concerns of the region – and their considerable economic implications – were shared to a much greater degree by New Zealand than Australia (whether the issue related to nuclear matters, waste and weapon disposal, climate change or drift-net fishing).

Trans-Tasman strategic concerns also grew apart during the 1970s and 1980s. Australia became increasingly preoccupied with possible security threats from its 'near north' and particularly China and Indonesia. These concerns help explain why Australia continued to give priority to maintaining an effective military alliance with the United

States. New Zealand's greater distance from Asia enabled it to feel more relaxed about its South Pacific location. When New Zealand had to choose between the ANZUS alliance and remaining nuclear-free it chose the latter – an unthinkable course for Australia. In doing so New Zealand identified with the strong anti-nuclear sentiments of other Pacific Island states.

But the most important factor explaining the difference between the way New Zealand and Australia felt about the region related to the make up of their people. The growing Polynesian nature of the New Zealand population – nearly a fifth of all New Zealanders by 1990 – allowed it to form a more relaxed relationship with its neighbouring islands, and calls into question Henningham's assessment about New Zealand not being 'of' the region. Geography also helped this process. Although large by Pacific Island standards, New Zealand's island nature helped it to identify with the ocean environment and resource concerns of other island states. Being 'small' (when compared with Australia and other outside powers) made New Zealand less 'threatening' to its neighbours.

But the 1980s also demonstrated that political rhetoric is not enough to establish a credible identity. This chapter opened with two decades of proclamations about accepting and celebrating New Zealand's Pacific location. But many challenges remained to be met for these claims to be justified. At home Pacific Islanders joined Maori as the disadvantaged section of society. Until this changes, claims about celebrating New Zealanders' Pacific identity will ring hollow. New Zealand's assistance to the region with both money and services also declined. Coming to terms with the realities of geography had a price tag New Zealand remained reluctant to meet.

Notes

1   *New Zealand Foreign Affairs Review* (hereafter *NZFAR*), July 1972, pp.38, 42.
2   *NZFAR*, December 1973, p.9.
3   *NZFAR*, October 1973, p.9.
4   *NZFAR*, October–December 1976, p.31.
5   David Lange, *South Pacific Security and Development: A Small State Perspective* (Honolulu, 1987), p.5.
6   J. Henderson (ed.), *Towards a Pacific Island Community*, Report of the South Pacific Policy Review Group, Wellington, May 1990.

7   Speech to the New Zealand Institute of International Affairs, 26 March 1991.
8   Anthony Haas, 'New Zealand: Pacific Island or Metropolitan Power?', in Ron Crocombe (ed.), *Foreign Forces in Pacific Politics* (Suva, 1983), pp.96–111.
9   Ron Crocombe, *Pacific Neighbours: New Zealand's Relations with other Pacific Islands* (Christchurch, 1992).
10 Vasantha Krishnan (ed.), *The Challenge of Change, Pacific Island Communities in New Zealand, 1986–1993* (Wellington, 1994), p.30. Five years later the number of Pacific Islanders had risen to 202,000, and was predicted to reach 327,000 by 2031.
11 *New Zealand Official Yearbook 1994* (Wellington, 1994), pp.93–4.
12 *New Zealand Official Yearbook 1994*.
13 See Krishnan, *Challenge of Change*, p.17.
14 Krishnan, *Challenge of Change*, p.18.
15 *NZFAR*, January–February 1972, p.63.
16 Krishnan, *Challenge of Change*, p.55–8.
17 Annex to the Report of the Defence Committee of Enquiry, *Public Opinion Poll on Defence and Security: What New Zealanders Want*, National Research Bureau, 1986.
18 Malcolm McKinnon, *Independence and Foreign Policy* (Auckland, 1993), p.275.
19 Hyam Gold and Alan Webster, *New Zealand Values Today* (Palmerston North, 1990), p.39.
20 *Insight New Zealand* poll regularly on this issue.
21 *NZFAR*, January–March 1997, p.63.
22 Mary Boyd, 'New Zealand and the Other Pacific Islands', in Keith Sinclair (ed.), *The Oxford Illustrated History of New Zealand*, (second edition, Auckland, 1996).
23 Kirk letter reproduced in Paul Harris and Stephen Levine, *The New Zealand Politics Source Book* (Palmerston North, 1994), pp.433–4.
24 *NZFAR*, June 1973, p.10.
25 Ministry of External Relations and Trade (MERT), 'The Operations in the South Pacific', Management Audit, Part II, 1989, p.3.
26 MERT, 'Operations in the South Pacific'.
27 MERT, 'Operations in the South Pacific'.
28 Henderson, *Pacific Island Community*, p.30.
29 *NZFAR*, January–March 1984, p.21.
30 Norman Kirk, *New Zealand and its Neighbours* (Wellington, 1971), p.13.
31 *NZFAR*, June 1973, p.10.
32 Mike Moore, *A Pacific Parliament* (Suva, 1982).
33 Henderson, *Pacific Island Community*, pp.24–7.
34 Bruce Brown (ed.), *Asia and the Pacific in the 1970s* (Canberra, 1971), p.83.
35 See Ken Ross, *Regional Security in the South Pacific* (Canberra, 1993), pp.60–8.
36 Commonwealth Consultative Group, *Vulnerability: Small States in the Global Society* (London, 1985).
37 New Zealand Government, *Defence Review 1978* (Wellington, 1978), p.10.
38 Quoted by Dalton A. West, 'Perspectives on Russia in the Pacific', in Eric Olssen and Bill Webb, *New Zealand Foreign Policy and Defence* (Dunedin, 1977), p.102.
39 *NZFAR*, July–September 1976, p.36.

40 Ramesh Thakur, 'New Zealand and the South Pacific', in *Contemporary Pacific*, Spring 1995, p.77.
41 Ross, *Regional Security*, p.1.
42 *NZFAR*, August 1973, p.13.
43 *NZFAR*, October 1975, p.3.
44 Thakur, 'New Zealand and the South Pacific', p.91.
45 McKinnon, *Independence*, p.275.
46 Henderson, *Towards a Pacific Island Community*, p.59.
47 MERT, 'Operations in the South Pacific', p.3.
48 *Canberra Times*, 29 September 1989.
49 *The Age* (Melbourne), 11 April 1992.
50 *Dominion*, 19 May 1972.
51 *New Zealand Herald*, 19 May 1992.
52 *New Zealand Herald*, 27 July 1992.
53 David Lange, *Nuclear Free – The New Zealand Way* (Auckland, 1990), p.162.
54 Lange, *Nuclear Free*, p.162.
55 Press Conference Transcript, 18 May 1987.
56 New Zealand Government, *Defence of New Zealand: Review of Defence Policy, 1987* (Wellington, 1987).
57 See Henry Naisali, 'Regional Trade', in Ramesh Thakur (ed.), *The South Pacific: Problems, Issues, and Prospects* (Dunedin/New York, 1991), pp.183–92.
58 Henderson, *Towards a Pacific Island Community*, p.85.
59 MERT, 'Operations in the South Pacific', p.3
60 *NZFAR*, April–June 1983, p.27.
61 Henderson, 'Operations in the South Pacific', p.111.
62 *New Zealand Official Yearbook* (Wellington, 1990), p.106.
63 *NZFAR*, April 1973, p.13; and Crocombe, *Pacific Neighbours*, p.71.
64 *NZFAR*, January–March 1991, p.22.
65 Henderson, *Towards a Pacific Island Community*, p.120.
66 Crocombe, *Pacific Neighbours*, p.70.
67 Stephen Henningham, *The Pacific Island States* (London, 1995), p.xv.
68 Richard A. Herr, 'Concluding Observations', in Thakur, *South Pacific*, p.210.

RODERIC ALLEY

The Public Dimension

NEW ZEALAND'S FOREIGN RELATIONS BETWEEN 1972 AND 1990 were subject to a growing array of public interactions. Some were controversial – most conspicuously over sporting contacts with apartheid South Africa and banning nuclear weapons from entering New Zealand. Others proved less visible and adversarial, fostering habits of consultation between non-governmental bodies and officials. Public expressions reflecting anxiety about immigration and race relations contrasted with those promoting social objectives, such as the advancement of women, conservation, and environmental stewardship. Notwithstanding dissimilarities, these activities often saw domestic interests interacting with counterparts abroad. These international links were cultivated to gain information, foster local encouragement, and promote ideas about how to formulate public strategies. Regardless of agenda, local groups did not hesitate to inform international audiences about New Zealand conditions that they deemed unsatisfactory. Subjecting New Zealand governments to adverse international publicity was viewed as a means of gaining added domestic leverage.

Electoral outcomes in New Zealand are rarely influenced by partisan differences over foreign policy. However, local concerns of voters about jobs, the cost of living, women's entitlements, race relations, and leadership performance can often assume international dimensions. By 1972, domestic interdependence with international developments was intensifying. Protest against domestic policies shaped by negatively perceived international dimensions grew more vociferous, wide-ranging, and uncompromising. Some campaigns adopted a specific objective, such as the Organisation to Halt Military Service. In seeking to end selective military service, this capitalised on the Vietnam War's unpopularity. Others pursued more wide-ranging objectives, including the 'Save Manapouri' mobilisation. That sought retention of the environmental integrity of a southern lake, with an associated energy project's pricing made subject to independent scrutiny. With its calls for responsible environmental management, and suspicion of foreign-based corporate enterprise, the Save Manapouri campaign shaped the 1972 formation of the Values Party. Although it failed to win seats in that year's General Election, the Values message of sustainable economic management, national self-reliance, and neutrality abroad helped to shape future public interaction on foreign relations

Within a year of the Kirk Labour Government's arrival in office, the country was hit by the accumulated impact of rapidly rising oil prices, British entry into the European Community, and persisting difficulties of external market access. Yet attributing the country's economic woes to international forces alone was unpersuasive. Harsher exposure to international economic instability confirmed public suspicions that volatile global forces were now afoot. Neither the Government nor its advisers, it seemed, had fully grasped or anticipated the seriousness of such challenges. Abjectly unprepared for the oil shocks, where else might the Government prove suspect in its reading of international developments affecting New Zealand's core interests? These were also the Watergate years, with outcry about governmental credibility *de nouveau*. As the unparalleled buoyancy of early 1973 plummeted into deep recession 18 months later, this uncertainty was relished and manipulated by opposition figures such as Robert Muldoon.

Labour's spectacular rout at the polls in 1975 was driven partly by hopes that Muldoon's pugnacious interventionism might steer New Zealand out of trouble. Subsequent attempts to insulate the country against further bouts of international oil price rises saw the inception of the so-called 'Think Big' policy of imported energy substitution, although this was accompanied by worsening inflation, high tax rates, fickle external prices for key commodities, and worsening external indebtedness. To a growing number of the disenchanted, afflictions from abroad were being aggravated by faltering policies at home. The Government's role as protector of New Zealand's core economic security was under heavier siege than at any time since World War II.

These developments set the scene for the Fourth Labour Government's robust post-1984 programme of deregulation, financial liberalisation, public sector downsizing, and sale of state assets. Like its predecessor's 'Think Big' policy, Labour did not foreshadow these decisive changes through its election campaign manifestos. The term 'capture', suggesting little compromise in the pursuit of ideology, entered the public discourse. Activists keen to further specific goals, many with international dimensions, responded by directing their social energy outside the party political system. Unable to combat 'Rogernomics', public activity looked to foreign relations objectives such as helping to end apartheid and banning nuclear weapons.

This, then, was the setting against which we may gauge the 1972–90 period's interaction between foreign relations and domestic public activity. These interactions are compared for their influence upon the formulation of agendas, shifts in public opinion, and responses to altering international conditions.

The Third Labour Government of 1972–75

After sweeping into office in late 1972, Labour faced an international system undergoing substantial re-positioning. Key features included a gradual, but now inexorable United States withdrawal from the Vietnam conflict, Britain's imminent entry to the European Community, and President Nixon's spectacular but unheralded initiation of a political dialogue with Beijing. The post-1947 Atlantic consensus built around economic reconstruction, political alignment, and military containment, now faced the substantive challenges of accommodating Japan's economic dynamism, Vietnam's facing down of American military might, and Beijing's demands for a seat at the highest tables. The 1971 Smithsonian Agreements, de-coupling the value of the United States dollar to gold, was a vivid illustration of how even the strongest economy was not immune from the volatility of intensifying economic interdependence.

The Kirk Government looked to public support for a more independent, principled conduct of foreign relations, accommodation of Asia Pacific's political realities through diplomatic recognition of communist China, and constructive small state advocacy of regional linkages fostering cooperation and partnership. An equity dimension was expressed through Kirk's belief that as 'we are seeking to create a more just society in New Zealand so we intend to work toward the same goal in the international community'.[1] To one observer, this approach 'struck a chord in public opinion (because) New Zealanders have long nurtured a hope that, instead of playing a merely passive or reactive role in international affairs, they might express openly and forcefully what they regard as their non-self-interested humanitarian feelings'.[2]

Immediate neighbourhood goals included enhancement of the newly formed South Pacific Forum and a marked increase in New Zealand's development assistance. Following recommendations from a 1974 conference of local and internationally based non-governmental organisations, the government established an Advisory Committee on External Aid and Development. This helped to examine, debate, and publicise development assistance questions. These years also witnessed a sharp rise in the number of Pacific Islanders entering New Zealand, many for temporary work purposes.[3] An unmet challenge lay in ensuring domestic attitudes towards this migration did not disturb regional South Pacific cooperation and partnership. This grew difficult as dispute over the status of lapsed temporary permit holders worsened, reaching a nadir in 1976. Despite denials from New Zealand cabinet ministers, police conducted hundreds of random checks of non-white people in major cities to ascertain their citizenship and resident status. This episode illustrated the 'power of domestically fostered concerns to collide with Pacific interests'.[4]

The 1973 dispatch of a frigate to Mururoa atoll to publicise internationally continued French nuclear testing was a high profile public action that, subsequently, Prime Minister Rowling believed helped persuade France to end its atmospheric nuclear weapons testing two years later.[5] Kirk articulated 'a widely shared belief that world peace and security depend on whether nuclear weapons can be limited and eventually eliminated, and that the continued development and proliferation of these devices increase tension and the risk of nuclear war'.[6] Mobilising international opinion for nuclear disarmament was an essential corollary, something conveyed by the Government's officials at the United Nations. Hence over nuclear disarmament, a 1974 statement claimed 'New Zealand does not subscribe to the view that Assembly resolutions which have behind them the weight of world public opinion are useless, merely because they are not accepted in advance by powerful countries whose policies they criticise'.[7]

The Kirk government's seemingly well managed 'postponement' of a planned 1973 visit to New Zealand by a Springbok rugby side from apartheid South Africa cost Labour traditional blue collar support at the polls in 1975. The National Party claimed the issue was less about apartheid sport than the right to travel overseas.[8] Although support for continuing sporting contacts with South Africa was effectively exploited by succeeding Prime Minister Muldoon, the principles motivating Kirk's cancellation set a benchmark that subsequent governments and the New Zealand public could not ignore.

The Muldoon Years 1975–84

Under Robert Muldoon's heavily centralised style of governance, the public dimensions of foreign relations were those of a leader seeking populist support for external conduct, amidst a climate of often embittered polarisation. Direct appeals to popular support were utilised when Muldoon demanded access to Japan's beef market in return for Japanese fishing in New Zealand's exclusive economic zone. Tokyo's tactics, Muldoon asserted, were those of a country trying to achieve by peaceful means what it had failed during World War II.[9] Popular sentiment was looked to in 1980 when the Soviet Ambassador was expelled for helping fund New Zealand's modest Socialist Unity Party. More conspicuously, it was enlisted again in support of the American-led boycott of the 1980 Moscow Olympic Games, orchestrated in retaliation against Soviet military intervention into Afghanistan. Public support for the United Kingdom over the 1982 Falklands conflict was also wooed. This resulted in the dispatch of a frigate for patrol duties normally assumed by the Royal Navy in the Indian Ocean, to free an equivalent British vessel for service in the Falklands. Contrary to official advice, Muldoon ruptured diplomatic relations with Argentina. In some instances, Muldoon reluctantly followed public opinion, as in 1979 over Indo-Chinese refugee acceptance and resettlement that was conducted in response 'to both internal and international pressures for increased official action'.[10]

Prime Minister Muldoon's attempted intimidation of domestic opponents and denigration of those he disliked abroad, inflamed public protest over foreign relations. This occurred in 1976 when he accused anti-nuclear protesters of supporting Moscow. In the same year, he broke convention by releasing to Parliament official advice tendered to the previous government. This warned against proceeding with proposals for a South Pacific Nuclear Free Zone Treaty not favoured by the United States.[11] Domestic protest against New Zealand's retention of sporting contacts with South Africa intensified following the Muldoon Government's unwillingness to condemn apartheid sport. This precipitated an African-led boycott of the 1976 Montreal Olympics, then compounded by Muldoon's studied refusal to follow the 1977 Commonwealth Gleneagles Agreement's recommendations urging practical steps to discourage South African sporting contacts. By the conclusion of his first parliamentary term of office in 1978, Muldoon had hardened public divisions leaving little ground for compromise over an issue that would split the country still further.[12]

In some instances the Muldoon Government utilised consultation processes deemed useful for the pursuit of external objectives while it disbanded others – the Commission for the Future following its 1982 report *Nuclear Disaster*, for example.[13] The consultative committee on development assistance was maintained, while in preparation for the 1978 United Nations Special Session of the General Assembly on Disarmament (UNSSOD I), a National Consultative Committee on Disarmament (NCCD) was established. Here, a cross section of interested non-governmental organisations exchanged views with officials about the priorities New Zealand ought to stress at the forthcoming Special Session. A resulting Green Paper published by the Government included a claim opposed by the NCCD. This asserted that

> as far as nuclear weapons are concerned, the reasoning of minor parties (ie New Zealand) would be simply that, in a world of nuclear weapon states, states without them enhance their security by alliance with those who have them.[14]

By contrast, the NCCD called on the government to dissociate itself from the use of nuclear weapons in any defence of New Zealand; establish a South Pacific Nuclear Weapons Free Zone; ban visiting warships failing confirmation that they were not carrying nuclear weapons; support a comprehensive test ban treaty; and encourage curbs on the international arms trade.[15] Although most of this was officially rejected, it served peace groups as a statement of objectives.

The NCCD statement clashed with security orthodoxy, the Government affording a higher priority to ANZUS than continuation of attempts to secure a South Pacific Nuclear Free Zone.[16] Yet when

Australia resumed this particular initiative at the South Pacific Forum in 1983, the Muldoon Government, increasingly aware of growing public support for nuclear disarmament, did not oppose it. It was evident that concern about nuclear weapons entering New Zealand was growing *before* Labour gained office. In March 1984, National's Deputy Prime Minister McLay told a Wellington audience that 'the very survival of mankind is threatened by the existence of nuclear weapons and the continuing arms race; . . . removing the threat of world war, a nuclear war, is the most acute and urgent task of the present day'.[17]

These concerns were not alleviated by American insistence upon neither confirm nor deny policies. At the 1982 ANZUS Council meeting, Washington had sought and secured a statement where members 'recognized the importance of access by United States naval ships to the ports of its treaty partners as a critical factor in its efforts to maintain strategic deterrence . . . They noted and accepted that it is not the policy of the US Navy to reveal whether or not its vessels are armed with nuclear weapons'.[18] In other instances, growth in support for the anti-nuclear policy was assisted by American retaliation. This occurred at the 1982 Labour Party conference, when the American Embassy issued a statement hoping that the sense of most New Zealanders would prevail and not support such policy.

The Fourth Labour Government 1984–90

The anti-nuclear policy of the Lange Government has been extensively analysed.[19] Accordingly, what further deserves note? This question is addressed by considering relevant public dynamics; party political dimensions; public review and evaluation activities; and finally institutionalisation. Before doing so however, two points deserve discussion.

First, and as a public question, New Zealand's divorce from ANZUS was never isolated from a widespread, long-standing and persistent cross-party public disapprobation of nuclear weapons testing. Shortly after entering office, the Lange Government received two messages. One was from the United States, indicating that it did not see how ANZUS could continue operating effectively should New Zealand prevent nuclear ship visits to its ports. The other came from Paris, indicating that the French Government would continue nuclear weapons testing until at least the end of the century. Although the first message gained most attention, the second was as crucial given its implications for American concerns. To the incoming Government and its supporters, the pronouncement from Paris epitomised what was obdurate about nuclear weapons state insistence that, so far as security questions were concerned, their interests would prevail regardless of South Pacific sentiment.

A second feature was the anti-nuclear policy's function as a lightning rod for independence aspirations previously perceived as blocked, waylaid, or threatened during the Muldoon years. Opportunities now existed to revisit and reapply the Norman Kirk principles of independent conduct before a public receptive to such initiatives. Shortly after winning office, Lange told a London audience that his government would 'be trying to stimulate a shift in public opinion which will ensure that a sporting tour to South Africa is as unthinkable in New Zealand as the presence of nuclear weapons'.[20]

The Anti-Nuclear Issue

Public dynamics

Much of New Zealand's anti-nuclear protest was decentralised and small scale, pursuing objectives such as creating local authority 'nuclear free zones' designed to support and legitimise the symbolic impact of anti-nuclear positions. This conformed to the distinctive 'do it yourself' pragmatism of New Zealand public organisational activity, coagulated opposition to actual nuclear ship visits, and exploited aspirations of independence and nationhood. Groups such as the New Zealand branch of the International Physicians for the Prevention of Nuclear War (IPPNW) capitalised on professional status and access to international contacts needed to draft informed submissions. The 1982 Parliamentary and Disarmament Arms Control Committee, established in response to growing alarm at current developments in the nuclear arms race, found the IPPNW 1983 submission sufficiently authoritative to include it in its report.[21]

The IPPNW's formation and the convening of the parliamentary select committee occurred as the nuclear arms race escalated through the United States Strategic Defence Initiative, popularly termed 'Star Wars'. Extending into 1983, this period saw Soviet-United States tensions heightened, arms control discussions stalled, and fissures evident within

NATO over nuclear deployments in Europe. Meanwhile, the United States continued its opposition to resolutions sponsored by Australia and New Zealand at the United Nations General Assembly calling for a comprehensive test ban treaty.

Table 1: Public opinion and nuclear-armed ship visits

Responses to the question: 'Do you agree that New Zealand should allow American ships equipped with nuclear weapons into New Zealand ports?' recorded in polls 1978–85 were:

Date	Agree	Disagree	Other	Pollster*	Sample	Area
1978	61.5%	31.5%	6.9%	L/S (a)	537	National
1982	49.0	41.0	8.0	K/W (b)	142	Auckland
1983	46.1	40.2	13.7	Heylen	1000	National
1984	30.4	57.4	12.3	NRB (c)	2000	National
1985	29.0	56.0	15.0	McNair	533	National
1985	30.0	59.0	11.0	NRB	2000	National

Key
(a) Levine/Spoonley
(b) Kjellstrom/Wilson
(c) National Research Bureau

Source: Campbell 1987 (see note 27)

The Political Party Dimension

Parties holding office in New Zealand regard consultation with the government as a vital function, conducted regularly via caucus meetings when Parliament is in session. When challenging, scrutinising, or otherwise holding the government's conduct to account via these meetings, backbenchers regard party and wider public support as critical to their effectiveness. Governments newly elected after considerable periods in opposition may also contain backbenchers harbouring suspicions about the capacity of officialdom to delay, dilute or derail party manifesto commitments.

These factors applied in 1984 when influential backbenchers such as Helen Clark and Jim Anderton believed that, on security policy, local officials shared more in common with American, British, and Australian policy élites than with the government that they were employed to serve. A submission supervised by Helen Clark for the 1986 Defence Committee of Enquiry (DCE) maintained that 'for too long the critical questions in defence and foreign policies and strategies have been debated within and decided by New Zealand's political, bureaucratic and military establishments. It is the view of the New Zealand Labour Party that there is a broad desire in the community for greater participation in the debate and development of policy on these matters. We sense too that the attitudes of what might be called the "Wellington establishment" are now somewhat removed from those commonly held in the community'.[22]

More colourfully, Prime Minister Lange regaled the 1988 Labour Party conference with descriptions of his initial encounters with officialdom over the anti-nuclear policy, namely, 'that it was taken for granted that we would change the anti-nuclear policy . . . when after several months it started to sink in we were serious , they started to get heavy. They told me our trade in Europe depended on our surrender to the doctrines of nuclear preparedness. They told me we would never get asked to the White House which is true but I have managed to live without it'.[23] Lange saw the need to build parliamentary and party support against local officialdom, whose corridors were viewed as the most likely means through which American and Australian attempts to eviscerate the anti-nuclear policy would proceed. A majority in caucus believed that, should the government proceed without party compliance, it risked alienating a significant core of informed, active and loyal support needed to avoid future electoral defeat. This was a key consideration behind the decision to legislate for the anti-nuclear ban.

Review and Evaluation

The most prominent attempt to engage the public dimension on nuclear disarmament and New Zealand security questions occurred with the Government's establishment, in 1985, of the Defence Committee of Enquiry headed by Frank Corner. This received and heard public submissions on New Zealand's defence policy, conducted polling on public attitudes to defence and security matters, and reported prior to a planned Defence Review.[24] An advance framework discussion paper raised questions about the most appropriate means of securing New

Zealand's security; relevant relations with the South Pacific and Australia; the scope for defence self reliance; and maintenance of the anti-nuclear policy.[25] When the DCE was established, Lange said that there would be little prospect that it would 'sing in unison'.[26]

Findings indicating strong support for both continued ANZUS membership *and* the government's anti-nuclear policies emerged as key results of the DCE. In 1985, the Heylen polling organisation detected approximately equal levels of support for maintaining the ANZUS alliance and accepting ship visits or, alternatively, maintaining the anti-nuclear position and quitting the alliance. The DCE posed a similar question, offering poll respondents options of a full, a qualified, or a no alliance arrangement, but with the anti-nuclear stance retained. The largest number (44 per cent) opted for a partial alliance with no nuclear ship visits, a full alliance including nuclear ship visits was supported by 37 per cent, while 16 per cent favoured no alliance. To the 44 per cent favouring qualified alliance, a further question was posed, namely: 'if that proves impossible what would be your next choice?' A majority of the 44 per cent (28 per cent) were for no alliance, but 15 per cent opted for a full alliance. Using scissors and paste, the DCE then took the last mentioned 15 per cent and added it to the original sample's 37 per cent wanting alliance retention, thus producing an overall 52 per cent wanting New Zealand within ANZUS and ship visits retained.

Confusing to many, this methodology engendered hostility between peace activists and the DCE. Prime Minister Lange's office intervened, attempting to have the report revised prior to publication.[27] Dispute over the DCE report and its polling methodologies failed to clarify who spoke with authority when interpreting what the New Zealand public wanted. However, majorities supporting continued ANZUS membership and closer defence ties with Australia, but opposition to nuclear weaponry in the defence of New Zealand were unmistakable. For experienced journalist Ian Templeton, the DCE offered Prime Minister Lange the negotiating option of postponing the anti-nuclear legislation, but he rejected this option because of 'domestic pressures'.[28] The Committee's attempt to advise the Prime Minister on negotiations, and its clear implication that the Government had not tried hard enough to resolve the impasse, also helps to explain why temperatures were raised over the report.[29]

Institutionalisation

To the New Zealand public, the nuclear ship ban's objective of nuclear disarmament was increasingly vindicated by international developments. Some were politically fortuitous, including the 1985 *Rainbow Warrior* bombing by French agents in Auckland harbour, and the 1986 Chernobyl nuclear plant disaster. Others signified that deep-seated international system changes were afoot such as the abortive but landmark Reagan-Gorbachev 1986 Reykjavik Summit which openly canvassed the possibility of comprehensive superpower nuclear disarmament; a continuing thaw in Soviet-US relations; and, in 1987, conclusion of the INF treaty banning intermediate range nuclear delivery systems. In the light of this treaty's comprehensive and intrusive verification requirements, American adherence to 'neither confirm nor deny' doctrines regarding the location of nuclear weaponry appeared increasingly inconsistent. These developments confirmed claims that New Zealand's anti-nuclear policy was running with, not against the tide of current international disarmament developments.

Institutionalisation through the Nuclear Free Zone, Disarmament and Arms Control Act of 1987 was of seminal importance. According to Clements this may have had 'irrational elements, but for many the Nuclear Free Act was a declaration of national independence'.[30] A receding Cold War saw the National Party prior to the 1990 General Election indicate that it would not repeal the 1987 legislation formalising the ban. This neutralised a key policy plank Labour was relying upon to mollify its core constituency, by now outraged at the impact that deregulation policies had exacted on New Zealand's increasingly threadbare welfare state.

The Frigates Dispute

The New Zealand Government's 1988 decision to join Australia in a joint frigate building project assumed public salience and generated unresolved controversy. Australian pressure to participate accumulated steadily following the 1986 rupture of security relations with the United States, and the 1987 Defence Review's confirmation that close links with Australia were an essential component of New Zealand's security profile. Opposition to participation also accumulated; the Just Defence lobby's 1986 14-point agenda called for a reappraisal of New Zealand's future security needs with resource protection in the 200 miles Exclusive

Economic Zone identified as a priority. Frigates were 'inappropriate and needlessly costly for this role ... and even incapable of performing effectively the military role for which they are designed. Alternatives should be found'.[31]

Prime Minister Palmer in 1989 believed the critical factor was 'Australia's insistence that the purchase was a litmus test of whether or not New Zealand was serious about trans-Tasman defence cooperation'.[32] Foreign Minister Marshall feared New Zealand refusal to participate in the frigate project would be construed as an act of bad faith by a country aligned to the West yet prepared to 'freeload' and jeopardize closer economic relations with Australia.[33] In November 1988, Opposition leader Bolger gained access to a Cabinet briefing that he released citing a message delivered three months earlier from Australian Prime Minister Hawke, and his Defence Minister Kim Beazley. This warned that New Zealand's failure to participate in the project would damage trans-Tasman economic and defence relations.[34]

Polling returns indicated solid majorities opposing the project. This was from cost grounds during conditions of economic difficulty, and resentment against perceived Australian pressure.[35] An October 1988 poll indicated that the proposed deal was opposed by 76 per cent of respondents, 57 per cent prepared to do so regardless of negotiated price of purchase. This was partly influenced by a belief that the New Zealand Navy sought the frigate purchase as a form of revived ANZUS arrangement, or as an expanded defence relationship with Australia.[36] Divisions of national opinion reverberated within the Government's parliamentary caucus. The dispute soured relations between the Government and the Labour Party, Party President Ruth Dyson regarding government conduct as a serious breach of promised consultation.[37]

The Public Advisory Committee on Disarmament and Arms Control (PACDAC), a statutory body established under the 1987 anti-nuclear legislation, also opposed the frigate purchase proposal. In November 1988, it called on the Government to indicate options open to New Zealand in maintaining its maritime security and publicise them before entering a long-term commitment.[38] This advice went unheeded, as did PACDAC's recommendation that New Zealand support an initiative in the United Nations General Assembly to have the International Court of Justice provide an advisory opinion on the legal status of nuclear weapons.

Antarctica

Dispute over the future management of Antarctica's resources provided a revealing, although often tortuous trail of official and non-governmental interaction on an issue of international significance. Following protracted negotiations, consultative parties to the Antarctic Treaty forged a consensus supporting a management regime designed to reconcile environmental protection needs with possible minerals extraction. Instrumental was senior New Zealand official Christopher Beeby. To his role as key adviser to the New Zealand Government was the added status of chair of the consultative parties' meetings. They were charged with formulating what emerged in 1988 as the Convention on the Regulation of Antarctic Mineral Resource Activity (CRAMRA). Opposing these developments was the Antarctic and Southern Oceans Coalition (ASOC), a grouping that maintained extensive links with international lobbies such as Greenpeace and Friends of the Earth.

The New Zealand Government saw a convention as necessary to avoid an unregulated scramble for Antarctic mineral and oil resources, an outcome that would inflame sovereign claimant/non-claimant differences and damage the Antarctic environment. The normative framework devised included regulations on prospecting, exploration and development; a commission comprising Antarctic Treaty Parties and countries sponsoring mining; regulatory supervision of the specific geological, environmental and technical aspects relevant to each application; and scope for advisory input from scientific, environmental and relevant intergovernmental interests.

In its entirety, this package was vehemently attacked by ASOC on grounds that commercial mining would necessarily undermine the intrinsic purpose of the Antarctic regime, namely the preservation of the Antarctic ecosystem and undisturbed scientific research. Proprietary mining rights would hinder the free flow of information from such research, and generate liability problems that the continent's unsettled legal status could not handle. Under these circumstances a total mining ban was justified.[39] Initially the New Zealand Government maintained 'arms length' relations with ASOC. This changed when it was apparent that this lobby was not only privy to negotiating details, but was playing an informal role advising recently joined consultative parties new to the mineral regime negotiations.

In early 1989 a significant development occurred when the Australian

Government switched tack to collaborate with France, Belgium, and Italy to bypass CRAMRA in favour of a total ban. Public determinants influencing this switch included the serious *Exxon Valdez* tanker oil spill of March 1989; the victory of five environmentalist candidates in the May 1989 Tasmanian state election; and publicity surrounding French explorer Jacques Cousteau's international efforts to gain over one million signatures for a 'Save Antarctica' campaign. By late 1989, a momentum favouring the French–Australian position at the expense of CRAMRA was evident. ASOC claimed New Zealand's rearguard attempt to salvage the convention was motivated by fears that abandonment would cost Wellington kudos after six years negotiating effort, by pique with the Australians 'at a time when New Zealand feels thoroughly bullied over frigates', and by a desire to accommodate the pro-mining stance of the United States as compensation for the anti-nuclear policy.[40] While the government won the negotiating round by completing CRAMRA in 1988, within two years it had lost the propaganda campaign needed to secure it.

East Timor

To interested constituencies, New Zealand's handling of the East Timor question was a barometer indicating official commitment to human rights. After Indonesia invaded the territory in 1975, lobbies such as the Auckland-based East Timor Independence Committee and the Wellington-based East Timor Independence Centre publicised documented human rights violations and political repression on the island. They called on the New Zealand Government to directly challenge Jakarta over such conduct, and insisted Indonesia accommodate UN expectations for peaceful discharge of the territory's self determination.

Although not condoning intervention, successive New Zealand governments recognized the territory's incorporation into Indonesia as a *fait accompli*. Protest groups noted that this contrasted with New Zealand's 1982 position at the United Nations, when its permanent representative insisted that 'the right to decide their own destiny belongs to the Falkland Islanders no less than to any other people. It is a right to which they have been forcibly deprived; it is a right which must be returned to them'.[40] As documentation of human rights violations in East Timor increased, New Zealand officials regarded Amnesty

International's reports of serious abuses as probably accurate. However public concern in New Zealand over East Timor remained effective only to the extent that governments were prepared to condemn human rights violations in general terms, but without calling for Indonesian withdrawal from the territory.

The Multilateral Arena

Through different representative bodies, the New Zealand public has long regarded intergovernmental multilateral settings as appropriate venues to promote demands and exert pressure on the New Zealand government. The UN has been viewed as an organisation accountable to citizens and taxpayers, not just governments and officials. Emancipation, welfare, development, and rule-based conduct by states have been regarded as essential for the promotion of international peace, order and justice pursued through multilateral means. Expansion of the UN's membership and circumference of activities has been accompanied by a proliferation of public interest constituencies concerned to distribute information and share lobbying strategies. This expanded between 1972 and 1990 as disarmament, environment, and human rights concerns enhanced their international public salience by utilising global networks that facilitated exchanges of knowledge, information, and promotional activities.

New Zealand public interest groups utilised intergovernmental settings to advance their objectives in a variety of ways. As UN conferences and their preparatory meetings increased, groups formulated domestic lobbying strategies accordingly. For those promoting the advancement of women, the UN sponsored conference sequence included major meetings in Mexico City (1975), Copenhagen (1980) and Nairobi (1985). In disarmament, key sequences included the five yearly review conferences of the Nuclear Non-Proliferation Treaty, and the UN General Assembly Special Sessions on Disarmament held in 1978, 1982 and 1988. These meetings afforded scope for non-governmental participation and international contacts; at the 1988 Special Session, a New Zealand NGO representative helped foster collaboration between those seeking to link South Pacific and Latin American nuclear weapons free zones.[42] Non-governmental attendance at these meetings by New Zealand representatives was a regular occurrence, sometimes within official delegations.

As this activity expanded, New Zealand officialdom regularised briefings with non-governmental representatives for purposes of information exchange, comparative evaluation of draft conference language, and consultation about local implementation of relevant outcomes. Governments used these meetings to gauge the strength of local NGO sentiment on particular issues, and sometimes forestall at source criticisms of New Zealand's official position.

New Zealand policy towards the formulation and possible adoption of international conventions added a further dimension of public interaction. Sometimes this was grist to local politics, as when the New Zealand Government – through its 1984 ratification of the Convention on the Elimination of All Forms of Discrimination Against Women – entered a reservation opposing paid maternity leave provisions.[43] When New Zealand presented its first report in 1988 under this Convention, it claimed that it led the world in establishing a Ministry of Women's Affairs as a separate autonomous department of state.[44] The period concerned also witnessed a growth in New Zealand's adherence to treaties and conventions requiring specific domestic compliance requirements. These could include stipulations for furthering public cooperation in implementation.

Institutional and legislative developments that helped to locate New Zealand domestic concerns against international standards included establishment of the Office of the Race Relations Conciliator (1973); the Human Rights Commission (1978); Freedom of Information Act (1982); Parliamentary Commissioner for the Environment (1986); and Office for the Commissioner for Children (1989). Although UN human rights procedures permitting non-governmental participation remained uneven, New Zealand groups utilised them to amplify their demands. In 1988, Maori representatives addressed the UN Commission on Human Rights and, from 1982, participated regularly in the UN Working Group on Indigenous Populations.[45] Within New Zealand, Waitangi Tribunal findings began relating local issues to international developments. Hence findings in the 1988 Muriwhenua fisheries claim case held 'that all peoples have a right to development as an emerging concept in international law' with possible application to indigenous peoples.[46]

The knowledge and experience acquired by New Zealand NGOs before multilateral fora during this period provided a platform for subsequent activity. For example, skills developed over nuclear disarmament helped inform the campaign to ban land mines. Intra-Commonwealth links developed in opposition to apartheid assisted subsequent non-governmental development and relief activity in Africa. Public groups opposed to French nuclear testing developed South Pacific contacts that furthered shared environmental concerns. Over environmental questions, public activity highlighted the lack of coordination among domestic agencies. This impeded New Zealand in meeting its full obligations under the Convention on the Law of the Sea.[47]

As the Cold War receded, public energies previously absorbed by the nuclear issue began to embrace activities aimed at rectifying distortions of gender inequality, environmental degradation, human rights violations, and negative social impacts of transnational corporate business activity. Other concerns included Central America's search for peace; Third World debt and development issues including community-based uses of technology; and the costs of structural adjustment upon developing countries. Here the more-market approach sweeping New Zealand provided a point of approximate reference. Public engagement also grew more project-specific, as over the campaign to engage the World Court on the legal status of nuclear weapons, designation of Antarctica as a world park in perpetuity, and a complete ban on whaling. Finally it deserves note that these were years of a steep decline in political party membership, activists turning to single issue campaigning as a preferred means of linking local to global concerns.

Comparative Assessments

What difference did public interactions make to New Zealand's foreign relations between 1972 and 1990? While evaluation is possible, it is complicated by idiosyncratic factors such as the contrasting values, styles and foreign policy fixations of Prime Ministers as different as Kirk, Muldoon and Lange. In different ways, each figure epitomised and amplified political upheaval unseen during the preceding Holyoake years. All three shook previous assumptions about New Zealand's place in the world, made foreign policy decisions that polarised the public, galvanised conflicting currents of sentiment, and attracted international attention. Political audience in some form or other motivated Norman Kirk's 1973 decision to send a frigate to witness French nuclear testing, Muldoon's electoral calculations during the 1981 South African rugby tour of New Zealand, and Lange's 1985 appearance opposing nuclear deterrence before the footlights at the Oxford Union. Prime Ministerial involvement in the conduct of New Zealand's foreign relations increased through greater international travel and conference opportunities and exposure through expanded international television news services. While these figures invigorated public involvement in foreign relations, it was an engagement of uncertain durability.

Another variable concerned the distinctive social dynamics surrounding the most controversial episodes identified: the Muldoon period in relation to sporting contacts with South Africa, and New Zealand's anti-nuclear policy during the first parliamentary term (1984–87) of the Fourth Labour Government. Over sporting contacts, the New Zealand Rugby Union was cast by its opponents as not only an apologist for apartheid, but a citadel of a New Zealand past viewed by critics as nasty and brutish if not short. This was the template that the 1981 Springbok tour brought into the homes, offices and work places of the nation when younger New Zealanders, women, professionals, and urban middle classes turned to the streets with an intensity that surprised even themselves. This was less a dispute about New Zealand foreign policy than a conflict over the symbols of an unproven national identity. For the first time in New Zealand's history, 'rugby was becoming a source of national embarrassment, not pride'.[48]

Idiosyncrasy of a different kind distinguished New Zealand's public quarrels over the anti-nuclear policy. Despite years of persistent under-resourcing, and through considerable effort, a cohort of foreign service officers took pride in what they viewed as a cachet of small state access and representation without parallel in Washington, London and Canberra, capitals of significance to New Zealand. These officials were reared in the Berendsen tradition of precepts that were unabashedly realist. Military power was what counted, New Zealand lacked influence and, in an uncertain world, alignment and its costs were the price for survival. Alliance, moreover, spelled indivisibility. After Labour gained power in 1984, figures such as McLean and Corner believed that hard-won access to the citadels of power was being needlessly frittered away through the popular expediency, naiveté, and inexperience characterised by the anti-nuclear policy. This was wasteful, disloyal, and even dangerous should it infect other, more important security arrangements involving United States relations with Japan and NATO.

Anti-nuclear sentiment had another view of indivisibility but not one confined to alliances, namely the global consequences of using nuclear weapons which, if doctrines of deterrence meant what they said, could never go ignored. As Lange told a San Francisco audience in October 1985, 'none of us anywhere can be defended against nuclear weapons'.[49] The impacts of atmospheric nuclear testing in the Pacific and the 1986 Chernobyl disaster were not outcomes manageable through calculations of state power and interest. Persistence by the United States in its neither confirm nor deny policy regarding the presence of nuclear weapons fitted uneasily within the broadening discourse of accountability, transparency, and human rights. Suspicions intensified that this policy was not military-based but a form of concealment designed to weaken opposition to policies of nuclear deterrence.

Evident throughout the period was a tension of continuing significance. This was manifest between official advice to the government claiming objectives would be better achieved by persuasion behind closed doors, and opposing activist expectations that New Zealand had more to gain by speaking out as a credible small state. An early illustration of that tension occurred when, shortly after winning office, Norman Kirk criticised the Nixon Administration for its Christmas 1972 bombing raid of Hanoi. This was kept private on the advice of officials aware of Nixon's potential for vindictiveness. By contrast, some public postures were gratuitous – Muldoon antagonised his officials by publicising the 'beef for fish' details in dispute with Japan, and through gratuitous attacks on President Carter and his family. Lange's unpredictability when making public statements also generated nervousness. The utterances of politicians complicated assessments about likely public or diplomatic impacts.

Conclusions

By 1990, the relationship between governments and publics in New Zealand over the conduct of foreign relations was more diverse, increasingly routine, and less confrontational. This was facilitated by the end of the Cold War and the dismantling of apartheid, and as consensus support for the anti-nuclear policy and self respect in race relations began to emerge. State sector restructuring left the foreign relations apparatus having to do more with less, necessitating solicitation of non-governmental advice for what it might offer. This was evident as the tempo and content of long running multilateral engagements increased throughout the period. What was recognisably 'foreign policy' in earlier years entwined more intensively with domestic issues through Closer Economic Relations with Australia, broadening Asia-Pacific links, and foreign relations conduct requiring active partnerships with business, commerce, education and science. In style and performance, New Zealand diplomacy gradually weaned itself from origins where a few key personalities remained dominant, assumptions about immediate access to the Prime Minister were constant, and formal traditions of bureaucratic hierarchy consistent. While wary of public engagement in controversies embroiling their political masters, officials grew less self conscious about promoting their objectives by going public.

Public bodies engaging foreign relations questions diversified in scope, increased their number, and fostered liaison with related and parent bodies. From 1972 to 1990, the local growth of organisations like Greenpeace and Amnesty International outstripped membership recruitment by the major political parties. Campaigning for environmental causes, human rights, and disarmament became more focused. The ending of the Cold War vindicated this approach and helped secure bipartisan support for New Zealand's anti-nuclear legislation. Attention to problems abroad highlighted neglected concerns at home over environmental management, race relations, the status of women, and violence in the community. Thus a slogan of these years – 'think globally and act locally' – was as significant for New Zealand's domestic needs as its external orientations.

Notes

1 Norman Kirk, 'Review of Foreign Policy 1973', in *New Zealand Foreign Affairs Review* (hereafter *NZFAR*), December 1973, p.32.
2 Keith Jackson, 'Norman Kirk – his role and influence: New Zealand's Third Labour Government', in *Current Affairs Bulletin*, Vol.51 No.10, March 1975. p.29.
3 Richard Bedford, 'Migration and Development in the Pacific Islands', in Ramesh Thakur (ed.), *The South Pacific: Problems, Issues and Prospects* (Dunedin/New York, 1991), p.158.
4 Malcolm McKinnon, *Independence and Foreign Policy: New Zealand in the World since 1935* (Auckland, 1993), p.264.
5 W. E. Rowling, 'New Zealand's Opposition to Nuclear Weapons', in *NZFAR*, October 1975, p.3.
6 Norman Kirk, 'New Zealand: A New Foreign Policy', in *NZFAR*, June 1973, p.4.
7 'Is the UN being Steamrollered?' Statement of New Zealand Permanent Repre-

sentative Templeton to the UN General Assembly, in *NZFAR*, December 1974, p.24.
8   McKinnnon, *Independence and Foreign Policy*, pp.242–3.
9   John Henderson, 'Foreign Policy and the Election', in *New Zealand International Review* (hereafter *NZIR*), September–October 1978, p.24
10 Alistair Bowie, 'Some Room at the Inn', in *NZIR*, January–February 1981, p.31.
11 Henderson, 'Foreign Policy', p.23.
12 Stephen Levine, 'Basic Choices', in *NZIR*, April 1979, p.14. Stephen Levine, 'Public Opinion and Foreign Policy', in *NZIR*, March 1980, p.21.
13 George Preddy, *Nuclear Disaster: A New Way of Thinking Down Under* (Wellington, 1982).
14 'Disarmament and Arms Control', Green Paper prepared for UNSOD I, Ministry of Foreign Affairs, Wellington, April 1978, p.37.
15 NCND Statement, Wellington, mimeo, April 1978.
16 *Report of the Ministry of Foreign Affairs, 1976*. Wellington, 1976, p.4.
17 J. M. McLay, 'Nuclear Arms in a Real World', in *NZFAR*, January–March 1984, p.12.
18 Anzus Council. *Communiqué*, 23 June 1982, in *NZFAR*, April–June, 1982, p.26.
19 See for example Stuart Mcmillan, *Neither Confirm Nor Deny: The Nuclear Ships Dispute between New Zealand and the United States* (Wellington, 1987); Michael Pugh, *The ANZUS Crisis, Nuclear Visiting and Deterrence* (Cambridge, 1989).
20 David Lange, 'Sporting Contact with South Africa', in *NZFAR*, July–September 1984, p.18.
21 *Report of the Disarmament and Arms Control Committee*, New Zealand Parliament (Wellington, 1985).
22 New Zealand Labour Party. Submission to the Defence Committee of Enquiry on the future of New Zealand's Strategic and Security Policies, 1986.
23 Speech to the 1988 NZLP Annual Conference, Dunedin.
24 Kevin Clements, 'The Defence Committee of Enquiry: A Unique Opportunity for Public Opinion', in Jonathan Boston and Martin Holland (eds.), *The Fourth Labour Government: Radical Politics in New Zealand* (Auckland, 1987), pp.214–41.
25 *The Defence Question*, New Zealand Government Paper (Wellington, 1985).
26 *The Dominion*, Wellington, 20 August 1986, p.1.
27 David Campbell, 'The Domestic Sources of New Zealand Security Policy in Comparative Perspective', Working Paper No.16, Peace Research Centre, Canberra, 1987, p.3.
28 Ian Templeton, 'Government Must Rally to the Nation's Defence', *Auckland Star*, 23 August 1986.
29 Templeton, 'Government Must Rally'.
30 Kevin Clements, 'The Last Broken Promise: Amending New Zealand's Anti-Nuclear Act', in *Pacific Research*, November 1991, p.9.
31 *Just Defence*, January 1986, Wellington, pp.1–4.
32 Cited in John Henderson, 'Changes in New Zealand Defence Policy', in Richard Kennaway and John Henderson (eds.), *Beyond New Zealand II. Foreign Policy Into the 1990s* (Auckland, 1991), p.89.

33 Katie Boanas-Dewes, 'Participatory Democracy in Peace and Security Decision-Making: the Aoteoroa/New Zealand Experience', *Interdisciplinary Peace Research*, Vol.5 No.2, 1993, p.96.
34 Andrew McClean, 'Lange Under Pressure on Frigates', in *Pacific Research*, November 1988, p.16.
35 Graeme Cheeseman, 'The Frigate Saga Continues', in *Pacific Research*, May 1989, pp.10–11.
36 McClean, 'Lange', p.16.
37 Boanas-Dewes, 'Participatory Democracy', p.98.
38 *New Zealand External Affairs Review*, October–December 1988, p.71.
39 David Schwartz, 'Pondering Antarctica's Future', in *NZIR*, November–December 1987, pp.12–13.
40 ASOC, *Antarctic News*, November 1989, p.3.
41 Ambassador Harland statement, *NZFAR*, April–June 1982, pp.60–1.
42 Comments of Llewelyn Richards, *Disarmament Possibilities*, Excerpts from the NGO Panel at UNSODD III, May–June 1988. UN Department of Disarmament Affairs, New York, 1988, pp.46–7.
43 Two other reservations entered were those relating to recruitment into or service in the armed forces (women not to serve in combat roles) and employment of women in underground work.
44 'Discrimination Against Women – New Zealand Report', Information Bulletin No.23, August 1988, Ministry of Foreign Affairs, Wellington.
45 Benedict Kingsbury, 'The Treaty of Waitangi: Some International Law Aspects', in I. H. Kawharu (ed.), *Waitangi. Maori and Pakeha Perspectives* (Auckland, 1989), p.121.
46 Kingsbury, 'Treaty of Waitangi', p.137.
47 Cath Wallace, 'An NGO Perspective', in Gary Hawke (ed.), *Guardians for the Environment* (Wellington, 1997), p.101.
48 Jock Phillips, 'New Zealand and the ANZUS Alliance: Changing National Self-Perceptions, 1945–88', in Richard Baker (ed.), *Australia, New Zealand and the United States* (New York, 1991), p.193.
49 David Lange, 'New Zealand's Anti-Nuclear Policies', Address to the Commonwealth Club of California, 25 October 1985, mimeo speech text, p.3.

EDITORIAL NOTE

References to the files of the Ministry of Foreign Affairs and Trade, and its earlier titles, pose some problems. Established as the Department of External Affairs in 1943, it was renamed the Ministry of Foreign Affairs (MFA) from 1 March 1970. It was renamed again as the Ministry of External Relations and Trade (MERT) from 1 December 1988, and renamed yet again as the Ministry of Foreign Affairs and Trade (MFAT) from 1 July 1993. From 1943 the Ministry's file numbers were prefixed by PM but this was dropped when it was separated from the Prime Minister's Department in 1976. Thereafter, no prefix was used by the Ministry itself. To show the origin of the files, references have been standardised under the initials of the current name, MFAT, plus National Archives (NANZ) box and references numbers where these are cited by the authors.

My thanks go to all the authors, many of whom had other pressing commitments, for accepting the Institute's invitation to contribute and meeting the timetable. I should thank especially Rachel Lawson, Acting Publisher of Victoria University Press, for her skill and energy in seeing the book through to publication. I am grateful also to the staff of the Turnbull Library for assisting my access to the Library's photo and cartoon collection, and to Malcolm McKinnon and Ian McGibbon for their advice and assistance.

Bruce Brown

LIST OF ACRONYMS

ABM	Anti-Ballistic Missile Treaty
ADB	Asian Development Bank
AMDA	Anglo-Malaysian Defence Agreement
Anzac	Australia and New Zealand Army Corps
ANZCERTA	Australia and New Zealand Closer Economic Relations Agreement
ANZUS	Australia, New Zealand, Unites States [Alliance]
APEC	Asia-Pacific Economic Cooperation
ASEAN	Association of South-East Asian Nations
ASPAC	Asia and Pacific Council
CAB	Commonwealth Agricultural Bureau
CABI	CAB-International
Caricom	Caribbean Community
CCCS	Commonwealth Committee for Cooperation in Sport
CD	Committee on Disarmament [UN]
CDR	Closer Defence Relations [Australia and New Zealand]
CER	*See* ANZCERTA
CFTC	Commonwealth Fund for Technical Cooperation
Chogm	Commonwealth Heads of Government Meeting
Chogrm	Commonwealth Heads of Government Regional Meeting
CFTQ	Country Specific Tariff Quota
CND	Campaign for Nuclear Disarmament
CoL	Commonwealth of Learning
CTBT	Comprehensive Test Ban Treaty
DEA	Department of External Affairs (1943–70)
DWFNS	Distant Water Fishing Nations
ECOSOC	Economic and Social Council of the United Nations
EEC	European Economic Community (later European Union)

LIST OF ACRONYMS

EU	European Union
FAO	Food and Agricultural Organisation
FFA	Forum Fisheries Agency
FPDA	Five Power Defence Arrangements
GATT	General Agreement on Tariffs and Trade
HoC	Head of Commonwealth
HoG	Head of Government
IBRD	International Bank for Reconstruction
ICBN	Intercontinental Ballistic Missile
ICJ	International Court of Justice
ILO	International Labour Organisation
IMF	International Monetary Fund
INF	Intermediate Range Nuclear Forces Treaty
JNZBC	Japan–New Zealand Business Advisory Council
JTC	Joint Trade Commission [New Zealand and China]
MAI	Multilateral Agreement on Investment
MERT	Ministry of External Relations and Trade (1988–93)
MFA	Ministry of Foreign Affairs (1970–88)
MFAT	Ministry of Foreign Affairs and Trade (1993–)
MFO	Multinational Force and Observers [in the Sinai]
NAFTA	New Zealand–Australia Free Trade Agreement
NAFTA	North American Free Trade Agreement [Canada, Mexico, USA]
NATO	North Atlantic Treaty Organisation
NCCD	National Consultative Committee on Disarmament [New Zealand]
NIEO	New International Economic Order
NGO	Non-Governmental Organisation
NPT	(Nuclear) Non-Proliferation Treaty
OAU	Organisation of African Unity
OECD	Organisation for Economic Cooperation and Development
OPEC	Organisation of Petroleum Exporting Countries
PACDAC	Public Advisory Committee on Disarmament and Arms Control [New Zealand]
PBEC	Pacific Basin Economic Council
PEEC	Pacific Economic Cooperation Conference
PFL	Pacific Forum Line

PIPA	Pacific Islands Producers Association
PSE	Producer Subsidy Equivalent
SADC	Southern African Development Community
SALT	Strategic Arms Limitation Talks
SARC	South Asian Association for Regional Development
SDT	Strategic Defence Initiative ['Star Wars']
SEATO	South-East Asia Treaty Organisation
SLBM	Submarine Launched Ballistic Missile
SMP	Skim Milk Powder
SMPs	Supplementary Minimum Prices
SOM	Senior Officials Meeting
Sparteca	South Pacific Regional Trade and Economic Cooperation Agreement
SPC	South Pacific Commission
SPNFZ	South Pacific Nuclear Free Zone
SPS	Sanitary and Phytosanitary Standards
TMD	Theatre Missile Defence
UDI	Unilateral Declaration of Independence [of Rhodesia, later Zimbabwe]
UNCLOS	United Nations Convention on the Law of the Sea
VRA	Voluntary Restraint Agreement [for exports]
WHO	World Health Organisation
WTO	World Trade Organisation

NOTES ON THE AUTHORS

Roderic Alley is Senior Lecturer at Victoria University's School of Political Science and International Relations. He has published on international relations in the Pacific, developments in Fiji, and disarmament and international security questions. He is the author of *The United Nations in Southeast Asia and the South Pacific* published by Macmillan in 1998. His next book, due for publication in 2000, deals with the interaction of domestic and international politics in Australia, New Zealand and the Pacific.

Bruce Brown QSO was Private Secretary to Walter Nash as Leader of the Opposition 1955 to 1957 and the Prime Minister from 1957 to 1959. He joined the Department of External Affairs in 1959. His postings included Deputy High Commissioner, Canberra, 1972–75; Ambassador to Iran and Pakistan 1975–78; Deputy High Commissioner, London, 1981–85; Ambassador to Thailand, accredited also to Vietnam, Burma and Laos, 1985–88; and High Commissioner to Canada, 1988–92. He was Director of the New Zealand Institute of International Affairs 1969–71 and again 1993–97 and currently chairs the Institute's Research and Publication Committee. His publications include *The Rise of New Zealand Labour* (1962); *The United Nations* (1966); historical contributions to the *Encyclopaedia of New Zealand* (1966); *Asia and the Pacific in the 1970s* (ed. 1971); and numerous articles and reviews.

John Henderson is Head of the Political Science Department and Chair of the Macmillan Brown Centre for Pacific Studies, at the University of Canterbury. He is a former director of the Prime Minister's Office (1985–89) and former Deputy Secretary-General of the Commonwealth Parliamentary Association. In 1990 he chaired the South Pacific Policy Review Group which produced the report *Towards a Pacific Island*

Community. He has previously held positions in the Politics Departments at Victoria University of Wellington and the University of Auckland. His primary area of research and teaching is on the politics of the Pacific Island region.

Stephen Hoadley has taught, researched and published for the past quarter-century on New Zealand's foreign relations. Amongst his publications are *The New Zealand Foreign Affairs Handbook* (1992); *Negotiating with Japan* (1993); *New Zealand and Australia* (1995); *The US-New Zealand Kiwifruit Dispute* (1997); and *New Zealand Taiwan Relations* (1998). He is currently writing a book on New Zealand–United States relations. He is Associate Professor of Political Studies at the University of Auckland and corresponding editor of *New Zealand International Review*.

Ian McGibbon ONZM is a Senior Historian at the Historical Branch, Department of Internal Affairs, Wellington. He has published extensively on New Zealand's defence and foreign relations, including the two-volume official history *New Zealand and the Korean War* (1992, 1996). He is currently editing the *Oxford Companion to New Zealand Military History*. He was awarded a LitD by Victoria University of Wellington in 1994, and three years later was made an Officer of the New Zealand Order of Merit for services to historical research.

W. David McIntyre OBE, professor of history at the University of Canterbury from 1966 to 1998, is a research associate in the University's Macmillan Brown Centre for Pacific Studies. He has reported the Chogms for the NZIIA since 1987. Among his twelve books are three on the Commonwealth: *Colonies into Commonwealth* (1966), *The Commonwealth of Nations 1869–1971* (1977); and *The Significance of the Commonwealth 1965-90* (1991). His trilogy on strategic history 'East of Suez' comprises *The Rise and Fall of the Singapore Naval Base* (1979); *New Zealand Prepares for War 1919-39* (1988) and *Background to the Anzus Pact* (1995).

John McKinnon, a graduate of Victoria University and of the London School of Economics, has been Director of the External Assessments Bureau in the Department of the Prime Minister and Cabinet,

Wellington, since 1995. He previously worked for the Ministry of Foreign Affairs and Trade, beginning his diplomatic career as a Chinese language student in Hong Kong in 1975, followed by a tour of duty in the New Zealand Embassy in Beijing. Back in New Zealand he was escort and interpreter for numerous delegations from China, and undertook similar work on a secondment with Fletcher Challenge Ltd in 1983. John McKinnon has also served in New Zealand missions in Washington, Canberra and in New York, where he was Deputy Permanent Representative to the United Nations.

Malcolm McKinnon holds the degrees of B.A. (Hons) and Ph.D. in history from Victoria University of Wellington and the degree of B.Phil. in international relations from Oxford University. He taught history at Victoria University from 1976 to 1990. He was editor of the New Zealand Historical Atlas project from 1990 to 1997, the *Atlas* itself being published in the latter year. He has written extensively on the history of New Zealand's foreign relations. He edited *New Zealand in World Affairs*, Vol. II (1957–1972); and is the author of *Independence and Foreign Policy: New Zealand in the World since 1935* (Auckland, Auckland University Press, 1993).

Merwyn Norrish was the Secretary of Foreign Affairs from 1980 to 1988. He joined Foreign Affairs in 1949. Among postings abroad, he served as New Zealand's Ambassador to the European Community from 1967 to 1972 and Ambassador to the United States from 1978 to 1980. Following retirement from Foreign Affairs, he chaired the Board of New Zealand on Air from 1989 to 1996.

Malcolm Templeton QSO, a career Foreign Service officer, served as New Zealand Permanent Representative to the United Nations from 1973 to 1978, then as Deputy Secretary of Foreign Affairs until 1984. On his retirement he was appointed founding Director of The Institute of Policy Studies at Victoria University for a three year term. Since 1987 he has been engaged in writing diplomatic history for the Ministry of Foreign Affairs and Trade. His published work includes books dealing with New Zealand's early diplomatic representation in Moscow, with New Zealand's role in the Suez crisis, and with New Zealand attitudes to race relations in South Africa. He has edited two books for the

Ministry, delivered a number of papers at the Otago University Foreign Policy School, and contributed an introductory chapter to *New Zealand in World Affairs* Vol. II 1957–72.

Ann Trotter ONZM, Emeritus Professor of History, University of Otago, is a graduate of the University of New Zealand and of the University of London where she completed her PhD at the London School of Economics. Her books *Britain and East Asia 1933-37* (1975) and *New Zealand and Japan 1945–1952* (1990) are concerned with international history in East Asia with particular reference to Japan. She edited 50 volumes, *Asia 1914–1939*, published between 1991 and 1997, in the series, *British Documents on Foreign Affairs*. In 1997 she was made an Officer of the New Zealand Order of Merit for services to historical research.

INDEX

Afghanistan, Soviet invasion of, 121, 155, 238, 299
Air New Zealand, hijacking of jumbo jet (1987), 128, 285
Albright, Madeleine, 67
Alley, Rewi, 228, 231, 242, 243
Aluminium production, 36–7, 214
Amnesty International, 309–10
Anderton, Jim, 303
Ansell, Graham, 255
Antarctic Treaty (1959), 71, 147, 239
Antarctica and Antarctic waters, 80, 120, 308–9
Anthony, Doug, 33, 182
Anti-Ballistic Missiles Treaty, 111
Anti-nuclear policy, 28–9, 30, 122–6, 138, 143, 144, 145, 157–65, 169–70, 195–6, 197, 210, 240, 281, 292, 300–1, 302–6, 312–13
Anzac frigates. *See* Frigates
'Anzac nationalism', 146, 148, 149, 157, 161, 162, 166, 169
ANZCERTA. *See* CER
ANZUS Council meetings, 122, 156, 158, 279, 301
ANZUS Treaty (1951), 30, 40, 113, 115, 122–5, 148–50, 152–3, 156–65, 210, 240, 281, 282, 292, 300–2, 305
Apartheid, 89, 95–7, 108
APEC, 51–3, 100, 221–2
Argentina, 28, 114
Armed services, structure and equipment, 118–21, 131–3
Armstrong, Lord, 98
ASEAN, 51, 52
Asia, trade with, 44, 45

Asian Development Bank (ADB), 207, 239, 246
ASPAC, 232
Atkins, R. B., 235
Attlee, Prime Minister Clement, 86
Australia: and ANZUS, 156, 291–2; defence cooperation with, 117–18, 129–31, 132–3, 165–6, 196–201; ratification of UN Covenants on human rights, 65; and South Pacific Forum, 100, 275, 287, 290, 291; and UNCLOS, 75; mentioned, 69, 70. *See also* CER; NAFTA; Trans-Tasman relations

Bai Xiangguo, 244
Bain, K. R., 101
Baker, James, 169
Balewa, Prime Minister Sir Abubakar Tafawa, 90
Ball, Margaret, 85, 86
Bayi, Filbert, 106
Beazley, Kim, 130, 168, 198, 307
Beeby, Christopher, 308
Beef exports, 39, 58*n*47, 207, 208, 209, 314
Bichan, Helen, 101
Bogor Declaration of Common Resolve (1994), 52
Bolger, Prime Minister Jim, 99, 137, 164, 199, 284, 307
Bougainville, 129, 278, 285–6
Boutros Ghali, Boutros, 78
Boyd, Mary, 273
Britain: entry to EEC (*later* EU), 21, 45, 92, 178–9, 213, 296, 297;

Britain *cont.* ratification of UN Covenants on human rights, 65; trade with, 23–31, 50–1; withdrawal from east of Suez, 112–13
Brooks, Peter, 101
Brownlie, A. D., 92
Brunei, trade with, 44
Buchanan, USS, 28, 122–4, 125, 143, 144, 145, 159–61
Butter exports, 24–5, 27, 44, 47, 50, 60–1

CABI, 102
Cairns Group, 47–8, 49
Caldicott, Helen, 122, 154
Cambodia, Vietnamese invasion of, 152, 236
Canada, 39, 65
Canberra Pact (1944), 195, 196
Car assembly plants, 37, 214
Carrington, Lord, 94
Carter, President Jimmy, 65, 150, 314
CDR, 117–18, 129–31, 166, 199–200, 201
CER, 32, 34–5, 117, 181–95; achievements of, 194–5; aviation services, 34, 193, 194; deferral list, 34, 185, 187–8; government purchasing, 185–6, 192; harmonisation of business laws, 193; industry agreements, 186–7; negotiation of (1978–83), 34, 181–8; review (1988), 34, 188–92; review (1992), 34, 193–4; six difficult issues, 184–6
Chan, Stephen, 98, 101
Cheese exports, 24–5, 43, 47, 50
Chernobyl disaster, 306, 314
Chile, 212
China, People's Republic of, 226–56; as threat, 115–16, 229; and APEC, 51; cultural exchanges with, 249–52; 'four modernisations', 237, 239; human rights, 68; investment, 248; Lange government's relations with, 239–44, 249; missile testing in Pacific, 237–8; Muldoon government's relations with, 234–9; participation in international organisations, 246; political and diplomatic relations with, 228–44, 281; preoccupied with Soviet Union, 232; recognition of, 228–30; relations with US, 115; scientific exchanges with, 251; signs Treaty of Rarotonga, 282; Tiananmen, 253–5; trade and economic relations with, 44, 244–9. *See also* Taiwan
Chogms, 85, 88–99; (Singapore, 1971), 87, 89, 90–1; (Ottawa, 1973), 87, 89, 91, 108; (Kingston, 1975), 89, 92; (London, 1977), 89, 92–4, 108; (Lusaka, 1979), 87, 89, 94–5, 104; (Melbourne, 1981), 89, 95–6; (New Delhi, 1983), 89, 96; (Nassau, 1985), 89, 96–7, 102; (Vancouver, 1987), 89, 97, 102; (Kuala Lumpur, 1989), 89, 97, 107; (Harare, 1991), 89, 98–9
Chogrms, 100
Clark, Helen, 242, 303–4
Clements, Kevin, 144
Clinton, President Bill, 51, 52
CND, 145, 147
Coates, Gordon, 23
Cold War, 30, 121, 134, 278–9
Coleman, Fraser, 282
Comalco, 36–7
Commission for the Future, 300
Commodity prices, 21, 179
Common Agricultural Policy (CAP), 26
Commonwealth, 85–110; inter-governmental organisations, 85, 100–3; professional associations, 103–6; Queen as Head, 85, 86–8, 93; regional organisations, 99–100; sport, 106–7. *See also* Chogms; Chogrms
Commonwealth Games, 85, 86, 106–7; (Christchurch, 1974), 92, 106; (Edmonton, 1978), 92, 107; (Brisbane, 1982), 34, 96; (Edinburgh, 1986), 107; (Auckland, (1990), 106
Commonwealth Parliamentary Association, 277

INDEX

Commonwealth Secretariat, 85, 100–1
Commonwealth Statement on Apartheid in Sport (1977), 93–4
Comprehensive Test Ban Treaty (CTBT), 69–70, 233
Compulsory military training, 119, 295
Conference on Disarmament, 70
Continental shelves, 74–6, 79
Convention on the Elimination of All Forms of Discrimination Against Women, 69, 311
Cook Islands, 65–6, 75, 100, 269, 270, 272, 273, 274, 275, 288
Cooke, Lord, 67
Cooper, Warren, 158, 199, 239, 249
Corner, Frank, 30, 91, 108, 115, 127, 304, 313
Council of Australian Governments, 35
Country Specific Tariff Quotas (CFTQs), 50
Crocombe, Ron, 268
Crooks, Air Marshal David, 128, 284

Davis, Premier Tom, 274
'The Day After', 153
Daysh, Zena, 105
De Klerk, President F. W., 97
Declaration of Commonwealth Principles (Singapore, 1971), 90–1
Defence Committee of Enquiry, 127, 200, 304–5
Defence Management Resource Review (1988), 131, 133
Defence policy, 111–43. *See also* Armed services; Australia: defence cooperation with; Frigates
Defence Reviews: (1978), 197, 278; (1983), 197; (1987), 127–8, 286, 306
Deng Xiaoping, 227, 235, 237, 238, 251
Denmark, 156
Development Finance Corporation (DFC), 215–16
Dillon Round. *See* GATT
Distant water fishing nations (DWFNs), 73, 74, 80–1, 211
Dong Biwu, 234

Donne, Gavin, 273
Douglas, Ian, 184
Douglas, Roger, 166, 167–8, 188, 215
Driftnet fishing, 79, 97, 211, 290
Dublin Declaration (10 March 1975), 24–5
Dumping, 212
Dunkel, Arthur, 49
Dutton, Roy, 96
Dyson, Ruth, 307

East Timor, 309–10
ECOSOC, 65, 68
EEC (*later* EC *then* EU): Britain's entry to, 21, 45, 92, 178–9, 213, 296, 297; trade with, 23–31, 50–1
Elizabeth II, Queen, as Head of the Commonwealth, 86–8
Endeavour Accord, 129, 286
Environmental issues. *See* Driftnet fishing; Nuclear weapons testing
Exclusive economic zones (EEZs), 74–6, 79, 120, 207–8, 289, 306–7

Faletau, Inoke, 105
Falklands War, 28, 114, 299, 309
The Fate of the Earth (Schell), 153
Federated States of Micronesia, 100, 275, 281
Fiji: and Commonwealth, 90, 102; coups (1987), 128, 278, 283–6; and South Pacific Forum, 100, 102; trade with, 44, 286, 287; mentioned, 69, 71, 163, 272, 275, 281
Finlay, Martyn, 70
Fish stocks, 79–80
Fishing zones, 74
Five Power Defence Arrangements (FPDA), 116
Food and Agriculture Organisation, 80
Food Security Act (US), 39
Forestry, 179–80, 214
Forum Fisheries Agency, 79, 276
France: International Court of Justice case against, 69, 70, 147, 233, 281–2; nuclear weapons testing, 69–72, 89,

France *cont.* 91, 122, 147, 233, 281–2, 298–9; possessions in the Pacific, 283; sinking of *Rainbow Warrior*, 143, 162, 163, 278, 282–3, 306
Fraser, Prime Minister Malcolm: calls for Chogrms, 100; at Gleneagles, 93; at Lusaka Chogm, 94; Nareen Declaration, 33, 182; relations with Muldoon, 34, 93, 181, 183, 184, 195; South Pacific Nuclear Weapons Free Zone, 71
Fraser, Prime Minister Peter, 86, 136
Freer, Warren, 227
Frigates, 120, 132–3, 166–9, 196, 198–9, 306–7. *See also* Falklands War; Mururoa

Gaddafi, Colonel, 164, 280
Galvin, Bernard, 93
Gandhi, Prime Minister Rajiv, 97, 98
Garland, Vic, 34
Garlick, Bill, 107
GATT, 45–51, 212, 246, 254; Dillon Round (1961), 25–6, 46; MFN status for Japan, 36; Tokyo Round (1973–79), 22, 25, 47, 181; Uruguay Round (1986–94), 22, 25, 30, 31, 39, 41, 47–51, 212
Genocide Convention, 65
George VI, King, 86
Gleneagles Agreement, 93–4, 300
Gorbachev, President Mikhail, 134, 279
Greenham Common protest camp, 153–4
Greenpeace, 145
Grenada invasion (1983), 96
Guam Doctrine, 117, 146, 150
'Guamist nationalism', 146, 168–9
Gulf War, 135–8

Haas, Tony, 268
Harare Commonwealth Declaration (1991), 98–9
Harland, Bryce, 29, 234
Hawaii, 275
Hawke, Prime Minister Bob: ANZUS and NZ's anti-nuclear policy, 124, 156, 161–2, 195–6, 197, 307; APEC initiative, 51; CER, 188, 189, 192; at Chogms, 97; relations with Bolger, 199; relations with Lange, 161–2, 195, 197; at South Pacific Forum, 290
Hawke Government, 124, 156, 165
Hayden, Bill, 124, 280
Heath, Prime Minister Edward, 23, 87, 90, 91
Helleiner, Gerald, 96
Henningham, Stephen, 291
Henry, Premier Albert, 273
Hensley, Gerald, 101, 199
Herr, Richard, 291
Highet, Allan, 250
Hijacking (Nadi, 1987), 128, 285
Holmes, Sir Frank, 181
Holyoake, Prime Minister Sir Keith, 23, 40, 90, 100, 206
Hong Kong, 44, 51
Howe, Sir Geoffrey, 29
Howell, Ron, 227, 249
Hu Yaobang, 237, 240–1, 241, 252
Hua Guofeng, Premier, 235, 237, 238
Huang Zhen, 250
Human rights, 63–9
Hungary, 102
Hussein, President Saddam, 43

ILO, 63, 64, 239
IMF, 246
Import licensing, 46
India, 70
Indonesia, 44, 68
Intermediate-range Nuclear Forces (INF) Treaty, 134, 306
International Court of Justice: case against France, 69, 70, 147, 233, 281–2
International Covenant on Civil and Political Rights, 64–8; Optional Protocol, 66; ratified by New Zealand, 65–6
International Covenant on Economic, Social and Cultural Rights, 64–8; ratified by New Zealand, 65–6

INDEX

International law, 62–84
International Physicians for the Prevention of Nuclear War, 302
International Sea-bed Authority, 77, 79, 81
Iran, 42–3, 152
Iraq, 42, 44, 135–8
Ireland, 102

Jamaica, 96
James, Colin, 181
Jamieson, Air Marshal Sir Ewan, 123, 124, 159, 160
Japan, 205–25; business with, 213–17; cultural and other exchanges with, 218–20; development aid to Pacific island states, 211; diplomatic relations with, 206–12; 'fish-for-beef' controversy, 38, 208, 209, 314; investment in NZ, 213–17; Most Favoured Nation status, 36; prejudice against, 222–3; trade with, 35–8, 212–13
Japan Advisory Council, 218
Japan–New Zealand Business Council (JNZBC), 213, 214, 215, 216, 217, 218
Jiang Qing, 236, 237
Johnston Island, 290
Jones, Sir Robert, 154, 155, 167

Kaunda, President Kenneth, 90
Kidd, Doug, 159
Kiribati, 75, 275, 279, 281, 291
Kirk, Prime Minister Norman: ANZUS, 113, 148–9; criticises Nixon Administration privately, 314; death (31 August 1974), 234; despatches frigate to Mururoa, 122, 147, 282, 298, 312; development assistance, 288–9; diplomatic representation, 228, 232; foreign policy, 267, 297–8, 302; friendships with African leaders, 91; ICJ case against France, 70; People's Republic of China, 229, 230, 231, 232, 244; postponement of 1973 Springbok tour, 92, 298–9;

South Pacific regionalism, 267, 273, 276, 277; mentioned, 35, 42. *See also* Labour Government (1972–75)
Kiwifruit, 251
Konsin Shah, 229
Korea, 44, 136
Kuwait, 135–8

La Varis, Ramon, 227
Labour Government (1935–49), 46
Labour Government (1972–75), 228–34, 297–9; ANZUS Treaty, 113, 148–9; economic woes, 296; ends National Service scheme, 119; foreign borrowing, 53; frigates to Mururoa, 122, 147, 282, 298, 312; Oceania, 273–4; People's Republic of China, 228–34, 244; ratification of UN Covenants on human rights, 64; ship visits, 148–9. *See also* Kirk, Norman; Rowling, Bill
Labour Government (1984–90): CER Review (1988), 188–92; defence and foreign policy, 122–37, 157–70, 303–4; economic policy and government management, 22, 53–4, 296–7; export incentives, 40–1; human rights issues, 66; People's Republic of China, 239–44, 249; removal of subsidies, 40; South Africa, 96; South Pacific Nuclear Weapons Free Zone, 71–2, 157, 282; Soviet Union, 155, 280. *See also* Anti-nuclear policy; ANZUS Treaty; Lange, David; Moore, Mike; Palmer, Sir Geoffrey; Ship visits
Laidlaw, Chris, 96, 101
Lamb exports, 25–6, 27–8, 42–3, 57n31
Lange, Prime Minister David: baby boomer Prime Minister, 114; anti-nuclear policy and ANZUS, 123, 125, 126, 157; on Anzac frigates, 133, 199; on Commonwealth, 96–7; on Defence Committee of Enquiry, 127, 305; first Fiji coup, 128, 284; Japan, 209, 211, 215;

Lange *cont.* meeting with Bill Hayden, 280–1; meetings with Shultz, 158, 164; Oceania, 128, 267, 281, 283, 284; on officialdom, 304; Oxford Union debate (1985), 126, 312–13; People's Republic of China, 239–40, 242–3, 244; relations with Hawke, 161–2, 195, 197; resignation, 125, 165; on 'threat' of Soviet Union, 155; Yale speech (1989), 125, 165; *Nuclear Free — The New Zealand Way,* 29, 133, 144. *See also* Labour Government (1984–90)
Latin America, trade with, 44, 45
Law of the Sea, 72–81, 120, 207
Lee Kuan Yew, Prime Minister, 90
Li Lairong, 239
Li Peng, Premier, 237–8, 244, 255
Libya, 280–1
Lini, Prime Minister Walter, 285
Liu Huaqiu, 255
Luxembourg Protocol, 24, 27, 31

McDowell, David, 101
Mace, Lt General Sir John, 129
McEwan, John ('Black Jack'), 180
MacGregor, John, 29
McKinnon, Don, 169, 268, 283, 289
McKinnon, Malcolm, 272
McLay, Jim, 155, 301
McLean, Denis, 313
McMechan, Peter, 103
Macmillan, Prime Minister Harold, 23
McMurtry, Roy, 107
Mahathir Mohamad, Prime Minister, 51, 67
Major, Prime Minister John, 98
Malan, Prime Minister Daniel, 86
Malaysia, 44, 52
Mandela, Nelson, 97, 99
Manila Treaty (1954), 116. *See also* SEATO
Mao Zedong, 234, 235
Maputo Declaration (1977), 93
Mara, Prime Minister Ratu Sir Kamisese, 284

Marshall Islands, 100, 275, 281, 291
Marshall, Prime Minister Sir John, 23, 113, 180, 229
Marshall, Sir Peter, 96
Marshall, Russell, 29, 126, 168, 254, 307
Mexico, 69
Middle East, trade with, 41–5, 45
Moore, Prime Minister Mike, 29, 137, 169, 188, 189, 249, 255, 277
Mugabe, President Robert, 95, 99
Muldoon, Prime Minister Sir Robert: ANZUS, 114, 152; biography awaited, 144; calls early election (1984), 154; on CER, 183, 184; at Chogm (London and Gleneagles, 1977), 92–6, 108; on Commonwealth, 108; defence policy, 113–14; exports to Japan, 37–8, 207–8, 314; lamb exports to EEC, 26, 28; meets Mao Zedong, 235–6; Oceania, 267, 276, 279; People's Republic of China, 234, 235–6, 238–9; pugnacious interventionism, 296; ratification of UN Covenants on human rights, 65; relations with Fraser, 34, 71, 181, 195; ship visits, 114–15; at South Pacific Forums, 71, 149; South Pacific Nuclear Weapons Free Zone, 71, 149; Soviet Union, 235, 238, 279; speech to UN General Assembly (1978), 65–6; Springbok rugby tour (1981), 95, 186, 312. *See also* National Government (1975–84)
Mulgan, Richard, 67
Mullins, Ralph, 113
Mulroney, Brian, 97
Multilateral Agreement on Investment (MAI), 63
Multinational Force and Observers (MFO), 114, 118, 135
Mururoa, frigate sent to, 122, 147, 282, 298, 312
Mutton exports, 44
Muzorewa, Bishop Abel, 94

NAFTA, 32–3, 34, 180–1, 183, 184
Nakasone, Prime Minister Yosuhiro, 209, 215, 220
Namibia, 97
Nareen Declaration, 33, 182
Nash, Sir Walter, 46
National Consultative Committee on Disarmament (NCCD), 300
National Government (1960–72), 23, 148
National Government (1975–84), 40, 41, 53, 54, 64–5, 149, 181–8, 234–9, 249, 271–2, 296. *See also* Muldoon, Robert
National Government (1990–96), 54–5, 137–8, 192–4
National Party, abandons opposition to anti-nuclear policy, 169–70
NATO, 121, 122, 153, 313
Nauru, 100, 275, 281
Nehru, Prime Minister Jahawarlal, 86
Netherlands, 156
New Caledonia, 275, 278, 286
New International Economic Order, 89, 92
New Zealand Bill of Rights, 66, 67
New Zealand Business Roundtable, 193
New Zealand Dairy Board, 36, 43, 44
New Zealand Olympic and Commonwealth Games Association, 96, 106
New Zealand Party, 154
NGOs, 86, 103–6, 310–12
Nigeria, 96
Niue, 65–6, 269, 270, 272, 273, 274, 288
Nixon, President Richard, 41, 115, 146, 226, 297
Non-Proliferation Treaty, 117
Noriega, Manuel, 169
Norrish, Merwyn, 158–9
Northey, Richard, 252
Norway, 75, 156
Nuclear disarmament, 298
Nuclear weapons, anti-militarist campaign against, 151–4
Nuclear weapons testing, 69–72, 89, 91, 122, 147–51, 233–4, 236, 281–2, 298–9, 301–2
Nyerere, President Julius, 94

Oceania, 267–94; development aid to, 211, 287–9, 298; diplomatic links, 234–5; economic issues, 286–7; environmental issues, 289–91; political links, 273–5; Polynesian links, 268–73; regional cooperation, 275–7; rise in sea levels, 290–1; strategic concerns, 277–83. *See also* South Pacific.
OECD, 63
O'Flynn, Frank, 127, 131, 158
Ohira, Prime Minister Masayoshi, 51, 210, 219, 221
Oil price shocks (1973, 1979), 21, 32, 33, 41–2, 152, 207, 296
Olympic Games: (Montreal, 1976), 92, 300; (Moscow, 1980), 153, 299
OPEC, 33, 41–2
O'Regan, Katherine, 252
Organization of African Unity, 96
Overstayers issue, 271–2, 298

Pacific Basin Community, 206, 210, 221
Pacific Basin Economic Council, 206
Pacific Economic Cooperation Conference, 221
Pacific Forum Line, 276
Pacific Island Producers' Association, 100
Pacific Island states. *See* Oceania
Pakistan, 68, 102
Palau, 275, 278
Palmer, Prime Minister Sir Geoffrey: on anti-nuclear policy and ANZUS, 160, 162; Anzac frigates, 133, 168–9, 192, 196, 198–9, 307; CER, 192; on Commonwealth, 97; driftnet fishing, 211–12; human rights, 63; Japan, 211–12, 215; Oceania, 267–8, 290; People's Republic of China, 243; as Prime Minister, 133, 137, 165, 196

Papua New Guinea, 69, 71, 280, 281, 286, 287
Patagonian toothfish, 80
Peace Movement New Zealand, 145, 153
Peacekeeping operations, 135
Pearson, Prime Minister Lester, 86
Pei Jianzhang, 232
Peoples' Commonwealth, 86, 108
Percival, Vic, 227
Perez de Cuellar, Javier, 78
Philippines, 44
'Pintado nationalism', 146, 148, 161–2, 168
Poland, 155
Pope, Jeremy, 96, 101, 107
Prebble, Richard, 166
Privy Council, 67
Producer Subsidy Equivalents (PSEs), 49
Protocol 18 (to Treaty of Rome), 24, 27, 31
Public Advisory Committee on Disarmament and Arms Control (PACDAC), 307
Public opinion on and involvement in government policy, 295–317
Punta del Este meeting (September 1986), 47, 48

Qiao Guanhua, 232, 233
Quentin-Baxter, R. Q., 72
Quigley, Derek, 131, 133

Rabuka, Lt Colonel Sitiveni, 128, 284, 285
Rainbow Warrior, 143, 162, 163, 278, 282–3, 306
Ramphal, Shridath (Sonny), 92, 93, 95
Ray, Robert, 199
Ready Reaction Force, 119–20, 132
Reagan, President Ronald, 78, 121, 155, 238
Remeliik, Haruo, 278
Renwick, Bill, 103
Rhodesia (*later* Zimbabwe), 89, 91, 94–5, 108

Richardson, Elliott, 77–8
'Rollback', 48
Ross, Larry, 153
Rowling, Prime Minister Sir Wallace (Bill), 42, 64, 71, 92, 149, 207, 234, 282, 298

Sali, Lazarus, 278
SALT, 111, 112, 121
Samoa. *See* Western Samoa
Sanitary and Phytosanitary Standards (SPS), 47
Saudi Arabia, 44
Save Manapouri campaign, 296
Sea-bed mining, 76–8, 81
SEATO, 116, 148, 232
Self-determination article (in UN Covenants on human rights), 68
Ship visits, 114, 115, 122–4, 125, 138, 148, 149–51, 154, 158, 301; US indemnifying legislation (1974), 115, 148
Shultz, George, 125, 158, 162, 164
Sinclair, Brian, 144, 145
Singapore, 44, 87, 89, 90–1, 116, 132
Sister cities, 218, 252
Skim milk powder (SMP), 43, 47, 50
Small, Tony, 241
Smith, Arnold, 87, 91
Social Credit Party, 154
Solomon Islands, 281, 288
Sope, Barak, 285
South Africa: arms sales to, 89, 90; sanctions against, 97; sporting contacts with, 89, 92–4, 95–6
South Pacific: defence, 119; trade with, 44. *See also* Oceania.
South Pacific Commission, 275
South Pacific Forum, 71, 79, 100, 149, 164, 238, 275–6, 282, 287, 290, 291, 298
South Pacific Nuclear Weapons Free Zone, 69, 71–2, 148, 157, 164, 241, 282, 300
Southeast Asia, Communist insurgencies in, 233
Southwest Africa, 89

INDEX

Soviet Union: invasion of Afghanistan, 121, 155, 238, 299; signs Treaty of Rarotonga, 282; as 'threat' in the Pacific, 150, 155, 278–80; trade with, 44, 45
SPARTECA, 287
Sporting contacts with South Africa, 89, 92–4, 95–6, 298–9, 312–13
Springbok rugby tour (1981), 34, 95, 186, 313
Sprott, Jim, 162–3
'Standstill', 48
Stevens, P. A., 101
Stock market crash (1987), 54
Strategic Defense Initiative ('Star Wars'), 134
Suharto, President, 51
Supplementary Minimum Prices (SMPs), 40, 54
Sutherland, Peter, 49
Sutton, Jim, 255
Sweden, 69

Taiwan, 44, 51, 228–30, 234–5, 238, 281
Talboys, Brian, 33, 153, 181–2, 182, 183, 249, 267, 272, 273, 279
Tanaka, Prime Minister Kakui, 207
Tanzania, 96
Tapsell, Peter, 253
Templeton, Hugh, 34, 144, 182–3, 183, 188
Templeton, Ian, 305
Templeton, Malcolm, 287
Terms of trade, 21, 60
Territorial seas, 73–5
Thailand, 44
Thakur, Ramesh, 279, 283
Thatcher, Prime Minister Margaret, 28, 87, 94, 97, 114
'Think Big' policy, 53, 296
Thompson, E. P., 153
Tiananmen, 227, 253–5
Tizard, Bob, 168
Tokelau, 270, 273, 288
Tokyo Round. *See* GATT
Tonga, 90, 100, 269, 270, 271, 272, 275, 279, 281, 282
Tourism, 212–13
Trade (NZ), 21–61; Asia, 44, 45; Australia, 31–5; Britain, 23–31, 50–1; Canada, 39; Europe, 23–31, 50–1; Iran, 42–3; Iraq, 42, 44; Japan, 35–8; Latin America, 44, 45; Middle East, 41–5, 45; South Pacific, 44; Soviet Union, 44, 45; United States, 38–41
Trans-Tasman relations, 177–204; defence cooperation, 117–18, 129–31, 132–3, 165–6, 196–201; diplomatic and political, 195–6, 291–2; economic, *see* CER; NAFTA
Trans-Tasman Travel Arrangement, 193
Treaty of Rarotonga (1986), 72, 164, 282
Treaty of Tlatelolco, 71
Trudeau, Prime Minister Pierre, 87, 91
Tuck, W. R., 101
Tuvalu, 275, 281, 291

UDI issue, 89, 94–5, 108
UN Charter, 63–4
UN Convention on the Law of the Sea. *See* UNCLOS
UN Economic and Social Council. *See* ECOSOC
UNCLOS, 62, 72–81, 289, 312; Part XI, 77–9; ratified by New Zealand, 79
United Nations: conferences, 310–12; peacekeeping and peace enforcement, 134–8
United States: human rights, 68; relations with China, 115; trade with, 38–41. *See also* Anti-nuclear policy; ANZUS Treaty; Ship visits
Universal Declaration of Human Rights, 64, 67–8
University of the South Pacific, 277
Uruguay Round. *See* GATT

Values Party, 296
Vanuatu, 129, 163, 278, 279, 280, 281, 282, 285
Vietnam, 114, 236
Vippsos, 106

Voluntary Restraint Agreements, 26, 39, 46–7

Wade, Hunter, 101
Wairakei golf course, sale of, 222–3
Walding, Joe, 231–3, 244, 248–9
Walker, John, 106
Wan Li, 243
Waring, Marilyn, 154
Watt, Hugh, 244
Western Samoa, 90, 100, 269, 269–70, 270–1, 272, 275, 281, 288
White, Robert, 144, 145
Whitlam, Prime Minister Gough, 35, 70
Wilson, Prime Minister Harold, 23, 92
Wilson, Margaret, 155
Wool exports, 43, 247
World Bank, 246
World Trade Organisation (WTO), 46, 50–1
Wu Xueqian, 240

Zeeuw, Art de, 49
Zhang Qunqiao, 235
Zhao Ziyang, Premier, 237, 238, 239, 240, 241
Zhou Enlai, Premier, 233, 234, 235
Zimbabwe (*earlier* Rhodesia), 89, 91, 94–5, 108
Zuleta, Bernardo, 72